Special Edition

Using

DYNAMIC

HTML

David Gulbransen
Kenrick Rawlings

Special Edition Using Dynamic HTML

Library of Congress Catalog No.: CIP Data available upon request.

ISBN: 0-7897-1482-5

99 98 97   6 5 4 3 2 1

Interpretation of the printing code: the rightmost double-digit number is the year of the book's printing; the rightmost single-digit number, the number of the book's printing. For example, a printing code of 97-1 shows that the first printing of the book occurred in 1997.

Screen reproductions in this book were created using Collage Plus from Inner Media, Inc., Hollis, NH.

Contents at a Glance

Table of Contents

III | Inside Dynamic HTML

VI | Real World Dynamic HTML

16   Pin the Tail on the Donkey   337

VII | Appendixes

A HTML Elements and Attributes 427

Credits

PRESIDENT
Roland Elgey

SENIOR VICE PRESIDENT/PUBLISHING
Don Fowley

ASSOCIATE PUBLISHER
David Dwyer

GENERAL MANAGER
Joe Muldoon

PRODUCT DEVELOPMENT SPECIALIST
David Gibson

MANAGING EDITOR
Sarah Kearns

ACQUISITIONS EDITOR
Steve Weiss

DEVELOPMENT EDITOR
Chris Cleveland

PRODUCTION EDITOR
Gina Brown

COPY EDITORS
Jenny Clark
Barbara Hacha
Brad Herriman
Karen Walsh

PRODUCT MARKETING MANAGER
Kourtnaye Sturgeon

ASSISTANT PRODUCT MARKETING MANAGER
Gretchen Schlesinger

TECHNICAL EDITOR
Yusuf Malluf

ACQUISITIONS COORDINATOR
Karen Opal

BOOK DESIGNER
Ruth Harvey

COVER DESIGNER
Sandra Schroeder

ILLUSTRATOR
Kevin Cliburn, Wil Cruz

PRODUCTION TEAM
Lori Cliburn, Kim Cofer,
Laure Robinson, Scott Tullis

INDEXER
Tim Wright

Composed in *Century Old Style* and *ITC Franklin Gothic* by Que Corporation.

Dedication

From David Gulbransen:

To my family: David, Anne, Mary and Matt.

From Ken Rawlings:

To my mother and father, Janet and Richard.

About the Authors

David Gulbransen has been performing Internet-related consulting and development for over eight years. He most recently served as the Manager of Information Systems at Dimension X, which was acquired by Microsoft in early 1997. In addition to his professional work David has contributed to *Java Unleashed* (by Sams.net), co-authored *Creating Web Applets with Java* (by Sams.net) and authored *The Netscape Server Survival Guide* (by Sams.net). David's most recent project is co-founding Vervet Logic, a provider of high performance web technology solutions, including channel development, Dynamic HTML, and custom application development. When he is not slaving behind a monitor and keyboard, David likes to place himself behind the camera as an amateur cinematographer.

Kenrick Rawlings has over ten years programming experience with C++ but abandoned it all with the alpha release of Java. He was a contributing author to *Java Unleashed* (by Sams.net) and co-authored *Creating Web Applets with Java* (by Sams.net) before turning his attention to Dynamic HTML. Ken recently co-founded Vervet Logic, which provides consulting and custom software development for cutting edge web technologies, such as Dynamic HTML and CDF channels. Between sleeping and coding, Ken enjoys cinema, techno-ambient music, and life outside of The City.

Acknowledgments

Thanks to Steve Weiss, Gina Brown, Chris Cleveland, and all the other folks at New Riders who helped make this a great title for Que. Thanks to Garth Bruce at Microsoft for the information. Special thanks to the folks at BlueMarble Information Services for the use of the space and bandwidth: Steve Volan, Luke Heidelberger, Jody Miller, Jeff Burkhart, Phil Foster, Rick Schmelz, Jodi Woods, and especially Nadia Kelley for being so cheerful! Thanks to our families and friends, without whom we would have collapsed halfway through this project. A very special thanks to Jim Causey, Scott Cramer, Carl Zahrt, and Ron Kuk for putting up with many late night dinners and excuses. And thanks to Stephanie Boys for taking some late night phone calls. Oh, thanks to Gary Numan and the MMB for the tunes. Thanks to Steve Simms for the late night cinema to keep us grounded in the real world. And thanks to the South Park gang, the spirit of Christmas is forever in our hearts.

We'd Like to Hear from You!

As part of our continuing effort to produce books of the highest possible quality, Que would like to hear your comments. To stay competitive, we *really* want you, as a computer book reader and user, to let us know what you like or dislike most about this book or other Que products.

You can mail comments, ideas, or suggestions for improving future editions to the address below, or send us a fax at (317) 581-4663. The address of our Internet site is **http://www.mcp.com** (World Wide Web).

In addition to exploring our forum, please feel free to contact me personally to discuss your opinions of this book: I'm **sweiss@newriders.mcp.com** on the Internet.

Thanks in advance—your comments will help us to continue publishing the best books available on computer topics in today's market.

Steve Weiss
201 W. 103rd Street
Indianapolis, Indiana 46290
USA

Introduction

Anyone familiar with the World Wide Web is undoubtedly aware of the constant state of flux that surrounds new web-related technology. As companies such as Microsoft and Netscape battle to gain market share, the weapons they employ are new techniques and applications, designed to increase the power of the Internet and Internet-based application development.

The latest advance on the web front comes in the form of Dynamic HTML, a collection of existing and new technologies that are designed to maximize the potential for web-based application development. With the advances that are being made with Dynamic HTML, web application and multimedia development promises to become easier and faster for the developer—and more robust and faster for the consumer. How Dynamic HTML accomplishes these goals is what is explored in this text. ■

Dynamic HTML

Dynamic HTML brings together a number of web technologies that work within an easily manageable structure. By leveraging existing technologies, such as Cascading Style Sheets, ActiveX, JavaScript, and VBScript, Dynamic HTML delivers an incredibly diverse range of applications. Dynamic HTML, however, is more than just a category for old technology. With new features such as data binding and data awareness, Dynamic HTML adds a level of extensibility that was previously unavailable to the web. Holding it all together is the Dynamic HTML Object Model, which opens the elements on a web page to scripting and manipulation in ways never before possible.

Why You Need This Book

Bringing together the technologies that Dynamic HTML encompasses is no small task. In addition to mastering several different technologies, it is necessary to understand how Dynamic HTML allows all the pieces to fit together and interoperate.

Getting the most out of Dynamic HTML involves mastering the following:

- Cascading Style Sheets
- Cascading Style Sheets Positioning
- Scripting—JavaScript or VBScript
- The Dynamic HTML Object Model
- Data binding and data awareness
- Implementing ActiveX Controls

This text will acquaint you with all the technologies used in Dynamic HTML. Each of the technologies is covered with a high level of detail, providing you with the knowledge you will need to use the technologies in accordance with Dynamic HTML. Then, in the final sections of the text, you will find some real-life examples. These examples will show you how to practically implement the theories and technologies discussed throughout this book.

How This Book Is Organized

This book is organized into six parts, each designed to acquaint you with everything you will need to begin developing your own Dynamic HTML pages and applications:

- Part I, "Dynamic HTML Basics" provides an introduction to Dynamic HTML. The chapters in this section are designed to showcase what can be accomplished with Dynamic HTML, and prime you for the examples and chapters to come.
- Part II, "Dynamic HTML Foundations," explores the fundamentals of Dynamic HTML. This part covers Cascading Style Sheets, JavaScript, the Dynamic HTML Object Model, and event handling. These are the foundations used to create Dynamic HTML content.

- Part III, "Inside Dynamic HTML," builds on the foundations provided in Part II and dives into Dynamic HTML creation—covering dynamic styles, layout and positioning, and dynamic content.

- Part IV, "Data Awareness," tackles data awareness and data binding, demonstrating how Dynamic HTML can be used to build complex database applications.

- Part V, "Multimedia and Dynamic HTML," moves from the world of Data Source Objects to interactivity and exciting animations. Part V explores the multimedia applications of Dynamic HTML, including the support for Microsoft's ActiveX Multimedia Controls.

- Part VI, "Real World Dynamic HTML," takes all the components of Dynamic HTML covered in previous parts and serves up some real world Dynamic HTML. Each chapter in this part provides a fully functional example of a Dynamic HTML application, complete with a detailed explanation of its creation.

- The Appendixes provide a comprehensive resource for the information provided elsewhere in the text. Comprehensive information on CSS, the Dynamic HTML Object Model, and alternate scripting languages can be found here.

Conventions Used in This Book

Because this book covers an array of scripting terms and components, it is important to distinguish them within the text. Scripting components such as objects, functions, methods, properties, and so forth are designated in *italic* text to help you distinguish them from normal text. Variables are set off by quotation marks("").

This book consists of a large amount of code. In complete examples of working code and in code snippets you may encounter this character, ➥. Within the constraints of printing, only a certain amount of characters can fit per line of text. The ➥ character designates that the line of code is a continuation of the line that precedes it. In cases of complete examples, you may find that the lines of code are numbered. These numbers are NOT part of the code—they are placed there to reference particular lines in the accompanying text within the body of the chapter.

N O T E   Notes provide additional information related to the topic at hand. ■

  Tips provide quick and helpful information to assist you along the way.

CAUTION
Cautions alert you to potential pitfalls or dangers in the operations discussed.

Dynamic HTML Basics

Dynamic HTML: A Defense

The World Wide Web has revolutionized the way that people use the Internet and interact with information. It would be impossible to achieve the level of Internet hysteria that exists today without the World Wide Web. Since its inception, the web has added compelling graphics, audio technology, limited interactivity (CGI and image maps) and has managed to capture the attention of many industries outside of computing. At the heart of the web is Hypertext Markup Language (HTML), the basic descriptive language that creates all the pages that advertise and inform through the web. As the web has matured, however, HTML has remained the same structurally. In fact, several HTML advances, such as tables and frames, have been embraced with mixed results. Although tables contribute formatting capabilities, they are a far cry from database applications. When you think of new innovative technologies that are changing the way the web is used, you probably think of ActiveX, Java, JavaScript, Visual Basic Script, and Cascading Style Sheets. No one ever talks of the revolutionary <BLINK> tag.

As technology has grown, stress has been placed on HTML to adapt. Incorporating all these technologies on some level has caused new tags to be created and has led to some changes in the way HTML is viewed. Those changes have finally come to the creation of a new web technology that is based in HTML—*Dynamic HTML*.

Limitations of Static HTML

Although HTML has been a landmark breakthrough for presenting text and graphics electronically to the largest possible audience, some drawbacks still exist.

Advantageous Features of Dynamic HTML

Learn how Dynamic HTML is revolutionizing information presentation on the web through the capability to specify typeface, position elements on a page, format page content, and alter page content at load time or runtime.

Style Sheets

Cascading Style Sheets arm Dynamic HTML with the capability to format web page content with smart design freedom and sensibility.

Scripting

Scripting languages provide the interactive backbone for Dynamic HTML with dynamic content generation and manipulation.

The Practicality of Dynamic HTML

Dynamic HTML changes the way web pages can be used, opening them up to serve as interfaces for multimedia and business applications, and creating new design methodologies that give designers more total control over their web-based content.

This chapter takes a look at some of the factors that have led to the development of Dynamic HTML (DHTML), and how the technology has become important to web development. As a web technology, DHTML offers the capability to create new and innovative web pages, which can act as interfaces to more complex and compelling web-based applications than were possible previously. The following parts outline some of the most compelling features of Dynamic HTML and how those features differ in different vendors' implementations.

- **Part II, "Dynamic HTML Foundations":** Covers the basics of Cascading Style Sheets, JavaScript, the Dynamic HTML Object Model, and Event Handling
- **Part III, "Inside Dynamic HTML":** Covers in detail the structure and implementation of dynamic styles, layout and positioning, dynamic content, and integration of multimedia
- **Part IV, "Data Awareness":** Covers the importance of data binding and data source objects
- **Part V, "Multimedia and Dynamic HTML":** Covers the integration of multimedia content with Dynamic HTML through the use of animation effects, CSS Positioning, transitions, filters, and ActiveX Controls
- **Part VI, "Real World Dynamic HTML":** Provides several models for implementing Dynamic HTML in real world scenarios

Let's take a look at the origin of Dynamic HTML, and at some of what Dynamic HTML has to offer.

The Limits of Static HTML

HTML is a great way to develop informative documents that are platform independent. It is fairly easy to create a web page that combines text and graphics in a single document by using HTML. CGI scripting and the inclusion of forms act as catalysts for more interactive experiences for the users, allowing them feedback mechanisms, and some rudimentary form of a user interface. Image map and CGI combinations have been used to create web-based games, and to create the illusion of a room or world that can be explored by clicking objects. Anyone comparing those types of interactive activities on the web versus the type of interactivity available on a CD-ROM will quickly find the experience lacking. Web-based interactivity often is slower because of the need to download information. This type of interaction is also pretty limited to simple, point-and-click interfaces. Without incorporating a Java applet or an ActiveX component, web-based interfaces can be pretty dull—and at the same time take quite an effort to produce.

Sure, animated GIFs can provide motion on a page, but only when a predefined motion path for objects is in a static area. With Dynamic HTML, the user could have the option of moving elements to a location of their choice. Developing complex user interfaces and layouts is also a tedious prospect; for example, the classic *one pixel spacer* technique has had to be used in the past for fine tuning layout control.

Web design has been limited by three major factors since the inception of HTML: text formatting, layout control, and the capability to dynamically alter document content. By refining these areas of web design, developers can take the web to the next level of user experiences.

Text Formatting Limits

Anyone who has ever tried to perform extensive text formatting with HTML has undoubtedly become frustrated by HTML's formatting limitations. This problem derives from the very inception of the web. The web was built to present information to a variety of clients quickly and easily. It was not designed for explicit layout and control of positioning, which, coincidentally, are the very elements that designers employ to create visually appealing designs. A quick lesson in HTML coding reveals that it is bad form to use a bold tag, <B>, when you should use a <STRONG> tag. The formatting for these tags is determined by the browser, which is exactly what makes HTML so portable—it's also what makes it so visually unappealing.

Out of desperation, designers have turned to a number of tricks for designing on the web. Many have used the technique of applying one pixel spacers to align elements on a page. Others have used tables to create a design grid. Neither is a very elegant solution, and both methods result in wasted time for the designer.

Designers have long been frustrated by HTML's formatting shortcomings. Many typographers were driven to new levels of insanity simply trying to indent a paragraph. To add insult to injury, the World Wide Web does not enable designers to control the font with which users set up their browser to display web pages. This lack of control can result in subtle differences from page to page and from browser to browser. As people began to use HTML tricks such as tables and alignment to create better layouts, the test formatting sometimes ended up confusing or unreadable.

Layout Control Limits

In addition to restrictions in the formatting arena, static HTML also prevents web designers from controlling content/text positioning and layout. Although HTML did make it easy to combine text and graphics, the resulting layouts were far less appealing than a newspaper or magazine layout. Positioning images was nearly impossible, as was wrapping text around images. With the <TABLE> tag, designers found a complicated way to incorporate some aspects of layout into HTML pages, but the process was quite tedious and still at the mercy of the browser.

The argument from many HTML purists was that the web was designed to be portable, and introducing mechanisms to provide strict layout control defeats that portability. The web is a new medium, after all, and should be designed as such. The problem is that sacrificing many of these layout elements prevented designers from creating copies of print design and from creating new interfaces that were unique to the web. Instead, web pages generally looked the same, with slight variations in graphical elements. The advent of tables and frames has contributed to the capability of the designer to create more distinct layouts. Tables have aided in the display and formatting of data, and frames have annoyed users everywhere with poor implementations.

With each successive preview release, however, browser manufacturers continue to improve the features that were improperly implemented the first time. Even frames have evolved to the point of being useful for "Table of Contents" and other types of navigation features.

Inability to Dynamically Change Content

HTML is also limited to rendering the contents of a web page, without allowing for changes after the page has been loaded. In fact, the problem goes even further than that: A web page with static HTML has no mechanism to adapt its layout to the browser being used to access it. If, for example, the user viewing a page resizes the window, the text might rewrap, but the images won't scale accordingly.

A concert promoter, for example, might want to have a page that showed the seating chart and stage layout for an upcoming concert. With static HTML, she could provide a GIF or JPEG image of the seating arrangement. With Dynamic HTML, however, it would be possible to show the seating layout, and to enable the user to click a potential seating section. Then, the layout could be altered to hide elements on the stage that would be obscured from that seat. By using Dynamic HTML, this user interaction could be done on the user's local machine, eliminating a complex application on the server.

The capability to dynamically change content from a single page is a very important feature of Dynamic HTML. It would be possible to provide similar content with traditional HTML. You could, for example, have an image map that represents the seats in the arena. When the user clicks an area, the map could pass the data on to a CGI script, which could then provide the browser with a new image based on the seating choice. You, however, can see that this would involve significantly more steps, and several interactions with the server, which could result in potential performance bottlenecks.

The capability to manipulate the contents of a page after loading is also important for user interface features. Altering text or dynamic text expansion, for example, can be used to make information more clear, or to provide explanations. Take a table of products that compares features and price points. At the top of each column in the header would be the title for that column, for example "MSRP." A user might be curious about what "MSRP" means, and with static HTML you could provide a hot link that takes the user to another page that would explain "MSRP." What if the words "Manufacturers Suggested Retail Price" display when the user passes the mouse pointer over the "MSRP" table header? Both scenarios serve the same purpose, however, traditional HTML would involve clicking and loading a new page. It involves a departure from the original page and data, for a simple term that should not require reloading a page to redefine.

Advantageous Features of Dynamic HTML

With the limits of static HTML hampering web page design, Dynamic HTML attempts to bring a new level of flexibility and development to the World Wide Web. Some of this is accomplished through the merger of existing technologies, such as Cascading Style Sheets and JavaScript. Some of Dynamic HTML's power comes from new features, such as data awareness and data binding.

Dynamic HTML arms the designer or information architect with the capability to control layout and information exchange that previously required complex or workload heavy server-side scripting or troublesome workarounds. Some of the features of Dynamic HTML include the following: layout precision, data awareness, dynamic styles, and dynamic content.

Layout Precision with Dynamic HTML

Creating visually appealing web pages without using some of the elements of traditional graphic design can be a daunting task. Designers rely on their capability to perform a few essential tasks when creating any sort of layout:

- Specifying typefaces
- Positioning images
- Formatting text

Without these options, the designers are severely limited in their capability to design well. It is much like asking a mechanic to fix your car with no wrenches. A skilled mechanic might still be able to do the job, but the quality of the work will suffer.

Font Specification   The capability to specify the typeface used on a page is one of the most fundamental aspects of any design. What if, for example, your company logo makes extensive use of a font that looks bad with Times Roman—the default font of many browsers. You could certainly have all your employees change their browser fonts, but that would be a hassle. You could put a disclaimer on the page noting that the page is best viewed with the Arial font. Most users, however, are not likely to take special steps to view a home page.

What if you could specify the name of the font that the browser was to use, assuming it were available. A number of fonts are automatically installed with Windows or the Macintosh operating system. These fonts could easily be used to design your web pages. Designers can specify a font that would be at least closer to their ideal by using the standard fonts.

Even the use of a standard font does not guarantee that the font will be installed on all user browsers. For dealing with this type of situation, the designer can specify a generic font family or style, such as sans serif, so that at the very least the font is closer to the ideal.

Altering Text   Dynamic HTML offers a unique dimension of text formatting: the capability to change text on-the-fly. This can be useful in creating user interface features, such as highlighting text links that are embedded in a document. You can change the color, size, and font of text in a Dynamic HTML document based on any number of factors, such as the amount of time after a page has loaded, or as a reaction to the user placing the mouse pointer closer to the text.

An example of this technique is imaging a page that loads with nothing but plain, black text. As time passes, say five seconds, the first link could automatically be highlighted in red. This would alert the page viewer to the link's presence and create a new interface for the web page. The page might even reveal more links as time progresses, showing a new link on the page every three seconds, designed to walk the reader through the page. The text could even change color when the user passes the mouse pointer over it. This could be used to create a text game, like a "word find" in which hidden links are embedded in the text.

Another way in which text manipulation could be used would be to replace the text on a page. You might, for example, have an interactive game that has several status indicators, such as "Number of Ships: 3." By using the power of Dynamic HTML and text ranges, you can actually replace the text on the page, changing "Number of Ships: 3" to "Only One Ship Left!" Chapter 10, "Dynamic Content," takes a closer look at text ranges and changing content.

Dynamic content, or the capability to manipulate a page text or HTML content on-the-fly and after the page has been loaded, is what makes DHTML so revolutionary. HTML has undergone several minor changes since its inception, but none have had the same potential to revolutionize the way web pages are designed as dynamic content has.

Absolute Positioning To create the most visually appealing layout, designers are usually very careful about the positioning of the elements that construct their designs. Static HTML does provide some level of positioning by using the <ALIGN> tag: align left, right, and center.

Aside from aligning elements the way you would format text in a word processing program, HTML provides little control for positioning elements on a page, based on the browser window size, or positioning the objects relative to each other. HTML simply flows elements on the page, and no mechanism for instructing the browser to position an element in a specific place exists, such as 50 pixels from the left side.

These types of positioning for elements can prove very useful for making the best use of the browser window, and for making sure that your pages are adjusted to the correct size for different resolutions. You might, for example, design a page by using a 15-inch monitor running 600×800, aligning your images for that sized window. When your page is viewed on a 17- or 20-inch monitor at 1024×786, users might find the layout chaotic, or be faced with a lot of wasted screen space. By taking advantage of positioning elements based on the screen size, you ensure that your page always looks correct for the appropriate sized window.

Z-Indexing Absolute (and relative) positioning enable the user to specify the location of elements on a page by specifying coordinates that essentially map to the X and Y axis. Another important aspect of positioning, however, is the Z-index.

Z-indexing is a means of assigning positioned elements to a layer on the page so that one element can overlap another, and the designer can control which element will remain on top.

Positioning elements with X and Y coordinates is fairly straightforward. A specified element can be assigned coordinates, and will be positioned on the loaded page according to those coordinates. This enables designers to position text anywhere on a page in relation to images, or to align two images together precisely. When you add Z-index positioning to X and Y coordinate positioning, you have a very powerful layout device.

Z-indexing enables designers to specify a position for an element along the Z axis. Although this might not seem like much, it is a great step forward in web design. By combining the capability to specify X and Y coordinates along with the capability to specify a Z position, new effects become possible. Using this technique enables images to be placed on the page so that they overlap. Imagine a map that has different areas of detail that are magnified when the mouse passes over them. With positioning, the detailed areas could be separate images with coordinates that are specified relative to the actual map. These elements could be located on a different layer, and when the mouse passes over them, the image of the detail area could be shown.

This type of application could be used for creating educational materials, such as geographic maps, or maps that include information about a region, such as political news or economic factors. It could also be used to create new user interface information for a particular site. Imagine a site index that was an image map that displays an icon representing the content instead of just showing a text description of an area on the site. The applications of positioning and Z-indexing are discussed more in Chapter 9, "Layout and Positioning."

Indexing and positioning can be combined to make layout for the web as flexible as layout for print. It was mentioned earlier that it might not be possible for an organization to duplicate their newsletter layout with the web. Positioning makes the transition between different mediums a little easier, allowing for a greater continuity among the design of different elements—print or electronic.

Data Awareness

Although it might seem like all the reasons that HTML was stifling are related to design, that is certainly not the case. Design innovations tend to come to the foreground because of their visual impact, but another area overlooked by HTML is that of incorporating data into web sites.

Since the web's inception, users have wanted to merge data applications and the web. The first forms of CGI scripts were designed to get input from the user, and to provide the user with some sort of feedback after filling out a form. As CGI scripting and server applications have matured, many applications have started making extensive use of data and the web.

Take travel sites, for example, that provide users with airline ticketing and reservations. Many of these sites enable a user to input data such as flight times and travel dates via a forms interface. This information is then fed back to the web server, where it is used in conjunction with a database application to look up information and then output it back to the user's browser.

Database applications play an important role in the development of the World Wide Web. As businesses turn to the web to access and input data into more traditional applications, a bridge is needed to bring data functions to the web.

Currently, HTML relies on a number of supporting technologies to achieve a poor form of data integration. Adding some form of interactive data to a web page would currently require extensive CGI scripting, or writing custom server-side includes. Of course, you could build data-based applications with ActiveX or Java, assuming that complex database programming is in your lexicon and schedule.

Dynamic HTML incorporates some new features that are designed to marry data access and web pages. Techniques such as dynamic table expansion eliminate the need to produce custom tables with CGI or server-side includes. Data awareness and data binding enable the development of some fairly advanced database interfaces without the extensive programming knowledge that might be required with Java or ActiveX.

Dynamically Producing Tables with Dynamic HTML   HTML tables helped bring data to the World Wide Web. Large amounts of information, such as product specifications or price comparisons, are generally best presented in a table for user viewing and analysis. Of course, HTML tables can be generated on-the-fly on the server side through a database server and server-side scripting. After the requested data is output to a script, the script builds a table and outputs the HTML table to the client browser.

What if the browser were able to accept the output directly from the database application and format a table dynamically? This scenario eliminates the server's scripting step, thereby decreasing the workload of the site's server, and increasing the speed of the transaction for the end user. The result is a better data interface for everyone, and that is exactly what Dynamic HTML is capable of achieving.

Dynamic HTML also enables tables to expand dynamically. This means that the user can view a page before all the data for the table is finished downloading from the server. As more table data loads, the table expands, resulting in a faster presentation of the overall page.

Imagine a pottery company, for example, that offered a set of plates with several different glazing options. With each glaze the price is different and some other slight variations need to be conveyed to a site visitor. Of course, the company could produce a new HTML file with a different table for each possible glaze, but this would require more HTML authoring each time a new glaze is introduced or discontinued. If the browser were capable of generating a table on-the-fly, the company would save time, and the user could easily explore all available options.

Dynamic table creation gives Dynamic HTML some distinct advantages over traditional tables—even tables that are generated by server-side applications. First, because the table is generated dynamically, based on the incoming data, it can also be regenerated dynamically. That means users could sort a table after it had been downloaded, a task that would require passing instructions back to the server, and regenerating a table on the server with traditional HTML. Because the data for the table is already incorporated into the page, that data does not need to be redownloaded. Instead, queries, filters, and sorting can be applied to the table, and then the table can be regenerated.

This capability to manipulate data in tables without contacting the server gives Dynamic HTML qualities that could be quite useful in business applications. The capability to perform data manipulation using local database engines as opposed to the server lowers the burden placed on the server and enables users to create customized data views dynamically. Dynamic HTML's data manipulation capabilities make it much easier to develop web-based database front ends and database applications. Working with tables, data awareness, and data binding are covered more in Chapter 11, "Introduction to Data Binding," and Chapter 12, "Using Data Source Objects."

Creating "Data Aware" Objects with Dynamic HTML   Dynamic HTML also uses a technique called data binding that enables HTML elements to be bound to certain database records. This enables records from a database to be incorporated into the HTML and displayed on the page as a part of the HTML element. This technique can be used to create customized HTML objects that are different for each user based on records generated by the database application.

Say, for example, that you had a company that produced gumballs, and you want to design a virtual catalog for your wares. You could create the catalog with the image of a gumball machine, with the knobs allowing you to select the merchandise that was displayed in the clear "dome" portion of the gumball machine. By using data binding, you could create controls that included the image of the merchandise, and bound those images to the gumball machine. You could also then build the controls of the gumball machine to control the image that was being displayed. The end result would be a nifty multimedia catalog based on data and images from the company's database. Chapter 12 talks more about data binding, and Part VI, "Real World Dynamic HTML," uses data binding to create an online catalog.

Dynamically Changing Pages after Loading

Dynamic HTML can be used to create pages that are dynamically generated at load time (for example, setting the font on a page). The font is specified as the page is loaded, and the font is actually changed before the page is finished loading. When the user accesses the page, the font is already set. The capability to alter the appearance of web pages at load time—based on layout instructions or data that is downloaded from the server—is one application of Dynamic HTML.

Another way in which Dynamic HTML can be used to create a truly dynamic experience is by changing the information on a web page at runtime, after the page has been loaded from the server. Imagine, for example, that you wanted to make a web version of the children's toy, Mr. Potato Head. It wouldn't be much of a user experience to see a different image of a completed face each time the page reloaded. Instead, you would want to create a user experience that is similar to the actual toy. This would involve a blank potato, and then the images of the parts for the face. You would want users to be able to click an element, say a nose, and drag it into position on the potato. This is what Dynamic HTML can provide: the capability to change data on a page after the page has already loaded.

Font and Color Manipulation   Of course, in addition to repositioning images, you can alter the qualities of text on your page. The font can be specified when the page is loaded, but the fonts in Dynamic HTML can also be changed on-the-fly. This allows for text effects, such as growing fonts or changing the color of fonts.

In fact, the entire color scheme of your pages can be altered by using Dynamic HTML. Elements that have color attributes can have those attributes altered after the page is already loaded, which can create a variety of user experiences based on a single page download. This type of content manipulation is covered later in Chapter 8, "Dynamic Styles."

Text Manipulation   In addition to altering the attributes of the text displayed on a dynamic web page, it is also possible to alter the actual text itself. This capability to replace text elements on demand can be very useful. Say, for example, that you want to create a text menu that expands as users pass over the items. You could create two descriptions for each item, one short and one long. The menu would be built using the short descriptions, with the longer ones waiting in the wings. By using Dynamic HTML, the menu could be designed to display the longer description if the user passes the mouse over a menu element. This type of text manipulation can be used to build complex user interfaces that are much quicker for the end user than building a complex component, such as a Java applet, to accomplish the same task. These sorts of content altering techniques are discussed in greater detail in Chapter 10, "Dynamic Content."

Style Sheets

You might already be somewhat familiar with Cascading Style Sheets (CSS) as a technology that has helped change the way that designers can approach managing web site and page design. Style sheets enable an incredible amount of flexibility in web page design. They also enable designers to add new levels of consistency to a site by enabling a design specification to be developed that can be applied to different areas of the site, or used as a template for other pages and sites.

Both Internet Explorer 4.0 and Netscape Communicator support Cascading Style Sheets. The current version of the standard, Cascading Style Sheets, Level 1 (CSS1) is administered by the W3C (World Wide Web Consortium).

Style sheets are the first leap forward in allowing designers freedom when designing for the web. Style sheets allow designers to develop styles that can be applied to entire areas of a site, and are the mechanism by which Dynamic HTML accesses many of the page formatting details that are used to create dynamic styles and content. The integration of CSS is a critical portion of Dynamic HTML, and CSS is covered in great detail in Chapter 4, "Cascading Style Sheets Primer."

Increasing Web Site Design Control with CSS

The first benefit of CSS is that it gives designers more control over web page layout and design. Using Cascading Style Sheets enables designers to specify color schemes, such as making all <H1> head levels green. Additionally, CSS solves some of the design problems that are typically associated with web layout, such as specifying whitespace, element spacing, and indents.

Creating Web Site Templates with CSS

Cascading Style Sheets are also an important step for the web because they enable the templatization of web sites. A style sheet can be created for the site, and then referenced by all the pages in it. Style sheet templates enable the content to be managed almost independently of the site's design. This management subsequently leads to a higher level of specialization for the site's content creators, helps bring consistency to a site, and helps create an overall graphic image.

Style sheets play a big role in Dynamic HTML because many of the features of Dynamic HTML are actually implemented through a combination of style sheets and scripting. In fact, some of the features, such as X,Y,Z positioning, are actually just different applications of the CSS Positioning standard. Dynamic HTML is a convenient way to group technologies together under one topic, to make implementation a little easier—and hopefully more straightforward.

Scripting

Another fundamental component of Dynamic HTML is a scripting language that is used to link elements together—a language that is used to manipulate elements after the page is loaded. Without a scripting language, many of the features that are touted with Dynamic HTML would not really be features at all. Of course, scripting languages can be used to add life to static HTML as well, but scripting is an integral part of Dynamic HTML. In fact, without scripting languages Dynamic HTML isn't very dynamic.

Sure, you can use positioning to animate graphic elements on a page, but not without a scripting language. If, for example, you wanted a graphic image to move from left to right across the page, you could do so with Dynamic HTML. The element could be positioned on the left as the page loads, and then the position could be shifted to the right by using scripting.

JavaScript

JavaScript is a scripting language developed at Netscape and designed to be structurally similar to the Java programming language. Because JavaScript was the first scripting language developed for use on the World Wide Web, it has become quite a popular language for scripting web sites. Therefore, it is supported by both IE 4.0 and Communicator, and remains a convenient way to script static HTML pages—and to control Dynamic HTML elements.

JavaScript is actually a powerful scripting language, but is fairly easy to learn. Many of the concepts and structures of JavaScript might be familiar to other web developers because they are based on Java syntax. The following shows a rudimentary JavaScript:

```
<SCRIPT language="JavaScript">

        document.write("Hello, world");

   </SCRIPT>
```

The script simply writes the words "Hello, world" in the browser window. It's only one line, but it still does quite a bit. Because of its simple syntax, power, and widespread use, JavaScript is an excellent choice for Dynamic HTML scripting. In fact, that's why it's the scripting language of choice in this book. You can learn more about JavaScript in Chapter 5, "JavaScript Primer."

VBScript

Visual Basic, Scripting Edition is a scripting language designed by Microsoft modeled after the Visual Basic programming language. Visual Basic (VB) is one of the most popular tools among corporate IS departments for creating in-house applications. Because of its popularity in the corporate world and its ties to other Microsoft products, Visual Basic also makes a good choice for scripting Dynamic HTML.

JavaScript and VBScript are very similar to each other, and there are advantages and disadvantages to both, which will be discussed in later chapters. If you already are familiar with one language, stick to it and don't spend valuable time trying to learn the other language. In spite of their different syntax, both scripting languages are well-suited for Dynamic HTML.

The Practicality of Dynamic HTML

Whenever you are evaluating a new Internet technology, there are always two fundamental reasons to adopt the new technology: the practical factors and the cool factors. As you can see from our feature summary, the cool factors certainly apply to Dynamic HTML. If you want to create hip, cutting-edge material for the World Wide Web, you will undoubtedly adopt Dynamic HTML. What about the practical reasons? Individuals might be able to justify learning a new technology based on merit, or because it adds a new creative dimension to their home pages, but businesses often need more solid, practical reasons before adopting a new technology. Dynamic HTML addresses this business sensibility in three areas: enabling compelling web presentations, facilitating site maintenance, and reducing server load.

Creating Compelling Web Sites

The single biggest practical reason for Dynamic HTML is that it helps create compelling web sites. This might seem like an overlap of the cool factors, and it is somewhat. Many people, however, are inundated with information on the web, and the only way to make that information stick out in their minds is to create new, innovative pages that capture their attention. You can certainly rely on older technologies to create visually appealing pages, but when other pages feature dynamic fonts, changing colors, or other special effects, it will be difficult to maintain your audience without all the bells and whistles.

Another type of compelling page is a page that contains very current data so that users are always aware of the changes. Waiting to download a table full of old, stale data is not nearly as compelling as viewing a dynamically generated table that expands as new data is received.

Easier Maintenance

It might seem that a lot of effort could go into creating web pages with Dynamic HTML, and that is an accurate statement. It is also important to remember that the features of Dynamic HTML lend themselves to making maintenance easier. If, for example, your pages are created with content from a database that is loaded and bound to Dynamic HTML objects, after the page design is specified, new data can be pumped into the same design. The same holds true for using style sheets as design templates. Style sheets enable you to design a site independent of the content, so updating the page doesn't mean redesigning it, as with earlier versions of HTML. An investment exists in developing the original design, but with style sheets and data binding, you can make surprisingly good use of existing resources after your site design is finished.

Lower Server Load

Finally, Dynamic HTML can take the burden of processing information off of your server and put it on the client. Animation, user interface elements, even simple data manipulation can be moved from the server and CGI scripts into Dynamic HTML scripts. This makes the overall interface faster for the end user because there is no need to reconnect to the server to update information. Instead, the data is all downloaded and presented according to the user's specifications. Sorting a table with static HTML involves sending the sorting parameters back to the server, generating a new table, and downloading the new table to the user's client—all the while adding load to your server and keeping the user in suspense. A Dynamic HTML table could be manipulated in near real-time on the user's machine, making everyone a winner.

From Here...

As you can see, the progression of technology used for the World Wide Web has created the demand for some new types of services, and new methods for designing and publishing web pages. Dynamic HTML addresses some of the issues that have plagued the web for years, which is a very long time in Internet years. Continue on to learn about some of the great new features that Dynamic HTML has to offer, and to see what you can look forward to creating in the future.

  ▪ Chapter 2, "Dynamic HTML Overview," takes a closer look at all the features that are promised by Dynamic HTML, and what Dynamic HTML has delivered. More detail is provided about some of the points that have been touched on in this chapter—to help you realize the potential that lies in Dynamic HTML.

- Chapter 3, "Microsoft versus Netscape," takes a look at the biggest issue facing Dynamic HTML—the standards battle between Netscape and Microsoft over the implementation of Dynamic HTML.

- Part II, "Dynamic HTML Foundations," examines the fundamental skills needed to start creating your own web pages with Dynamic HTML, to ensure that you have the skills you will need to work with Dynamic HTML, and have all the resources available at your disposal.

- Part III, "Inside Dynamic HTML," begins an in-depth look at Dynamic HTML.

Dynamic HTML Overview

Dynamic HTML offers a new set of extensions to HTML, merged with supporting technologies, that enable the creation of new and compelling web-based documents and applications. Dynamic HTML allows the creation of real-world business applications, and multimedia applications that were impossible to create with static HTML. Dynamic HTML also makes it easier to develop many features for the web that were difficult and time consuming with static HTML.

It is easy to talk about Dynamic HTML as if it were simply one thing: a new version of HTML that adds all the features discussed in this book; however, Dynamic HTML is much more than that. It is really a collection of technologies designed to work together.

Dynamic HTML relies on Cascading Style Sheets as a mechanism for altering the stylistic content of a page. Without CSS, many of the color effects, font effects, and other style attributes would not be so easy to alter. Dynamic HTML also makes extensive use of CSS Positioning. Layering and animation effects are a result of CSS Positioning. Finally, Dynamic HTML uses JavaScript and VBScript, scripting languages that get their bite in Dynamic HTML through the Dynamic HTML Object Model. By combining all these technologies, you create what is referred to throughout this text as Dynamic HTML.

Object Model

The Dynamic HTML Object Model enables all HTML elements on a page to be treated as objects.

Scripting

Scripting is an essential part of instructing Dynamic HTML elements how to behave.

Cascading Style Sheets

CSS provide the glue for Dynamic HTML web pages, and are a means for controlling web page layout and element styles.

Load Time/Runtime Content Alteration

Dynamic HTML can manipulate page content during its download to the browser (load time). Microsoft's version of Dynamic HTML can also manipulate the data after the page is loaded (runtime).

Text Effects

Dynamic HTML allows for a variety of text effects.

Multimedia/Animation

Dynamic HTML can create animation, transparency, lighting filters, and blending effects.

Data Awareness/Data Binding

Data awareness and data binding enable Dynamic HTML to work directly with data from database servers.

As you read on to discover the features of Dynamic HTML, be sure to keep in mind that many of these topics will require more extensive outside reading or reference on your part. This text covers all the technologies of Dynamic HTML and discusses the core Dynamic HTML entities in great detail. Knowledge of some of the other topics, however, is quite helpful in exploiting the technology to its fullest extent. Whenever possible, you are provided with an overview of auxiliary technologies, but to cover them all comprehensively would really require a three book set. So read on to discover what Dynamic HTML is about. ▓

Defining Microsoft Dynamic HTML

What would a web technology be without a little friendly competition? Dynamic HTML is certainly no exception to this rule. Of course, both Microsoft and Netscape are developing competing standards for Dynamic HTML, and the two standards are not compatible. This text purposefully covers the Microsoft implementation of Dynamic HTML—largely because of Microsoft's willingness to submit their specification to the World Wide Web Consortium (W3C) and the more "dynamic" nature of their technology. Chapter 3, "Microsoft versus Netscape," provides a comparison of the technologies so that you can get a better idea of how the two technologies stack up, side-by-side.

N O T E Although Microsoft has chosen to submit Dynamic HTML to the W3C, it still has not been ratified as a standard. When, and if, it finally is, there may be some minor changes to the technology, and more browser vendors will support Dynamic HTML. Until then, you should consider the Microsoft Dynamic HTML covered in this book to be a proprietary format, for use in conjunction with Internet Explorer 4.0. ▓

So, what is Microsoft Dynamic HTML? It is really a combination of new HTML attributes, JavaScript or VBScript, and Cascading Style Sheets that work together to provide the features outlined in this chapter. This chapter discusses Dynamic HTML features specific to Microsoft Dynamic HTML. For a comprehensive analysis of Netscape's implementation of Dynamic HTML compared to Microsoft's implementation of Dynamic HTML, refer to Chapter 3. Part II, "Dynamic HTML Foundations," moves on to cover the other technologies that you'll need to make Dynamic HTML work.

In addition to creating a glue that binds existing web technologies together, however, Dynamic HTML does have a few tricks of its own up its sleeves. Data binding and data awareness are both new features that Dynamic HTML brings to the playing field; however, one of the most important and revolutionary aspects of Dynamic HTML is the Dynamic HTML Object Model.

The Object Model

Object-based technologies are not new to computing, and they are not new to the World Wide Web. Dynamic HTML is one of many technologies that uses an object model to implement the technology's features and how they interact with each other. In fact, Dynamic HTML's Object Model gives it many of the capabilities that make Dynamic HTML a compelling new technology.

The advantage of Dynamic HTML is that all the elements on the page are treated as programmable objects. An image could be an object. So could a chunk of text, or virtually any type of element that you might place on a web page. These objects have events that can be handled, and methods and properties that can be manipulated through scripting.

The capability to script Dynamic HTML objects is one of the strongest aspects of Dynamic HTML. The capability to script an object enables one element to influence the behavior of another. With scripting, for example, you could create an object that passed its position to another object, so that when one object moved, the other object moved in relation to the first object. The same technique could be applied to data objects, such that the value of one object influences the value or properties of another object.

The following example demonstrates a real-world scenario of how objects are used with Dynamic HTML. Suppose you were designing a page for a car dealership that had an image of a car that was for sale on the page. To the right of the car's image might be a list of features. As the user passes their mouse pointer over each of the features, that feature could be automatically highlighted on the image. To do this, each of the tags that describes a feature needs to be able to capture the event from the mouse movement. Then through a script, it needs to be able to control the state of the image. All this is accomplished through the object model.

Taking advantage of the object model allows Dynamic HTML to become even more than mere extensions to HTML. Although the Dynamic HTML Object Model is not particularly complex, it is important to understand how objects relate to each other, and how they handle events, such as mouse clicks and mouse movements. The Dynamic HTML Object Model is discussed in detail in Chapter 6, "Dynamic HTML Object Model."

On the surface, the Dynamic HTML Object Model might seem like it is a complicated model for working with HTML, but quite the contrary is true. The Dynamic HTML Object Model is quite simple: it exposes HTML elements on a page as objects. In spite of its simplicity, the object model adds an important feature to Dynamic HTML—event bubbling. Event bubbling is discussed in Chapter 6, but the most important thing to learn about it now is that Dynamic HTML objects can either deal with events (such as mouse clicks) or they can "bubble" up to another object. If, for example, you pass the mouse over an image, and the image has not been scripted to handle the event, then the event is passed up the chain to the next object, such as the document. This type of event handling can help you develop some complex user interfaces without having to develop complex event handling routines. Event handling is covered in more detail in Chapter 7, "Event Handling."

Exposing the elements on a page through the object model and providing elements with the capability to capture events makes it easier to develop interfaces. But develop interfaces using what? There needs to be a mechanism to create the interaction between elements that have been described, and that mechanism is scripting.

Employing JavaScript or VBScript with Dynamic HTML

Dynamic HTML needs a tool to make many of the *dynamic* changes previously discussed. HTML tags offer one level of dynamic interaction, but the capability to script Dynamic HTML objects gives the technology more power.

If, for example, you wanted to take two elements and link them so that they move together, you would need some sort of mechanism to communicate position information from one object to the other. The mechanism that you would use is a scripting language, such as JavaScript or VBScript.

N O T E Microsoft refers to JavaScript as *JScript,* however, Microsoft is the only entity supporting JavaScript to do so. Because the language is referred to by its full name in all other documentation, and other outside texts, it is referred to as JavaScript in this text.

JavaScript is a scripting language developed by Netscape—and is included in the Navigator and Communicator software. Microsoft also offers support for JavaScript in Internet Explorer 4.0, and it can be used as a scripting language for Dynamic HTML components.

JavaScript is a useful scripting language because of its widespread support, its easy-to-use object model, and its syntax based on the Java programming language. If you are not already familiar with JavaScript, you can learn more about it in Chapter 5, "JavaScript Primer."

In addition to allowing Dynamic HTML scripting with JavaScript, Microsoft has also developed a scripting language based on Visual Basic called *VBScript*. VBScript offers many of the same features and extensibility as JavaScript, but might be a better choice for individuals who are already familiar with Visual Basic. In actuality, the scripting languages are not that different. If you have a mastery of one, learning the other should not prove a difficult task. If, however, you are already comfortable with one of the languages, there is no compelling reason to learn the other one. After all, both languages can accomplish the same tasks. Why reinvent the wheel?

Although VBScript is not covered extensively in this book, Appendix C, "Using VBScript Instead of JavaScript," contains a detailed comparison of the two scripting technologies.

Communicating Between Objects

Scripting is the principal method that enables communication between Dynamic HTML objects. To create complex new user interfaces and new designs that take advantage of Dynamic HTML's capabilities, you will need to rely on using different elements together. It might be possible to use one simple Dynamic HTML object to add a new font to your page, or to create some other design aspect. But generally, you want to use more than one Dynamic HTML object in conjunction with another.

To communicate information from one Dynamic HTML object to another, you need to employ a scripting language. To manipulate Dynamic HTML objects, you also need to use a script to pass the parameters to the Dynamic HTML object—or to manipulate the parameters.

Putting the Dynamic in Dynamic HTML with Scripting

Dynamic HTML wouldn't be very dynamic without the incorporation and functionality of scripting. Without the capability to script Dynamic HTML, many of the features would be reduced to load time features, without the capability to change items on-the-fly, which is the power of Dynamic HTML. Without scripting, it might be possible to specify a new font, but it wouldn't be possible to change the font size of a link when the mouse passed over it. It would be possible to position elements in a layout, but not to move them relative to each other.

If, for example, you wanted to change the size of a font after the page was loaded, how would you pass along the point size to your text element? After the page is loaded, the point size cannot be changed without using a script that will increase the point size of the font based on whatever event you specify, such as a mouse-over or click.

The Importance of Cascading Style Sheets

In an effort to address many of the design issues problematic for the early web, Netscape and Microsoft, among several other influential companies, collaborated to develop a technology called *Cascading Style Sheets (CSS)*. Cascading Style Sheets represents a way of defining attributes for HTML elements, and applying those attributes to the entire page, or even to an entire site.

A style enables web authors to set an attribute for an HTML tag that can be applied globally. The <STYLE> tag, for example, could be used to set the indent for a page to ten spaces. A style can also be used to establish guides for a specific element, such as specifying that all <H2> tags should be displayed in red. By defining a style once in the document, and applying it to all the elements, authors can save time coding, and easily change attributes by assigning a single <STYLE> tag to an HTML element—rather than manually changing every occurrence of the HTML element in a document.

Another advantage of Cascading Style Sheets is that individual style tags can be grouped together into a single file. This file could contain all the style elements for a page design, and would be referred to as a *style sheet*. The style sheet can then be included in any file using the <LINK> tag, or an *@import* statement. This enables the actual style definitions to reside in a physical file that is separate from the HTML page to which it is being applied. This gives designers incredible flexibility to define a global style sheet for a site, and then manipulate individual styles on a page by page basis by including one style sheet in several different HTML pages.

So how do Cascading Style Sheets fit into Dynamic HTML? First, CSS can be used to control the appearance of HTML elements—what would happen if you could script changes to style sheets? Well, you'd get Dynamic HTML. In fact, the link between Dynamic HTML and Cascading Style Sheets is so tight that it would be almost impossible to separate CSS from Dynamic HTML.

You might recall mention of layout and positioning with CSS that is taken advantage of by Dynamic HTML. In fact, Dynamic HTML layout, and X-,Y-, and even Z-index positioning are all directly from style sheets. The Cascading Style Sheets specification enables absolute and relative positioning of HTML elements, and establishes a Z-index for layering. Dynamic HTML makes use of these positioning features by combining them with JavaScript to dynamically change the positioning of an object. Similarly, animation effects can be created by manipulating the positioning parameters of a style sheet with JavaScript or VBScript code.

Chapter 4, "Cascading Style Sheets Primer," covers the implementation of Cascading Style Sheets and provides a tutorial on working with style sheets, because it is such an essential component to Dynamic HTML. Chapter 9, "Layout and Positioning," discusses the issues of Cascading Style Sheets Positioning in greater detail.

Adapting Content for the Browser

Using load-time Dynamic HTML enables you to configure your page for a particular browser. You can query the browser to see how the user environment is set. Changing your page's color scheme, changing the display font, and adjusting your content to the size of the browser window are all examples of how to use Dynamic HTML at load time so that your pages are presented in the best light to the end user. Because first impressions are so important, this certainly adds a new dimension to designing for the web.

Controlling Content at Load Time

One of the most apparent applications of Dynamic HTML is to change the appearance of a web page at load time, depending on the conditions established by the end user, or their browser. You might, for example, have a graphic that you want to be scaled to fill the entire browser window when the page loads. Because you really have no way of knowing how big the user's monitor might be, or how big they might have set their window, you cannot know how big your image should be. The way to solve this problem is to have the image scaled dynamically at load time. Your script could obtain information about the browser's window size while the image was loading. The image could then be scaled appropriately, and then displayed to the user. Because all this happens as the page is loading, and before the user offers any real input, this is referred to as a load-time feature. Of course these types of manipulations are not limited to images. Text, and even color schemes, could also be altered on-the-fly to give more choices to the user as to how a page is viewed.

Customizing Content for the User

Most of the Dynamic HTML features that you will take advantage of at load time involve preparing your page to be viewed for a particular user or browser. You could use a browser cookie, for example, to determine whether a user had visited the page before, and if they had, you could use a Dynamic HTML script to alter the page presentation for them. This would enable you to have a "new user" version of the page constructed and displayed on-the-fly.

N O T E Browser *cookies* are text files that are stored on a user's machine that enable the web server to store information about the user locally so that on future visits the content of the page can be adjusted to that user. Cookies are used extensively to keep track of all sorts of information, although the most common use is to track what online advertisements a user has seen. That way, when a user revisits the site, the server can check the cookie and make sure the user is greeted with ads they haven't seen. ▪

Part
I
Ch
2

This type of manipulation can help you create pages that are designed to communicate on a more intimate level with the site's visitor. It can create the illusion that a web page was designed specifically for the user, or it can help keep a user returning to the site because the information is customized and relevant.

Dynamically Altering Content at Runtime

In an effort to make Dynamic HTML as "dynamic" as possible, Microsoft implemented many features that enable HTML objects to be manipulated both before and after the page has loaded. This runtime feature is a catalyst for making the content that you have created truly dynamic—in the sense that even after the page has loaded, the content can be changed and manipulated.

This type of content manipulation allows several new features that were not possible before, such as dynamically expanding outlines, changing text content, and repositioning objects.

Expanding an Outline View

Enabling changes at runtime allows for more flexibility in the presentation of information to users. You might, for example, have some content that is presented in the form of an outline. Although it is possible to have the entire outline displayed on any normal HTML page as text, it would be more visually attractive, not to mention functional, to enable the outline to be expanded and collapsed by clicking an element in the outline. Figure 2.1 shows an example of how you can use expanding outline views to create an index for your site.

This type of effect is one example of how you can manipulate the content of a web page at runtime, and provide the user with more flexibility over how they view the data that is contained on your pages.

Changing Text Content on an Already Loaded Page

Another way to manipulate text on a page involves replacing the default text with new text—based on a mouse event. You could, for example, have some text that was a riddle, and when users clicked the riddle, the text of the riddle would be replaced by the text of the answer. Changing the text on the page can open the door to building complex user interfaces and menu systems by changing and replacing text in addition to the expanding and collapsing of outlines previously mentioned. The techniques for altering text in this manner include event handling, which is covered in Chapter 7, "Event Handling," and *textRange* objects, which are covered later in Chapter 10, "Dynamic Content."

FIG. 2.1

The Internet Explorer site index demo shows collapsing outlines in action. When the user clicks a major heading, the minor outline points are exposed.

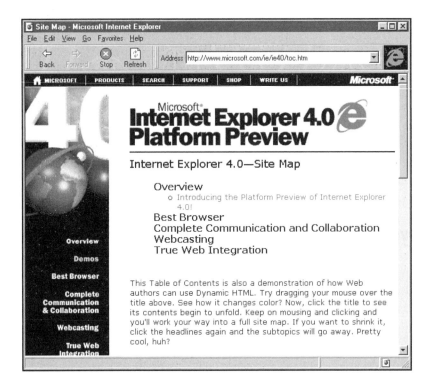

Changing Object Position on a Page

Finally, one of the most compelling reasons for Dynamic HTML is the capability to change the layering and positioning of objects at runtime. This allows the user to grab elements and reposition them on a page, without reloading the page or the elements.

The technique of moving elements on a page could enable the creation of any number of different user interfaces, or even the creation of customized games. Figure 2.2 shows a Mr. Potato Head style game called Alien Head, in which the user can move various fruits and vegetables to create an "Alien Head."

In fact, this capability to move elements on the page dynamically will be the technique used to create the Pin the Tail on the Donkey game that you will build in Chapter 16, "Pin the Tail on the Donkey."

More practical applications can also be built around this capability, such as training applications that involve dealing with complex diagrams. Another application would be to create children's educational games involving matching different graphic elements.

FIG. 2.2

The Alien Head demo enables the user to dynamically position page elements at runtime.

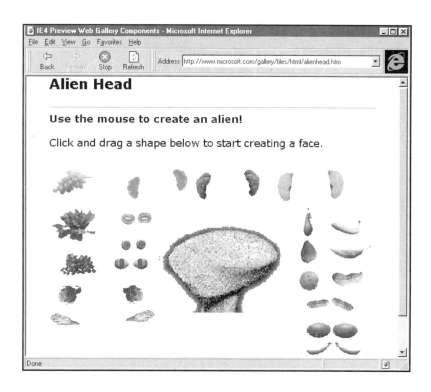

Dynamic HTML and Multimedia

The capability to reposition elements on the page and the capability to change the position of those elements leads to a higher level of multimedia with Dynamic HTML. After all, creating an animation is simply moving an image on the screen—add a soundtrack playing in the background and you are on your way to multimedia presentations with Dynamic HTML. In fact, Dynamic HTML has some special allowances for multimedia, including animation, and ActiveX Controls to enable filtering, transparency, and a variety of other multimedia effects. You can find out more about the integration of high-level multimedia with Dynamic HTML in Chapter 13, "Introducing Multimedia."

Animation Effects

Several mechanisms currently exist that can be used to create animations on the web. One type of animation is supported through *animated GIFs* (showing several different images in rapid succession so that the image appears to be moving). This type of animation would be appropriate for making a cartoon character's mouth move, for example; however, what if you wanted to move a cartoon character across the screen?

Images can be positioned with X and Y coordinates by using Cascading Style Sheets, and those coordinates can be manipulated with scripting languages. Therefore, by using animated GIFs and Cascading Style Sheets together, you can produce some complex animations.

Dynamic HTML also offers some new multimedia components in the form of ActiveX Controls that enable you to create path animations and manipulate images on-the-fly. Some of these effects are demonstrated on the Microsoft site, as shown in figure 2.3.

FIG. 2.3

The animation demo showcases Dynamic HTML's capability to animate 2D objects with layering and positioning.

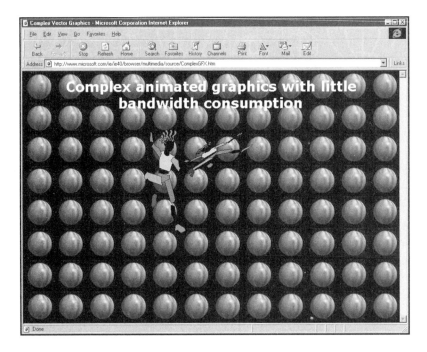

The animation example in figure 2.3 shows the manipulation of two images using one of the ActiveX Multimedia Controls to set the images in motion. Although the effect is not the same as an animated GIF, it enables a greater range of motion and loads faster. You can create quite complex animations that require little time to download, and even less time to actually start in motion.

Filtering, Blending, and Alpha Channel Graphics

Animation is not the only graphical effect that is offered through Dynamic HTML. With the incorporation of ActiveX Controls, a variety of fairly advanced graphics techniques are also available.

It is possible to apply lighting filters and blends to light sources with Dynamic HTML so that you can create an artificial tint to images on your page, or easily create the illusion of a spotlight, or other light source that appears to be illuminating your page or a single element. Dynamic HTML offers Alpha Channel support, which allows you to easily create transparent images or text. Combined with overlapping, you can use these techniques to create a variety of different transitions. You can use transparency with the Alpha Channel to dissolve text into an image, or to create a watermark effect with a logo on your page. By combining filters, lighting effects, and animations, Dynamic HTML helps bring the web one step closer to the multimedia capabilities of CD-ROMs. The ActiveX Mulitmedia Controls that are a part of Dynamic HTML are covered in greater detail in Part V, "Multimedia and Dynamic HTML."

Data Binding: The Power of Dynamic HTML

One of the most powerful aspects of Dynamic HTML is the capability to handle and manipulate data. Data binding is a Dynamic HTML technique that enables authors to take data directly from a database application on the server, and assign the current record to an HTML object. This allows the data to be displayed as if the data were a part of the original HTML code. Data binding allows the author to build a web-based interface to database applications—a function that was previously limited to high-powered web development tools such as Java.

Prior to Dynamic HTML, merging database applications with the web was a slow and tedious process. Along with building a custom interface between the web server and the database, interface problems would involve complex CGI workarounds, or customized application development with a technology such as Java. With data binding, the web can actually be used as the interface to business applications. The capability to include database records directly into HTML code provides simple solutions for previously complex tasks. Figure 2.4, for example, shows data being read from the server and incorporated into a simple browsing interface.

Part

I

Ch

2

FIG. 2.4

The Microsoft data binding demo shows how data can be dynamically incorporated into an HTML object for display.

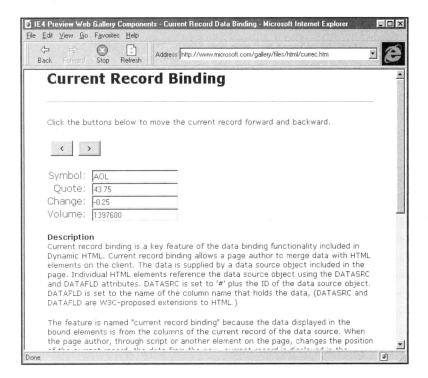

This type of simple interface could certainly be expanded, and eventually developed into a more robust database front-end. The result would be a database application that could be accessed via the web. The benefits for developing database systems are pretty far reaching, as companies could develop simple database applications with web-based interfaces not only for customers via the Internet, but also for internal applications. As more users begin to use web mechanisms for intranet application development, the combination of data tools and the web make intranet applications a viable and appealing alternative to customized in-house application development with C or Visual Basic.

Creating Tables On-the-Fly

Data can be incorporated into web pages automatically by using the table generating features of Dynamic HTML. Dynamic HTML has the capability to take data rows from database servers and convert them automatically into HTML tables. This offers two distinct advantages over traditional HTML table generation. First, the tables generated by Dynamic HTML are expanded dynamically. This means that as soon as the browser receives data, it begins to build the table so that the user does not have to wait for the entire table to download before they can start seeing data.

Secondly, tables that are generated by Dynamic HTML can be manipulated at the browser level. Dynamic HTML-generated tables can be queried, sorted, and filtered, all without contacting the original data source—more importantly, without reloading any of the table data or HTML code. This might not seem like a big deal, but let's look at an example of a customer database with 100 customers in it. With traditional HTML, the table would need to be downloaded and drawn. After the table is complete, let's say the user wanted to sort by reverse alphabetical order. This would involve contacting the data source, passing it the new data parameters—with which it would sort the data—create a new table, and redownload the table information.

With Dynamic HTML, after the data is downloaded, the data could be sorted in reverse alphabetical order by passing the instructions to the table script. The table is sorted and redrawn all on the clients machine, without ever contacting the server.

Making Elements Data Aware

Dynamic HTML also allows HTML elements to be created that are *data aware*. Data awareness is just another way of saying that certain HTML objects are designed to receive input from data objects as a part of their HTML code. You could, for example, build an index card that would display the customer's name at the top and the address below. The name and address information would actually come from the database server, but would be read by the browser as if they were part of the HTML page. This gives Dynamic HTML the power to create database interfaces.

Data binding and awareness make the creation of data aware form fields possible. These fields accept input that are automatically processed by the proper script to be pushed onto the proper data server source. This provides a sort of feedback mechanism, or more importantly, the means to update records in the database, and not just to display them, as shown in figure 2.5.

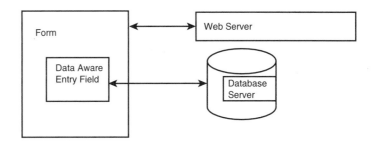

FIG. 2.5
Data awareness
enables data
application creation
with Dyanmic HTML.

Application Building with Dynamic HTML

It might seem like all these Dynamic HTML features are just designed to add new cool elements to web pages, and that certainly is one application for many of the new features of Dynamic HTML. Animation and text effects could add some spice to some of the dull web sites that are available on the net. In addition to these seemingly superficial web design improvements, Dynamic HTML harnesses a lot of potential in other areas.

Keep in mind that many business are beginning to rely on the Internet more—for both external and internal business applications. Until now, building web-based interfaces for many business applications required the use of a language such as Java, which is capable of reading data from servers without being unreasonably slow. Dynamic HTML opens another door to creating user interfaces for a variety of complex applications, not the least of which are business databases.

Because of the flexibility and the blending of different web technologies to create Dynamic HTML, very little can't be done with some variant of Dynamic HTML. Only time will tell what innovations Dynamic HTML will bring to application and interface development, but as more people turn to the net as a resource, Dynamic HTML's strength in interface creation should place it in a good position.

From Here...

Don't feel overwhelmed if your head is spinning from all this Dynamic HTML information. A lot of different components of Dynamic HTML make up a large number of new features. Because Dynamic HTML is not one single technology, it can be difficult to pin down what is and what is not Dynamic HTML. Don't worry if you don't feel that you are an expert.

The following chapters guide you through more detailed coverage of the components of Dynamic HTML:

- Chapter 3, "Microsoft versus Netscape," compares the features of Dynamic HTML supported and implemented by Netscape Communicator versus the features supported and implemented by Internet Explorer 4.0. Be prepared for a battle to the finish!

- Part II, "Dynamic HTML Foundations," covers the technologies that you will need to develop Dynamic HTML pages. This part consists of four concentrated chapters:
  - Chapter 4, "Cascading Style Sheets Primer" covers the basics of understanding and using Cascading Style Sheets.
  - Chapter 5, "JavaScript Primer," covers the basics of understanding and using JavaScript, one of the preferred scripting languages used by Dynamic HTML.
  - Chapter 6, "Dynamic HTML Object Model," talks about the object model used by Dynamic HTML that treats all HTML elements on a page as mutually aware objects.
  - Chapter 7, "Event Handling," covers the importance of event handling in Dynamic HTML-generated web sites.
- Part III, "Inside Dynamic HTML," takes you through the ins and outs of implementing specific features of Dynamic HTML.

CHAPTER 3

Microsoft versus Netscape

What would new standards be without a little competition? Well, this is a much debated topic in the computing industry. Some argue that by competing for the dominant position in new technology, the technology itself advances faster. Others argue that this rapid development and competition hurts users of the technology. Web developers are either forced to choose a side, and face the possibility of choosing wrong, or hedge their bets and develop on two platforms. Advocates of cooperation argue that by working together, companies can create solid technologies based on standards that would enable web developers to easily develop cross-platform and cross-product web sites.

As you can see from the preceding chapters, Dynamic HTML is an attempt to compensate for many of the problems that existed with previous versions of HTML. A great deal of potential exists in web development for Dynamic HTML technologies, and that has led to the common reaction in the computing industry—both Microsoft and Netscape are developing competing standards for Dynamic HTML.

Understanding Dynamic HTML

What makes Dynamic HTML so dynamic anyway? Learn how the marriage of existing technologies is paving the way for the next generation of web content.

Scripting Languages

JavaScript or VBScript? Figure out which one is the best for you and if either have a future with the evolution of Dynamic HTML.

Style Sheets

Cascading Style Sheets and JavaScript Style Sheets. What are the advantages of each? Which style sheets are worth your time and effort? Make this decision for yourself.

Microsoft's Role in Dynamic HTML

As usual with groundbreaking new technologies, Microsoft has ventured into some proprietary applications of Dynamic HTML. Learn what they are and what they can do for you.

Netscape versus Microsoft

A handy chart that delivers the information you need on which Dynamic HTML features are supported or not supported by the latest browser efforts in the ongoing struggle between these cybergiants.

Dynamic HTML is suffering the same fate as other web technologies. You only need to look at ActiveX and Java to see how intense the battle for web standards can get. This chapter takes a look at the differences between Microsoft's and Netscape's implementations of Dynamic HTML and how those differences might affect your web site development. Hopefully, this analysis will help you decide which implementation to follow. ▤

Working with the W3C Consortium

The World Wide Web was developed to allow the exchange of information easily between researchers—regardless of the type of computer they were using or their location. Of course, in the original stages of development, there were only a few browsers with limited features. Even in the early stages of web development, standards were crucial to ensure that newly developed browsers were capable of displaying the same information as their predecessors.

The two primary standards of the web are the Hypertext Transfer Protocol (HTTP) and the Hypertext Markup Language (HTML). Without some common ground for these basic web technologies, HTML documents that were created for one web browser would not necessarily work with another browser. As a result, an organization called the World Wide Web Consortium (W3C) has been working to ensure that the technologies that are used on the web are standardized in some fashion. Nonetheless, the existence of a standards organization has not stopped vendors from attempting to implement their own special features. A classic example of this is the infamous Netscape <BLINK> tag. Netscape has a history of implementing special tag support into versions of Netscape Navigator software and then attempting to use their wide support base to manipulate their innovations into the standard. Of course, Microsoft employs similar techniques, and the resulting mixed support for additional features has led to the all too familiar "This page best viewed with…" message that is frequently seen on web pages.

Unfortunately, this message violates the basic spirit of the web. Tim Berners-Lee, developer of the web at CERN, offers this opinion on using proprietary features:

> "This comes from an anxiousness to use the latest proprietary features, which have not been agreed upon by all companies. It is done either by those who have an interest in pushing a particular company, or it is done by those who are anxious to take the community back to the dark ages of computing when a floppy from a PC wouldn't read on a Mac, and a WordStar document wouldn't read in WordPerfect, or an EBCDIC file wouldn't read on an ASCII machine. It's fine for individuals whose work is going to be transient and who aren't worried about being read by anyone."

Unfortunately, users of Dynamic HTML are forced to choose between Microsoft's proprietary implementation of Dynamic HTML, or Netscape's proprietary implementation of Dynamic HTML. Committing to one over the other will involve some tough decisions; however, the most important aspect to consider is the features of which you want to take advantage. Adaptations later will undoubtedly be necessary if a standard causes variations, but the benefits of being an early adopter can result in a higher profile for your pages.

The only hope that looms on the horizon for web developers is Microsoft's recent standards-friendly stance on web technologies. Microsoft has already submitted a draft specification of their implementation of Dynamic HTML to the W3C for consideration as a standard. Of course, the W3C could accept part or all the Microsoft draft, or they could merge the technology with Netscape's to create a hybrid. The fact that Microsoft has already submitted their technology for consideration as a standard is a demonstration of their commitment to make the technology work across the web.

Netscape has also contributed their technologies to the W3C in the past, but Netscape generally has tried to strong arm the standards organization slightly by continuing to support proprietary implementations. In the case of Dynamic HTML, Netscape has not submitted their standard at all, in spite of the fact that Netscape often touts their solutions as *open* standards. You can be assured, however, that if a Dynamic HTML standard is adapted, both companies will likely alter their technologies to comply with the basic standards—and then continue to contribute their own special features. Until then, you will have to hedge your bets on the technology and features that you want to implement, and the strength you feel each company wields in the development community.

Part

I

Ch

3

This standards debate does not end with Dynamic HTML. If you remember that Dynamic HTML is actually based on several different technologies all tied together, the technologies used to author Dynamic HTML (such as scripting and style sheets) are also the subject of standards debates.

Defining "Dynamic" in Dynamic HTML

A central issue in the debate between Microsoft's and Netscape's implementations of Dynamic HTML is what *dynamic* means. A useful way to extrapolate this definition is to examine the process by which web pages are loaded:

1. The user specifies the address of the site and/or the page that they want to view by clicking a link or specifying an address.

2. The client (that is, Netscape or Internet Explorer) contacts the site's web server to request information.

3. The server determines from the initial request what pages should be downloaded to the client, and sends those pages, graphics, and other page elements to the client.

4. The client interprets the HTML and any other special instructions (such as Java applets or ActiveX Controls) and displays the page.

Each of these steps presents opportunities for the browser and the server to pass information to each other that could be used to customize the page information that is eventually displayed. When the client initially contacts the server, the client gives the server some information about the client's configuration, such as the client version and the IP address of the client. You may have seen pages that display some information about your client, such as displaying "Greetings 199.18.207.25", or something along those lines. This is an example of passing information between the client and the server. The information passed between the client and the server is the same information that is used in a server's log files.

Any time information is exchanged between client and server, the information can be manipulated. The content of a web page, for example, could be changed on the server by randomly rotating the page that was served after each contact—subsequently resulting in the creation of a novelty page. A better application of this opportunity to change web page content would be to alter content based on client information instead of some arbitrary content change.

A limited amount of customization can be performed based on information passed between the client and the server, most of which requires the intervention of CGI scripts or preprocessed information that is included by the server. Both of these techniques consume server resources because processing must be done on the server. These techniques also slow down the page loading for the user, because the client must wait until the information from the server is downloaded before displaying the page.

Additionally, it would be beneficial to be able to change some characteristics of web pages that cannot be determined from the information passed between the client and the server while the page is loading. Scaling a page to fit within the size of the browser window is a good example. Previously, the design of a page needed to be independent of the window size. Of course, the text flow might have been altered when the user resized the window, but the size of the graphic elements would not change, so the layout of the page would be adversely affected.

This is one area where Dynamic HTML allows a new type of control over content. Dynamic HTML as implemented by both Netscape and Microsoft enables the manipulation of pages before they have been downloaded by the browser, based on information fed to the server by the user. The Netscape Dynamic HTML demo shown in figure 3.1 is an example of how Dynamic HTML can be used to manipulate pages.

FIG. 3.1

The Netscape Stella Chelsea Associates demo resizes the window based on information the user enters about the resolution of their monitor.

Dynamic HTML enables you to define page attributes (such as size, element layout, and font style) that can be changed by browser specifications, entered by the user, while the page is loaded, and then displays those changes immediately. This is one of the benefits of Dynamic HTML.

Both Microsoft's and Netscape's implementations of Dynamic HTML offer the capability to alter web pages at load time. What occurs after load time is where the two implementations begin to diverge.

Netscape essentially defines *dynamic* as the capability to alter web page content at load time. Under the Netscape Dynamic HTML paradigm, you can alter the layout of a document, position page elements, and alter the typeface and style of fonts used on your web pages at load time. Unfortunately, this load time restriction severely limits what can be accomplished after the page has been loaded. To compensate for the lack of changes that can be made to content at runtime, Netscape supports layers, which can be shown and hidden at runtime, but many of the features that are supported by Microsoft's implementation of Dynamic HTML at runtime aren't possible.

Microsoft's implementation of Dynamic HTML adopts all the same features as Netscape's Dynamic HTML. The Microsoft implementation adjusts positioning and layout at load time. It also specifies font attributes at load time. In addition to the supporting features of Netscape's Dynamic HTML, Microsoft's Dynamic HTML also offers a host of other features, such as the capability to dynamically alter style sheets (dynamic styles), the capability to create *textRange* objects to alter page content (dynamic content), the capability to dynamically sort table content (data binding), and the capability to associate HTML elements with database functionality (data awareness).

Of course, even the syntax for implementing Dynamic HTML features are incompatible between Netscape's and Microsoft's versions. The fundamental difference between Netscape's Dynamic HTML and Microsoft's Dynamic HTML, however, is that Microsoft defines the term *dynamic* as the capability to alter the content at runtime *in addition to* at load time. Microsoft's Dynamic HTML enables the font attributes to be altered after the page has been loaded. Microsoft's Dynamic HTML also enables elements to be repositioned after the page has loaded. This type of manipulation could be used to create multimedia transitions and animated content. Many push channels created by using the CDF, for example, are also created by using Dynamic HTML techniques. Figure 3.2 shows the font and element position changes made at runtime.

Allowing the manipulation of page elements and content after the web page has been loaded is an example of how Microsoft has made Dynamic HTML more dynamic. Microsoft's implementation of Dynamic HTML makes a number of applications of the technology possible that are unfeasible with Netscape's version of Dynamic HTML. Some of the possibilities enabled by Microsoft's runtime Dynamic HTML include interactive pages and complex user interfaces for web-based applications.

FIG. 3.2
The Acrobats with Style demo shows how graphics can be manipulated with Dynamic HTML after the page has loaded.

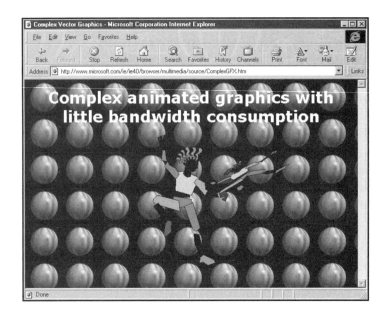

Scripting: JavaScript and VBScript

The glue that holds Dynamic HTML together is the scripting language that binds elements together, and manipulates the content. Without a solid scripting environment, Dynamic HTML fizzles quickly.

Of course both Microsoft and Netscape support scripting, and both support some web standards. For example, JavaScript, the default scripting language of the web is supported by both versions of Dynamic HTML, although Microsoft likes to refer to JavaScript as JScript.

The 1.1 version of JavaScript is a supported scripting language for Dynamic HTML for both Netscape Communicator and Internet Explorer 4.0. Netscape, however, has expanded JavaScript with a number of extensions designed to be used in conjunction with their push technology called Netcaster. Netcaster actually supports JavaScript version 1.2. This should not affect much of the development work being done with Dynamic HTML, but it is always a good idea to keep these kinds of discrepancies in mind when developing content for the web.

Even though Microsoft supports JavaScript for Dynamic HTML, they also elected to support their proprietary scripting language—Visual Basic Script (VBScript). The decision to support VBScript allows a little bit of flexibility in scripting choices, but was largely incorporated to capitalize on the popularity of Visual Basic among corporate and small application developers. Because Visual Basic has an extensive development community, supporting a scripting language based on the popular language makes Dynamic HTML scripting more accessible to Microsoft's installed user base. If you already have experience with Visual Basic, this can be a boon; however, if you do not, JavaScript is a very straightforward scripting language and well supported as well. Without doing additional development in Visual Basic, JavaScript is a stronger choice.

There are also some other differences in the supplementary technologies that each implementation supports. Netscape has extensive Java support, with JavaScript and supporting Java applets that can control Dynamic HTML objects. Microsoft also has JavaScript support, VBScript support, and support for Java applets and ActiveX Controls. In fact, many of the advanced multimedia features for Microsoft Dynamic HTML require the use of ActiveX Controls to work properly. Netscape has announced that in future versions they do plan to offer ActiveX Controls; however, the current Communicator release does not offer support for ActiveX Controls.

The bottom line here is that Netscape supports two widely supported technologies—JavaScript and Java. Microsoft supports these two technologies, in addition to adding a number of proprietary technologies, such as VBScript and ActiveX Controls. What this means is that you can develop your Dynamic HTML using Java-related technology, such as applets and JavaScript, and it will be relatively easy to port your pages between Netscape Communicator and Internet Explorer. Relying on ActiveX and VBScript to develop your pages, however, restricts your audience to Internet Explorer users.

Part
I
Ch
3

Cascading Style Sheets and JavaScript Style Sheets

Without scripting, Dynamic HTML might not be dynamic, but style sheets play an equally important role in creating Dynamic HTML-generated sites. All the layout features in Dynamic HTML are implemented through style sheets.

Style sheets offer the support to create different font styles, to specify different fonts in HTML documents, and to provide more flexibility to control all the similar elements on a site without modifying each element individually. Additionally, style sheets are responsible for the object positioning methods in both vendors' implementations of Dynamic HTML.

The positioning aspects of style sheets are what enable Dynamic HTML to reposition elements on a page, based on the information that is received from the browser at load time. Additionally, style sheets provide the mechanism for creating layers. With layers, elements can be overlapped, or hidden and revealed, to create a number of different effects. In figure 3.3, for example, layers are used in Internet Explorer to create a new style of web-based interface. By creating buttons that are linked to the layers through scripts, the layers can be revealed or hidden through user interaction, creating a user interface that is built on Dynamic HTML.

The capability to manipulate positioning and to control layers is essential to the functionality of Dynamic HTML, and the most widespread type of layering is found in Cascading Style Sheets.

FIG. 3.3

The Lakes and Sons example demonstrates layers and dynamic positioning.

NOTE   Throughout the text, you will see references to HTML tags, objects, and elements. Keeping track of these might seem confusing at first, but it is really quite simple.

An HTML tag is the markup tag used to define how text should look. <H1>, for example, is an HTML tag used to create a headline. After you have created the headline:

```
<H1>This is an element</H1>
```

the tag, and the text it is formatting is an HTML element. Finally, by exposing the element through the Dynamic HTML Object Model, the element can become an object with more properties that can be manipulated:

```
<H1 ID="myheadline">This is an object</H1>
```

The Cascading Style Sheets (CSS) specification is a means of defining style attributes and assigning those styles to various HTML objects, such as specifying a color for all <H2> heads, or assigning a basic font type to all the text elements on a page. Cascading Style Sheets offer an incredible degree of flexibility for altering and controlling layout and design because style sheets can be globally applied to all the pages on a site, or included in each file individually. This feature is particularly powerful, because it gives designers the power to separate the design of the site from the content. This means that content can be easily edited without a lot of aesthetic reformatting. It also means that the design or look of a site can be completely re-vamped without complex content editing, because style sheets allow the separation of content and design elements.

By creating a standard CSS for a site, the site can easily maintain a high level of consistency among the elements on a site, and site redesigns are simplified by altering the style sheet file instead of altering each page individually. The power of style sheets, however, comes from the capability to apply a global style to pages, and then override the style by specifying inline styles for specific pages within the web site. This creates flexibility in creating special elements, which could be used to construct a user interface, for example.

Microsoft's and Netscape's versions of Dynamic HTML offer support for Cascading Style Sheets. This is a boon for designers for several reasons:

- **Cascading Style Sheets are simple to use**—The format and syntax for CSS is straightforward and easy for designers to grasp. It affords them the control they are used to with other graphic design software.

- **Cascading Style Sheets have been in widespread use for a while on the net**—Because designers and developers are familiar with the Cascading Style Sheet specification, the development work involved in learning a new support technology to use CSS and Dynamic HTML is lower.

- **Cascading Style Sheets are a W3C specification**—Because the CSS specification has been recommended for industry-wide adoption by the W3C, the use of Cascading Style Sheets is supported by leading browsers. It also means that no variants need to be used when designing with CSS for Netscape or Internet Explorer.

These reasons make CSS an obvious choice for support in Dynamic HTML. For that reason, both Netscape and Microsoft use the CSS specification for Dynamic HTML, which bolsters Microsoft's claim to support standards, and lends standard support to Netscape.

Although both vendors offer CSS support, Netscape also offers support for a proprietary technology called JavaScript Style Sheets (JSSS). JSSS offers many of the similar features to CSS, but uses a syntax that is based on the JavaScript language. For developers who are familiar with JavaScript, this might be an easier syntax to learn, however, because JSSS is not supported by any browser other than Netscape, your sheets are limited to use in Navigator and Communicator. For that primary reason, JSSS makes a poor choice for general web development. Although it might prove to be a good choice for corporate intranets—where the content will only be viewed with Netscape products—JSSS can be a viable alternative to CSS. For general purpose Internet application, however, CSS is clearly a superior choice for style sheet implementations, the CSS specification will be covered in Chapter 4, "Cascading Style Sheets Primer."

Part

I

Ch

3

Microsoft Specific Features of Dynamic HTML

In many instances, Netscape and Microsoft offer one common technology, and then offer their own competing technologies as an alternative. This is the case with scripting languages. Both companies offer the JavaScript scripting language, and Microsoft offers the alternative VBScript. For style sheets, both vendors offer Cascading Style Sheet support, and Netscape also offers support for JavaScript Style Sheets. Generally speaking, it is better to stick with the widely supported standards than to adopt proprietary solutions.

A number of features, however, are only supported by Microsoft's implementation of Dynamic HTML. A number of these technologies have already been discussed. Microsoft's Dynamic HTML has the capability to reposition objects on a page dynamically, at both load time and runtime.

Microsoft also offers a host of multimedia effects, such as filtering, blending, and transparency, which are only available through a combination of multimedia objects and ActiveX Controls. These types of features make it possible to use Microsoft's Dynamic HTML to create new web-based multimedia applications and to create new web-based users interfaces that are difficult, if not impossible to create using Netscape's technology. Multimedia effects are covered in detail in Chapter 15, "Multimedia Filters and ActiveX Controls."

The most significant differences, however, lie in the data technologies supported by Microsoft that are not available by Netscape's Dynamic HTML. These features give Dynamic HTML the power to integrate web content with information from databases, without extensive server application development or CGI scripting—the result is an increase in speed and functionality for the end user.

The first technology that is supported by Microsoft Dynamic HTML is data awareness. *Data awareness* provides features such as dynamic table generation, which enables HTML tables to be populated automatically by table data provided directly from a database server. Dynamic table generation eliminates the need to hard code large, complex tables, or to slow user interaction by generating tables on the server side through CGI scripts. This increases the speed for the end user, and enables you to provide more dynamic types of data through web services.

Imagine, for example, a small stock brokerage that wants to create a portfolio management tool. Of course, the portfolio tool could be developed by using CGI scripts that would query a database of stock prices, reloading the data each time the customer refreshed the page. Of course, this would put a heavy load on the firm's server, and wouldn't be very fast for the customer. With Dynamic HTML, the firm could create a portfolio management tool that used data awareness and data binding to create tables that contained the data related to each holding in the portfolio. The customer could then sort or change the view of the data without contacting the server. Another important aspect would be that specific fields that change rapidly, such as "current price," could be updated independently of the rest of the data, lowering the demands on the server, and increasing the speed for the customer.

Dynamic tables are also progressively displayed, or dynamically expanded, so that the table and page load as soon as the first data from the server is received. This enables the end user to view the page content almost instantly, but as more table data is downloaded, the table expands to accommodate the new data.

The second aspect to Microsoft's Dynamic HTML support is the capability to perform data binding. *Data binding* enables specific data records to be bound to HTML objects. This enables the incorporation of live data from a database server into active HTML objects. Figure 3.4 shows an example of how live data can be integrated into HTML objects.

Data binding makes it possible to create web-based interfaces for web applications. Previously, this could only be accomplished through complicated programming and CGI scripting to offer a similar level of functionality. Remarkably, this method still does not come close to rivaling the performance of Dynamic HTML. By utilizing data binding, through data source objects and the tabular data control, an astonishing degree of data flexibility can be achieved with Dynamic HTML, with increased speed and efficiency. Chapter 11, "Introduction to Data Binding," and Chapter 12, "Using Data Source Objects," cover these data techniques in detail.

Of course, to take advantage of these data features, you are forced to use the Microsoft implementation of Dynamic HTML. Netscape's Dynamic HTML does not offer any comparable data support.

FIG. 3.4
Data binding enables
data records to be
displayed in HTML
objects.

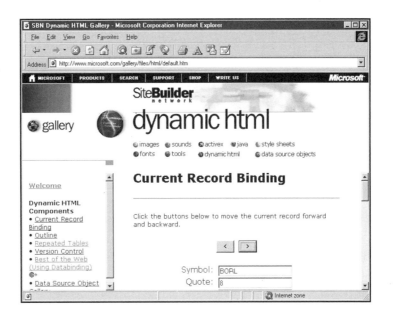

Feature Comparison Chart

All this discussion of the different features of Dynamic HTML will undoubtedly have you wondering what features are supported by which browser. Keep in mind that in the war between
browsers, the feature set is always changing and these features could change even further if a
standard is elected by the W3C. To clarify what features are currently supported, table 3.1
shows a list of the features of Dynamic HTML, and which features are supported by Microsoft
and which are supported by Netscape.

Table 3.1   Netscape versus Microsoft Dynamic HTML Feature Support

Dynamic HTML Feature	Netscape Support	Microsoft Support
Object Model	Yes	Yes
Event Generation	Yes	Yes
Event Bubbling	No	Yes
Load Time Manipulation	Yes	Yes
Runtime Manipulation	No	Yes
Dynamic Styles	No	Yes

continues

Table 3.1 Continued

Dynamic HTML Feature	Netscape Support	Microsoft Support
Cascading Style Sheet Positioning	Yes	Yes
JavaScript Style Sheet Positioning	Yes	No
Canvas Mode	Yes	Yes
Java Applets	Yes	Yes
ActiveX Controls	No	Yes
JavaScript	Yes	Yes
VBScript	No	Yes
Data Awareness	No	Yes
Data Binding	No	Yes
Multimedia Extensions	No	Yes
Backward Compatibility	No	Yes
Submitted Proposal	No	Yes
Available for Windows, UNIX, and Mac	Yes	Yes
Free Third-Party Licensing	No	Yes

Both Netscape and Microsoft support the Dynamic HTML Object Model and event generation; however, only Microsoft's Dynamic HTML supports event bubbling, which is covered in Chapter 7, "Event Handling." Event bubbling enables events that are generated by a Dynamic HTML object to be passed to its parent object for handling.

Likewise, both versions support load-time modifications, such as specifying fonts and other formatting information; however, only Microsoft supports runtime modifications that enable Dynamic HTML to perform multimedia effects and dynamic styles, such as changing the fonts on-the-fly, or moving images.

Cascading Style Sheets are supported in both implementations, as are Java applets, and the JavaScript scripting language. Netscape also offers support for its proprietary JavaScript Style Sheets, while Microsoft offers proprietary support for its Visual Basic scripting language, VBScript.

Only Microsoft offers any type of data support through data aware objects and data binding, which enables data records to be bound to specific HTML objects.

Finally, Microsoft has proposed its version of Dynamic HTML to the W3C as a web standard, and offers free licensing of the technology to third-party developers and vendors. Microsoft has also ensured that their version of Dynamic HTML degrades to older browsers to display dynamic content statically so that the information is not lost, although its dynamic qualities might be.

From Here...

This chapter points out the slightly different implementations of Dynamic HTML offered by Netscape and Microsoft. Microsoft hopes to make their implementation the Internet standard by submitting it to the W3C, but Netscape offers some interesting technologies as well.

Part I, "Dynamic HTML Basics," covered all the types of applications and features of Dynamic HTML that are discussed at greater length throughout the rest of the book. If you have read about a technology in this section, rest assured that a more detailed explanation with solid examples lies in the chapters ahead. This chapter provided a comprehensive overview of the Dynamic HTML technology so that you have an idea of how technologies from different vendors compare. Because of the support for standards, and the complete features of Microsoft's Dynamic HTML, this book concentrates on those features. It is, however, not a complicated task to adapt these techniques to Netscape's Dynamic HTML implementation.

Part II, "Dynamic HTML Foundations" looks at the technologies and concepts that make Dynamic HTML tick. These chapters will provide you with comprehensive coverage of the core technologies that encompass Dynamic HTML, and how those technologies function on their own, and in conjunction with DHTML. The chapters in this section of the book are as follows:

- Chapter 4, "Cascading Style Sheets Primer," covers the basics of understanding and using Cascading Style Sheets.

- Chapter 5, "JavaScript Primer," covers the basics of understanding and using JavaScript, one of the preferred scripting languages used by Dynamic HTML.

- Chapter 6, "Dynamic HTML Object Model," talks about the object model used by Dynamic HTML that treats all HTML elements on a page as mutually aware objects.

- Chapter 7, "Event Handling," covers the importance of event handling in Dynamic HTML-generated web sites.

Dynamic HTML Foundations

CHAPTER 4

Cascading Style Sheets Primer

Style Values

Learn about style values and how to assign them.

Cascading Style Sheets

Learn the fundamentals and primary components that provide dynamic design and layout capabilities.

CSS Syntax

Discover numerous ways to incorporate Cascading Style Sheets into your basic HTML vocabulary.

CSS Positioning

Introduce yourself to the object-oriented design and layout capabilities provided by CSS Positioning.

Part I, "Dynamic HTML Basics" discussed how Dynamic HTML is not so much a new type of HTML, as it is a collection of technologies that are designed to work together to help you manipulate the content of web pages. Technologies such as Cascading Style Sheets and JavaScript are essential parts of Dynamic HTML. Without these technologies, many of the features of Dynamic HTML would not exist. JavaScript, covered in Chapter 5, "JavaScript Primer," is used to change the properties of HTML dynamically. To take advantage of this capability to treat HTML elements dynamically, however, there needs to be a mechanism for assigning styles to elements that can be changed. Cascading Style Sheets provide a mechanism for creating styles that can be applied to pages or even entire sites. This chapter covers the basics of Cascading Style Sheets to give you an example of what can be accomplished with the technology, so that in later chapters you are prepared to integrate Cascading Style Sheets with Dynamic HTML. ■

The Elements of Style

Web design with HTML has never been as strong as graphic designers would have liked. With the goal of the web being communication among many machines and browser types, features that would aid graphic design were often initially overlooked. This was certainly acceptable for early incarnations of the World Wide Web. Because the early adopters were often researchers and educators, there was still an emphasis of content over form. However, as the web has expanded into the personal and commercial realms, there has also been an increase in the attention paid to the style and design of web pages. Commercial interests are better served with pages that are aesthetically pleasing as well as informational, and as more individuals use web pages as forms of personal expression the nature of web page design has shifted.

For many designers, the structural limitations of HTML have caused many headaches and design compromises. Whereas with print design the designer has total control over the appearance of material, the web lends itself to viewer modifications. Compounding the problem with HTML was a lack of graphic design and typographic controls, so the designer had no means with which to modify font structure, precisely layout images and text, or even to control the flow of text on a page. As HTML matured and tables were introduced, many designers found compromises and workarounds to the problems of design, however Cascading Style Sheets represent the first step in HTML toward answering the design problems for the World Wide Web from the designer's perspective.

A number of different style properties can be defined with Cascading Style Sheets. Some of the types of elements that can be specified in style sheets include the following:

- Fonts
- Backgrounds
- Text
- Borders
- Lists

The following sections go into more detail as to how these elements can be manipulated and customized with Cascading Style Sheets.

Fonts

CSS brings designers the capability to manipulate fonts used on web pages, and in later chapters how Dynamic HTML exploits these CSS properties for its font manipulation is discussed. Some of the font attributes that can be changed with CSS include: font family, style, weight, size, and color.

Backgrounds

Background styles for elements can also be specified and manipulated with CSS. This capability can help minimize the tedious task of developing and laying out multiple GIF images and manipulating elements around the background with complex tables. Some background elements that can be manipulated include: background color, transparency, images, scrolling, and positioning.

Text

CSS offers the most design advances in the treatment of text. Because HTML has never been designer-friendly, many designers may find the typographic control that style sheets introduces to be one of the most compelling reasons to adopt Cascading Style Sheets.

CSS enables designers to fine-tune the following attributes of text: word spacing, letter spacing, text styles, alignment, transformations, margins, and padding. When used in conjunction with font properties, the text properties bring traditional typography to the web with the aid of CSS.

Borders

You can use CSS to manipulate the border properties of various HTML elements as well. This can include image borders or table borders. The attributes that can be altered include color, style, and width.

Lists

Formatting lists has always been awkward with HTML. CSS offers some relief with the capability to specify list style, images, style types, and style positions. All these elements enable you to customize how various list elements appear, and how they are altered depending on the order in which they appear in the list.

Of course, this list of customizable properties afforded by CSS is by no means complete. For a more complete overview of the properties defined by CSS and the details of the specification, see Appendix B, "CSS and CSS Positioning Attributes."

Defining Cascading Style Sheets

A Cascading Style Sheet is simply a set of definitions for how each of the HTML elements on a page should be rendered, or how they should appear to the user in the browser window. In straightforward HTML, each HTML tag has attributes that can be used to assign a value for the characteristics of the element the tag is used to define. The following code, for example, assigns values for the width and alignment attributes:

```
<HR WIDTH=85% ALIGN=LEFT>
```

The preceding line displays a horizontal rule line that has a length 85% the width of the window, and is aligned with the left side of the window. The attributes define the style of that element. Many HTML tags have attributes that can be used to define a style for a particular element, and style attributes can be manipulated in several different ways.

In the previous horizontal line example, for instance, the WIDTH and ALIGN attributes define how the horizontal rule line element appears. The WIDTH and ALIGN attributes within the <HR> tag have no effect on any elements outside of this particular element, which renders a line across the screen. Before CSS, designers were limited to specifying each of the attributes on a tag by tag basis. Of course, this adds a lot of drudgery and time to site development, and it also creates a huge headache if you want to change all the attributes for one element throughout a site. Changing each of the references by hand is quite tedious, and even using search and replace methods in an HTML editor can be tiresome.

The solution to specifying tags individually begins with the STYLE attribute. Returning to the horizontal rule line example, the attributes of the <HR> tag are used to set the characteristics of the horizontal line:

```
<HR WIDTH=85% ALIGN=LEFT>
```

Now take a look at a slightly different way to set the attributes of an HTML element. Take the paragraph tag <P>, for instance. Before the development of CSS, it was only possible to use <P> by itself to begin a new paragraph. In CSS, it can be used to specify many attributes, such as the color, font, and indention of the paragraph. You can use the STYLE attribute with the <P> tag to indent text as shown in figure 4.1. The HTML code for specifying text attributes in this example is as follows:

```
<HTML>
<BODY>
<P>
This is a plain paragraph.
<P STYLE="TEXT-INDENT: 30">
This is the paragraph indented.
</P>
</BODY>
</HTML>
```

The example in figure 4.1 shows that although one of the <P> tags is a standard HTML tag, the other makes use of the STYLE attribute to add indentation. Styles used in this manner are called inline styles. *Inline styles* enable you to use the STYLE attribute to customize elements; however, inline styles do not eliminate the necessity of specifying style values for a group of elements, such as all <P> tags on the page.

FIG. 4.1

Text formatting with and without inline styles.

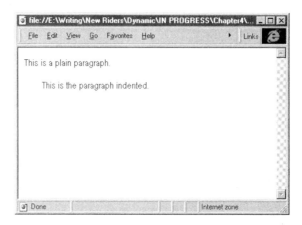

N O T E When referring to an inline style, the term simply means that that particular style definition appears in the HTML file with the HTML code it is being applied to. As you will see later, CSS allows style sheets to be imported using the "@import" syntax, in which case the style is no longer inline.

The CSS specification, however, allows for the specification of styles as style blocks in the <HEAD> of HTML files. This enables you to specify a style globally for a document, as shown in the following lines of HTML code:

```
<HTML>
<HEAD>
<TITLE>Sample HTML with Styles</TITLE>
<STYLE>
P { COLOR: GREEN; TEXT-INDENT: 30; FONT-FAMILY: SANS-SERIF}
</STYLE>
</HEAD>
<BODY>
<P>
This is a paragraph on a page with a global style.
</BODY>
</HTML>
```

Figure 4.2 demonstrates how style blocks globally specify a style for consistency throughout a document.

FIG. 4.2

A CSS style defined in a style block.

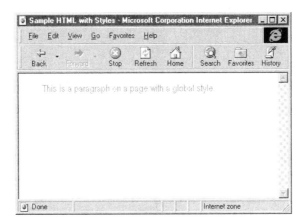

In this example, the style is defined for the entire document, so that whenever the <P> tag is used, the COLOR and TEXT-INDENT attributes are automatically applied to that element. Assigning styles this way has its disadvantages.

- Style blocks group all the styles in one location, so page content and page style can be easily separated or edited.
- CSS allows for multiple style specifications through classes.

These features of CSS are discussed later in the chapter in the section titled "Importing Style Sheets."

Part

II

Ch

4

Another important aspect of the Cascading Style Sheets (CSS) specification is that it is a standard that has been adopted by the World Wide Web Consortium (WC3). As such, the CSS specificaton is supported by both Netscape Communicator 4.0 and Microsoft's Internet Explorer 3.0 and higher. This can eliminate many development hassles, and enables you to develop style sheet–based designs that work on multiple browsers with little modification.

Style Sheet Syntax

Now that you have an idea of what style sheets are, take a look at how styles and style sheets are defined in syntax.

Style sheets are collections of style properties that can be assigned to individual elements to add style attributes to a tag that might not have been flexible before. With traditional HTML, the <P> tag only represents a new paragraph, for example. Style sheets enable you to define a property such as font or color with a specific value. The basic syntax for specifying style for an element is as follows:

```
<TAG STYLE="style: value"> blah </TAG>
```

In this case, <TAG> represents a standard HTML tag, the *style* is a CSS property, and *value* is a property value that is accepted for the tag. To define a paragraph with green text, for example, you would use the following syntax:

```
<P STYLE="COLOR: GREEN"> Blah </P>
```

This sets the color of the text within the paragraph tags to green; however, other paragraph tags on the page are not affected by the assignment.

N O T E CSS properties and their values are not case-sensitive. COLOR and color, for example, are equivalent. Being consistent with tags, however, helps keep them separated from content text. This may help others to read your code more easily.

You might notice that syntax used to assign the color is slightly different from standard syntax. Rather than using an equals sign "=" to assign values, the CSS specification uses a colon ":". For instance:

```
<P STYLE="COLOR=GREEN"></P>
```

is *not* correct. Assigning the value as "COLOR: GREEN" on the other hand, would be correct. The style attribute must also be in quotation marks so that it is recognized as the style assignment, and not as part of another attribute in the tag.

CAUTION

Browsers might recognize some style assignments that are made with an equals sign (=) rather than a colon (:). You should get into the habit of using the colon right away, even if your browser recognizes an equals sign. Using the colon ensures the compatibility of your code in other browsers, and also makes sure that your code adheres to the standard for CSS.

Specifying Styles in the <HEAD> Section

Now that you know that single style assignments are not the most efficient way to define styles, you are probably interested in specifying styles for your entire HTML file. You accomplish this by placing the <STYLE> tag near the beginning of your HTML file. The <STYLE> tag must be located within the <HEAD> tag, so that it can be parsed before the remainder of the HTML code on a page. Because the <STYLE> tag specifies a block of styles, it must also have a terminating (</STYLE>) tag as shown in the following lines of HTML code:

```
<HTML>
<HEAD>
     <STYLE>
     style definitions
     </STYLE>
</HEAD>
</HTML>
```

The actual definition of the style for an element looks somewhat different as well:

```
<STYLE>
P { COLOR: BLUE; TEXT-INDENT: 30}
</STYLE>
```

As you can see, some new elements are used when creating a global style, and a slightly different format to establish the style. Here, the "P" is referred to as a selector that selects the paragraph tag for a style property. The style itself consists of two separate property definitions, "COLOR: BLUE" and "TEXT-INDENT: 30". Multiple property definitions are separated by a semicolon (;). The entire style assignment for the paragraph element is contained within curly braces "{ and }" that signify the beginning and ending of the style for the element. Because there are only two properties in this example, they appear on the same line; however, this is not a requirement. The following syntax is also acceptable:

```
<STYLE>
P { COLOR: BLUE;
    TEXT-INDENT: 30}
</STYLE>
```

In fact, as your styles become more complex, using multiple lines and indentation will make your code much easier to read.

TIP Because not all browsers support CSS, you might want to use HTML comments to enclose your style definitions so that they are not displayed by some browsers as text. For example:

```
<STYLE>
<!—
P { COLOR: BLUE; TEXT-INDENT: 1in}
—>
</STYLE>
```

The preceding code allows CSS-enabled browsers to process the style information, and enables older browsers to ignore the <STYLE> tag as an unknown tag—and then ignore the definitions as an HTML

continues

Part

II

Ch

4

continued

comment. Using the HTML comments can be a good way to easily maintain some level of backward-compatibility with older browsers, without sacrificing new features or investing in costly redevelopment. The practice of including comments in CSS HTML code is covered in more detail later in the section called "Comments."

Specifying Styles with Multiple Selectors

In some instances you might want to assign the same style to multiple elements. You might want to assign the same font styles to all your headlines, for example, by using the various <H> tags (H1, H2, H3). You can use multiple selectors just as you would multiple properties by separating the selectors with commas. To make all the headlines on a page blue, for example, you would write your HTML code as in the following:

```
<HTML>
<HEAD>
<STYLE>
        <! —
        H1,H2,H3,H4,H5,H6 { COLOR: BLUE }
        —>
</STYLE>
</HEAD>
<BODY>
<H1>This is Blue</H1>
<H3>This is Blue too! (Trust me!)</H3><BODY>
</HTML>
```

Assigning the same properties and values to all the <H> headers identified as selectors can be a convenient shortcut when elements have similar style attributes, as shown in figure 4.3.

FIG. 4.3

Defining styles by using multiple selectors can make the definitions more efficient.

Linking Style Sheets From Other Documents

Now you know how styles can be created by using inline styles, and how they can be defined as style blocks in the <HEAD> section of a document. Both of these methods are easy ways to utilize styles in your site, but another way is by linking style sheets.

Assume that there are some types of styles that you might want to define for all the HTML documents on a site, and the pages for the site might span multiple directories, and almost certainly multiple HTML files. You could write a series of style blocks to define all the styles for your site, and then copy those blocks into each page on your site. Doing this would not only be tedious, but it would also make each HTML file larger and harder to read.

CSS provides an easy solution—you can create a file with a .css extension that contains your style definitions and then import or link that file to an existing HTML page. Assume, for example, that you have created a file on your site called *"globalstyle.css"*, which contains all the style information for your site. One way in which you can import this file into your HTML page is to use the <LINK> tag. The link tag *must* be located between the <HEAD> tags in your HTML for the link to be properly processed, as shown in the following lines of HTML code:

```
<HTML>
<HEAD>
<LINK REL="stylesheet" HREF="globalstyle.css" TYPE="text/css">
</HEAD>
</HTML>
```

N O T E   When using the <LINK> tag to import a style sheet, it is important that the <LINK> tag appear in the <HEAD> of the HTML document. The reason for this is the manner in which HTML pages are processed by the browser. The pages are read and rendered in a linear fashion, beginning with the <HEAD> and then following on to the <BODY>. Because the linked style sheet will cause the browser to alter how elements in the <BODY> are rendered, the browser must have the style sheet information before it begins to process the <BODY>, and the only way to force the browser to do this is to include the <LINK> in the HTML file <HEAD> section.

This <LINK> tag uses several attributes to link a style sheet to the document in which it is used. The REL attribute specifies the type of relationship the specified link represents. In this case, the linked document is to be a *stylesheet* so that is the relationship that is specified. Next, the link needs to know where the style sheet is, as denoted by the file name, or the complete URL to the style sheet. If the page is in the same directory, the file name should be fine, but in other instances, for example if the style sheet were in a different directory than the file, you might want to use the full URL to be sure. Finally, the TYPE attribute defines the type of style sheet that is being linked. In the preceding code example, the type is *"text/css"* because we are using a Cascading Style Sheet. What if the site were using JavaScript Style Sheets? This is where the difference might be indicated.

In fact, you can use multiple <LINK> statements in your HTML file to specify the style sheets to be included in your page. You could, for example, have a site with different color schemes defined for styles as defined in the following <LINK> statements:

Part
II
Ch
4

```
<LINK REL=stylesheet HREF="pastel.css" TYPE="text/css">
<LINK REL=stylesheet HREF="rainbow.css" TYPE="text/css">
<LINK REL=stylesheet HREF="midnight.css" TYPE="text/css">
```

If each of the files in the preceding code contained different style definitions, then one site style could be created by using all three files. For purposes here, however, assume that each one of these files uses the same selectors, just different values. In this case, if all three of these <LINK> statements were included in one file, then the browser would use the style sheet file specified in the last listed link as the default for the style sheet. The other choices for styles would not be used by default, but some browsers offer support for allowing the user to specify a file. Permitting a choice for the user enables you to add an additional level of customization where the user can choose a style that is most aesthetically pleasing to them, resulting in a user experience that meets your design needs and satisfies the user.

> **CAUTION**
>
> If you are using multiple <LINK> tags to build a global style sheet, keep in mind that none of the files can contain conflicting selectors. If selectors conflict the default style attributes from the *last* link listed are used for the conflicting selector.
>
> Also keep in mind that if you are using the <LINK> tag to import style sheets, you will not be able to override your global styles with inline styles. To override global styles with inline styles, you will need to use @import, as described in the following section.

Importing Style Sheets

In addition to the <LINK> tag, another way you can associate a style sheet with a web page without using a large series of style blocks is to use the "@import" statement. The "@import" statement directs the browser to import the style sheet that is associated with a file. The following HTML code shows how you would load a style sheet by using the @import statement:

```
<STYLE type="text/css">
        @import URL("globalstyle.css");
</STYLE>
```

The @import statement indicates that the style sheet to be used on this page is the *"globalstyle.css"* file. The type attribute for the <STYLE> tag indicates that the type of style sheet being defined (in this case, imported) is a Cascading Style Sheet. This is important, because it is possible to use other types of style sheets for some browsers. Netscape Communicator, for example, supports JavaScript Style Sheets.

Just as you can use the <LINK> tag to link multiple style sheets, you can also use the @import statement to import multiple style sheets as shown in the following HTML code:

```
<STYLE TYPE="text/css">
        @import URL("globalstyle.css");
        @import URL("specialstyle.css");
        @import URL("pagestyle.css");
</STYLE>
```

In the preceding example, three separate style sheets are combined by using multiple @import statements. As is the case with the <LINK> tag, if conflicting selectors are in the imported style sheets, the style specification in the last file is used. If, for example, the following selector appears in the globalstyle.css style sheet:

```
P {FONT-FAMILY: ariel; COLOR: red}
```

but the style specification in the pagestyle.css style sheet contains a conflicting selector, such as:

```
P {FONT-FAMILY: serif; COLOR: blue}
```

the style from the pagestyle.css style sheet is used rather than the style from the globalstyle.css style sheet, resulting in paragraph text being displayed as blue text in a serif font.

The @import statement and the <LINK> tag do exactly the same thing, but appearances can be deceiving, especially in this case. The <LINK> tag can *only* be used to import style sheet definitions. It cannot be combined with local definitions, but the @import statement can. This is actually a powerful tool because you can use an imported style sheet and then override specific style declarations with a locally defined selector for use on a specific page as demonstrated in the following example:

```
<STYLE type="text/css">
        @import URL("globalstyle.css");
        P {COLOR: black};
        H1 {FONT-FAMILY: sans-serif};
</STYLE>
```

In this example, the local style declaration overrides the globalstyle.css style sheet selector for paragraphs or for any Level 1 heads. Similarly, you could use an inline style to override an imported style for one specific element on a page.

This type of flexibility allows you to combine imported style sheets and local declarations so that you can customize your styles specifically for various pages. This is the very flexibility for specifying design elements that designers have been requesting for years, and it brings a new level of control to web-based design.

Defining "Cascading" in Cascading Style Sheets

Several types of style sheets are available to various browsers; however, Cascading Style Sheets offers some unique features. One of these features is "cascading," which is so compelling it is advertised in their name. So what exactly is "cascading," and where does the cascading part come into play?

The idea of cascading is simple. Rules determine how one style declaration can override another. The order in which styles are defined, for example, is important in determining what style is used. This is how you can use multiple <LINK> statements—and also how you can use multiple @import statements combined with local declarations to override global style settings in a particular document.

Part

II

Ch

4

Assume, for example, that you have a style sheet called "global.css" as defined in the following HTML code:

```
<STYLE TYPE="text/css">
<!—This file functions as a global style sheet —>
P {COLOR: green; FONT-FAMILY: sans-serif}
H1,H4,H5 {FONT-FAMILY: serif; COLOR: blue}
H2,H3 {FONT-FAMILY: serif; COLOR: red}
</STYLE>
```

This style sheet specifies that all paragraph text will be in a sans-serif font, such as Ariel or Helvetica, with the color set to green. The style sheet continues to define Level 1, 4, and 5 headers to be in a serif font, such as Times, with a color of blue. Finally, Level 2 and 3 headers are also in a serif font, but the color is set to red.

Now, say that you have one page where you want to override the definitions for the colored heads, and make all the headlines black. You could do this in one of two ways.

The first way to override the style sheet definition is to create another style sheet, called "local.css" (defined in the following code example) that overrides the style definitions from the "global.css" file:

```
<STYLE type="text/css">
<!—This file introduces some conflicting definitions —>
H1,H2,H3,H4,H5 {FONT-FAMILY: san-serif; COLOR: black}
</STYLE>
```

After establishing the font specifications in the "local.css" style sheet, if you use the following import methods with your HTML file, the "local.css" attributes will override any selectors that it has in common with "global.css":

```
<HTML>
<HEAD>
<STYLE TYPE="text/css">
@import URL("global.css");
@import URL("local.css");
</STYLE>
</HEAD>
</HTML>
```

The style sheet overrides results from an ascending hierarchical order established for processing style definitions. In this case, importing the "local.css" style sheet after the "global.css" style sheet creates a style definition conflict. Because of the style sheet ascending hierarchy, style definitions specified in the "local.css" style sheet are used.

Another way would be to use a style block, or an inline style to override the imported style sheet, as demonstrated in the following HTML code:

```
<HTML>
<HEAD>
<STYLE TYPE="text/css">
@import URL("global.css");
H1 {FONT-FAMILY: sans-serif; COLOR: black}
```

```
</STYLE>
</HEAD>

<H1> This head has been overridden in a style block</H1>
<P STYLE="COLOR: black">
The color of the paragraph text has been overridden by an in-line style.
</P>
</HTML>
```

In the preceding code, the @import statement is being used to import a global style sheet. The style block that immediately follows the @import statement, however, redefines the style for <H1> and overrides the imported style sheet. Then, later in the code, the <P> style is overridden by specifying a style attribute directly in the tag. The results of this code are shown in figure 4.4.

FIG. 4.4
Although the color for the head and the paragraph are defined in a style sheet, they are overridden by other specifications.

Part
II

Ch
4

Establishing a protocol for how the definitions are processed is an essential part of Cascading Style Sheets. These rules are summarized in table 4.1.

Table 4.1   Style Sheet Declaration Processing Hierarchy

Method	Precedence
<LINK>	Last style sheet linked overrides previous style sheets.
@import URL	Last style sheet linked overrides previous style sheets.
Style blocks	Overrides imported styles.
Inline styles	Overrides imported styles and style blocks.

You can think of it this way, hierarchically, inline styles have the highest priority, followed (in order) by style blocks, @import statements, and links. If you think about how the HTML file is structured, this makes sense and follows a pretty logical order. The <LINK> and @import statements come first, so after they are loaded and parsed by the browser, a style block can be defined, and because that comes next, it can override linked and imported styles. Finally, because inline styles are defined in the body of the HTML file, they are parsed last, and therefore, override all previous style definitions. This is cascading, and one of the reasons that CSS is so powerful. It allows you to produce completely customized styles for your sites, and alter those styles for special circumstances on an as-needed basis.

Understanding CSS Inheritance

In addition to having the style definitions cascade, CSS also incorporates a form of inheritance that can simplify the process of defining styles. The examples used in this chapter so far have all consisted of selectors that have mirrored individual elements as demonstrated in the following simple line of code:

```
P {COLOR: red};
```

In the preceding line of code "P" represents the paragraph tag. Some more general HTML tags, however, can be used to describe HTML pages such as the <HEAD> tag, or the <BODY> tag, which can both be used to describe different areas of an HTML document as shown in the following lines of code:

```
<STYLE>

BODY {FONT-FAMILY: sans-serif;
     COLOR: green;
     TEXT-ALIGN: justify;}
</STYLE>
```

This example specifies the style characteristics for the <BODY> HTML tag. The font will be a sans-serif font, green, and justified. So what does that mean for text used within the <BODY> tag? Well, the <P> tag is a "child" tag of the <BODY> tag—which is called the parent. This means that <P> inherits the properties that are defined for the <BODY> tag, or in other words, the <P> tag will be in a sans-serif font, green, and justified.

Although this might not seem like a big deal, it can be used as a shortcut to simplify your style sheet creation. By specifying styles for parent tags, such as the <BODY> tag, you can easily pass style properties on to other styles that you are going to use on your pages. For details about what properties are inherited, refer to the Cascading Style Sheets specification in Appendix B.

Comments

Finally, it is always useful to be able to add comments to any type of coding. Comments enable you to document the code that you have written so that others can easily determine what your code does.

CSS uses one form of the C/C++ notation for comments, placing "/*" at the beginning of a comment, and "*/" at the end of the comment. You can see how comments are denoted in the following:

```
<HTML>
<HEAD>
<STYLE>
```

```
        /* This line is a comment. */
H1,H2,H3,H4,H5 { COLOR: blue }
</STYLE>
</HEAD>
</HTML>
```

Getting in the habit of commenting your code is a good idea, not just for others, but also for yourself. You might need to go back and modify an extensive style sheet definition someday, after having long forgotten exactly how you wrote it. Comments are a good way to find your way around a definition, and a good way to make sure you remember important or tricky details of a particular style sheet.

CSS Properties Divisions

Cascading Style Sheet properties are divided into five broad categories for classification. These classifications include font, color and background, text, box, and classification. The purpose of these classifications is to bring elements together into categories that make sense for documentation, but also to aid in understanding how each property inherits values from another property. Here is a breakdown of each of the divisions and the types of properties they contain. Detailed explanations of the properties can be found in Appendix B.

Font

The font properties relate to the type and style of fonts that are used on a web page. These properties enable you to manipulate the font face, style, size, and weight of a font being used, and include properties such as the following:

- **font**—A generic font property that can be used to specify multiple style properties with one tag, such as size, family, style, and so on.
- **font-size**—Enables designers to specify font-sizes.
- **font-weight**—Enables manipulation of the font weight, ranging from light to normal to bold (or heavy).
- **font-variant**—Enables you to specify a variant of a font family, such as small caps.
- **font-style**—Enables you to specify the style of the font, such as bold or italics.
- **font-family**—Enables you to specify a generic font family for the font, such as serif or script, to avoid using explicit font names.

Color and Background

The color and background properties can be used to alter the appearance of a page's background, or they can be applied to HTML elements to change the attributes of that element, such as changing the color of a border or font. Some of the color and background properties include the following:

- **color**—A flexible and powerful property that can be used to alter the color value for nearly any HTML element, ranging from a border to a table cell or a font.

- **background-color**—Enables you to specify a color that will function as the background color of an element. Although the property is often applied to a page as a whole, it can also be used for specific elements, such as a positioning container.

- **background-image**—Functions similarly to the background-color property, but enables you to specify an image that is to be used in the background, rather than a solid color.

Text

The CSS text properties exist to alter the appearance of text on the page. These properties can be used to refine the typesetting on a page, or to create specific text effects. Some of the text properties are included in the following list:

- **word-spacing**—Enables you to assign a unit of measurement to the amount of whitespace that appears between words in text.

- **letter-spacing**—Enables you to alter the amount of whitespace that exists between letters of text.

- **text-transform**—Enables the application of special effects to a group of text, such as making the text all lowercase, or capitalizing the text.

- **text-align**—Enables the designer to alter the alignment of text elements so that they are aligned with the left or right side of the page, for example.

- **text-indent**—Enables the creation of a standard indention so that elements such as paragraphs will consistently be indented the same number of spaces.

Box

The box properties are used to assign property values to elements that essentially exist in a "box," such as blocks of text, the page, images, or positioning containers. These properties enable the designer to manipulate attributes such as the margins, table cells, or borders.

- **margins**—The margin properties include margin, margin-top, margin-bottom, margin-left, and margin-right. These properties are used to define margins for elements using the units of measurements and can be applied to individual elements or the entire page.

- **padding**—Similar to margin properties, padding establishes a "buffer zone" around elements to prevent them from overlapping. Padding properties include padding, padding-top, padding-bottom, padding-left, and padding-right.

- **borders**—The border properties include border-style, border-width, border-top, border-bottom, border-left, and border-right. These properties are used to alter the border attributes for elements.

- **width**—Used primarily with CSS Positioning to specify the width of a positioning container. This property is covered extensively in Chapter 9, "Layout and Positioning."

- **height**—Used with CSS Positioning to define the height of a positioning container. This property is also covered extensively in Chapter 9.

Classification

Finally the classification properties are used to create special classifications for elements on the page. The *display* property, for example, is used to classify whether an element is *visible* or *hidden*. These properties become increasingly important with dynamic styles later in Chapters 8 and 9.

- **display**—Alters the appearance of an element by enabling the designer to classify an item as *visible* or *hidden*. This can be used to create dynamic content by choosing what elements on a page a reader may or may not be exposed to.

- **list-styles**—Enables designers to specify how lists are to be formatted, including the style of bullet points used.

Values

CSS properties accept values in a variety of formats, ranging from predefined keywords to percentage values. It isn't necessary to know all the value types that can be specified with a particular property at this stage in learning CSS, but it pays to be a little more familiar with some value types, such as measurement units, colors, and font attributes. After you have mastered these values, you can use the reference in Appendix B to look up the specific values that can be assigned to each property.

Specifying Measurement Units

Many of the CSS properties accept values for length or other measurements based on a number of different unit systems such as inches (in) or points (pt). Table 4.2 shows the various types of measurements that are accepted by CSS.

Table 4.2   CSS Measurement Units

CSS Abbreviation	Measurement
pt	Points
pc	Picas
ex	X-height
em	M-width
mm	Millimeters
cm	Centimeters
in	Inches
px	Pixels

Part

II

Ch

4

Because CSS is widely regarded as a tool for designers, many of the measurement values that are accepted are rooted in desktop publishing. Values such as points, picas, ems, and x-height all have their roots in graphic design and typography. More commonly used measurements are inches and centimeters.

To specify letter spacing, you could use picas to specify the distance between individual letters as shown in the following HTML code:

```
<HTML>
<HEAD>
<STYLE>
        P { LETTER-SPACING: 2pc }
</STYLE>
</HEAD>
<P>
SPACE
</HTML>
```

The output for this code displays the word "SPACE" something like figure 4.5:

FIG. 4.5

Specifying the distance
between characters.

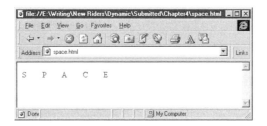

The measurement is defined by following a numerical value with the abbreviation for the measurement unit. In addition to being used for letter and line spacing, the units of measurement are used with elements such as borders to define widths, or fonts to define size. The units of measurement will also be important for positioning in later chapters.

Specifying Color

Defining color with Cascading Style Sheets is an important feature for web design and Dynamic HTML. Defining color in CSS can be accomplished in many ways.

The first method is to use a predefined natural language label. These predefined values are limited, only about 128 inches in all. The values are listed in Appendix F, "Browser-Safe Hexadecimal Chart."

Although these predefined color values do come in handy, in some instances you need finer control over the color on your web pages.

One alternative is defining the color with a hexadecimal value for color, in the format of "#RRGGBB" where "RR" is a value for the red component, "BB" blue, and "GG" green. This is really a variant of RGB color definition, but is helpful because of the widespread usage of hexadecimal values on the web.

Finally, you can define color by using the RGB values, either as integers or as percentages. You could define blue, for example, as:

```
COLOR: RGB(0, 0, 9)
```

which would mean the red value was 0, green 0, and blue 9. Of course, it would be a very bright blue! Similarly, you can use the same syntax, but replace the integers with percentages as in the following:

```
COLOR: RGB(100%, 0%, 100%)
```

In this example, the mixture of 100% red, 0% green, and 100% blue would produce purple.

Having the option of natural language color names can make it easy to use highlighting colors in a pinch. For finer design control, and the capability to specify custom color, the finer controls of RGB values are very handy.

Specifying Font Values

Another flexible design aspect of Cascading Style Sheets is that they offer the capability to specify information about the fonts that are going to be used on your pages. You can specify font family, style, size, weight, and other attributes to get you more typographical control over how your web sites appear. Say, for example, that you want to produce a site that has all sans-serif fonts, but you want the headlines to be in italics. You could use the following styles to make this a reality:

```
<STYLE>
H1,H2,H3,H4,H5 {FONT-FAMILY: sans-serif; FONT-STYLE: italic}
</STYLE>
```

In this style, the *FONT-FAMILY* property specifies that the typeface used for headlines should be a sans-serif font. In addition, the heads are italicized with the *FONT-STYLE* property. Table 4.3 summarizes the CSS properties that are available when working with type.

Table 4.3   CSS Font Properties and Values

Property	Accepted Values
FONT-SIZE	*integer, percentage*
	xx-small, x-small, small, medium, large, x-large, xx-large
FONT-FAMILY	*family name*
	serif, sans-serif, cursive, fantasy, monospace

continues

Part
II

Ch

4

Table 4.3 Continued

Property	Accepted Values
FONT-STYLE	normal, italic, oblique
FONT	font-size, font-family, font-style
COLOR	*color*

You will notice that some of the font properties can take a variable, such as "*family name*" but also have specific values, such as "serif". This is because specifying an explicit font name might not produce a useable result. You, for example, could use *FONT-FAMILY* to specify that you want your body text to appear in the "Garamond" font; however, what happens if you specify Garamond font and the user does not have that font installed?

One alternative would be to specify that you want the browser to use a "serif" font—which Garamond is. Then the browser will choose a serif font that is installed on the system, and use that to display the font. By using a generic family name, the designer can exert some control over the design of the page without worrying about what the user has installed. However, that doesn't solve our original problem, which was a designer who wants to use Garamond, but can't be sure that font is installed. To address situations like this, CSS provides an even greater degree of flexibility. Although one solution was to just use the generic font name, another would be to use a specific font, but to also provide an alternative if the font is not available. This is no problem for CSS. You can use multiple values with some of the font properties as shown in the following HTML code:

```
<STYLE>
P {FONT-FAMILY: helvetica, sans-serif; FONT-STYLE: italic}
</STYLE>
```

The style definition in the previous example instructs the browser to use "Helvetica" as the text font, provided the user has it installed on his system. If Helvetica is not available, the browser substitutes a generic sans-serif font as described in the font specification.

Advanced CSS

Now that you have the basics of CSS under your belt, there are some other advanced features that will become important as you learn how Dynamic HTML exploits CSS to manipulate objects. Some of these advanced features include the use of classes and element IDs that enable you to specify multiple styles for HTML elements, or pseudo classes for commonly manipulated HTML elements.

Specifying Styles with Classes

With CSS you can specify different styles for an HTML element by employing classes to identify different styles for the same element. Classes enable you to create versions of a style that can be applied by using the CLASS attribute in conjunction with the style in the text.

To define a class, you append a class name to the style selector in the style sheet. To define a class for a head, for example, you could use:

```
H1.classname {COLOR: red}
```

that defines a class called "classname" that defines the color as red. The following line of code demonstrates how to specify a class in an HTML tag:

```
<H1 CLASS=classname>This head would be red.</H1>
```

You can also define a class that is not associated with a specific tag, by omitting the selector:

```
.specialtext {COLOR: fuchsia}
```

The preceding line of code specifies a style class called *.specialtext* that is not associated with a specific selector or HTML tag. This enables you to apply this style to different HTML tags by using the "CLASS" attribute. This *.specialtext* class could then be applied to multiple HTML elements, for example:

```
<H1 CLASS=specialtext>A Fuchsia Heading</H1>
<P CLASS=specialtext>Fuchsia body text as well!</P>
```

Here, the style we created called *.specialtext* is applied to both an <H1> tag and a <P> tag by assigning them the style's class name. The result is that both elements display the same style characteristics from the same style definition, even though they are different tags.

You can define as many classes as you want, but keep in mind that if you define multiple classes for an element, you need to use the CLASS attribute to specify which style should be applied to an element as demonstrated in the following HTML code:

```
<HTML>
<HEAD>
<STYLE>
     P.REDTEXT {COLOR: red; FONT-FAMILY: sans-serif}
     P.GREENTEXT {COLOR: green; FONT-SIZE: 25}
     .blue {COLOR: blue; FONT-FAMILY: serif}
</STYLE>
</HEAD>
<BODY>
<P CLASS=REDTEXT>
This text will be red and sans-serif.
</P>
<P CLASS=GREENTEXT>
This text will be green, and larger.
</P>
<P CLASS=blue>
This text will be blue and a serif font.
</P>
</BODY>
</HTML>
```

Part

II

Ch

4

The results of which are shown in figure 4.6.

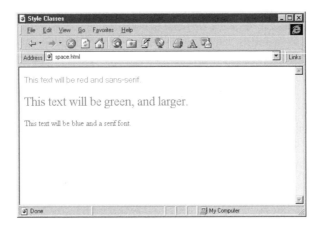

Specifying Styles with Element IDs

Element IDs (sometimes called selector IDs) work similarly to classes, but they are limited to use for only one element. IDs are specified by using the pound sign (#) followed by the ID name and definition as shown in the following syntax:

```
#elementid {FONT-FAMILY: serif}
```

In this declaration, the ID "elementid" will have a font family that is a serif font. To use this style in your document, you would use the ID attribute as follows:

```
<P ID="elementid">This is a serif font</P>
```

Unlike the CLASS attribute, however, each element ID must be unique. The following, for example, is *not* valid:

```
<P ID="elementid">This is a serif font</P>
<H1 ID="elementid">This is not recommended</H1>
```

The code is invalid because the ID is meant to provide a mechanism for overriding a style for a particular element. For broader style applications, stick to using classes. Of course, you can use both in the same document for added flexibility as demonstrated in the following HTML code:

```
<HTML>
<HEAD>
<STYLE>
     #abc345 {COLOR: blue}
     P.redtext {COLOR: red}
</STYLE>
</HEAD>

<P ID=abc345>
This text will be blue.
```

```
</P>
<P CLASS=redtext>
This text will be red.
</P>
<!— The following line is illegal and will not work —>
<H3 ID=abc345>It is not recommended to use multiple IDs</H3>
</HTML>
```

Pseudo Classes and Elements

In several instances HTML already provides for a special style of its own. The fact that links are highlighted and underlined is an example of a style that already exists before it is even specified in your style sheet. To accommodate for some of these special circumstances, CSS provides some special classes called *pseudo classes* that are used explicitly for modifying some of these cases. The three pseudo classes that are currently available include the following:

- **:link**—This pseudo class represents an element that functions as an HTML link, such as **<A HREF="http://www.myserver.com/mypage.html">**.

- **:active**—When a link is clicked, the link becomes a member of the active pseudo class, although this is generally a temporary state.

- **:visited**—Finally, after a link has be visited, the visited link becomes a member of the visited pseudo class.

These pseudo classes can be appended to other style selectors, and used to create a style for specific elements, such as the Anchor tag as demonstrated in the following code:

```
A:link {COLOR: green}
A:link IMG {BORDER-COLOR: blue}
A:visited {COLOR: gray}
```

These declarations define all the HREF links in a document as green and any images that serve as links as having a blue border. In addition, the :visited pseudo class defines any links that have been visited to have a color of gray. Of course, because these pseudo classes are actually elements that are already monitored to see if they have been clicked by the browser, it is not necessary to use any special notation in your HTML code. After a pseudo class is defined, it applies to all elements of that type.

In addition to the pseudo classes, there are also pseudo elements that function as special selectors. That is, they can be used to apply special style attributes to HTML elements that are prdefined by the browser, but are not actually used in standard HTML. The pseudo elements currently used include the following:

- **:first-letter**—The first letter pseudo element represents the first letter in a block of text.

- **:first-line**—The first line pseudo element represents the first line in a block of text.

These pseudo elements can be manipulated to produce special text effects, such as a dropcap or a tagline as demonstrated in the following example:

```
<HTML>
<HEAD>
```

Part

II

Ch

4

```
<STYLE>
     P.TAGLINE:FIRST-LINE {TEXT-TRANSFORM: UPPERCASE}
     P.DROPCAP:FIRST-LETTER {FONT-SIZE: 200%; FLOAT: LEFT}
</STYLE>
</HEAD>
<BODY>
<P CLASS=TAGLINE>
This paragraph has a tagline, so that all the characters on the first
➥line of the paragraph will appear in capitals.
</P>
<P CLASS=DROPCAP>
This paragraph starts off with a dropcap.
</P>
</BODY>
</HTML>
```

N O T E At press time the current version of Internet Explorer 4 was not properly rendering pseudo elements. You will want to test your current version of IE to ensure proper support for these CSS features. ▓

The pseudo classes and pseudo elements enable the CSS specification to be altered to accommodate different standard elements easily. By combining pseudo classes and pseudo elements with selectors you can create a variety of interesting text effects.

Nesting Elements

Sometimes in your HTML coding you might want to *nest* elements, that is, place one HTML element inside another similar element. One of the best examples of nesting is lists that resemble an outline structure as shown in figure 4.7.

FIG. 4.7

Nesting HTML elements.

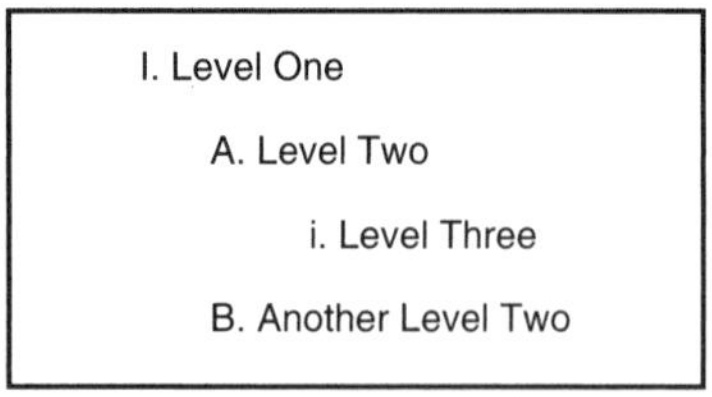

```
I. Level One

    A. Level Two

        i. Level Three

    B. Another Level Two
```

This could be created by placing a list within a list. Just as you can create a list within a list, you can also specify a STYLE property within a STYLE property. So, assuming that you have a list, and you want the first level elements to be all bold words, you would use the following HTML code to create a list STYLE where all the list items were boldface:

```
UL LI {FONT-STYLE: BOLD}
```

This code would result in the first item in the list appearing in boldface.

Now, suppose that following an outline format, you wanted to nest a second list below the bold-face list, but this one you wanted to appear in italics. You can actually nest the STYLE definition as well:

```
UL UL LI { FONT-STYLE: ITALIC }
```

This would create the output that is shown in figure 4.8.

FIG. 4.8

Nesting style definitions.

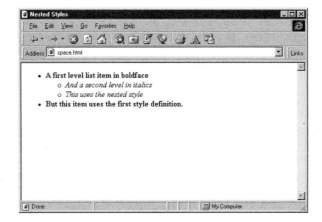

Your capability to nest items on multiple levels is not limited, but practically speaking, it is not recommended to nest too deeply. Implementing nesting in the HTML file just follows the natural order that you would nest elements as shown in the following example:

```
<HTML>
<HEAD>
<TITLE>Nesting Styles</TITLE>
<STYLE>
UL LI { COLOR: RED; FONT-STYLE: ITALIC }
UL UL LI { COLOR: BLUE; FONT-FAMILY: SANS-SERIF; }
</STYLE>
</HEAD>
<BODY>
<UL>
<LI>This list item would appear in red and italicized.
<UL>
<LI>This nested list item would appear in blue, sans-serif font.
</UL>
<LI>This list item would also appear in red and italics.
</UL>
</BODY>
</HTML>
```

Part
II

Ch

4

Figure 4.9 shows the output for the previous HTML code, where the styles defined for list items are nested styles, and the list elements are also nested.

FIG. 4.9

Nested elements can be customized with nested STYLE properties.

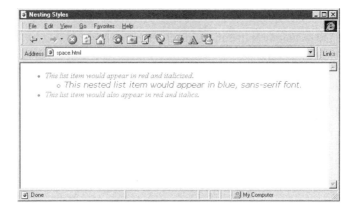

As you can see, nesting is not a complicated process, but it does add a great deal of flexibility to style sheets.

CSS Positioning

The Cascading Style Sheet specification actually does not contain any mechanisms for positioning elements, although this is an important mechanism for making web pages dynamic. Although CSS does provide mechanisms for aligning text or changing text appearance, it does not allow for the explicit positioning of elements in a given location on the page. That is what CSSP, or Cascading Style Sheets Positioning, is for. Because positioning has become so important for web design, both static and dynamic, some extensions to CSS, known as CSS Positioning have been proposed by Microsoft and Netscape.

In fact, CSS Positioning forms the basis of many aspects of positioning and animating objects in Dynamic HTML. Because it is not a part of the CSS1 specification, the CSS Positioning specification is not discussed here; however, it is covered explicitly in Chapter 9 where it is appropriate to the Dynamic HTML concepts being discussed.

Where to Learn More About CSS

Obviously, it is impossible to cover all the aspects of Cascading Style Sheets in one chapter. Although this chapter tried to touch on all the major details of CSS, and provide you with the widest possible coverage of properties and values, there is still much that can be learned about CSS, and much you will want to learn to make the most out of Dynamic HTML. This chapter should serve as a primer, to get you started, and prepare you for some of the examples that will follow in later chapters. If you are interested in the specifics of different properties, their values, and their inheritance, you can consult Appendix B.

To learn even more about the CSS specification, or to read the specification itself, you can consult the W3C at **http://www.w3c.org**.

To learn more about the specifics of the CSS in relation to Microsoft, you can check out the Microsoft web site at **http://www.microsoft.com/workshop/author/css/css-f.htm**.

Finally, a number of very good texts cover Cascading Style Sheets, including one from Hankon Lie and Bert Bos of the W3C: *Cascading Style Sheets* (Addison-Wesley).

From Here…

Now that you have the foundations you need to create style sheets using the Cascading Style Sheet specification, you are ready to move on to learning about some more of the technologies that you will need to be familiar with to begin working with Dynamic HTML.

After you are familiar with the basics of the technologies covered in the chapters that follow, you will be able to use Dynamic HTML more quickly and efficiently. The increase in your ability to comprehend how Dynamic HTML functions will more than make up for the time out you have taken to understand the core technologies. Although this might seem like a lot of groundwork, it is essential for understanding how the underlying technologies tie together to create Dynamic HMTL. From here, you will delve into the following areas:

- Chapter 5, "JavaScript Primer," covers the basics of understanding and using JavaScript, one of the preferred scripting languages used by Dynamic HTML.
- Chapter 6, "Dynamic HTML Object Model," talks about the object model used by Dynamic HTML that treats all HTML elements on a page as mutually aware objects.
- Chapter 7, "Event Handling," covers the importance of event handling in Dynamic HTML-generated web sites.

JavaScript Primer

For something to be dynamic, there needs to be another mechanism in place to provide instructions and direction. In the real world, for instance, the number of places an automobile could go are pretty much limitless. Without someone controlling the car (starting it up, pressing the accelerator, turning the steering wheel, and so on), however, it will not go anywhere. It is the person sitting in the driver's seat who decides the purpose and destination of the automobile.

Scripting languages are the drivers of Dynamic HTML. The combination of HTML and Cascading Style Sheets provides you with unprecedented control over the look and feel of your web pages; however, by themselves, the technologies are static and unmoving, much like an automobile without a driver. Scripting languages enable you to bring interactivity and motion to your HTML and CSS.

So what is a scripting language? At its essence, a *scripting language* is a programming language, such as C, C++, Java, or FORTRAN. For many people, however, the thought of programming is somewhat scary. Scripting languages try to make the prospect of programming a little less frightening.

Scripting languages, such as JavaScript and Visual Basic Scripting Edition, have been designed to open up the world of programming to those people who are not programmers by profession or training, and who are easily put off by the complex syntax of a language such as C++ or Java.

Think of a scripting language as a programming language stripped down to its essence. It might not be powerful enough to write a modern word processing program in, but it's probably more than powerful enough for any basic programming that you might need for your web page—with the added bonus of comprehension by normal human beings. ■

Validating the Use of JavaScript with Dynamic HTML

Dynamic HTML is quite open in terms of the scripting languages that it supports. Future web browser designers could use whatever scripting language is popular at that time and still reap all the benefits of Dynamic HTML.

Internet Explorer 4.0, however, includes two scripting languages that can be used with Dynamic HTML: JavaScript and VBScript. The fact that IE 4.0 comes with support for two scripting languages immediately begs for an answer to the question: Which scripting language should I use?

N O T E   Microsoft always refers to the implementation of JavaScript in Internet Explorer as *JScript* instead of *JavaScript*. This can cause some confusion, because Netscape always refers to it as JavaScript. In any case, to keep confusion to a minimum, it will be referred to as JavaScript throughout this book. ■

There are many arguments for and against each scripting language. The commercial version of Visual Basic (the parent language of VBScript), for instance, is one of the best selling programming environments of all time, and vast multitudes of programmers use it every day. Thus, a huge pool of talent is best served by having a scripting version of Visual Basic available to them.

JavaScript, on the other hand, is currently the de facto scripting language of the web due to its inclusion in Netscape Navigator 2.0 and above and Internet Explorer 3.0. Although more programmers know Visual Basic, more web programmers know JavaScript. Moreover, VBScript is currently available only in Internet Explorer.

N O T E   Although we don't have a strong opinion either way on scripting languages, we had to decide on one of the two to focus on to keep things from getting too confusing. We chose to concentrate on JavaScript, mainly due to its massive acceptance and familiarity on the web.

The use of VBScript with Dynamic HTML in Internet Explorer 4.0 is covered in Appendix C, "Using VBScript Instead of JavaScript." ■

Introduction to JavaScript

If you've ever programmed in any other languages, JavaScript should be fairly straightforward for you to learn. If not, don't worry; it's pretty easy. Listing 5.1 is a simple program that gives you an idea of how JavaScript looks:

Listing 5.1   A Simple Hello World Program in JavaScript

```
01. <HTML>
02. <HEAD>
03.     <TITLE>
04.     Hello World in JavaScript
05.     </TITLE>
06. </HEAD>
07. <BODY>
08.
09.     <SCRIPT language="JavaScript">
10.
11.         document.write("Hello, world");
12.
13.     </SCRIPT>
14.
15. </BODY>
16. </HTML>
```

The first thing you should do is take a look at the HTML in line 9 that surrounds the JavaScript program. If you've used basic HTML before, everything looks pretty standard until you get to the line that says:

```
<SCRIPT language="JavaScript">
```

The <SCRIPT> tag is just a standard HTML tag. The <SCRIPT> tag instructs the program to take everything contained within (that is between this and </SCRIPT>) and treat it as a script to be executed. The scripting language to be used is specified by the *language* attribute, which in this case is set to JavaScript (if Visual Basic Scripting Edition was used instead, the *language* attribute would be set to VBScript).

Line 11 is the only line that actually contains JavaScript code:

```
document.write("Hello, world");
```

This line tells the browser to write the string "Hello, world" to the browser document window. As you can see in figure 5.1, "Hello, world" shows up just as if you had included it as part of the HTML code.

In fact, you can use JavaScript to output any HTML you like, not just plain text. Try replacing the JavaScript from the previous example with the following:

```
<SCRIPT language="JavaScript">

    document.write("<H1>Hello, world</H1>");

</SCRIPT>
```

Make sure that you reload the HTML page to ensure that the script is updated. Note that now "Hello, world" is displayed as an HTML heading rather than as regular text (see figure 5.2).

FIG. 5.1

Output from the "Hello World" script.

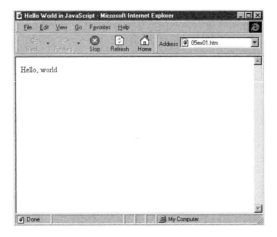

FIG. 5.2

"Hello, world" to HTML.

In the sections that follow, the different syntax elements that make up a JavaScript program will be covered. These elements include the following:

- **Statements**—Statements are the lines of code from which JavaScript programs are built.
- **Blocks**—Blocks enable you to group statements.
- **Comments**—Comments enable you to annotate your code with remarks.
- **Data**—Data is the actual information upon which your programs work.
- **Expressions**—Expressions enable you to perform operations on data.
- **Variables**—Variables give you a place to store your data.
- **Functions**—Functions are used to group your code into sections with a name.
- **Flow Control**—Flow control enables your program to take different courses of action at runtime.

- **Objects**—Objects enable you to group together your data and functions.
- **Arrays**—Arrays enable you to hold a great deal of data and access individual elements easily.

Statements

JavaScript programs are made out of statements. What is a statement? Technically *statements* are a group of one or more items and symbols on a line. Put simply, however, a statement is a line of code. You've already written a statement:

```
document.write("Hello, world");
```

Note that this line ends with a semicolon. In JavaScript, a semicolon is a way of saying that the statement has ended and the script can be executed. Semicolons are normally used at the end of each line, but you can place multiple statements on a line if each is separated by a semicolon. If you don't like the idea of putting semicolons at the end of all your statements, you'll find that you can usually leave them off without generating an error. It's best, however, to get in the habit of using semicolons because it can make tracking down errors easier and is generally considered to be better form.

Blocks

It is quite common in programming to want to group many statements together so that they can be treated as one entity—this is often done with functions and in conditionals, which are discussed later in this chapter.

This grouping of statements together into one entity is called a *block*. A block is created by surrounding all the statements that it will contain with brackets ({ and }). The following code snippet is a block:

```
{
    document.write("This is the first statement");
    document.write("This is a second statement");
    document.write("All these statements are part of a block");
}
```

Note that the statements inside the block are indented compared to the brackets that surround it. Although not required, doing this is a common coding convention that makes your code more readable and easier to modify.

Part
II

Ch
5

Comments

Even though JavaScript is fairly readable for a programming language, it certainly isn't English and therefore can become quite confusing. Moreover, it's easy to use complicated logic in a program that might not be readily apparent the first time someone else reads the code to your program.

To remedy this situation, JavaScript enables you to comment your code. Comments are completely ignored by the JavaScript interpreter, so you can type whatever descriptive text you want. You can write single-line or multiline comments.

The process of commenting code is something that most programmers know they should do, but all too often they forget. It's a good idea to keep in mind, however, that it may not be someone else who has to figure out your code in the future. It may be you in a year or two, having completely forgotten what it was you were trying to do.

In general, it doesn't make sense to try to comment every line in your program. A good general benchmark is that if you had to spend more than a few minutes figuring out how to write a section of your code, write a comment about it, because that means you'll have to spend just as much time figuring out the code when you revisit it later.

Single-Line Comments

If you just need to add a small amount of description to the code you are writing, a single-line comment is probably the best option. Placing "//" before your text makes it a single-line comment:

```
// The following line writes "Hello World" to the browser window
document.write("Hello World");
```

You can also join a line that contains a JavaScript statement and a single-line comment into one line:

```
document.write("Hello World");    // Write "Hello World" to the browser window
```

If you do this, make absolutely sure that you put the comment *after* the JavaScript code, otherwise that code will not be executed. After you're used to programming in JavaScript this fact can be used to your advantage, enabling you to selectively comment out a line or two of your code if you think it is unneeded or is causing problems.

Multiline Comments

Sometimes one line of commenting isn't enough room for the description you want to provide. In this case, you can use a multiline comment. Multiline comments are specified by surrounding the commented text with "/*" at the beginning and "*/" at the end:

```
/*
    This comment is of the multiline type. It can contain as
    many lines of comments as you want. Repeat to yourself,
    Commenting is a good thing, Commenting is a good thing."
*/
```

You need to be careful when using multiline comments to make sure that you do not put one inside of another, because this causes an error. The following, for example, is not valid multiline commenting in JavaScript:

```
/*
    This is a standard multiline comment. So far, so good
    /* This is multiline comment, which by itself
    would be fine */
*/
```

The reason that enclosing one multiline comment within another generates an error is that the end of a multiline comment is signified by "*/" and the JavaScript interpreter treats anything between the "/*" and the "*/" as comments, therefore the second "/*" is ignored and not recognized as the beginning of another comment.

Data

One of the basic tenets of programs is that they have to work on data. What is data? *Data* is any type of information with which you are working. Data can be words, such as "Hello There" or numbers, such as 42 or 381.33. In any case, different programming languages enable you to work on different kinds of data.

JavaScript has six fundamental data types: string, number, Boolean, function, object, and Null (see table 5.1). The sections following this table discuss the string, number, Boolean, and Null types. Functions and objects are discussed later in this chapter.

Table 5.1 JavaScript Fundamental Data Types

Data Type	Example
String	"Hello", "A String", 'He said, "hello"'
Number	12, 372.33, 0xff
Boolean	true, false
Object	document, window
Function	computePrimes(), addName()
Null	null

Strings

A string is any grouping of characters together that are surrounded by either double quotation marks(") or single quotation marks('). Strings are used anytime you want to use text in a program. Here are a few examples of strings:

```
"Hello World"
```

```
"Microsoft Dynamic HTML"
```

Usually double quotation marks are used to denote strings. If you want to include double quotes in the string itself, use single quotation marks instead:

```
'A string that contains "double-quotes"'
```

Numbers

JavaScript is quite flexible in the ways it enables you to represent numbers. Many programming languages make you decide ahead of time what type of number you will be using. You, for instance, might need to specify whether a number is an integer or a floating point number.

JavaScript, however, treats all numbers the same: they're just numbers, whether they're whole integers or not. Here are a few examples of numbers in JavaScript:

```
72      // The decimal integer 72
32.4    // The floating point number 32.4
.327    // The floating point number .327
```

Booleans

A *Boolean* is the simplest data type available. A Boolean value has only two possible values—true and false. They are often used to represent whether something has been done.

An example of when a Boolean might be used is when you want to keep track of whether the users have clicked an image previously. The first time they click the image, you might want to do something special such as running an animation or playing a certain sound. The second time they click, however, you might want to do nothing. The most straightforward way to keep track of this information would be through a Boolean that is set when the image is clicked.

Null

The final JavaScript data type is quite special. The Null data type only has one possible value: null. When a variable is set to *null* it means that it has no value. Variables are often set to null when a value was to have been returned to a function but instead no value was generated.

Expressions

Data by itself can be pretty useless. Normally you want to do something with the data. Maybe you want to divide two numbers by each other, add two numbers together, or perhaps you want to check to see whether two sets of numbers added together are equal to one another. These are all uses of *expressions*.

This may sound a bit confusing at first, so consider a practical example. Say you were given a temperature in degrees Fahrenheit and wanted to convert it to Celsius. You would use the following process to do this:

1. Start with the degrees in Fahrenheit (F).
2. Subtract 32.
3. Multiply the number by 5.
4. Divide the number by 9.

This process can be turned into a mathematical representation instead of the longhand version just shown. This mathematical representation would be

```
(F-32)*5/9
```

This representation is known as an expression.

Numeric Expressions

A *numeric expression* is the rudimentary sort of mathematical operation that you're accustomed to, except written out in its full form. The numeric expression for two plus three, for instance, is:

```
2 + 3
```

The common operations that can be used on numbers in JavaScript are listed in table 5.2.

Table 5.2   Common Numerical Operators

Operator	Example	Definition
+	3 + 3	Addition
–	12 – 4	Subtraction
*	22 * 3	Multiplication
/	18 / 4	Division
%	18 % 4	Modulo: The remainder after division. The result here would be 2, because 4 goes into 18 4 times, with a remainder of 2.
–	–(12 * 3)	Unary Negation: The negative of the expression that follows. The result, for example, would be –36. The negative of a negative is a positive.

If you have an expression that contains more than one set of operations, you can group them together with parentheses ('(' and ')'). This dictates the order in which the expressions are evaluated. Figuring out the order to carry out the operations in the following expression, for instance, could take a while:

```
36 * 12 % 15 - 32 * 12 / 3
```

This is a valid expression, and if you looked in a JavaScript reference manual for operator precedence you could probably figure it out; however, it would be much easier to just use the following:

```
((36 * 12) % 15) - (32 * 12) /3))
```

Logical Expressions

A *logical* (or Boolean) *expression* is an expression that when evaluated returns a result of either true or false. Boolean expressions can be generated in several ways, but the most common way is to use logical or comparison operators (see table 5.3).

Part
II

Ch
5

Table 5.3 Logical and Comparison Operators

Operator	Name	Usage
&&	And	(exp1 && exp2) returns true if both exp1 and exp2 are true, otherwise returns false.
||	Or	(exp1 || exp2) returns true only if either exp1 or exp2 are true.
!	Not	(!exp) returns false only if exp is true, or true if exp is false.
==	Equal	(exp1 == exp2) returns true only if exp1 is equal to exp2.
!=	Not equal	(exp1 != exp2) returns true only if exp1 is not equal to exp2.
>	Greater than	(exp1 > exp2) returns true only if exp1 is greater than exp2.
>=	Greater than or equal	(exp1 >= exp2) returns true only if exp1 is greater than or equal to exp2.
<	Less than	(exp1 < exp2) returns true only if exp1 is less than exp2.
<=	Less than or equal	(exp1 <= exp2) returns true only if exp1 is less than or equal to exp2.

A few examples of Boolean expressions follow:

```
true && false
```

This expression evaluates to false because one of the sides is not true and the AND operator (&&) requires both sides to be true for the expression to be true.

```
26 < 50
```

The preceding expression, however, evaluates to true because 26 is indeed less than 50.

```
(26 < 50) || (45 < 10)
```

By using the OR operator(||),this expression is a little less restrictive than the AND operator (&&) in that it needs only one side to be true for the expression to evaluate to true.

```
!(10 != 4)
```

Finally, the preceding expression evaluates to false. This type of expression requires a little bit of thought: 10 doesn't equal 4, which is true, but the NOT operator (!) gives the opposite, which is false.

In a Boolean expression, any numeric expression that evaluates to 0 is regarded as false, otherwise it is regarded as true. Although this sounds pretty confusing, the following examples might clear this up:

```
(2 + 2)
```

Because 2 plus 2 equals 4, which isn't 0, this expression—if used where a Boolean expression is expected—returns true, while

```
(2 - 2)
```

returns false because it evaluates to 0, which is regarded as false.

Numeric expressions can also be combined with logical operators, as in the following:

```
(2 - 2) || (2 + 2)
```

The preceding expression evaluates to true, because the right side of the expression evaluates to true, and the OR operator (||) requires only one side of the expression to be true for the expression to evaluate to true.

Variables

Having data and expressions is fine, but not of much use if you can't store them somewhere. *Variables* enable you to define places to store this data. Think of a variable as a storage container: it always contains something, but the thing it contains can change over time.

Over the course of this section, two aspects of working with variables will be presented. First, the methods for creating and naming variables will be discussed. Next, methods for changing the value that is held in variables will be shown.

Defining and Naming Variables

It's extremely simple to define a variable in JavaScript: think of a name for the variable that you want to define and then put **var** before it. Here's an example:

```
var position = 10;
```

This code creates a variable named position and gives it an initial value of 10. You can also create a variable without an initial value, but if you do so, be careful not to access the variable before it has had a value placed in it.

You can name a variable just about any name you can imagine, as long as you follow these rules:

1. The variable name cannot be a reserved word (see table 5.4).
2. The first character in the name must be an alphabetic letter or an underscore (_).
3. Characters subsequent to the first character in the variable name can be alphabetic letters, numbers, or underscores.

Part

II

Ch

5

Table 5.4   JavaScript Reserved Words

abstract	boolean	break	byte	case
catch	char	class	const	continue
default	delete	do	double	else
extends	false	final	finally	float
for	function	goto	if	implements
import	in	instanceof	int	interface
long	native	new	null	package
private	protected	public	return	short
static	super	switch	synchronized	this
throw	throws	transient	true	try
typeof	var	void	while	with

Here are a few examples of valid variable names:

```
var x_location;
var _loc;
var choice32;
var answer_42;
```

Here are a few examples of variable names that are invalid:

```
var 99balloons;     // Violates rule 2
var eggs$bacon;     // Violates rule 3
var $fred;          // Violates rule 2
var package;        // Violates rule 1
```

Another thing to be aware of is that JavaScript is case-sensitive. This means that two variables can appear to be the same, but are not recognized as such by the browser. The following, for example, are two entirely different variables:

```
var testResult;
var TestResult;
```

This can be a source of *major* headaches during debugging sessions, so just repeat over and over in your head: "JavaScript is case-sensitive. JavaScript is case-sensitive."

Where you define your variable dictates where it can be used later. A variable defined in a function can only be used inside that function definition, for example. This type of variable is known as a "local" variable because it is specific to that function.

On the other hand, if you declare a variable outside of your functions, it can then be used by all the functions you define. This type of variable is known as a "global" variable because it can be used throughout your entire program.

Changing the Value of a Variable

To give a variable a new value after it is created, the assignment operator (=) is used. The variable name is listed on the left-hand side of the statement and an expression containing the value it is to be assigned is listed on the right-hand of the statement. Consider a simple example, assuming that the variable currPosition has already been created:

```
currPosition = 10;
```

This statement changes the value of currPosition to 10. Variables can hold any type of valid data—remember the data types listed earlier in the chapter?—so you could also change *currPosition* to a Boolean or string value, as in the following:

```
currPosition = true;
currPosition = "foobar";
```

All the expressions so far are made up of constant data, but a variable could also be used in the expression. The interpreter just substitutes the value of the variable into the expression. Therefore, assuming currPosition has the value 10, the statement

```
currPosition = currPosition + 10;
```

sets the value of currPosition to 20, adding 10 to the current value of the variable.

It turns out that this type of variable assignment is executed frequently. So often, in fact, that there are special assignment operators for all the common numeric operations (+, –, *, /, and %). These are constructed by adding an equal sign immediately after the operator without adding a space between the two. Therefore,

```
currPosition += 10;
```

is completely equivalent to the earlier example, setting *currPosition* to its current value plus 10.

It has been a while since there was an example to try in Internet Explorer. Listing 5.2 ties together some of the concepts from the last few sections in an example program. Figure 5.3 that follows shows the output from this program.

Part

II

Ch

5

Listing 5.2   Changing Variable Contents in JavaScript

```
01. <HTML>
02. <HEAD>
03.     <TITLE>
04.     JavaScript Example 2
05.     </TITLE>
06. </HEAD>
07. <BODY>
08.
09.     <SCRIPT language="JavaScript">
10.
11.         var myValue = 18;
12.         document.write("Initial Value is: ");
13.         document.write(myValue);
```

continues

Listing 5.2 Continued

```
14.          myValue += 2;
15.          document.write("<p>Then after adding 2, value is: ");
16.          document.write(myValue);
17.          document.write("<p>But, is that greater than 19: ");
18.          document.write(myValue > 19);
19.
20.      </SCRIPT>
21.
22.  </BODY>
23.  </HTML>
```

FIG. 5.3

Output of a script that changes variable contents.

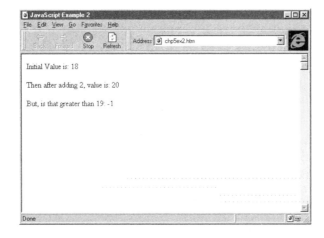

Most of this code should be pretty straightforward to you by now. The most important thing at this point is to focus on three significant lines of code in this example. The first significant line occurs on line 11 between the <SCRIPT> paired tag:

```
var myValue = 18;
```

This sets up a variable named *myValue* and gives it an initial value of 18. Because this value is stored in a variable, it's kept in memory while the next statements are executed:

```
myValue += 2;
```

Remember that this is the short version of

```
myValue = myValue + 2;
```

as described in the previous section about assignment operators. This statement sets *myValue* equal to the current value, which is 18, plus 2, which is 20.

Line 18 prints to the documents the result of checking whether *myValue* is greater than 19:

```
document.write(myValue > 19);
```

No statements between *document.write (myValue > 19);* and the previous statement change the value of *myValue*. As a result, *document.write (myValue > 19);* prints the result of a logical expression that asks whether *myValue* (currently 20) is greater than 19, which it is. Therefore, "true" is printed.

Functions

So now you know how to write programs and could conceivably even write large programs; however, they would become large and unruly quite quickly. It would be nice if you could break up those larger programs into smaller sections that perform small and well-defined actions.

Programs are broken up this way with functions. A *function* is a block of code—remember blocks from earlier in the chapter—with a defined name that may or may not take one or more arguments. Functions are called by name, which takes the form

```
foo(bar);
```

The parentheses enclose any arguments that the function may take. In this instance the function named *foo* takes one argument named *bar.*

Functions can also return values, although they do not always do so. You don't necessarily have to do anything with these returned values, but they usually return a value for a good reason, so it's best not to ignore them. Functions that return values can be placed in an expression in the same manner that data or variables can be.

Built-In Functions

Most of the functions you will be calling as you program in Dynamic HTML are related to the Dynamic HTML Object Model, which will be discussed in the next chapter. However, the JavaScript language itself includes a few useful built-in functions, listed in table 5.5, of which you should be aware.

Part
II

Ch
5

Table 5.5   Useful Built-In JavaScript Functions

Function	Description
escape(*charstring*)	Returns the conversion of *charstring* into a form that displays in the browser without HTML markup.
eval(*codestring*)	Evaluates *codestring* as JavaScript code, returning anything that JavaScript returns.
isNan(*numvalue*)	Returns true if *numvalue* is not a number, otherwise returns false—used with parseFloat and parseInt.
parseFloat(*numstring*)	Returns *numstring* converted to a floating point number. If it cannot be converted, returns the reserved value NaN.

continues

Table 5.5   Continued

Function	Description
parseInt(*numstring*)	Returns *numstring* converted to an integer. If it cannot be converted, returns the reserved value NaN.
unescape(*charstring*)	Returns the conversion of *charstring* back into a form that displays in the browser with HTML markup (the opposite of escape).

Start by looking at one of the functions that's built into JavaScript. This function is called *eval* and takes one argument, called *codestring*:

```
eval(codestring)
```

The eval*(codestring)* function takes a string as an argument and evaluates it as a JavaScript expression. It is actually run through the JavaScript interpreter and whatever output it generates is returned as the return value of the function. Listing 5.3 shows the *eval()* function in action:

Listing 5.3   Evaluating String Arguments as JavaScript Expressions

```
01. <HTML>
02. <HEAD>
03.     <TITLE>
04.     JavaScript Example 3
05.     </TITLE>
06. </HEAD>
07. <BODY>
08.
09.     <SCRIPT language="JavaScript">
10.
11.         var convertMe = "2+2";
12.         convertMe = eval(convertMe);document.write(convertMe);
13.
14.     </SCRIPT>
15.
16. </BODY>
17. </HTML>
```

Figure 5.4 shows the output from this example. Note that the string "2+2" isn't printed, but instead "4" is printed, which is what "2+2" would evalute to in a JavaScript expression.

The important line to pay attention to in this example is

```
convertMe = eval(convertMe);
```

As discussed earlier, the *eval()* function enables you to evaluate arbitrary strings as JavaScript expressions and find out to what they evaluate. This means that you can use the *eval()* function as sort of a calculator or logical statement analyzer that is always available to your programs.

FIG. 5.4
Using the eval()
function.

User-Defined Functions

Say you use *eval()* often before printing to the web page. In fact, you use it all the time, and frankly it has gotten to be a pain making sure that you always remember to use *escape()* first.

Luckily, it turns out that you can define your own functions. A function is defined by combining a function statement and a block of code to associate with that function. The function statement consists of the word function, followed by parentheses containing the name of the function.

Call the function *printEval()* and have it take one argument called *theText*. You don't need to worry about making it do anything yet, so just follow it with a blank block:

```
function printEval(theText)
{
}
```

This is a valid function definition, although it doesn't do much. Now, what do you want to do inside the function? You want to print out the string *theText* after sending it through the *eval()* function. The following code shows this addition to the function:

```
function printEval(theText)
{
    theText = eval(theText);
    document.write(theText);
}
```

The following code in listing 5.4 uses the user-defined *printEval()* function. The output from this code should be the same as from the preceding example:

Part

II

Ch

5

Listing 5.4 Incorporating User-Defined Functions in JavaScript

```
01. <HTML>
02. <HEAD>
03.    <TITLE>
04.     JavaScript Example 4
05.    </TITLE>
```

continues

Listing 5.4   Continued

```
06. </HEAD>
07. <BODY>
08.
09.     <SCRIPT language="JavaScript">
10.
11.         function printEval(theText)
12.         {
13.             theText = eval(theText);
14.             document.write(theText);
15.         }
16.         var convertMe = "2+2"
17.         printEval(convertMe);
18.
19.     </SCRIPT>
20.
21. </BODY>
22. </HTML>
```

If you're paying close attention, you may be wondering what happens to the variable *convertMe* after you pass it to the *printEval()* function on line 17. Use the *document.write()* function to write out the value of *convertMe* after making the call to *printEval()* in the main body of the script. After all, the best way to learn is by doing!

Returning Values from Functions

The *printEval()* function from the previous section performs an action but doesn't return any data. Data can be returned from a function by using the keyword *return*, followed by the data to be returned. The following simple function takes a number and returns the square of that number to the calling expression:

```
function square(inNum)
{
    return (inNum * inNum);
}
```

You are not limited to returning numbers via *return*. In fact, any of the data types listed earlier in the chapter can be used as a return value.

Now, if you want to use this function, you could include a call in the main body of the script or another function that calls the square function, for example:

```
var squared;
squared = square(4);
```

After executing this code, *squared* would have the value 16. Why is this? The function *square()* takes one argument: the value to be squared. Then it returns that value squared as the value of the function.

Flow Control

The discussion of JavaScript to this point in the chapter presents the scripting language as a linear mechanism—it starts at the first statement, goes to the next, and so on.

Programming is, in many ways, about making decisions. What you do in one circumstance may well not be what you do in another. Also, you may want to do something over and over and over, but up to this point, the only way to do that would be to place the statements you want to repeat in a function, and then call that function over and over—or worse, cut and paste the statements you want to call repeatedly.

The concept of diverting what the program does at a given point, based upon differing conditions, is called *flow control*. JavaScript gives you quite a bit of control over the program flow through conditional statements, such as "if...else" and repetition statements, such as "for" and "while" loops.

Suppose, for instance, that you're driving along and come to a fork in the road. You must decide at that point whether to take the fork to the left or the fork to the right. Which one do you take? Flow control is the mechanism that JavaScript uses to make decisions like these.

if and if...else

The most basic concept in flow control is branching based upon a conditional expression. This might sound complicated, but all it means is to use a logical expression—explained earlier in the chapter—to decide whether to follow one path or another.

An *if* statement is constructed by using the keyword *if* followed by a logical expression inside parentheses, and then the statement (or block) to execute if that logical expression is true. The following code shows a few concrete examples of *if* statements in action:

```
var x = 10;
var y = 25;
if (x < y)
    document.write("x less than y");
if (x != y)
    document.write("x doesn't equal y");
if (x >= y)
    document.write("x greater than or equal to y");
if (x == y)
    document.write("x equals y");
```

In the first case "*x less than y*" is printed to the page, because 10 is less than 25, which is true, so the statement included in the *if* statement is executed. By the same logic, the second *if* statement causes "x doesn't equal y" to be printed to the screen. For the final two *if* statements, nothing is printed, because the logical expressions that follow are false, so the next statement is not executed.

Part
II

Ch
5

Notice in the description of how to construct an *if* statement that a block of code can follow the logical expression as well. Applying the same x and y variables from the previous example (10 and 25, respectively), take a look at the following example:

```
if ((x == y) || (x < y)) {
    document.write("x less than y ");
    document.write("or x equals y");
}
```

In this case "x less than y or x equals y" is printed because the logical expression is true—work it out in your head if it isn't immediately obvious, because it's this sort of thinking that helps you acclimate to understanding conditionals—and the block that follows the *if* statement contains two statements, which are then executed in order.

You can also construct an *if...else* conditional statement by adding the *else* keyword to the end of an *if* statement. In this case, the program executes the statement (or block) following the logical expression if the expression is true or the statement (or block) following the *else* keyword if the expression is false. Applying the same x and y variables from the previous examples (10 and 25, respectively), take a look at the following example:

```
if (x == y)
    document.write("x equals y");
else
    document.write("x doesn't equal y");
```

In this case "x doesn't equal y" is printed. Why? The logical expression is false because 10 doesn't equal 25, so the statement following the expression isn't executed; however, because the expression was false, the statement following the *else* keyword is executed, which prints "x doesn't equal y."

for Loops

The *for* loop is the most basic of looping statements. It enables you to execute a statement (or block) a set number of times, based upon a counter and expression to compare that counter against.

A *for* loop is constructed by starting with the keyword *for* followed by a specification of a counter variable. This counter variable is used by the *for* loop to keep track of where you are in the loop.

Next comes the test case, which determines whether the loop will be executed.

Finally, there is the statement (or block) to execute every time the loop is run.

That sounds a bit complicated, so try constructing a simple *for* loop. Suppose you want to print out every number from 1 to 10. The *for* loop you might use to do so would be as follows:

```
for (var count = 1; count <= 10; count++)
{
    document.write(count);
    document.write("<br>");   // Print a break to separate lines
}
```

For a better view of what's occuring in the previous code, the following list breaks this transaction down into its component parts:

- **Counter variable:** The counter variable is set to *var count = 1*, which sets up a new variable to use for this loop and sets it to 1. This part is only executed once.

- **Test case:** Before the loop is executed each time, the logical expression *count <= 10* is tested. Therefore, the loop will be executed until the count is no longer less than or equal to 10. After the test case fails, the *for* loop exits and the next statement following the *for* loop construction is executed.

- **Action taken after execution:** At the end of each execution of the loop, the statement *count++* is called. In this loop, 1 is added to the count each time (*count++* is also the same as *count = count + 1* or *count += 1*).

- **Statement/Block to execute:** Each time the test case is satisfied, this statement (or block) is executed. Here, this is the block that is enclosed within the curly braces ({}).

Although this *for* loop is simple, you could certainly get more complicated in the logic of the loop. You could, for example, have the loop start at 64 and then divide the counter variable by 2 until the counter variable equals 1:

```
for (var count=64; count >= 1; count = count / 2)
```

> **CAUTION**
>
> In some instances making the logic of your loops or conditionals more tricky makes sense. Always use caution before doing this sort of thing, because it can make debugging more painful later. In general, when considering making things more complicated, ask yourself if you could do this in a more simple manner.

while Loops

A *while* loop is much like a *for* loop except it has only a test case. Therefore, you must make sure that conditions change over the execution of the *while* loop to ensure that the test case eventually fails (returns false).

A while loop is constructed by using the *while* keyword, followed by a test case—much like the one in the *for* loop—and finally the statement (or block) to execute if the test case is true. Before each time the statement(s) of the *while* loop is executed, the test case is checked.

Consider a metaphor that exists in the real world. Your car will only drive when it has gas in it. In a way, you could think of your car's engine as a *while* loop that evaluates to "while there is gas, run the engine."

You will want to initialize the counter variable outside the *while* loop, assuming you are using a counter variable and not some other means of testing for completion, and somewhere inside the *while* loop you will want to make sure that the counter variable is updated.

The following code constructs a *while* loop that behaves the same way as the first *for* loop example:

```
var count = 1;
while (count <= 10)
{
    document.write(count);
    document.write("<br>");  // Print a break to separate lines
    count++;
}
```

First, before getting to the *while* loop itself, the counter variable *count* is created and initialized to 1. This is done because no section in the *while* loop is set aside for creating and initializing the counter variable. Next, the test case is checked inside the *while* loop. Then, if the test case is true, the body of the loop—the statement or block that follows—is executed. Note that 1 is added to count at the end of the body, making sure that the condition in the test case will change after each run through the loop.

> **CAUTION**
>
> Use *while* loops with caution. It's easy to forget to increment the counter in a *while* loop, which can result in a loop that just repeats forever—often referred to as an infinite loop. Always make sure that whatever is being checked in the test case is updated each time the loop is executed, or at least is guaranteed to update at some point.

break and continue Statements

For the most part, using loops as they were designed is more than enough power over the control of execution in your program. On occasion, however, you may find yourself writing the body of the loop and wishing there was some way you could skip to the next iteration of the loop or break out of the loop entirely. This possibility is provided by the *continue* and *break* statements.

The first example examines the *break* statement. The following example is a repetition from the section on the *for* loop, but updates the *for* loop so that when the counter variable gets to 5, the *for* loop exits completely:

```
for (var count = 1; count <= 10; count++)
{
    if (count == 5)
        break;
    document.write(count);
    document.write("<br>");  // Print a break to separate lines
}
```

In this example, each time the loop is executed it checks to see whether *count* is equal to 5. If it isn't, the loop continues as normal. If, however, it is equal to 5, the *for* loop is exited. It is important to note that not just the iteration through the loop is exited, but the entire *for* loop is broken out of and it will not loop again. Therefore, only the numbers 1 through 4 are printed.

The following code examines the *continue* statement. The *continue* statement doesn't break you out of the loop entirely, it just skips the rest of the body of the loop for that iteration as demonstrated in the following:

```
for (var count = 1; count <= 10; count++)
{
    if (count == 5)
        continue;
    document.write(count);
    document.write("<br>");  // Print a break to separate lines
}
```

This is similar to the previous example demonstrating the *break* statement. The numbers 1 through 4 print out first. The *continue* statement executes on the fifth time through the loop because *count* is equal to 5, which causes the number 5 not to be printed. Unlike the *break* statement, however, the *for* loop continues, and the numbers 6 through 10 print.

> **CAUTION**
>
> Using the *continue* statement inside a *for* loop is usually fairly safe; however, be sure to use *continue* statements inside a *while* loop with a great deal of caution. It is quite easy to end up with an infinite loop if you execute a *continue* statement before the variable that is tested is updated.

Objects

Object-oriented programming (OOP) has been a hot topic in computer programming for quite a while now, and every new self-respecting computer language includes some kind of support for objects. JavaScript is no exception.

If you're accustomed to the object-oriented programming models of C++ or Java, you're in for a bit of surprise. JavaScript doesn't support advanced OOP concepts such as inheritance or polymorphism. Instead, it tries to keep things as simple as possible by stripping things down to the bare minimum.

One of the core tenets of OOP is called encapsulation. Encapsulation sounds like a complicated term, but it's actually quite a simple concept. If you're accustomed to writing big programs, you know that it's easy to end up with an overwhelming number of functions and variables that can be hard to manage.

Encapsulation is simply the process of wrapping up those functions and variables into different packages, called *objects*. The variables become known as *properties* of the object, and the functions are then known as *methods*. Don't let the terms *properties* and *methods* get you confused; just think of them as variables and functions wrapped up inside an object.

Properties and methods are the core elements from which objects are built. Start by taking a look at methods in more detail.

Part II

Ch 5

Methods

As mentioned previously, a *method* is just a function that is contained inside of an object. This is a pretty abstract concept, so let's start by considering a real world example.

Say that you want to use an object that represents an automobile. Someone driving an automobile can perform several basic functions: push the gas pedal, push the brake, steer the wheel right, and steer the wheel left. This functionality would be made available to the user of the object via its methods:

- *pushGas()*
- *pushBrake()*
- *steerRight()*
- *steerLeft()*

Because these are methods and not functions, they could not be called by themselves. Instead, to call a method you must prefix it with the name of the object you want to call the method upon, separated by a period.

So, if you had one of these automobile objects that was named *myCar*, you would tell the automobile to steer right by using the following statement:

```
myCar.steerRight();
```

This statement calls the *steerRight()* method of the *myCar* object, causing the car to turn to the right. At this point you may be asking yourself where the data that represents the automobile is stored. The answer to that question is in the properties of the object.

Properties

When methods are called, those methods usually act upon some sort of data contained in the object. That data is called *properties*. A property is simply a variable that is contained inside of an object.

Consider the automobile example again. The methods that have been presented together model two aspects of the automobile's state at any given time—speed and direction.

This data would be contained inside the object via its properties. Assume that the object contains the following two properties to model this state: *speed* and *direction*.

Now, you could modify the speed of the automobile represented by the object *myCar* directly by modifying the *speed* property. Properties are modified like any other variable, except that, much like methods, the property name must be prefixed by the name of the object you want to modify the property of, separated by a period. Therefore, if you want to set the speed of the *myCar* object to 25, you would use the following statement:

```
myCar.speed = 25;
```

Now that you understand how you might use an imaginary object, take a look at an actual object built into the JavaScript language.

Built-In Objects

JavaScript includes a few objects itself—Dynamic HTML adds a great deal more, but that is covered in the next chapter. One of the more common of these objects is the *Math* object. The *Math* object includes quite a few methods for doing higher-level mathematical calculations and also includes a few properties that contain common mathematical constants.

One of the common mathematical constants that the *Math* object contains is *PI*. Let's say you wanted to write a small function that determined the area of a circle:

```
function area(radius) {
    return (radius * radius * Math.PI);   // Area=PI*Radius Squared
}
```

This function simply takes one argument, "radius," and then returns the value of PI times it squared, which is the formula for the area of a circle.

The *Math* object also includes methods for mathematical operations. It includes the *sqrt()* method, for instance, which determines the square root of the number passed to it. The following example uses this method to print out the square root of 10:

```
var myNumber = Math.sqrt(10);
document.write(myNumber);
```

To learn more about the other built-in objects in JavaScript, see the formal JavaScript documentation—World Wide Web addresses are provided for these documents in the "JavaScript Resources" section of this chapter.

User-Defined Objects

Defining your own objects is a bit tricky. The first step is to write a function that contains all the properties and, if desired, methods of the object. You then set the properties inside the object with the *this* statement. Assume that you want to define an employee object that contains the employee's name, age, and salary. You would define this object as follows:

```
function employee(name, age, salary)
{
    this.name = name;
    this.age = age;
    this.salary = salary;
}
```

It's important to note that at this point you haven't created the object. Instead, you've created a function that makes the objects. Think of it as an object "cookie-cutter." This "cookie-cutter" is referred to as the object's constructor. Using this "cookie-cutter" to create an object is known as *instantiation*.

To actually make objects, you need to call the new statement with a call to *this* constructor following it. So, if you want to create an employee object with the name "Fred Jones", age 28, salary $35,000.00, and assign it to the variable *myEmployee*, you would use the following code:

```
myEmployee = new employee("Fred Jones", 28, 35000)
```

Then you could reference the object properties as follows:

```
empName = myEmployee.name;
empAge = myEmployee.age;
empSalary = myEmployee.salary;
```

If you're using one object extensively in a section of your program, there is a shorthand way to access this object that enables you to avoid typing the name of the object before the properties when referencing them.

To do this, you use the *with* statement, followed by the name of the object to be used by default when referencing properties, and a block of statements that use this object. The following, for instance, executes the same actions as the previous example:

```
with (myEmployee)
{
    empName = name;
    empAge = age;
    empSalary = salary;
}
```

Now that the *myEmployee* object is being used in the *with* statement, the references to the *empName*, *empAge*, and *empSalary* properties are all automatically assumed by JavaScript to be properties of the *myEmployee* object.

Objects are useful to group together methods and properties into one data structure. The final element of JavaScript syntax that will be covered, the array, is also one that groups things together.

Arrays

Assume you want to keep a list of 25 numbers. How would you go about keeping this list? You could create 25 different variables to do so, but that would be unwieldy. You could make the situation a little easier to handle by taking those 25 variables and encapsulating them in an object, but it would still be an arduous process.

The correct thing to do in this situation is to use an array. An *array* contains several pieces of data that are referred to as *elements*. Arrays enable you to hold an arbitrary number of elements without defining beforehand what these elements will hold.

An array is created much like an object, using *Array* as the constructor, with the number of elements that it will hold as the argument for that constructor. Assume you wanted to create an array called *allNames* that holds 5 different names. You would create it in the following manner:

```
allNames = new Array(5);
```

Now, if you want to assign values to the different elements of the array, list the number of the element that you want to access in brackets([and]) following the name of the array as shown in the following code:

```
allNames[0] = "Fred";
allNames[1] = "Mary";
allNames[2] = "John";
allNames[3] = "Tim";
allNames[4] = "Mark";
```

The number that is used to refer to individual elements of an array is known as the element's array index. This index number enables each element to be addressed uniquely. Array indexes start at 0 and count up to the position of the last element of the array.

N O T E Referring to elements in an array may not be an obvious process because people are used to starting to count beginning at 1. The first element of an array is always at position 0, not position 1. Therefore, the last position of an array with 5 elements is 4, not 5. ▦

An Example JavaScript Program

After familiarizing yourself with the concepts in this chapter, you should now be familiar with most of the components of JavaScript. The following program ties together many of the JavaScript concepts you've learned in this chapter into a single working application.

The code in Listing 5.5 prints out a different greeting based on whether it is during the morning or not, then it prints out the name of the day of the week for today (see fig. 5.5 for sample output).

Part
II

Ch
5

Listing 5.5   Printing Output Based on Date in JavaScript

```
01.  <HTML>
02.  <HEAD>
03.      <TITLE>
04.      JavaScript Example 5
05.      </TITLE>
06.  </HEAD>
07.  <BODY>
08.
09.      <SCRIPT language="JavaScript">
10.
11.      var today = new Date();
12.
13.      if (today.getHours() <= 12)
```

continues

Listing 5.5 Continued

```
14.          document.write("<p>Good Morning!");
15.      else
16.          document.write("<p>Good Day!");
17.
18.      document.write("<p>Today is a ");
19.      var todaysNum  = today.getDay();
20.      var todaysName = dayName(todaysNum);
21.      document.write(todaysName);
22.
23.      function dayName(day)
24.      {
25.          var names = new Array(7);
26.
27.          names[0]= "Sunday";
28.          names[1]= "Monday";
29.          names[2]= "Tuesday";
30.          names[3]= "Wednesday";
31.          names[4]= "Thursday";
32.          names[5]= "Friday";
33.          names[6]= "Saturday";
34.
35.          return names[day];
36.      }
37.
38. </SCRIPT>
39.
40. </BODY>
41. </HTML>
```

FIG. 5.5

A JavaScript date
program.

This program builds upon the JavaScript *Date* object, one of JavaScript's built-in objects. When you create a new *Date* object, all the information about today's date and time is stored in that instance of the object. One of the methods contained in that object is *getHours()*, which returns the current hour of the day in military time.

Therefore, after you have the information about what hour of the day it is, you can use a conditional statement to determine whether or not to say "Good Morning!" or "Good Day!", as demonstrated in lines 11–16:

```
11.    var today = new Date();
12.
13.    if (today.getHours() <= 12)
14.        document.write("<p>Good Morning!");
15.    else
16.        document.write("<p>Good Day!");
```

The next step is to determine the day of the week. You can get that information from the *Date* object you've created via the *getDay()* method on line 19:

```
var todaysNum  = today.getDay();
```

This code generates a number that corresponds to the name of the day of the week in relation to today. Table 5.6 establishes the correlation between the number and the name of the day.

Table 5.6   Numbers for the Days of the Week

Number	Day
0	Sunday
1	Monday
2	Tuesday
3	Wednesday
4	Thursday
5	Friday
6	Saturday

Because you wouldn't want to print "Today is a 3," you need to convert the day number into the corresponding name. Because this is the sort of thing that you might want to do on a regular basis, this would be a perfect place to use a function.

The function *dayName()* takes a day in number form and represents it in the variable *day.* The first thing the *dayName()* function does is create an array with 7 elements, one for each day of the week:

```
var names = new Array(7);
```

Next, the *dayName()* function places the name of the day of the week into the corresponding element in the array:

```
names[0]= "Sunday";
names[1]= "Monday";
names[2]= "Tuesday";
names[3]= "Wednesday";
```

Part
II

Ch
5

```
names[4]= "Thursday";
names[5]= "Friday";
names[6]= "Saturday";
```

Finally, the *dayName()* function looks at the position in the array corresponding to the value passed into the function. It then returns the name of the day needed by returning the value associated with that position in the array.

```
return names[day];
```

This is a little tricky, so you might want to think it through a few times. If you look at table 5.6, you'll see that Wednesday corresponds to the number 3. Therefore, by placing "Wednesday" in the element that will be returned by addressing the number 3 in the array, you can easily retrieve that data.

Now all you need to do is use the *dayName()* function to convert the number for today into its corresponding name:

```
var todaysName = dayName(todaysNum);
```

This example has covered many of the important JavaScript concepts that will be used throughout this book. First, although you will usually not have to create your own objects, you will have to use those provided by Dynamic HTML. Quite a bit of work was done with the Date object, which reflects the sort of process that will be shown later.

Second, it is important to become familiar with the process of creating functions and their use. A great deal of the work that you will do in creating your own dynamic web pages involves the addition of functions that will be called when certain actions are taken by the user. This process is known as event handling, and will be discussed in great detail in Chapter 7, "Event Handling."

JavaScript Resources

JavaScript was originally created by Netscape, and for the final word on general JavaScript issues, the Netscape documentation is the best place to look:

`http://developer.netscape.com/library/documentation/index.html`

For documentation on JavaScript and JavaScript features unique to Internet Explorer 4.0, or to make sure that a specific JavaScript feature is implemented in Microsoft's version of JavaScript, go to:

`http://www.microsoft.com/jscript`

From Here...

As mentioned in the beginning of the chapter, the use of a scripting language is essential to Dynamic HTML because it is the tool that is used to drive Dynamic HTML.

This chapter covered a lot of information. Don't feel overwhelmed if you don't understand everything about JavaScript right now. The important thing is that you understand the basics and return to this chapter if you're confused by any JavaScript code presented later. From here, the following topics are covered in the next chapters:

- Chapter 6, "Dynamic HTML Object Model," talks about the object model used by Dynamic HTML that treats all HTML elements on a page as mutually aware objects.

- Chapter 7, "Event Handling," covers the importance of event handling in Dynamic HTML-generated web sites.

Part

II

Ch

5

Dynamic HTML Object Model

The fact that Dynamic HTML has something called an object model might sound a bit imposing at first, but don't worry, it's actually pretty simple. Using an object model means you just have to look at something you're quite used to and comfortable with in a new and more powerful way.

What is an object model? It's the result of breaking up something into objects. For instance, if you were to simulate all the components of an automobile via objects (an engine object, a transmission object, and so forth), you would then have an automobile object model for your simulation.

The Dynamic HTML Object Model applies this same process to the web browser and the HTML pages that are contained within it. The Dynamic HTML Object Model enables you to access aspects of the browser, such as its history, as well as aspects of the web page it is currently viewing, such as the HTML elements that make up that page.

The Object Hierarchy

The first aspect of the Dynamic HTML Object Model you need to know is the Object Hierarchy. The Object Hierarchy, contained within the *window* object, contains all aspects of the current window and document that is being shown in the browser.

Collections

Collections are objects that Dynamic HTML uses to group the elements of an HTML document together.

Elements

The *element* is the basic way that HTML is broken up. The *element* object is just the representation of an HTML element as a scripting object.

window Object

At the core of the Dynamic HTML Object Model is the *window* object. The *window* object contains all the information about the state of the browser window and all that it contains.

document Object

The *document* object contains all the information about the HTML document that the browser is currently viewing. Any portion of the HTML document that you want to access with scripting is contained here.

Although this is definitely a positive development, there is concern that the object model Microsoft uses will not be the same as other browser vendors. One of the more arduous aspects of working with the World Wide Web is the seemingly endless diverging standards for how to do things. The World Wide Web Consortium (W3C) is trying to ensure that this doesn't happen with object models by creating a standard object model called the W3C Document Object Model.

Microsoft has built the Dynamic HTML Object Model on the foundation proposed by the W3C for the Document Object Model. Microsoft has also made it clear that they intend to follow future W3C standards regarding the object model. ■

Viewing HTML Documents as Collections of Objects

Think of all the HTML pages you have written in the past. When you sit down to write a page, you have to break sections of it up into separate logical pieces. For instance, even a simple standard HTML document would have two sections:

- The header (<HEAD>)
- The body (<BODY>)

Through this process of creating a BODY and HEAD, you are used to having some structure to your HTML document. Other than breaking up your document into these two pieces, however, you probably think of the rest of your HTML document as the rest of the HTML elements added in a linear fashion.

The Dynamic HTML Object Model presents the HTML page and the browser itself as a large collection of objects. By doing this, you can access any portion of the page that you want by descending into the collection of objects and retrieving the portion you want.

For example, the Dynamic HTML Object Model contains an object called body that enables script writers to access the elements in the BODY of the document directly. It also contains an object named location that enables script programmers to find out information about the page currently being viewed, such as the page's URL or the protocol used to view it.

This type of programmatic capability to retrieve the state of the page will become quite valuable later in the book when you start changing the content or style of page elements on the fly. For instance, you might want to limit your changes to the head or the body of the document. The Dynamic HTML Object Model provides you with the tools to achieve this.

Language Independence in the Dynamic HTML Object Model

Object models are a standard way of breaking up complex data into manageable pieces, but in the past object models have been tied to one specific language. The Microsoft Office Object

Model, for instance, is an object model for the entire Microsoft Office Suite. Through this object model, programmers access and change the state of the applications and documents contained within them.

One of the big disadvantages of an object model such as the Microsoft Office Object Model, however, is that it is tied to a specific programming language, which in this case is Visual Basic for Applications. Therefore, you cannot use other common programming languages, such as Java or Pascal.

This causes problems in two ways. First, a different object model must be developed for each language, which is essentially reinventing the wheel over and over. Second, a language-dependent object model focuses too much attention on the language used and not enough attention on the project at hand.

The Dynamic HTML Object Model strives to make this a non-issue by being completely language independent. You can just as easily access and use the object model with VBScript as you can with JavaScript. With a little more work you can also access and use the object model with Java or C++.

Making the Dynamic HTML Object Model language independent should be an important contributor to its success because it doesn't force developers to make the difficult choice of selecting a standard language for Dynamic HTML development. If your favorite scripting language is JavaScript, great; but if you're a VBScript proponent, you're not left out in the cold.

Building Upon Netscape's Efforts

If you're used to using JavaScript in Netscape Navigator to do programming with forms, the Dynamic HTML Object Model should seem quite familiar to you. Microsoft originally incorporated Netscape's object model into Internet Explorer 3.0 with minor additions. With Internet Explorer 4.0, however, Microsoft has extended Netscape's object model to cover almost every conceivable aspect of the browser and the HTML document that resides within it.

Netscape Navigator 2.0 and up enable you to access forms and form elements by a straightforward syntax. If, for instance, you had a form called *entry* with a text field called *user*, you could access the value of that field in the following manner:

```
document.entry.user.value
```

Dynamic HTML takes this process to its logical extreme. The current URL that the browser window is viewing, for instance, is contained in an element called *location* in the *window* object:

```
window.location
```

In the same way, the entire body of the HTML document is contained in a collection of objects called *all*, which is contained in the *document* object that is contained in the *window* object:

```
window.document.all
```

Part
II

Ch
6

Understanding the Dynamic HTML Object Model

Now that you have an idea of what an object model is and how it may be used, it's time to take a look at the specifics of the object model Microsoft has implemented for Dynamic HTML inside Internet Explorer 4.0.

The core of the Dynamic HTML Object Model is its Object Hierarchy. The Object Hierarchy is shown in figure 6.1. The Object Hierarchy is where all of the objects that you will need to access and modify the state of the browser and the HTML page are stored.

FIG. 6.1

The Dynamic HTML
Object Hierarchy.

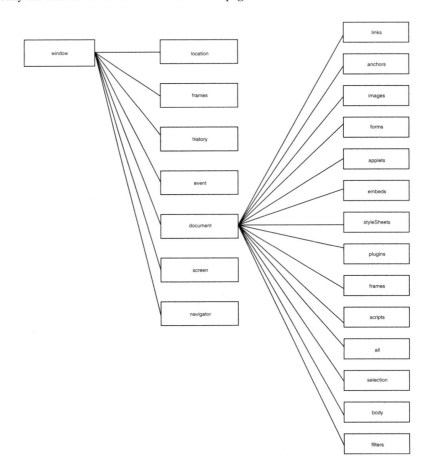

The first point to note about the hierarchy is that all of the objects in the hierarchy are contained within the *window* object. Therefore, to get to the document that is contained inside the current window, you use the *document* object contained within the *window* object.

The second important point to note about the hierarchy is that in addition to objects, which you're familiar with, there are also things in the hierarchy known as "collections" that haven't been discussed yet.

Therefore, before discussing the Object Hierarchy in greater detail, take some time to learn what a collection is so that when the different collections are considered, they will be familiar to you.

Collections

A *collection* is a set of things grouped together by the Dynamic HTML Object Model. A typical HTML document, for example, is a collection of links, frames, forms, and other elements such as images.

Think of a collection as a wrapper around a large number of objects. You normally wouldn't use a collection in and of itself, but instead you could use it to access the objects that it contains.

Consider a real world example. Suppose that there was an object that represented a candy shop that you were running. You might use a collection to represent your inventory that contained objects representing the candies that you currently have in stock.

Collections are mainly used for grouping like things together. This enables you to access things that are similar to one another on a page quickly and easily.

This is a bit theoretical, so perhaps you should consider an example of a collection that might be useful to you as a programmer. One of the core collections contained in the Dynamic HTML object model is the *document.all* collection. This collection, which contains all the HTML elements on a given HTML page, is discussed later in this chapter.

Accessing Collection Elements

Because collections are used to group elements, it makes sense to have ways to access those elements from the collection. Elements can be extracted from all Dynamic HTML collections via the three methods described in table 6.1.

Table 6.1   Collection Methods

Collection Access Methods	Description
item (string)	Returns all the elements in the collection with the specified name or id. If more than one element is returned, a collection containing those elements is returned.
item (number)	Returns the element in the collection at the position specified as the argument.
tags (tagName)	Returns a collection containing only the specified tag.

Part
II

Ch
6

The *item (string)* method enables you to access elements in the collection by specifying the element's name or id. For instance, suppose an element exists in your HTML document with the name "myElement". You could return that element by using the *item ()* method with the name of the element "myElement" as an argument as demonstrated in the following line:

```
document.all.item("myElement")
```

N O T E   If more than one element matches the name or id that you pass to the *item()* method, a collection containing all the elements that match the given criteria is created. Then what is returned by the *item()* method is not an element, but actually another collection. You would then use one of the collection methods again, such as *item()*, to retrieve the elements from that collection.

The second way to extract an element from a collection is to use a number as an argument to the *item ()* method to return that element, assuming you know exactly where in the collection an element is located. The first element of the *document.all* collection, for example, is the HTML element. Therefore, you could access the HTML element with the following code:

```
document.all.item(0)
```

Much like an array, the first element in a collection is always located at position 0. This is important to remember, because it is easy to get confusing bugs if you forget this and try to access it at position 1. If you access an element at position 1, instead of returning the first element of the collection, the second element will be returned. The *tags(tagName)* method enables you to retrieve all the elements in the collection that use the specified tag. The value returned is another collection that contains all of these elements. The *tags(tagName)* method uses the name of the tag as an argument to search for it as the element.

Suppose, for example, that you want to get a collection of all elements in the document that use the <P> tag. You would then use the following code:

```
document.all.tags("P")
```

Returning the Length of a Collection

Collections only have one property—*length*. This property enables you to know how many elements are currently contained within the collection.

Let's expand on the previous example. You've already learned how to get a collection that contains all the elements in the document with the <P> tag; however, how do you determine the number of paragraph tags in the document?

The following example counts the number of paragraphs in an HTML document. Figure 6.2 shows the output from listing 6.1.

Listing 6.1   Using the *document.all* Collection to Count HTML Elements

```
01. <HTML>
02. <HEAD>
03.    <TITLE>
04.        Special Edition Using Dynamic HTML, Chapter 6, Example 1
05.    </TITLE>
06. </HEAD>
```

```
07. <BODY>
08.    <P>This example demonstrates collections in Dynamic HTML
09.    <P>There are 4 paragraphs in this document
10.    <P>And we're using the tags method to return a collection
11.    <P>Then using the length property to count the paragraphs
12.    <SCRIPT language="JavaScript">
13.        var pgraphs = document.all.tags("P");
14.        var numpgraphs = pgraphs.length;
15.        alert(numpgraphs + " total paragraphs");
16.    </SCRIPT>
17. </BODY>
18. </HTML>
```

FIG. 6.2
Counting
paragraphs with the
document.all
collection.

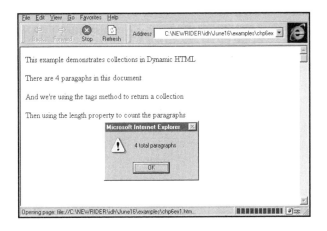

The first important thing to pay attention to in this example is that the body text of the document contains four <P> tags. Therefore, *document.all* contains four paragraph elements.

The *tags()* method of the *document.all* collection specifies a subcollection containing all the <P> tags. This collection containing the <P> tags is assigned (returned) to the variable *pgraphs* as shown in the following code:

```
var pgraphs = document.all.tags("P")
```

The number of <P> tags in the <P> tag collection is then determined using the collection's *length* property on line 14. Because this collection contains all the tags in the document that are of the <P> tag type, the length of this collection is the number of paragraphs in the document:

```
var numpgraphs = pgraphs.length;
```

Finally, the *alert()* function on line 15 is called to show the number of paragraphs in the document, which in this case is four:

```
alert(numpgraphs +_" total paragraphs");
```

A method of the *window* object, *alert()* pops up a message box containing the string passed as an argument. The *window* object is at the very top of hierarchy of the object model.

Part
II

Ch
6

Elements

The elements that are returned through collections in Dynamic HTML are the same HTML elements that you're used to using with regular HTML. The difference is that they are now objects that you can manipulate and from which you can return information.

This may seem strange, but it makes quite a bit of sense. For instance, every element in a collection is defined by a certain type of tag. Therefore, it is completely logical to make an element an object with a property that contains the name of its tag.

In the same way, it follows that an element object should know its ID or CSS style. The element object wraps all this information up for you, and an element object is created for every HTML element in the document.

If you placed an <H1> element in your HTML document, for example, a corresponding object would be created in the object hierarchy. This object is known as the tag's element object. This distinction may be a bit confusing. However, all you need to remember is that the element you placed in your document and its corresponding element object are the same thing. The difference is that the element object is accessible via the Dynamic HTML Object Model.

Like any object, these element objects have methods and properties. These methods and properties enable you to find out the information that makes up the element that it represents. There are certain properties and methods that will be present for all element objects, and these will be discussed next.

Element Properties

All HTML elements in the Dynamic HTML Object Model are guaranteed to have a set of properties associated with them, no matter what their type. This standardization means that you can write functions that can depend on a core set of properties without worrying about what type of HTML element is being accessed. Table 6.2 lists these core properties. These properties can contain any valid variable type, such as a String, an Integer, a Boolean, or even an Object.

Table 6.2 Element Properties

Property	Description
document	The document that contains this element
id	The id of this element
left	The position of this element in relation to the left side of the window
top	The position of this element in relation to the top of the window
tagName	The name of the tag that this element is an instance of (always uppercase)
style	An object containing the style of this element
parentElement	The element that contains this element
ClassName	Returns the class specified for this element

The following example in listing 6.2 demonstrates a few of these core properties in action. Figure 6.3 shows the output from listing 6.2.

Listing 6.2 Determining HTML Element Properties

```
01. <HTML>
02. <HEAD>
03.    <TITLE>
04.        Special Edition Using Dynamic HTML, Chapter 6, Example 2
05.    </TITLE>
06. </HEAD>
07. <BODY>
08.
09.    <P id=para left=100 top=100>
10.    Basic element properties in JavaScript
11.
12.    <SCRIPT language="JavaScript">
13.        var pgraph = document.all.tags("P").item(0);
14.        document.write("<P>id : " + pgraph.id);
15.        document.write("<P>tagName : " + pgraph.tagName);
16.        document.write("<P>top : " + pgraph.top);
17.        document.write("<P>left   : " + pgraph.left);
18.    </SCRIPT>
19.
20. </BODY>
21. </HTML>
```

FIG. 6.3
Looking at the properties of an element.

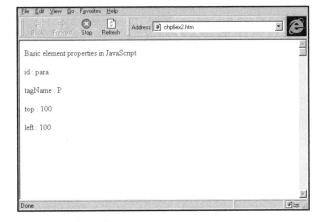

Part

II

Ch

6

Most of the code here should be familiar to you. You may remember the use of inline styles from Chapter 4, "Cascading Style Sheets Primer." Inline styles used in the preceding code set the id and the left and top style of the element.

Later, in the JavaScript portion of the document, these properties are retrieved by accessing the properties of the element. Note that the generic *tags()* method of the *document.all* collection retrieves the element instead of accessing the element by its ID.

The four properties accessed as shown in figure 6.3 are a few of the more important generic element properties as follows:

```
pgraph.id
pgraph.tagName
pgraph.top
pgraph.left
```

The *id* property is what uniquely identifies each HTML tag on the page, although more than one tag can have the same id. This not a required attribute of the tag, so you do not have to specify it. In such a case, the *id* property will be equivalent to "" (or a blank string) when you access it through your script; however, there will always be some value for the property, so you can always check for it.

The *tagName* property simply specifies the type of tag this element is. Therefore, for a <P> tag it would be "P", for an <IMG> tag it would be "IMG", and so on.

The *top* property represents the number of pixels from the top of the window at which the element has been positioned. From the example, this element has been given a top position of 100, so the top property is returned as 100 as well.

Much like the *top* property, the *left* property is the number of pixels from the left-hand side of the window at which the element has been positioned. This element has also given a left position of 100, so its *left* property is 100.

In addition to these core properties, additional properties may exist that a particular element can access. A Button element, for instance, has a property called *disable* that can be used to allow the button to be clicked or not, depending on its value.

Element Methods

In addition to the properties present in elements, there are also methods that all elements are guaranteed to have. These elements allow you to perform actions upon the element in question, such as making sure that it is currently viewable in the browser window.

Two important methods are guaranteed to be present in every element object: *contains()* and *scrollIntoView()*.

The *contains()* method is used with HTML elements that can contain other HTML elements, such as a <DIV> element or a <SPAN> element. This method provides a quick and convenient way to determine what is and is not contained within an HTML element. The *contains()* method is called by passing the object containing the element to search for as the argument:

```
element.contains(searchElement)
```

The *contains()* method then returns a Boolean value indicating whether the element being searched for is contained within the element that was specified for searching. The *contains()* method returns true if the element is found and false if it is not.

The second important method is *scrollIntoView()*. This method makes sure that the element that is being called on is brought into the portion of the window visible to the user by scrolling it. The *scrollIntoView()* method takes a Boolean argument that determines whether the element scrolls to the first line of the display (if the argument is true) or the last line of the display (if the argument is false). The following statement would scroll the element to the first line of the display:

```
element.scrollIntoView(true);
```

The *window* Object

At the very foundation of the Dynamic HTML Object Model is the *window* object. The *window* object contains everything that is accessible to programs via the object model: the elements, frames, images, browser window history, and almost anything else that you might need to access through the browser.

A breakdown of the most important collections, methods, and properties available in the window object is listed in table 6.3. You've already become familiar with properties and methods and their uses, and events are covered in the next chapter.

Table 6.3   Components of the *window* Object

Collections	Frames
Methods	item, navigate, blur, focus, alert, confirm, prompt, setTimeout, clearInterval, setInterval, showHelp, execScript, clearTimeout, close, open, scroll, showModalDialog
Properties	document, location, history, navigator, event, visual, client, closed, defaultStatus, dialogArguments, dialogHeight, dialogLeft, dialogTop, dialogWidth, length, name, offscreenBuffering, opener, parent, returnValue, screen, self, status, top, window
Events	onfocus, onload, onunload, onblur, onhelp, onerror, onbeforeunload, onresize, onscroll

The basic structure of the window object is shown in figure 6.4. You can see that the window object is the root of the object model and that all the other objects are contained in the *window* object.

N O T E Complete details on the properties and methods for all of the objects in the Dynamic HTML Object Hierarchy are available in Appendix D, "Scripting Objects, Collections, Methods, and Properties." ▪

Part
II

Ch

document Object

The *document* object contains all the information pertaining to the HTML document. This includes all the tags in the document, collections of all the common types of elements, and methods to access the textual content of the document. In fact, the *document* object is so important that it is covered in detail in a later section.

FIG. 6.4
Structure of the window object.

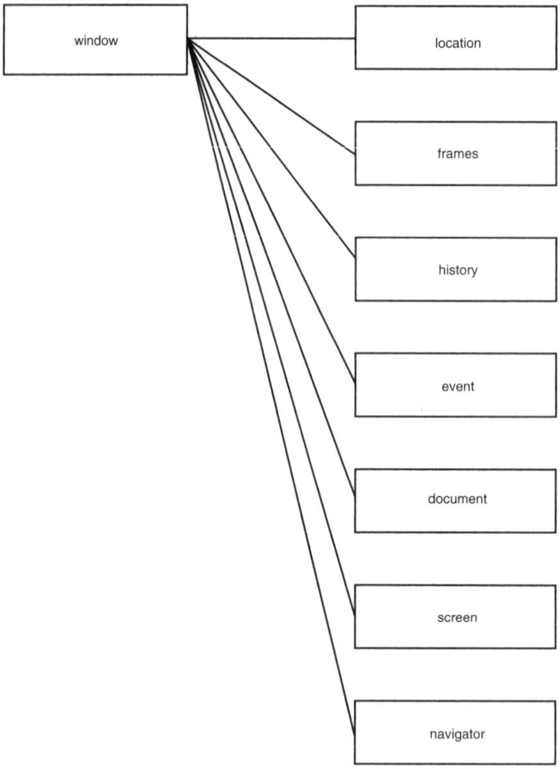

location Object

The *location* object contains all the information on the location that the window is currently displaying and all the details on that location (the port, the protocol, and so on). In addition, this object also contains a method that causes the page to reload.

Take a look at the important properties of the *location* object:

- **href**—The *href* property is the entire URL of the current page. Using this property, you can specify the location of other URLs. This is the equivalent of typing the URL in the Address box in IE. For instance, to go to the Internet Explorer page from the current page, you would use: *location.href* = "**http://www.microsoft.com/ie**";.

- **protocol**—The protocol is the method that the browser uses to retrieve the URL. For the Internet Explorer web page, the protocol is *http:*. Other common protocols are *file:* and *ftp:*.

- **host**—The hostname is the name of the host machine on which the current URL is located. In the case of the IE site, the hostname is *www.microsoft.com*. If there is a port specified in the URL (such as *"www.micrsoft.com:8888"*), it is included.

- **hostname**—The name of the host machine on which the current URL is located. Unlike the *host* property, the port is not included, even if specified.
- **hash**—The *hash* property includes the section of the URL following the hash character ('#') if any.
- **search**—The *search* property includes the section of the URL following the question mark character ('?') if any.
- **port**—If a specific port is specified in the URL, its value is located in the *port* property.
- **pathname**—This property contains the path to the specified location on the host. For the Internet Explorer example, this is: *ie*.

The *location* object also contains two methods:

- **reload()**—The *reload()* method takes no arguments and simply causes the current page to be reloaded. This behavior is exactly the same as if you were to hit the Reload button on a web browser.
- **replace(URL)**—The *replace(URL)* method takes one argument—an URL. It then causes the browser to replace the current document with the one specified by the *URL* argument.

history Object

The *history* object contains all the URLs the user has visited during a session—a session being every time Internet Explorer is launched. This will also be referred to from here on as the history list.

One property is supported by the *history* object: *length*.

The *length* property specifies how many URLs are contained in the current history object. The URLs saved are identical to those shown in the browser's history list.

The *history* object also has three methods: *back()*, *forward()*, and *go()*.

The *forward()* and *back()* methods enable the browser to be moved backward and forward in the history list programmatically. The *back()* method is identical to hitting the Back button in a browser window. Similarly, the *forward()* method is identical to hitting the Forward button in the browser window. Neither method takes any arguments. Therefore, to go back one URL in the history, use the following code:

```
window.history.back();
```

In addition, the *window* object is always the default object when scripting. Therefore, if you like, you can leave off the window object reference:

```
history.back();
```

The *go()* method enables you to go to a specific place in the browser history by passing an argument indicating where you want to go. The *go()* method can be called in two ways. The first way is to pass a partial URL to go to. If, for instance, you knew that you had been to part of

Part

II

Ch

6

the Internet Explorer site and wanted to go back to where you were, you would call the *go()* method in the following manner:

```
window.history.go("http://www.microsoft.com/ie");
```

Or:

```
history.go("http://www.microsoft.com/ie");
```

This would take you to the URL in the history list that contains "**http://www.microsoft.com/ie**". Note that this does not need to be the full URL; it just needs to be a part of it.

The second way to use the *go()* method is by specifying a number that corresponds to the location in the history list where you want to go. To go to the first location in the history list, for example, you would do the following:

```
window.history.go(1)
```

Or:

```
history.go(1);
```

> **CAUTION**
>
> It is important to remember that the first position in the history list is indicated by 1, rather than the 0 that you use when you access collections or arrays.

frames collection

The *frames* collection contains all the frame windows contained in the current window being displayed in the browser. It is important to note that what is contained in the *frames* collection is not the frame elements themselves, but the window objects associated with those frames.

Let's consider an example. Let's say you wanted to retrieve the name of the first frame contained in the current window. You would use the following code:

```
window.document.frames(0).name;
```

screen Object

When designing content for the web, it is often aggravating to not know the abilities and size of the screen on which the content will be displayed. For instance, if you knew that the screen you are working on is only 640 by 480 pixels, it would be nice to know this ahead of time if you are planning to render content that will require 800 by 600 pixels.

The *screen* object allows you to retrieve this sort of information. The following properties are available to you:

- **height**—The height of the screen in pixels.
- **width**—The width of the screen in pixels.
- **colorDepth**—Contains the number of color bits per pixel for the screen.

- **bufferDepth**—Specifies whether or not there is an offscreen basket.
- **updateInterval**—Specifies how often, in milliseconds, the screen is updated.

navigator Object

The *navigator* object enables you to access general information about the browser program. It is important to figure out at runtime what the browser does and does not support, in addition to being able to make decisions based upon which browser you might be running.

For instance, Netscape Communicator does not support a great deal of the functionality contained in Internet Explorer 4.0. If you were to try and use this functionality, errors would be generated. Therefore, you might want to check ahead of time to see whether the functionality you desire is available before using it.

There is also the unfortunate fact that although standards programs are supposed to act the same, in reality they don't. By checking the type of browser you are working with ahead of time—along with the knowledge of the incompatibilities between browsers—you can adjust for those differences at runtime, rather than having to distribute entirely different versions of the program.

Five important properties are supported by the *navigator* object.

- **appName**—Returns the name of the browser that is processing the script. The *appName* property is accessed in the following manner:

  ```
  navigator.appName
  ```

  In the case of Internet Explorer, the value of the *appName* property is "Microsoft Internet Explorer".

- **appVersion**—Returns the version number of the browser and is accessed in the following way:

  ```
  navigator.appVersion
  ```

  In the case of IE 4.0, the following is returned: "4.0 (compatible; MSIE 4.0; Windows 95)". The first part of the information returned is the major and minor version number of the browser, separated by a period—any additional information about this version of the browser is returned inside parentheses. Note that one of the extra pieces of information returned is the name of the platform that the browser is running on, which in this case is Windows 95.

- **appCodeName**—Supplies the application's code name for compatibility reasons to show that the browser is compatible with Netscape Navigator, which was the dominant browser for several years. The value returned by IE 4.0 is "Mozilla", which is the code name of Netscape's browser.

- **userAgent**—Supplies the user agent, which is the exact string that is sent via HTTP as the user-agent header when communicating with a web server:

  ```
  Mozilla/4.0 (compatible; MSIE 4.0; Windows 95)
  ```

Part

II

Ch

6

Note that once again "Mozilla" is sent, along with a version number. This is for compatibility reasons because quite a bit of content on the web checks to see whether you are running a new version of a Netscape browser, and uses that information to determine your browser's capabilities.

■ **cookieEnabled**—Returns whether "cookies" are supported in this browser. *Cookies* simply store information on your machine to customize future trips to that server. There has been quite a bit of debate, however, over the security risks posed by cookies, so many browsers now enable you to turn cookies off. The *cookieEnabled* property enables you to know whether cookies have been turned off. The value of this property in a default installation of Internet Explorer 4.0 is "true". This means that cookies are indeed enabled in the browser running the script.

■ **javaEnabled**—Returns true if the Java Virtual Machine is available in the browser and false otherwise.

event Object

The *event* object makes available information on the current event that is being processed. An *event* is the browser's way of telling you that the user is interacting with the browser.

Chapter 7, "Event Handling," discusses events and event handling in more detail.

The following properties are available in the *event* object:

■ **altKey**—True if the Alt key is pressed when the event was fired, false otherwise.

■ **button**—The mouse button that has been pressed: 0 if no button was pressed, 1 if the left button was pressed, 2 if the right button was pressed, and 4 if the middle button was pressed.

■ **cancelBubble**—True if the current event should bubble up the event hierarchy, false otherwise.

■ **clientX**—The X position of the mouse relative to the client area of the window.

■ **clientY**—The Y position of the mouse relative to the client area of the window.

■ **ctrlKey**—True if the Control key was pressed when the event was fired, false otherwise.

■ **fromElement**—The last element that the mouse was over before it was over this one.

■ **keyCode**—The code of the key that was pressed when the event was fired.

■ **offsetX**—The X position of the mouse when the event was fired relative to the container that received the event.

■ **offsetY**—The Y position of the mouse when the event was fired relative to the container that received the event.

■ **reason**—The current condition of the data transfer object. Can be one of three states: 0 if the data was transferred successfully, 1 if the data transfer was aborted, and 2 if there was an error in the data transmission.

■ **returnValue**—The return value from the event.

- **screenX**—The X position of the mouse relative to the size of the screen rather than the browser window.

- **screenY**—The Y position of the mouse relative to the size of the screen rather than the browser window.

- **shiftKey**—The state of the Shift key when the event was fired. The value is true if it was pressed, false otherwise.

- **srcElement**—The element that originally fired the event that is now being handled.

- **srcFilter**—The filter object that fired the onfilterchange event.

- **toElement**—The element that the mouse moved to after it left the current one.

- **type**—The name of the event as a string. The name of the event is retrieved without the "on" prefix. Therefore "onmouseover" would just be "mouseover."

- **x**—The X position of the mouse object when the event was fired relative to the nearest parent object that was positioned with CSS Positioning.

- **y**—The Y position of the mouse object when the event was fired relative to the nearest parent object that was positioned with CSS Positioning.

The *document* Object

Whereas the *window* object contains all the pertinent information about the state of the browser window, the *document* object contains all the information you might want about the document that the browser is currently showing. Figure 6.5 shows the relationship between the *document* object and the objects it contains.

The *document* object can be accessed in two ways. The first and more correct way to access it is through the *window* object—remember that the *document* object is contained by the *window* object. Therefore, to access the *"all"* collection of the *document* object, use the following syntax:

```
window.document.all
```

For compatibility with older browsers, however, an alternate way to access the *document* object is by using the keyword *document* by itself, followed by any methods or properties you may want to access. This is due to the fact that the default object when scripting is the current *window* object. In the case of the previous "all" example, you would use the following syntax:

```
document.all
```

This provides the same information that is returned if you had appended the *window* object before it, which is the *document* object that the browser window is currently viewing. The procedure you use is largely a matter of preference: If you want to be as specific in your code as possible, use *window.document.all*, otherwise just use *document.all*.

All the collections, methods, properties, and events supported in the *document* object are shown in table 6.4. The entire HTML document that is being viewed is contained inside this object and can be accessed via the collections contained within it.

FIG. 6.5
Structure of the
document object.

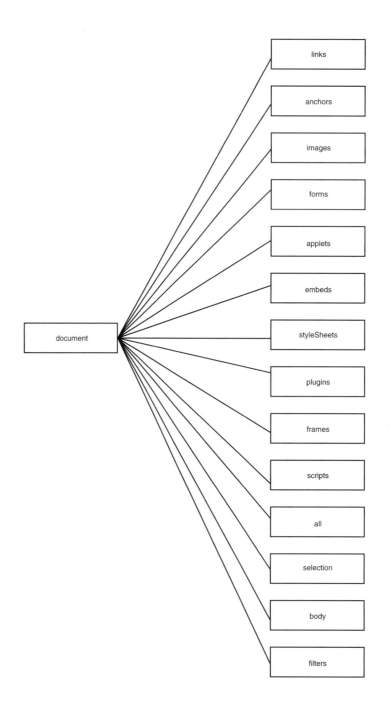

Table 6.4 The *document* Object

Collections	anchors, links, forms, all, applets, frames, images, scripts, embeds, plugins
Methods	close, open, clear, write, writeln, rangeFromText, rangeFromElement, execCommand, queryCommandEnabled, queryCommandText, elementFromPoint, queryCommandSupported, queryCommandState, queryCommandIndeterm, createElement
Properties	alinkColor, linkColor, vlinkColor, mimeType, title, bgColor, link, vLink, aLink, cookie, lastModified, charset, location, referrer, fgColor, activeElement, strReadyState, domain, URL, fileSize, fileCreatedDate, fileModifiedDate, fileUpdatedDate
Events	onclick, onmouseover, ondblclick, onkeypress, onmousedown, onmousemove, onmouseup, onkeydown, onkeyup, onmouseout, onreadystatechange, onhelp, onbeforeupdate, onafterupdate

In addition to the data that makes up the HTML page, the *document* object also has a great deal of useful information about the document itself, which is exposed through the *document* object's properties. The following list takes a closer look at a few of the more important properties:

- **linkColor**—This property is the color in which standard links are displayed. This value is given as a hex RGB value preceded by a "#". The default link color in IE 4.0 is #00000FF, which is the hexadecimal value for blue.

- **vlinkColor**—The color in which visited links are displayed. This value is also given as a hex RGB value. Its default value is #FF0000, which is the hexadecimal value for red.

- **alinkColor**—The color in which links are displayed after the mouse is pressed on them, but before the mouse button is released. The value is given in hex form. The default color value for IE 4.0 is also #FF0000.

- **activeElement**—The element that currently has the focus.

- **URL**—This documents the entire URL as a string.

- **mimeType**—The MIME standard enables you to specify different viewers for different types of content. For instance, the MIME type of a TIFF image is "image/tiff". The standard MIME type for HTML documents in IE 4.0 is "text/html".

- **title**—The *title* property is simply the name given to the document inside the HTML <TITLE> tag.

- **bgColor**—The *bgColor* property defines the background color of the document. The default color is the hexadecimal value for white (#FFFFFF).

- **cookie**—The *cookie* property stores the value of the cookie for the current page. On a standard HTML page without a cookie, this value is blank. This property can also be used to create a cookie for the current page.

- **lastModified**—The *lastModified* property gives the date and time this document was last changed. For instance, if the file was last modified on June 16, 1997 at 11:24 a.m., the value of this property would be "06/16/97 11:24:00".

- **charset**—The charset is the character set with which this document is encoded. For browsers using the English language, this value will be "iso-8859-1", which is the standard character set for English.

- **location**—The *location* property is simply the URL that contains this document. If, for instance, you were viewing the Internet Explorer page at microsoft.com, this value would be "**http://www.microsoft.com/ie**".

- **referrer**—The URL of the page that was viewed previous to this one. For example, had you viewed the main Microsoft page before viewing the Internet Explorer page, this value would be "**http://microsoft.com**". If there is no referring page, then the value of this property is blank.

- **fgColor**—The *fgColor* property contains the color that HTML text will use in the document by default (if the text color is not specified for that section of text). This value is also specified as an RGB hex number.

- **strReadyState**—The *strReadyState* property enables you to know whether or not the page has been completely downloaded. It has four possible values. The first value is "uninitialized", which is the value when the document is first beginning to load. As it loads, the value changes to "loading". Then, when enough of the document is loaded that it can be interacted with—for instance, links can be clicked before images are done loading—the value changes to "interactive". Finally, when the document is finished loading, the *strReadyState* property changes to "complete".

- **domain**—The *domain* property provides the domain name of the web server that is supplying the document. In the example of the Microsoft web server, this value would be "**www.microsoft.com**". If you are not loading the document from a web server, then this value is blank.

- **fileSize**—The *fileSize* property is the length of the document loaded in bytes.

- **fileCreatedDate**—The *fileCreatedDate* property provides the day on which the file was created. Unlike the *lastModified* property, *fileCreatedDate* spells out the date. So, a sample date might be "Monday, June 17, 1997".

- **fileModifiedDate**—The *fileModifiedDate* is the day on which the file was last modified. This is much like the *lastModified* property, except that it does not give the time at which the document was last modified. Like the *fileCreatedDate* property, the date is spelled out in long form.

- **fileUpdatedDate**—At first glance the *fileUpdatedDate* property might appear to be the same as the *fileModifiedDate* property; however, this is not the case. The *fileUpdatedDate* property provides the date that the file was last reloaded by the local browser from the remote server. Like *fileCreatedDate* and *fileModifiedDate*, *fileUpdatedDate* spells out the date in long form.

selection Object

Much like a text editor or word processor, Internet Explorer enables users to select text inside the document. This is done by holding down the mouse button and dragging the mouse pointer over the text that the user wants to select.

Information about the text the user has currently highlighted with the mouse is available in the *selection* object. This can be useful if you want to do some action based upon what the user has selected, perhaps highlighting it or changing its font.

The *selection* object has one property—*type*, which defines the type of selection. This can be one of two values: 0 if there is no selection insertion point, or 1 if the selection is a text selection and there is in fact an insertion point

The *selection* object has three methods as follows:

- **clear**—Clears the contents of the selection.
- **createRange**—Creates a text range over the selection.
- **empty**—Deselects the current selection.

body Object

The *body* object contains information about the HTML elements that make up the visible part of the HTML document in the current browser window. The *body* object corresponds to the BODY element in the HTML document.

Here are the properties contained in the *body* object:

- **accessKey**—The accelerator for the body.
- **background**—The picture in the background of the body.
- **bgColor**—The background color for the body.
- **bgProperties**—The properties for the background picture, such as whether the picture scrolls on the page.
- **bottomMargin**—The bottom margin in pixels for the body of the page.
- **className**—The CSS class name associated with the body of the page.
- **clientHeight**—The height of the body in pixels.
- **clientWidth**—The width of the body in pixels.
- **document**—The document object for the body.
- **id**—The CSS Identifier for the body.
- **innerHTML**—The HTML code between the start and end tags of the body.
- **innerText**—The HTML code between the start and end tags of the body represented purely as text.
- **isTextEdit**—Whether the text range can be edited. True if it can, false otherwise.

- **lang**—The ISO code for the language being used. Note that this is not the scripting language, but the actual written language being used.
- **language**—Specifies the computer scripting language in which the current script is written.
- **leftMargin**—The left margin for the entire page represented in pixels.
- **offsetHeight**—The height of the body in pixels, relative to the parent.
- **offsetLeft**—The left position of the body in pixels, relative to the parent.
- **offsetParent**—The object that contains the body and provides the offset.
- **offsetTop**—The top position of the body in pixels, relative to the parent.
- **offsetWidth**—The width of the body in pixels, relative to the parent.
- **parentElement**—The parent element of the body.
- **parentTextEdit**—The next element in the object hierarchy on which a text range can be created.
- **rightMargin**—The right margin for the entire page represented in pixels.
- **scroll**—Whether the scroll bars are on or off. If "yes" they are on, if "no" they are off.
- **scrollHeight**—The scrolling height of the body in pixels, including content that is not visible.
- **scrollLeft**—The amount in pixels between the left edge of the body and the left edge that is currently visible to the user in the browser.
- **scrollTop**—The amount in pixels between the top edge of the body and the left edge that is currently visible to the user in the browser.
- **scrollWidth**—The scrolling height of the body in pixels, including content that is not visible.
- **sourceIndex**—The position of the body in the document's source index.
- **style**—The inline style sheet for the body .
- **tabIndex**—The tab index for the body.
- **tagName**—The tag for the current element (the body tag).
- **text**—The text color for the body.
- **title**—A tooltip for the body.
- **topMargin**—The top margin for the entire page represented in pixels.

Here are the methods contained in the *body* object:

- **blur**—Causes the *body* object to lose mouse and keyboard focus.
- **click**—Simulates the user clicking the mouse button.
- **contains**—Returns true if the element passed as an argument is contained in the body, false otherwise.
- **createTextRange**—Creates a text range over the body.
- **focus**—Causes the body to receive mouse and keyboard focus.

- **getAttribute**—Returns the value for the attribute passed as an argument.
- **insertAdjacentHTML**—Inserts HTML code passed as an argument into the body.
- **insertAdjacentText**—Inserts text passed as an argument into the body.
- **removeAttribute**—Removes the attribute passed as an argument from the body.
- **scrollIntoView**—Scrolls the body into view.
- **setAttribute**—Sets the attribute passed as an argument.

As mentioned previously, the *document* object contains the entire contents of the page in its various collections. Figure 6.5 shows the relation of the various collections to the document object. Each of these collections is described in more detail in the sections that follow.

all Collection

The *all* collection is perhaps the most important part of the *document* object. It is where all the elements that make up the document are stored.

The most straightforward way to use the *all* collection is by accessing an element of the document via its id. For instance, assume you had the following tag in your HTML document:

```
<P id=mainPara style="font-weight: italic "> Dynamic HTML
```

You could then access that element through the *document.all* collection by using the id of the tag:

```
var elem = document.all("mainPara")
```

To verify that you now have the correct element selected, you can use a logical expression in an *if* statement:

```
if (mainPara == elem)
{
      document.write("Selected correct element");
}
```

If you want to access the elements of the page in a more general manner, you can select the elements via the *tags()* method of the collection. Therefore, if you want to find all instances of the <H1> tag inside your document, you would use the following code:

```
var allH1 = document.all.tags("H1");
```

This would return a collection containing all the desired <H1> elements in the document.

Several elements will always be present in the *document.all* object, even if you do not specify them in the HTML document explicitly. These are known as Implied Elements. The four Implied Elements are:

- **HTML**—The HTML element is usually specified by the <HTML> tag at the top of the document and surrounds the rest of the elements, indicating that they are HTML.
- **HEAD**—The HEAD element is specified by the <HEAD> tag at the top of the document and contains any elements that will not be part of the visible BODY portion of the document.

- **BODY**—The BODY element is the main section of the HTML document and is specified by the <BODY> tag. The BODY section of the HTML document is where the elements that make up the content of the document are found.

- **TBODY**—Finally, the TBODY element is where the content of tables can be found. Unlike the previous three Implied Elements, which are recognized explicitly by most HTML authors, TBODY is one to make sure you remember is implied.

anchors Collection

The *anchors* collection contains all the elements that contain an <A> tag in them. Anchors are normally used in documents to specify hyperlinks, as in the following example:

```
<A HREF="http://www.microsoft.com">The Microsoft Site</A>
```

applets Collection

The *applets* collection is a slight misnomer for what it actually contains. From the name, you would expect the *applets* collection to contain only applets, Java applets in particular.

Instead, the *applets* collection contains what Microsoft defines as all the objects in the document. Once again, this is a bit confusing, as an actual <OBJECT> tag is defined in Dynamic HTML, and the meaning in the *applets* collection is more encompassing than just elements that use the <OBJECT> tag.

Instead, the objects that are contained in the *applets* collection include the following:

- **applets**—Elements with the <APPLET> tag.
- **embeds**—Elements with the <EMBED> tag.
- **images**—All images in the document, usually specified with the <IMG> tag.
- **objects**—Any element that uses the <OBJECT> tag.
- **intrinsic controls**—These are the controls that are built into Internet Explorer 4.0 by default.

forms Collection

The *forms* collection contains all the forms present in the document. A form is defined as an element that uses the FORM HTML tag. Dynamic HTML will enable you to place user interface controls outside of a form, but it is important to note that these controls will not be present in the *forms* collection.

images Collection

The *images* collection contains all the images in the document. An image is defined as an element that used the IMG HTML tag. Images that are produced without an IMG tag, such as from a Java applet or ActiveX Control, will not be present in this collection. All these images are also contained in the *applets* collection.

links Collection

The *links* collection contains all the hyperlinks in the document. This collection contains all the elements in the *anchors* collection, plus all the elements that use the <AREA> tag.

frames Collection

The *frames* collection contains all the frames in the document. Frames are considered windows themselves in HTML, so this collection contains *window* objects instead of the actual frame element objects.

scripts Collection

The *scripts* collection contains all the scripts in the document. The scripts themselves are represented and can be retrieved as pure text.

embeds Collection

The *embeds* collection contains all the embedded content (plugins) in the document. Plugins are programs that have been integrated into the browser to increase its functionality. The Real Audio Player is a good example of a plugin.

plugins Collection

This is an alias for the *embeds* collection.

filters Collection

The *filters* collection contains all the Dynamic HTML Multimedia Filters for the document. A filter enables the visible aspect of any element to be modified on the fly. For instance, there is a blur filter that causes the content of an element to become blurry. Dynamic HTML Multimedia Filters are covered in detail in Chapter 15, "Multimedia Filters and ActiveX Controls."

styleSheets Collection

The *styleSheets* collection contains all of the style sheets for this document. A style sheet is contained for each occurrance of a LINK or style element present in the document.

Part

II

Ch

6

TextRange Object

In addition to the Dynamic HTML Object Hierarchy, there is a special object that is used quite often when working with the Object Hierarchy. This object is the *TextRange* object and is used to represent areas of text in your document.

At a core level, all HTML files are constructed out of pure text. This text normally has a great deal of style associated with it, but at its core it is still pure text. *TextRange* objects enable you to access this pure text directly.

Take a look at the following HTML code that defines a few tags that are rendered in different sizes and styles:

```
<BODY>
    <H1>Example</H1>
    <H2>TextRange</H2>
    <P><B>This Example Examines Text Ranges</B>
</BODY>
```

If you were to create a *TextRange* object for the <BODY> tag, it would contain the following value:

```
"Example TextRange This Example Examines Text Ranges"
```

The simplest way to think of text ranges is by considering what the value of the text is after all the tags are stripped away. In other words, the core textual information contained in the HTML that you are considering.

TextRange objects are discussed and used heavily in Chapter 10, "Dynamic Content." Dynamic content is a method by which you can actually change what is being shown on the page in real-time. *TextRange* objects enable you to find the text in the document that you want to change.

From Here...

This chapter discussed the many ways in which the Dynamic HTML Object Model can be accessed. Although the material presented here might not seem too exciting, it is the structure upon which Dynamic HTML is accessed and modified.

The benefits of the Dynamic HTML Object Model are covered in much greater detail when you learn how to use it to modify the style and content of the document in realtime. You'll learn about these concepts in the following chapters:

- Chapter 7, "Event Handling," covers the importance of event handling in Dynamic HTML-generated web sites.
- Chapter 8, "Dynamic Styles," will cover the process of changing the style of your HTML elements on the fly.

Event Handling

One of the foundations of Dynamic HTML is its capability to interact with the user. *Event handling* is the procedure by which user interaction is accomplished. Any time your script gets information from the user, it is using event handling.

Event handling can become quite complicated, but at its core it is simple. Your program specifies what types of interactions with the user that it is interested in. Whenever the user performs one of those actions, your program is notified that the action occurred.

In Dynamic HTML, you not only specify what type of interaction you are interested in, but also the scope of the interaction. You can specify, for instance, that you only want to be notified of certain actions that occur to a specific HTML element, perhaps an image or a range of text. Or, if you prefer, you can specify that you want to receive notification of actions for the entire HTML body. ■

Event Handling

Discover what events are and how you can use them to make your HTML pages interactive.

Binding to Events

Learn three different ways to attach events to your HTML elements: binding via element, SCRIPT...FOR, and VBScript special syntax.

window.event Object

Discover how to use the window.event object to find out a great deal of specifics about the event that was performed.

Default Actions

Many HTML elements have default actions associated with them. Dynamic HTML enables you to override these actions if you choose. Techniques for doing this are discussed in this chapter.

Event Bubbling

Learn how Dynamic HTML not only fires events based on the elements that they occur on, but how it also sends the event to the parents of the element. Find out how to control this process.

Events

The most fundamental concept in event handling is that of the event itself. An *event* is a notification from the browser that the state of things has changed in some way, normally by the user performing an action.

All sorts of events can be generated and in turn, dealt with by scripting. Many of the more common events and how to handle them with scripting languages are covered later in this chapter. Although many types of events exist, basic events can be broken down into four distinct types.

- **Keyboard Events**—The most basic keyboard event is generated by the user hitting a key. There are, however, distinct events for the pressing of a key and the releasing of a key, and events for pressing combinations of keys, such as the A and the Shift key, for instance. An event for the pressing of the help key exists as well.

- **Mouse Events**—Mouse events are the most common types of events in Dynamic HTML because the main way that users interact with web pages is through the use of a mouse. Much like keyboard events, events for clicking the mouse button, pressing it, and releasing it are all separate—in addition, there is an event for the user double-clicking the mouse button. Finally, events can be generated by the movement of the mouse, regardless of whether or not the mouse button is clicked.

- **Focus Events**—Events can be generated when an element gains focus and when it loses focus. If you're not familiar with the concept of focus, it is discussed further in the section "Focus and Selection Events," but for now it is sufficient to know that focus is a concept used to describe with which element on the page the user is currently interacting.

- **State Change Events**—These events are not necessarily generated by user interaction. Instead, state change events can be generated when the state of the document changes in some important way. An event, for instance, can be generated when the document has loaded enough that the user can interact with it, or another event can be generated when the document has completely finished loading.

A few of the more common events that are used in Dynamic HTML have been discussed, such as *onclick*, *onmouseup*, and *onmousedown*. These are a subset of a class of general events in Dynamic HTML that will probably be the events that you use most.

These general events are available for every element in the document. Individual elements may have additional events that are specific to them, but the general events are guaranteed to be accessible for every type of element.

The general events that are guaranteed to be available for every element are the mouse and keyboard events. In addition to these types of events, the focus and state change events are covered and the types of elements that they can be used with are discussed.

Mouse Events

The mouse events are all related to the user performing some sort of action with the mouse. The user can perform two general types of actions with the mouse: click one of the mouse buttons or move the mouse pointer around inside the browser window.

The first events covered in this section are those events generated when the user clicks the mouse button. These mouse button–related events are delivered in a designated order as follows:

1. *onmousedown*
2. *onmouseup*
3. *onclick*
4. *ondblclick*

Next, you will learn about the events generated when the user moves the mouse. Much like the mouse button–related events, mouse movement–related events are called in a specific order:

1. *onmouseover*
2. *onmousemove*
3. *onmouseenter*

onmousedown

The *onmousedown* event fires when the user presses a mouse button while over an object. One important subtlety of the *onmousedown* event is that it is called before the *onclick* event.

onmouseup

The *onmouseup* event fires when the user releases a mouse button while over an object. Unlike the *onmousedown* event, the *onmouseup* event is called after the *onclick* event.

onclick

The *onclick* event fires when the mouse button is pressed and released while over an object. Information about the mouse button that was pressed is available from the *window.event.button* property (see the later section, titled "window.event Object").

ondblclick

The *ondblclick* event fires when the mouse button is clicked twice while over an object. The mouse button must be clicked within the amount of time that the system allows for a double-click.

Part

II

Ch

7

onmouseover

The *onmouseover* event fires when the user moves the mouse pointer into the range of the object. It is then not fired again until after the user moves the pointer out of the object and then back into it again.

Dynamic HTML always remembers the last element that the mouse pointer was over before it entered the current element. The object representing this element is available in the *window.event* object as *window.event.fromElement*.

onmousemove

The *onmousemove* event fires whenever the user moves the mouse pointer within the range of the object. It is important to keep the event handler for this event as small as possible because a large number of *onmousemove* events can easily be generated if the user moves the mouse quite a bit.

onmouseout

The *onmouseout* event fires when the user moves the mouse pointer out of the range of the object. It doesn't fire again until after the user moves the pointer back into the range of the object and then back out again. This means that for every one time the *onmouseout* event is fired, the user must have moved the mouse into the range of the object.

Dynamic HTML always remembers the next element that the mouse pointer entered after it leaves the element that receives the *onmouseout* event. The object representing this element is available in the *window.event* object as *window.event.toElement*.

Keyboard Events

Keyboard events are events generated whenever the user presses a key on their keyboard. Events exist not only for the action of typing a key on the keyboard, but also for the pressing down of the key and for the releasing of the key.

Similar to the mouse movement events, the keyboard events also are generated in a specified order:

1. *onkeydown*
2. *onkeypress*
3. *onkeyup*

onkeydown   The *onkeydown* event is generated whenever the user depresses a key, but before it is released. The value of the key that was depressed is available from the *window.event* object as *window.event.keyCode*. The value contained in *keyCode* is the UNICODE value associated with the key.

onkeypress   The *onkeypress* event is generated whenever the user presses and releases a key. The value of the key that was pressed is available from the *window.event* object as *window.event.keyCode*. The value contained in *keyCode* property is the UNICODE value associated with the key.

In addition, the *altKey*, *ctrlKey*, and *shiftKey* properties are available from the *window.event* object. Each of them is a Boolean property that is set to true if the corresponding modifier key is pressed at the same time as the key that generated the event.

onkeyup   The *onkeyup* event is generated whenever the user releases a key that has been depressed. The value of the key that was released is available from the *window.event* object as *window.event.keyCode*. The value contained in the *keyCode* property is the UNICODE value associated with the key.

onhelp   The *onhelp* event is a special event that is fired when the user is requesting help by pressing a help-related key on the keyboard. Dynamic HTML defines two keys as being help-related. First is the HELP key. Second is the F1 key, which is a traditional key used for help in Windows. Either of these keys will generate the *onhelp* event.

Focus and Selection Events

The *focus* and *selection* events give you general information about how the user is interacting with the document. These events are special in that they are notifying you of actions that do not normally signal to an application that a response is required. You, however, might want to keep track of every action the user is doing, so having access to these events could be quite useful to you.

The first of these types of events are the *focus* events. Focus events are generated when a user signifies to the application that they are interacting with a certain element on the page. This is done by either clicking the element or navigating to it with the Tab key. This concept may sound a bit abstract, so consider a real-world example. Go to the File, Open Menu command in Internet Explorer. Now hit the Tab key a few times. Notice that a different control is highlighted each time you hit the Tab key. Each time you hit the Tab key, a different control recieves the focus.

Selection events, on the other hand, are generated whenever the user drags the mouse over elements on the HTML page. Whenever the user clicks and drags the mouse over a range of elements in the page, selection events are generated. The sections that follow provide descriptions of the focus and selection events.

onfocus   The *onfocus* event is fired whenever an element receives the focus from the user. This is done by the user either clicking the element or navigating to it via the Tab key.

onblur   The *onblur* event is fired whenever an element loses the focus from the user. This event is generated after the element loses focus via the user clicking another element or navigating to another element with the Tab key.

Part

II

Ch

7

onselectstart   The *onselectstart* event is fired when the user has indicated that he wants to start a selection. This is done by the user clicking at the start of the section that they want to select.

onselect   The *onselect* event is fired whenever the user actually makes a selection. This is done by the user holding down the mouse button and moving it over the elements that he wants to select. The fact that the selection has been made is indicated by the select area appearing in reverse video. For instance, if normal text on the page is black on a white background, the text would change to white on a black background when selected.

ondragstart   The *ondragstart* event notifies the script that the user is indicating that he wants to move a selected area. This is done by the user pressing down with the mouse button on an area that has been selected and moving the mouse.

State Change Events

State change events enable you to find out the current state of the document. The state of the document reflects how far along the document is in loading. Because Internet connections vary in connection speed, the amount of time it takes to load a document is not known ahead of time. These events enable you to find out where the current document is in that process.

onreadystatechange   The *onreadystatechange* event is fired whenever the document reaches a milestone in its loading process. This enables the script to follow the document throughout its entire loading and make decisions based upon that information.

When the *onreadystatechange* event is fired, the current state of the document can be accessed via the *readyState* property of the *document* object. The *readyState* property can have the following values:

- **complete**—The document is completely loaded.
- **interactive**—The document can be interacted with even though it is not fully loaded.
- **loading**—The control is currently being loaded.
- **unitialized**—The document is in the process of downloading.

onload   The *onload* event is fired when the document has finished loading. This means that not only has the HTML file for the current document been loaded, but all the elements on that document have been loaded. This means that all elements that require their own connections to the server (such as images and applets) must have finished loading.

onunload   The *onunload* event is fired when the browser unloads the document. The document is unloaded whenever the document that the user is viewing changes. This is done by the user specifying that a new URL should be loaded into the browser. In addition, the *onunload* event is fired when the refresh button is clicked, which reloads the document.

onabort Event

The *onabort* event is a special event used only with images (IMG elements). It is fired when the loading of the images is stopped. The loading of an image can be stopped under two circumstances: if the user clicks the stop button in the browser, all images being loaded are stopped; if the user clicks a link in a page before all images are loaded, the loading of those images stops.

Event Firing

When an event is performed that your program is looking for, there has to be a process by which your program is notified that the event has happened. This process is known as *event firing*.

Event firing can be thought of as the bridge between the actions that are taking place and your program. When an event happens, the browser takes note of whether the document is event aware for any of the events, and if so, fires the appropriate response to the event to the document. When an event is fired, the element that wants to receive that event has a procedure called on it that has been bound to that event.

Consider a simple example: an image is receiving mouse click events. The first time that the user clicks the image, an event is generated that informs the image that it has been clicked. It is important to realize that an event is generated not only the first time that the user clicks the image, but *every* time the user clicks the image.

You might, for instance, want to cause an element on your page to appear or disappear whenever an image is clicked. In effect, you are then making this image a button that interacts with the user. Because you want to do something every time the image is clicked, it's important that you receive a new event every time the user clicks it.

Event Handlers

An event is fired after it has been generated by the browser. As mentioned previously, event firing can be thought of as a bridge. The event handlers for the document are the other side of that bridge. Event handlers are procedures written in a scripting language that are called when events are fired.

The *event handler* is a user-defined procedure in your script that is called when events are fired. It can be written in any language that can interface with and support the Internet Explorer 4.0 scripting mechanism. Normally, however, JavaScript or VBScript is used because they are built into Internet Explorer 4.0.

Because events can be generated for all sorts of elements on the page, and even for the document itself, event handlers are defined not in a general sense, but instead they are bound to the element that will receive the event. If, for instance, you have an image that you want to receive events, write an event handler for the actions you want performed and then bind that event to the image element (binding is discussed in greater length in the section, "Binding to Events"). If you want to implement the button scenario previously described, for instance, bind the *onclick* event to the image that you want to respond when clicked.

Part

II

Ch

7

Figure 7.1 shows how events, event firing, and event handlers work.

FIG. 7.1
The event handling
process.

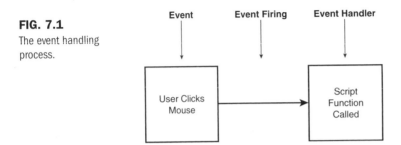

Figure 7.1 depicts an event that is generated, in this case, by the user clicking an image. The browser then fires an event, notifying the document that an event has occurred. Finally, the event handler for the image is called, letting the image know that it has been clicked.

Event Handling Prior to Dynamic HTML

The capability to interact with the user is not unique to Dynamic HTML. In fact, the capability to do primitive event handling has existed since the introduction of JavaScript in Netscape Navigator.

Because the methods that Dynamic HTML uses to do event handling are derived from JavaScript, it would be advantageous to take a quick look at how JavaScript handles events. Listing 7.1 displays the entire HTML and JavaScript code for this interaction. The code segments that follow are numbered corresponding to their placement within the final listing.

Prior to Dynamic HTML, the primary method for using and receiving events was to use them with objects inside forms. The following example defines a simple form for this purpose:

```
11. <FORM NAME="info">
12.    Name:
13.    <INPUT TYPE="text" name="user" value="">
14.    <INPUT TYPE="button" name="show" value="Click Here">
16. </FORM>
```

This code defines a form that contains two objects: a text entry field and a button. Before the advent of inline scripting languages, forms were used mainly for communicating information to CGI scripts, which is, in fact, still a common use for them.

Beginning with JavaScript, however, you were able to use forms interactively without communicating data back to the server. This is an important consideration, because communication on the Internet (especially with a modem) can sometimes be quite slow.

Inline scripting languages enabled you to define event handlers for the objects inside forms, and execute specific scripting code for those objects. This functionality enabled the page to be interactive.

The following example defines a function called in JavaScript "Greet" that opens an alert box with a different greeting, depending on whether a name is passed to it:

```
19. function Greet(name)
20. {
21.    if (name.length == 0)
22.        alert("Hello stranger");
23.    else
24.        alert("Hello " + name);
25. }
```

The *Greet(name)* function is the event handler and is called whenever the interaction that you are looking for is performed. In this case, the interaction you want is the user clicking the Click Here button in your form, as defined in the previous code.

The way that events are bound to objects in a form in JavaScript is by adding the function call, with its arguments, as an attribute to the GUI object. In this case, the GUI object is the Click Here button, and the event that you want is the *onclick* event that is fired when the user clicks the button.

Now bind the *Greet(name)* function to your form by adding the event handler function, *onclick* to the button in the form definition:

```
11. <FORM NAME="info">
12.     Name:
13.     <INPUT TYPE="text" name="user" value="">
14.     <INPUT TYPE="button" name="show" value="Click Here"
15.             onclick="Greet(document.info.user.value)">
16. </FORM>
```

Now, when the Click Here button is clicked, the *Greet(name)* function is called. Note that the value that is passed to the *Greet(name)* function depends on the value of another object in the form, the text entry field with the name attribute of "user." The events for the user field are also not defined, because the only time you are interested in doing something special is when the button is clicked. The final code for the interaction created in the three preceding excerpts, ready to be executed in Internet Explorer, is displayed in listing 7.1. The output from this example is shown in figure 7.2.

Listing 7.1   Recording User Input with Event Handling

```
01. <HTML>
02.
03. <HEAD>
04.     <TITLE>
05.         Chapter 7, Example 1
06.     </TITLE>
07. </HEAD>
08.
09. <BODY>
10.
11.     <FORM name="info">
12.         Name:
```

Part

II

Ch

7

continues

Listing 7.1   Continued

```
13.        <INPUT TYPE="text" name="user" value="">
14.        <INPUT TYPE="button" name="show" value="Click Here"
15.               onclick="Greet(document.info.user.value)">
16.    </FORM>
17.
18.    <SCRIPT language="JavaScript">
19.    function Greet(name)
20.    {
21.       if (name.length == 0)
22.          alert("Hello stranger");
23.       else
24.          alert("Hello " + name);
25.    }
26.    </SCRIPT>
27.
28. </BODY>
29. </HTML>
```

FIG. 7.2

Basic JavaScript event handling.

Although this method of event handling is certainly powerful, and added quite a bit of client-side scriptability to HTML forms, it is lacking in a fundamental way: it only works with forms.

Being limited to objects in forms originally made sense because forms contain elements that are obviously part of a user interface. However, this limitation keeps the document from responding to more subtle events, such as the user moving the mouse over an image or a piece of text. It is precisely this type of event handling that is now facilitated by Dynamic HTML.

Event Handling in Dynamic HTML

Event handling in Dynamic HTML is done in much the same way as with previous versions of HTML that supported inline scripting, but with many important extensions. Events can be bound to any HTML element, or even to the document itself; there is also greater selection of events is available.

You should consider several things when you use event handling in Dynamic HTML. The most important aspect to consider is where you want the event information to go. You have many options in this respect. You can have the event handled by the following components:

- Element on which it occurs
- Container that it resides in (for example, <DIV> or <SPAN>)
- Body of the document (<BODY>)
- HTML element (<HTML>)
- Other places in the *document* Object

The element that receives the event depends on the design of your program and what you want to achieve. The hierarchy in which events can occur is discussed later in the "Event Bubbling" section, which should make these design decisions clearer.

For now, consider the first option: defining event handlers based on individual elements. In this procedure, the most straightforward way to define an event handler is by including them via inline attributes, through the following syntax:

```
<tagname event_type="event_handler()">
```

The "tagname" is the name of the tag you are using (for example, <H1>, <P>, <IMG>, and so on); "event type" is the kind of event that you are looking for; and "event_handler" is the function to call when that event occurs on the element.

Event Handling in Action

Listing 7.2 at the end of this section is a concrete example of setting up an event handler based on individual elements. For starters, this example begins with a pretty basic <H1> tag:

```
<H1>Some Header Text</H1>
```

Here's where the real power of event handling becomes apparent. Note that this element is not in a form and doesn't have an ID attribute to be uniquely identified on the page. It's the same as any other <H1> element you might have written in the past. But because you can add events on an element by element basis, adding an event that doesn't occur in a form is easy.

Part

II

Ch

7

The following code applies the boilerplate from the previous example to fire an event when the user clicks on the element and to call the JavaScript *hClicked()* function when it is clicked with the mouse:

```
11. <H1 onclick="hClicked()">Some Header Text</H1>
```

Pretty straightforward, isn't it? The following code writes the JavaScript function to call when the image is clicked. In this case, a popup alert box tells the user that the header has been clicked:

```
13. function hClicked()
14. {
15.    alert("Header Text element clicked");
16. }
```

Now every time the user clicks on the <H1> element with the mouse, the following sequence occurs:

1. A mouse click event is generated.
2. The mouse click event is fired.
3. The browser checks to see if this event is being handled by the element that the mouse is over.
4. Because the H1 element has an event handler, that function is called. In this case, *hClicked()* is called.
5. The *hClicked()* function brings up an alert box informing the user that the element has been clicked.

Take a look at this code in the context of a legal HTML document. Figure 7.3 shows the output from this document when the user clicks on the <H1> tag.

Listing 7.2   Responding to User Interaction with Event Handling

```
01. <HTML>
02.
03. <HEAD>
04.    <TITLE>
05.        Chapter 7, Example 2
06.    </TITLE>
07. </HEAD>
08.
09. <BODY>
10.
11.    <H1 onclick="hClicked()">Some Header Text</H1>
12.    <SCRIPT language="JavaScript">
13.    function hClicked()
14.    {
15.        alert("Header Text element clicked");
16.    }
17.    </SCRIPT>
18.
19. </BODY>
20. </HTML>
```

FIG. 7.3
Event handling on
arbitrary HTML
elements.

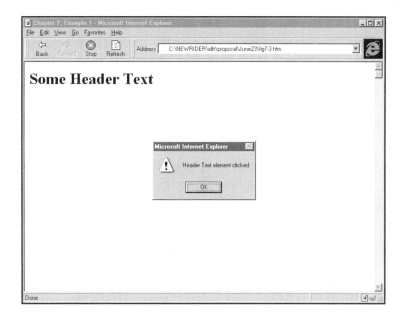

Compare the script in listing 7.2 to the script in listing 7.1 that performs a similar action with methods prior to Dynamic HTML. You should take note of several things:

- You didn't have to use a form.
- The element that has an event attached to it is not what is normally considered a user interface element.
- The syntax for binding the event is surprisingly similar.

The last point is perhaps the most important. Microsoft has taken great pains to make Dynamic HTML as familiar as possible to frequent users of HTML.

Netscape had already defined a method for event handling for forms. When Microsoft decided to add the capability for any element on the page to bind events on the tag itself, they chose to use a standard, and a known way, to extend traditional event handling rather than coming up with their own proprietary way to do things.

Binding to Events

Binding a function to an event is just the standard Dynamic HTML way of referring to the process of assigning an event handler to a specific element for a specific event.

Although the method of binding event handlers to events on elements is quite natural, Dynamic HTML is actually quite flexible in the manner in which it enables you to bind events.

Part
II

Ch

7

Three ways to bind a function to an event are:

- Through elements
- Through the SCRIPT...FOR method
- Through VBScript special syntax

These techniques are covered in the sections that follow.

Binding Events via Elements

You've already learned about the process of binding event handling procedures to an element for a specific event in the "Event Handling in Action" section. All you need to do is assign the name of the event handler via the attribute that is associated with the event.

Suppose, for instance, you had an image that you wanted to fire an event handler called *imgClick()*, which is to be called whenever the mouse is clicked on the image. You would use the following syntax to do this:

```
<IMG SRC="image.gif" onclick="imgClick()">
```

When would this type of event handling be useful? If you were building an online music catalog, for example, you might want special information to be displayed when the user clicks the image of a CD.

What do you do, however, when you want to add more event handlers to an element? All you need to do is add another attribute containing the name of the event and the function to be called. Let's add an event handler called *imgUp()* that is called when the mouse button is released over the image:

```
<IMG SRC="image.gif" onclick="imgClick()"
                     onmousemove="imgUp()">
```

Binding Events via SCRIPT...FOR

Binding event handlers via element binding is the standard way to bind events. It also has many advantages. First, element binding uses a simple syntax. Second, and in many ways more importantly, it lets you see what events are bound to a specific element just by looking at the element on the page.

Why, then, should there be alternate ways to bind events? This is because binding event handlers via element binding is limited to languages that are built into the browser.

This may not seem important for most cases, and for simple Dynamic HTML it is not. If, however, you use Dynamic HTML to design world-class applications—as Microsoft has made clear they see as the future of Dynamic HTML—you may want to have events bound to other languages, such as Java. Also, the computer language in vogue always seems to change, so it's a good idea to have a method of binding events that doesn't make the assumption that either JavaScript or VBScript is being used.

Secondly, you can bind events to more than just HTML elements. In fact, if you remember the definitions from the beginning of the chapter, you can bind events to the document itself. This means that it is entirely possible that there might not be an HTML element to include the event name attribute and the handler to call.

It is for these reasons that the *SCRIPT...FOR* method of assigning events was created. This method enables events to be bound to page elements (and objects in the Dynamic HTML Object Model hierarchy, such as the *document* object) separate from the section of the HTML document where the code for handling these events is created. Start by using the previous image example from the "Binding Events via Elements" section, but without defining any events:

```
<IMG SRC="image.gif">
```

Now you want to assign an event handler to be called whenever the image is clicked, but you face a dilemma. How do you refer to this page element from somewhere else in the HTML document?

Obviously you need to have some way of assigning a name to the element. Such a method is the ID attribute.

The ID attribute enables you to give individual identification names to each element. It's quite easy to use: just add "id=" and then the ID that you want to give to the element. For this example, you want to give the <IMG> tag an ID of "myImg," and you can do so as follows:

```
<IMG ID="myIMG" SRC="image.gif">
```

You now have a way of referring to the element from anywhere on the page. Take a look at the syntax for the *SCRIPT...FOR* binding method:

```
<SCRIPT FOR=id EVENT="event_type" LANGUAGE="language"
    // Code to be executed when the event
    // is fired.
</SCRIPT>
```

Three important attributes are being set here. The first is the FOR attribute, which specifies the id of the element or object to which the event handler contained within the <SCRIPT> paired tag is being bound. It is important to remember to use the id of the element here ("myIMG") and not the name of the tag (<IMG>).

The second attribute being set is EVENT in which you specify the event to which you will be binding to the event handler. Although the same information is being given, specifying the event is a little trickier than using the binding to element method. With the EVENT attribute, the name of the event is treated as if it were a function, rather than an attribute. This means that when referring to the event in JavaScript, you should follow the name of the event with parentheses, enclosing any arguments that the event may take. For instance, handling a mouse click event using the SCRIPT...FOR method would be similar to:

```
<SCRIPT FOR="some_element" EVENT="onclick()" LANGUAGE="JAVASCRIPT">
//Code to handle the event
</SCRIPT>
```

Part

II

Ch

7

N O T E When specifying the the EVENT attribute it is important to note that JavaScript is case sensitive. Therefore, you need to list the events in all lowercase, otherwise the event handler will not be bound. VBScript does not have this limitation and you can capitalize however you want, such as *OnClick()*, *onClick()*, and so forth.

The third attribute that you need to set is the LANGUAGE attribute. This attribute specifies the name of the language that is being used with the event handler. In the case of Internet Explorer 4.0, the two scripting languages that will be used most often are JavaScript and VBScript.

The following code specifies the *SCRIPT...FOR* method of binding for the IMG that was defined previously:

```
<SCRIPT FOR=myImg EVENT="onclick()" LANGUAGE="JavaScript">
    // The same code that would have made up the function
    // imgClick() in the previous example of binding via
    // element.
</SCRIPT>
```

In general, it is probably a better idea to use the binding via element method over the *SCRIPT...FOR* method. In those cases where it is necessary to use *SCRIPT...FOR*, however, such as handling events in the document object that do not result from the user interacting with elements on the page, you should include a comment that says the code is binding to an element or object by its ID.

Binding Events via VBScript Special Syntax

Microsoft has done a good job throughout Dynamic HTML of making the procedures for doing things as language neutral as possible. One exception, however, is the VBScript special syntax for binding events. In addition to the standard methods of binding events, VBScript has a proprietary method called the VBScript Special Syntax.

The VBScript Special Syntax is similar to the *SCRIPT...FOR* method of binding, except that it is much simpler and not as much information needs to be supplied for it to handle an event.

The syntax is straightforward. You begin by specifying a SCRIPT block with a LANGUAGE attribute specifying VBScript. You then write the VBScript subprocedure that you want to define, using a special naming convention that binds the subprocedure to the element:

```
<SCRIPT LANGUAGE="VBScript"
    Sub elementID_eventType()
        ' The code for the event handler '
    End Sub
</SCRIPT>
```

It is important to note the way in which the subprocedure has been named. The first part of the name is the ID of the element for which you want to handle an event. Then comes an underscore character "_". Finally, the type of the event that you want to handle is listed, followed by parentheses and any arguments that the event might take.

To clear this up, take a look at a concrete example. The following example replicates the event binding of the last two examples (from "Binding Events via Elements" and "Binding Events via SCRIPT...FOR") with this new syntax:

```
<SCRIPT LANGUAGE="VBScript"
   Sub myIMG_onclick()
         ' The code for the event handler, equivalent to
         ' the script "onClick()" from the previous examples
   End Sub
</SCRIPT>
```

Seeing this code by itself in a Dynamic HTML page can be quite confusing if you're not aware of this syntax. Why? Because using this syntax is not necessary to specify the name of the event handler in either the element itself, or the SCRIPT element that surrounds the code. Instead, the event is bound automatically just by its name. JavaScript programmers that are used to binding explicitly may not be accustomed to automatic binding.

The special circumstance that is happening in VBScript special syntax is that by defining the subprocedure inside your script with a special name, that subprocedure is *automatically* bound to the event that corresponds to its name. How does this happen? The VBScript interpreter checks for function names of the form and goes ahead and does the binding work for you when the document is loaded.

N O T E The decision on whether to use the VBScript special syntax is an especially difficult one. It is undeniably convenient; however, this method works *only* in VBScript, which goes against the grain of the rest of the language-neutral Dynamic HTML philosophy.

The best advice is to follow your intuition. If you are a Visual Basic programmer, the *elementID_eventType()* method of specifying events will seem quite natural to you. If, however, you are not experienced with Visual Basic, it may take a little more time to understand the logic behind this syntax. In any case, if you do decide to use VBScript-specific syntax, make a point of commenting it so that other programmers, who may not be aware of the syntax, know what is going on. ▪

window.event Object

When events are passed in Dynamic HTML, not much information is passed along with them. For instance, the *keypress* event only informs you that a key has been pressed, but not the specific key that has been pressed.

Because this information is not passed directly, there has to be an alternative way of obtaining it. This, and much more information, is made available via the *event* object, which is a child of the *window* object in the Dynamic HTML Object Model that was discussed in the previous chapter. The *event* object can be accessed as an object contained by the *window* object (that is, window.event).

The *event* object has many properties that are useful for event handling situations where more information is needed. Many of the properties are useful only in certain situations. The *keyCode* property, for instance, would probably not be useful when you receive a mouse click event.

Although certain properties of the *window.event* object are not pertinent to some events, the *window.event* object is made available to all events. This is done to maintain consistency and to make sure your generic even handler never expects an object that does not exist. The *event* object consists of the following properties:

- *keyCode*
- *altKey*
- *ctrlKey*
- *shiftKey*
- *button*
- *cancelBubble*
- *fromElement*
- *returnValue*
- *srcElement*
- *toElement*
- *x*
- *y*

The following sections cover each of the event object's properties in greater detail.

keyCode Property

Although it is nice to know that a key has been pressed via the *keypress* event, sometimes it is important to know what key was pressed. The *keyCode* property gives you this information.

Suppose, for instance, that you were writing a game that took keyboard input. You might want to have the game perform a different action depending on which key was pressed. The *keyCode* property enables you to discern this information.

If a key has been pressed during an event, the *keyCode* property contains the value of that key as an integer. This integer value is the key's UNICODE keycode.

The values that are generated for keys vary from language to language. The codes for each language and a further discussion of UNICODE is available at **http://www.unicode.org**.

altKey Property

When an event is generated, the browser checks to see if the Alt key has been pressed. This information is then placed in the *altKey* property, which is a Boolean value set to true if the Alt key was pressed and false if it was not.

The altKey property can be used in a variety of ways. The first and most obvious way is to detect if an Alt+*Key* combination was pressed by the user (that is, detecting if the user hit Alt and X at the same time).

This property is also useful if you want to check to see if the Alt key has been pressed while another type of event has occurred. You might, for instance, want to do one action if just the mouse button is pushed, and another if the Alt key was being pressed when the mouse button was clicked. The *altKey* property enables you to check for these actions.

ctrlKey Property

The *ctrlKey* property is similar to the *altKey* property. The *ctrlKey* property contains a Boolean value that is true if the Ctrl key was held down during the event, or false if the Ctrl key was not held down during the event.

shiftKey Property

The *shiftKey* property is similar to the *altKey* and *ctrlKey* properties. The *shiftKey* property contains a Boolean value that is true if the Shift key was held down during the event, or false if the Shift key was not held down during the event.

button Property

When you receive an event that in some way indicates that the mouse has been clicked (*onmousedown*, *onmouseup*, and so on), you may know that a mouse button was clicked, but not which mouse button.

The *button* property enables you to retrieve the information regarding what mouse button was clicked. This is useful if you want to perform a different action, depending on which mouse button was pressed.

Assume, for example, that you wanted to create a user interface control that causes information to appear when the user clicks the left mouse button on the element and causes it to disappear when the user clicks the right mouse button on the element. The *button* property enables you to discern which button was pressed.

The *button* property contains a number that has one of four values that range from 0 to 3. The meanings of the values are as follows:

- **0**—No mouse button was pressed
- **1**—Only the left mouse button was pressed
- **2**—Only the right mouse button was pressed
- **3**—Both mouse buttons were pressed

Part

II

Ch

7

cancelBubble Property

All events in Dynamic HTML have the capability to "bubble" up through the element containment hierarchy until it finds an event handler. The *cancelBubble* property is a readable and writable property that enables you to set or read whether the event will continue to bubble up.

Don't worry about understanding what it means to "bubble" up through the containment hierarchy at this point. Event bubbling is covered in detail later in this chapter. For now, just be aware that events are not limited to the elements with which they occur.

fromElement Property

When moving the mouse pointer around over your window, the mouse pointer crosses over many different elements. The standard property for specifying which element the mouse last moved over before moving onto the one receiving the event is the *fromElement* property.

When a mouse-related event fires, you know that the mouse pointer has moved over the element that received the event. You do not know, however, what element the mouse pointer was last over before it moved over the element where it currently resides.

The *fromElement* property enables you to find out what element was passed over last by the mouse pointer. The value of the *fromElement* property contains the last element passed over as an *element* object (*element* objects are discussed in Chapter 6, "Dynamic HTML Object Model").

This property could be very useful in a wide variety of circumstances, most notably multimedia applications and games. Whether or not you see an obvious use for it currently, make a point of remembering the *fromElement* property because when it is needed, it will save you quite a bit of work.

returnValue Property

Sometimes you may want to return a value from an event. This can easily be done in JavaScript by assigning a return value to the event handler that you've defined. Then the caller of that event handler can decide whether or not to use or ignore the value that is returned.

Return values are useful for changing the default actions for elements. By changing the *returnValue* property to false for a HREF link, for example, the default action (going to the link specified by the HREF) would not be executed.

Unfortunately, some languages do not enable event notification via procedural routines. This is a problem, because Microsoft wants to keep Dynamic HTML as language neutral as possible. The solution was to enable return values in a property.

The *returnValue* property is a writable property that enables your event handler to dynamically set the value that is to be returned by setting the property. The *returnValue* property does not expect a certain type of data because you could expect to return almost any type of information to the *returnValue* property from your event handler.

srcElement **Property**

Event bubbling was mentioned previously in the description of the *cancelBubble* property. The *srcElement* property is also related to the bubbling of events throughout the containment hierarchy. Event bubbling is covered in further detail later in this chapter.

The *srcElement* property contains an object that is the HTML element that first received the event. For instance, the <BODY> may be getting this event. When the event handler for this event checks to see what element the event started on, the element might be an <IMG> buried deep within it.

This means that you can write event handlers that are "generic." You might want to hide any element that is on the page if it is clicked, for instance. The event handler in the <BODY> can use the *srcElement* property to find out what element was originally clicked and hide that element.

toElement **Property**

The *toElement* property is similar to the *fromElement* property. When the *mouseout* event fires, you know that the mouse pointer has left your element. You do not know, however, what element the mouse pointer then entered.

The *toElement* property enables you to find out what the next element the mouse pointer passed over is. The value of the *toElement* property contains that element as an *element* object.

You might use this property if you had an application where it was important to keep track of all the elements over which the mouse pointer passed. The event handlers for each object could then use the *toElement* property to communicate this information to each other.

x **Property**

When an event is fired, you may want to know what the current position of the mouse is at that time. The *x* property lets you find out this information.

The *x* property contains the x-position of the mouse at the time the event fires. This coordinate is calculated relative to the edge of the document and not relative to the edge of the screen. This means that you can treat your document as the coordinate space you have to work on without worrying where the browser is currently placed on the screen.

This property could be quite useful in a game program. You might want to move a ship to wherever the mouse pointer has moved to, for instance. This property provides you with the x-position where the mouse pointer currently resides.

y **Property**

Much like the *x* property, the *y* property lets you find out the y-position of the mouse at the time the event fires. This coordinate is also calculated relative to the edge of the document rather than relative the to the edge of the screen.

Part
II

Ch
7

Much like the *x* property, the *y* property could be quite useful in a game program. You might want to move a ship to wherever the mouse pointer has moved to, for instance. This property provides you with the y-position where the mouse pointer currently resides.

Overriding Default Event Handling

The capability for your scripts to handle events on HTML objects is a relatively new capability in web browsers, but event handling in general has been going on behind the scenes in browsers since they were first developed.

A straightforward example of event handling going on in browsers is what happens when you click an anchor (<A>) link in. The browser records that the user has clicked on the anchor element, fires a mouse click event on that element, and then checks to see if it has a default action to perform for a click on the anchor element. In the case of the <A> tag, the browser knows to go to the URL specified by the tag.

You've already seen how you can use event handling to do this sort of thing with whatever elements on your page that you want; however, Dynamic HTML also enables you to override the default behavior of tags that have built-in event handling mechanisms.

Overriding default behavior is actually quite simple. It only requires that you make sure to do two things:

> Provide an event handler for the event that triggers the default behavior (for example, *onclick* for clicking an anchor).
>
> Set the *window.event.returnValue* to false.

By fulfilling these two requirements, the default action is cancelled, and whatever code you place in the event handler is executed instead. The first requirement is pretty straightforward. Because you are overriding the behavior for a certain action, it makes sense that you would want to write an event handler for that event.

The second requirement is a little more subtle. To make the browser not perform the default action for the element for that event, you have to inform the browser not to take the action, or else it performs both actions. The signal to the browser to not perform the default behavior is setting the *returnValue* property of the *window.event* object to false.

The following syntax uses this technique to disable the capability for a user to click an anchor link:

```
<HTML>
<BODY>
<A id=myAnchor onclick="aClicked()"
   HREF="http://yourmachine.com"
   onclick="aClicked()">
Your Machine
</A>
```

```
<SCRIPT LANGUAGE="JavaScript">
function aClicked() {
    window.event.returnValue = false;
}
</SCRIPT>
</BODY>
</HTML>
```

When this code is loaded into Internet Explorer, the anchor link looks like a normal link. It is underlined (unless you've turned link underlining off), it uses the link colors, and so on. However, when you click it, it does nothing.

The important line to pay attention to in this example is:

```
window.event.returnValue = false;
```

This line sets the *returnValue* property of the *window.event object* to false. As mentioned previously, setting this to false causes the browser to forgo the default action it would have otherwise taken, which in this case would have been to follow the link.

In this example you didn't have the event handler do anything but cancel the default behavior. You could, however, easily add additional code to the event handler to provide your own behavior.

Providing at least some sort of event instead of the default action is probably a good idea, because users generally find it disconcerting if interface elements that they are accustomed to functioning in a certain manner stop working. For instance, using the previous example, many users would assume the browser had stopped working and restart it. Even if all you want to do is disable the behavior, try to provide some sort of information (perhaps in an alert box, or in the status bar) that mentions that this element has been disabled.

Overriding default actions for elements can create confusion, but it can also be quite powerful. Suppose, for instance, that you were designing a kiosk application. You may want to only allow links to be followed if the user has identified himself or if a password has been supplied. By overriding default actions for an anchor link, you can check for this verification before allowing the link to be followed.

Event Bubbling

So far, all the event handling covered has focused on receiving events for individual elements. Most of the time, event handling individual elements is more than sufficient.

For those times when handling events for individual elements isn't sufficient, Dynamic HTML has the capability to bubble events up the HTML containment hierarchy. First, let's define what is meant by the containment hierarchy. The following HTML code is an example:

```
<HTML>
<BODY>
    <DIV id=myGroup>
        <H1>The Image</H1>
```

Part

II

Ch

7

```
      <IMG src="image.gif">
   </DIV>
</BODY>
</HTML>
```

The containment hierarchy is defined simply by what is contained within each other. If you examine the preceding HTML code and pay attention to where tags begin and end, you'll notice that the <HTML> tag surrounds every other tag.

The next most inner tag, the <BODY> tag, surrounds the <DIV> tag. Finally, the <DIV> tag surrounds the <IMG> and the <H1> elements. This containment hierarchy is shown in figure 7.4.

FIG. 7.4

Examining event bubbling.

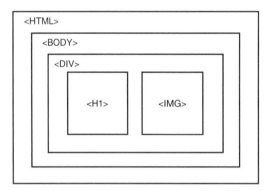

Event bubbling is the process of traversing up this containment hierarchy, starting at the element that receives the event. Suppose you click the <H1> tag in the example. The browser then performs the following actions:

1. Checks to see if the <H1> element has an event handler for the *onclick* event type. If so, executes it.

2. Checks to see if the <H1> element's parent, the <DIV> element, has an event handler for this event type. If so, executes it.

3. Checks to see if the <DIV> element's parent, the <BODY> element, has an event handler for this event type. If so, executes it.

4. Checks to see if the <BODY> element's parent, the document object, has an event handler for this event type. If so, executes it.

The judicious use of event bubbling can make your programming life much easier, because it frees you from having to bind event handlers for every individual element.

Assume, for instance, that you want to have the JavaScript function *doUpdate()* called anytime the <IMG> or <H1> elements in the previous example are clicked. To do this without event bubbling requires you to bind each of them as follows:

```
<h1 onclick="doUpdate()">The Image</h1>
<img src="image.gif" onclick="doUpdate()">
```

Because these two elements fall hierarchically within a <DIV> paired tag, however, and you know that events bubble up the containment hierarchy, you can instead place the event binding in the DIV tag as follows:

```
<div id=myGroup onclick="doUpdate()">
  <h1>The Image</h1>
  <img src="image.gif">
</div>
```

Now, when the user clicks on the <H1> element or the <IMG> element, the browser checks to see if they have *onclick* event handlers. They do not.

However, next the browser checks to see if the parent of the <H1> and <IMG> elements has the event handler. It does, so the browser then executes the <DIV> element's *onclick* handler to handle the <H1> and <IMG> element events. This provides the same behavior as binding to each individual element, without using nearly as much code.

The savings in code and complexity in this example is relatively minimal. Event bubbling, however, can be a huge time saver with an event-rich document. Imagine having several hundred elements that you want to use similar event handlers for and having to assign event handlers individually for all them.

Discovering Where the Event Bubbling Started

Because event bubbling traverses all the way up the hierarchy, quite a few event handlers may end up being called. If you are writing an event handler for high up in the hierarchy, it may sometimes be advantageous to know where the event bubbling started.

The *window.event.srcElement* property enables you to find out this information. When you receive an event that has been bubbled, the *srcElement* property contains the HTML element that first received the event before it started to bubble.

Canceling Event Bubbling

Dynamic HTML bubbles events to the top of the containment hierarchy by default, so even if the event is handled at the element level, it still makes it all the way up to the document object.

This may sound confusing, so consider how event bubbling works in the initial event bubbling example. The event handling always starts at the element where the event occurs, so if you clicked the H1 element, it would fire an *onclick* event for the <H1> element. It would then fire the *onclick* event for the <DIV> element that surrounds the <H1> element. What if you only wanted the event to be delivered to the <H1> element and not to the <DIV> element? Canceling event bubbling enables you to do this.

Normally, it makes sense to let Dynamic HTML use this default behavior. You may find an instance, however, where you want to stop event bubbling at a specific point in the hierarchy. Dynamic HTML enables you to do this with the *window.event.cancelBubble* property.

Part

II

Ch

7

The proper way to use the *cancelBubble* property is to bind an event handler at the point in the hierarchy that you want the event bubbling to stop. Then, in the event handler, set the *window.event.cancelBubble* property to true.

The following syntax adds this behavior to the previous example, and causes the event bubbling to stop at the <DIV> element. First, here is the <DIV> element itself:

```
<DIV id=myGroup onclick="doUpdate()">
  <H1>The Image</H1>
  <IMG SRC="image.gif">
</DIV>
```

Now you want to cancel bubbling in the *doUpdate()* function. This causes events to cease bubbling after the <DIV> element:

```
<HTML>
<BODY>
<SCRIPT LANGUAGE="JavaScript">

function doUpdate() {
   window.event.cancelBubble = true;
}

</SCRIPT>
<DIV id=myGroup onclick="doUpdate()">
  <H1>The Image</H1>
  <IMG SRC="image.gif">
</DIV>

</BODY>
</HTML>
```

By canceling event bubbling in the <DIV> element, you are guaranteeing that the only event handlers that will be called if a user clicks inside of the <DIV> element are the event handler for the <DIV> and the event handler for any element that is nested inside of it. Therefore, you can now write event handlers for the <BODY> element knowing that they will never be called for the <DIV> element that has canceled event bubbling.

From Here...

The discussion on event handling in Dynamic HTML is the end of the Dynamic HTML foundations section of this book. Although the material that has been presented in this chapter has certainly been interesting, the truly exciting material is yet to come.

The next part, "Inside Dynamic HTML," covers the truly dynamic portion of Dynamic HTML by changing the style and content of the document on the fly. Like many topics, however, learning the foundations first will make learning the exciting material easier. The chapters in this section consist of the following:

   ▪ Chapter 8, "Dynamic Styles"—The dynamic styles chapter will show you how to change the CSS style of any HTML element on the page on the fly.

- Chapter 9, "Layout and Positioning"—The layout and positioning chapter will give you the capability to specify exactly where on the page you want elements to be placed.
- Chapter 10, "Dynamic Content"—The dynamic content chapter will show how Dynamic HTML can be used to actually change HTML elements and the contents of those HTML elements on the fly.

Part

II

Ch

7

Inside Dynamic HTML

Dynamic Styles

With a background in scripting (either JavaScript or VBScript) and a familiarity with Cascading Style Sheets, you are ready to begin using the features of Dynamic HTML. It might seem that the previous chapters have discussed many different technologies, but have side-stepped addressing Dynamic HTML directly. That perception might be somewhat accurate; however, Dynamic HTML is not just one technology. Without the Dynamic HTML Object Model, event handling, scripting, and style sheets, Dynamic HTML would not exist.

This chapter covers the implementation of the collection of Dynamic HTML features known as *dynamic styles*. Dynamic styles are just as the name would imply, dynamically changing the characteristics of style elements on the page, as opposed to the characteristic changes provided by static HTML.

Changing the style of fonts on a page, for example, is a dynamic style. Of course, you can use Cascading Style Sheets to change the style of a font on the web page; however, if you want to change the style of the font *after* the page has loaded, you will need to make use of Dynamic HTML. This chapter covers the basics of font manipulation, hiding and showing elements, and positioning. Then you will be ready to apply those skills to more advanced concepts in later chapters. ■

Changing Font Attributes

Dynamic HTML provides mechanisms that enable you to alter the attributes of the fonts on your web page, including the font family, font style, and font color.

Hiding and Showing Elements

Dynamic HTML enables you to display or hide elements based on layering and in conjunction with mouse events.

CSS Positioning

By incorporating the Cascading Style Sheets Positioning specification, Dynamic HTML enables absolute positioning, relative positioning, and the capability to specify many layout attributes, including Z-indexing.

Changing Font Attributes

One of the simplest ways you can add dynamic content to your web pages is through the use of Dynamic Fonts. You can use Dynamic Fonts to provide a host of different effects for your pages, ranging from links that change color as you pass over them to fonts that switch styles or grow in size as the mouse pointer passes over them. Follow along with this section and discover some of the basics of manipulating fonts by dynamically changing font attributes.

Changing Font Styles

Establishing a dynamic style starts with the *style* object. The *font* property belongs to the *style* object and has the following values: size and face. The elements used in the examples in this section inherit their properties in the following manner:

```
Style  —> Font  —> size, face
```

What does this mean in terms of specifying attributes? Well, in JavaScript you would use the following syntax to specify the element that you are going to alter:

```
mytext.style.color
```

In this example, *mytext* corresponds to the ID of the element you were specifying, *style* refers to the object, and *color* refers to the value.

The first task when changing an attribute is to define the new value in a JavaScript function, as in the following:

```
function mytext_onmouseover() {
    mytext.face = "serif";
}
```

This block of code specifies a function called "*mytext_onmouseover()*", which sets the "*face*" value for the "*mytext*" element equal to "*serif*".

The code used to produce the effect of flipping between a serif and sans-serif font as the mouse passes over it is shown in listing 8.1.

Listing 8.1   Altering the Font Style Value with Dynamic HTML

```
01.    <HTML>
02.    <HEAD>
03.    <TITLE>Changing the Font Family</TITLE>
04.    </HEAD>
05.
06.    <SCRIPT LANGUAGE="JavaScript">
07.
08.    function mytext_onmouseover() {
09.        mytext.style.fontFamily = "serif";
10.    }
11.
```

```
12.    function mytext_onmouseout() {
13.        mytext.style.fontFamily = "sans-serif";
14.    }
15.
16.    </SCRIPT>
17.
18.    <DIV id=mytext  style="font-family: serif;font-size: 16pt"
19.    onmouseover="mytext_onmouseover()"
20.    onmouseout="mytext_onmouseout()">
21.    Flipping between serif and sans-serif faces.
22.    </DIV>
23.
24.    </BODY>
25.    </HTML>
```

Figure 8.1 shows the results of the final Dynamic HTML code demonstrated in listing 8.1.

FIG. 8.1

Using Dynamic HTML to alter the font-family based on a mouse event.

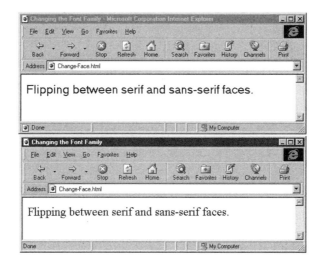

There is nothing particularly special about the appearance of the code, but what makes it different and dynamic is that the Dynamic HTML Object Model exposes the element in the styles used on the page, which means that style settings can be manipulated with a scripting language. Two simple functions define the fontFamily value, one with *onmouseover()* and one with *onmouseout()*. If you recall from Chapter 7, "Event Handling," when mouse events used to trigger the change are detected by the element, they call the functions specified by lines 8–14:

```
onmouseover="mytext_onmouseover()"
onmouseout="mytext_onmouseout()">
```

Executing these functions changes the fontFamily value to produce the style change in the font face that is possible with Dynamic HTML!

Changing Font Sizes

Changing the font face can be a very useful tool for designers, enabling them to match the face to a logo, for example. With dynamic styles, however, you can use a method similar to the one used to alter font style to dynamically manipulate the font size of text elements on your pages. This can be used to create "growing" or animated text, or highlight key words or phrases in a document.

In the following listing, the JavaScript functions are used to manipulate the *size* property when the mouse moves over and off the element, resulting in growing and shrinking text. The code in listing 8.2 will produce the results shown in figure 8.2.

Listing 8.2   Altering the Font Size Value with Dynamic HTML

```
01. <HTML>
02. <HEAD>
03. <TITLE>Font SizeChanges</TITLE>
04. </HEAD>
05.
06. <SCRIPT LANGUAGE="JavaScript">
07.
08. function mytext_onmouseover() {
09.         mytext.style.fontSize = "5";
10. }
11.
12. function mytext_onmouseout() {
13.         mytext.style.fontSize = "2";
14. }
15. </SCRIPT>
16.
17. <DIV id=mytext STYLE="font-size=2; color=blue;font-family=sans-serif"
18. onmouseover="mytext_onmouseover();"
19. onmouseout="mytext_onmouseout();">
20. This is a Dynamic Size Change!
21. </DIV>
22.
23. </BODY>
24. </HTML>
```

In listing 8.2, the functions shown in lines 8–14 are used to alter the fontSize property defined in line 17. These functions are called when the users pass their mouse pointer over the text on the screen, causing the font size to increase as demonstrated in figure 8.2.

FIG. 8.2
Using Dynamic HTML
to alter the size of
fonts.

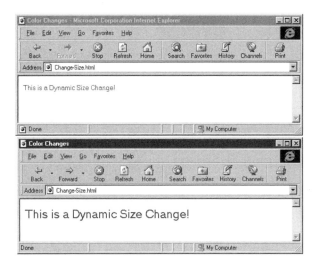

Changing Font Colors

You can also change the *color* attribute using the same technique used for the *style* and *size* attributes. Because *color* is also a value of the *font* property, it can be manipulated by JavaScript as well. The benefit of this is that you can use the font color to accent areas of your pages and links, or to draw attention to important words or phrases. The code in listing 8.3 results in text that changes color with mouse events.

Listing 8.3   Manipulating Color Schemes with Dynamic HTML

```
01.    <HTML>
02.    <HEAD>
03.    <TITLE>Color Changes</TITLE>
04.    </HEAD>
05.
06.    <SCRIPT LANGUAGE="JavaScript">
07.
08.    function mytext_onmouseover() {
09.         mytext.style.color = "red";
10.    }
11.
12.    function mytext_onmouseout() {
13.         mytext.style.color = "blue";
14.     }
15.
16.     </SCRIPT>
17.
18.    <H2 id="mytext" style="color: blue; font-family: sans-serif"
19.    onmouseover="mytext_onmouseover();"
20.    onmouseout="mytext_onmouseout();">
21.    This is a Dynamic Color Change!</H2>
22.
23.
24.    </BODY>
25.    </HTML>
```

Figure 8.3 represents the output from listing 8.3. Although the figure is in black and white, you can get the general idea.

FIG. 8.3
The color of the font changes as the mouse passes over the text.

The event handles in lines 19 and 20 in listing 8.3 are used to call the functions you have defined to change the color of your font when the mouse passes over the text. The functions, as defined in lines 8–14, then modify the color *style* property to achieve the effect of changing the color of the text, as shown in figure 8.3.

As you can see, altering the properties and values of HTML elements with Dynamic HTML does not have to be complicated; however, this does not mean that it cannot be powerful. In fact, the capability to directly access objects on a page after load time is a very powerful feature. As you explore Dynamic HTML further in the ensuing chapters, you will learn that the same techniques that enable you to change the color of fonts also enable you to use complex ActiveX Multimedia Controls and incorporate live data into your site.

These text effects can be used to create some complex user interfaces, such as a dynamic table of contents for a site. Other important techniques also exist that can be used with dynamic styles, such as the capability to show and hide elements on the page. When combining dynamic styles with these text effects, you can create complex interfaces, such as expanding outlines that feature color changes and other effects to highlight text.

Hiding and Showing Elements

The capability to selectively hide and reveal elements on your pages is an essential part of Dynamic HTML. With the capability to selectively choose which site elements are revealed and when they are revealed to your audience, you can create new user interfaces and user interactions with your site that were not possible before Dynamic HTML.

You could hide text elements on your page, and only reveal them when users passed their mouse pointer over a specific area on the page, to create a "treasure hunt," for example. Using the same functionality, you could keep some resources more private.

More importantly, you could use this technique to hide information that wasn't necessary to the user and that cluttered the user interface. If you had a bulleted list, for example, and you wanted to conserve space, only expanding the list with user interation, you could hide the expanded text under normal circumstances. When users pass their mouse pointers over a point they are interested in, the expanded text displays on the screen.

By selecting which elements the user has access to and when, you can create a whole user experience that is dependent on how the information on your site is revealed. To accomplish this Dynamic HTML makes use of the CSS Positioning property for *"visibility"* and enables you to link the visibility of elements to mouse input from the user. This enables you to hide and reveal elements on a page based on what the user is doing, a great way to build user interfaces and interactivity!

Visibility

Hiding and showing elements with Dynamic HTML is a function of the *visibility* property. With this property, you can specify whether or not an element is "visible" or "hidden." If the element is selected to be visible, it appears on the page with the other elements, and if it is hidden, the element will not be drawn at all. Do not operate under the assumption that hiding elements reduces your download time because hidden elements are still downloaded to the page; they just have not been rendered to your screen. Until you perform some task that is designed to change that attribute, the elements will remain hidden.

Revealing Information Based on Mouse Events

Hiding and showing elements is another straightforward feature of Dynamic HTML. Like other specifications, what makes the feature special and dynamic is that objects can be set to visible or hidden even after the page has loaded. In fact, the elements can be configured to alter their styles based on user interaction.

Take a look at the following JavaScript function, for example:

```
function picture_onmouseover() {

        picture.style.visibility = "hidden";
    }
```

This function specifies that if the mouse enters its element (*picture*), the element identified as *picture* will have the visibility value set to hidden, causing it to disappear.

Although you might want to make objects and elements disappear on a timing control, a majority of the time you will want to set the attribute based on mouse events, such as *onmouseover()*, *onmouseout()*, *onmouseclick()*, and so on, just as you would with text effects, such as modifying a font's size and color.

With this in mind, take a look at a page that draws some text and an image, and then hides the image based on the *onmouseover()* event when the user passes the mouse pointer over the text. The code for this interaction is shown in listing 8.4.

Listing 8.4 Hiding an Image Based on *onmouseover()* Events

```
01. <HTML>
02. <HEAD>
03. <TITLE>Color Changes</TITLE>
04. </HEAD>
05. <BODY>
06. <SCRIPT LANGUAGE="JavaScript">
07.
08. function picture_onmouseover() {
09.     picture.style.visibility = "hidden";
10.     }
11.
12. function picture_onmouseout() {
13.     picture.style.visibility = "visible";
14.     }
15.
16. </SCRIPT>
17.
18.
19. <DIV STYLE="color=blue; font-family=sans-serif;"
20. onmouseover="picture_onmouseover();"
21. onmouseout="picture_onmouseout();">
22. Pass over the text, and watch me disappear!
23. </DIV>
24. <P>
25. <IMG ID=picture src="picture.gif"  visibility="visible">
26.
27. </BODY>
28. </HTML>
```

Figure 8.4 shows the end result of a user interacting with the appearing/disappearing image as specified in listing 8.4.

As you can see, this code is similar to the code used to manipulate text with mouse events. There are two JavaScript functions defined in lines 8–14 to hide and display the element in question. The image in line 25 has the visibility property set to visible, and when the proper mouse event is handled in lines 19–23, the appropriate images are shown or hidden by altering the visibility property.

Designing a Hide and Display Peek-A-Boo Game

As you can see, hiding and showing elements is not a difficult task. The only difficult aspect is coordinating the display of multiple images and such. To follow up on the concepts you've learned so far, follow along with the design of a Dynamic HTML Peek-A-Boo game. In this game, both images are displayed when the page loads, but as the user passes the mouse pointer over the first image, the second image disappears and vice versa. It is not a complicated game, but it does deal with the issues of coordinating multiple elements, and it introduces a new tag—the <DIV> tag.

FIG. 8.4

Hiding the picture based on an *onmouseover()* event and the accompanying text.

The <DIV> Tag   This example introduces a new tag that can be used with CSS and Dynamic HTML called the <DIV> (division) tag. This tag provides a mechanism for grouping style properties together for elements that might not have them in common, or for elements to which you might want to apply JavaScript functions.

Here's one way you might use the <DIV> tag:

```
<DIV id=example STYLE="position:absolute; left:10%; top:30%; z-index: 1;
visibility:hidden; font-size: 7; color=green">
What a great tag
</DIV>
```

In this example, the <DIV> tag specifies several properties that will be inherited by nested elements, such as the text, if the style is inheritable. With the <DIV>'s ID attribute, you can use scripting to manipulate the tag's styles, which can be inherited by any nested elements, such as text. Although the tag is commonly known as the division tag, it can be used to group elements together so that properties can be applied to the elements as a group rather than as individual elements. This can dramatically reduce the amount of scripting necessary to manipulate the elements, and also provides you with a more convenient mechanism for specifying the elements that contain properties you want to manipulate.

Coding the Peek-A-Boo Game   The Peek-A-Boo game consists of five parts: three nearly identical JavaScript functions and two similar <DIV> tags.

When the page first loads, both of the images are displayed normally, and they simply wait for the user to pass the mouse pointer over one of the images. The code snippets from the final listing that follow for listing 8.5 are numbered according to their placement within the final syntax for the Peek-A-Boo game.

Each of the <DIV> tags specifies one of the "areas" on the page, which consists of a line of text and an image:

```
31. <DIV onmouseover="peek_onmouseover();"
32. onmouseout="everyone_onmouseout();">
33. <FONT id=mytext color=blue face=sans-serif>
34. Peek-A-Boo!
35. </FONT>
36. <P>
37. <img id=picture src="picture.gif">
38. </DIV>
```

This preceding syntax uses the <DIV> tag to treat both the line of text and the images in the same way for mouse events. Grouping all the elements together into the paired <DIV> tag, and then specifying the mouse event results for the <DIV> tag itself rather than for each separate element, preserves a great deal of space and time.

In addition to the grouping of the elements, a series of three functions are created to perform nearly identical tasks, as shown in the following syntax:

```
08. function peek_onmouseover() {
09.
10.     mytext.style.visibility = "visible";
11.     picture.style.visibility = "visible";
12.     cattext.style.visibility = "hidden";
13.     kitty.style.visibility = "hidden";
14. }
```

Each of the functions is designed to show or hide a combination of the images and text. The first function, *onmouseover()*, is set to display the top image while hiding the bottom image when the mouse pointer is over the elements. Another function, *aboo_onmouseover()* (appearing in lines 23–28 in listing 8.5), reverses this procedure for the bottom image, completing the "peek" and "boo" sections of the game.

If the mouse is not over either picture, however, all the images on the page should be displayed. Here, the elements can share one function, *onmouseout()*, that shows all the images on the page:

```
16. function everyone_onmouseout() {
17.     mytext.style.visibility = "visible";
18.     picture.style.visibility = "visible";
19.     cattext.style.visibility = "visible";
20.     kitty.style.visibility = "visible";
21. }
```

That's all there is to it! Listing 8.5 shows the code for the final assembled product.

Listing 8.5   The Dynamic HTML for the Peek-A-Boo Page

```
01. <HTML>
02. <HEAD>
03. <TITLE>Peek-a-Boo</TITLE>
04. </HEAD>
05. <BODY>
06. <SCRIPT LANGUAGE="JavaScript">
07.
08. function peek_onmouseover() {
09.
10.     mytext.style.visibility = "visible";
11.     picture.style.visibility = "visible";
12.     cattext.style.visibility = "hidden";
13.     kitty.style.visibility = "hidden";
14. }
15.
16. function everyone_onmouseout() {
17.     mytext.style.visibility = "visible";
18.     picture.style.visibility = "visible";
19.     cattext.style.visibility = "visible";
20.     kitty.style.visibility = "visible";
21. }
22.
23. function aboo_onmouseover() {
24.     mytext.style.visibility = "hidden";
25.     picture.style.visibility = "hidden";
26.     cattext.style.visibility = "visible";
27.     kitty.style.visibility = "visible";
28. }
29. </SCRIPT>
30.
31. <DIV STYLE="visibility: visible" onmouseover="peek_onmouseover();"
32. onmouseout="everyone_onmouseout();">
33. <FONT id=mytext color=blue face=sans-serif>
34. Peek-A-Boo!
35. </FONT>
36. <P>
37. <img id=picture src="picture.gif">
38. </DIV>
39.
40.
41. <DIV STYLE="visibility: visible" onmouseover="aboo_onmouseover();"
42. onmouseout="everyone_onmouseout();">
43. <FONT id=cattext color=blue face=sans-serif>
44. I see you!
45. </FONT>
46. <P>
47. <img id=kitty src="kitty.gif">
48. </DIV>
49.
50. </BODY>
51. </HTML>
```

Figure 8.5 shows the screen appearance for the Peek-A-Boo example described in this section.

FIG. 8.5

The Peek-A-Boo game deals with hiding multiple elements.

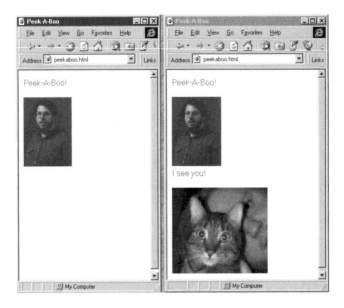

Collapsible Outlines

Now you can see how to use Dynamic HTML to manipulate HTML objects on the page by using scripting languages and style sheet specifications. This is the power of Dynamic HTML—the capability to alter objects on the page. This is really a result of the Dynamic HTML Object Model, which exposes HTML elements so that they can be manipulated.

Now you have seen how you can change the style properties of various elements using scripting languages. You've seen how you can alter the font properties of an element, or how you can show or hide elements based on user interaction. You should also be a little more familiar with how you can use mouse events so that they control how your changes are implemented.

There are a number of different effects that you can create on your pages by combining these techniques. One effect that you might feel has fantastic practical applications is a collapsible outline.

The concept of a "collapsible" outline is probably one you are very familiar with already. For example, Windows Explorer uses a variation of a collapsible outline to display the items on your computer when you explore your hard drive.

As another example you could have a table of contents for your site that lists the areas on the site, down to the individual pages as shown in figure 8.6.

FIG. 8.6

A typical web site table of contents.

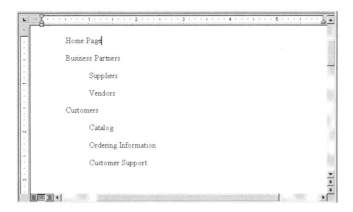

This type of outline view might be a useful navigation tool, but for large sites, it could quickly become so large that its usefulness would be limited. One way to avoid this pitfall is to display only the major headers on the page and hide the other information until the user clicks a header of his or her choice. Using this setup, customers wouldn't have to scroll through pages that were indexed for Business Partners just to get to a customer service page. To follow up on this scenario, take a look at what is involved in constructing a collapsible outline with Dynamic HTML.

First, you will need to decide how you want your outline to function. You could make the elements expand as the mouse passes over elements, but that might be quite busy and confusing for users. For purposes here, the following example uses the *onclick* and *ondblclick* events, so that users can click an element to expand it, and double-click an element to hide it.

The following syntax contains the function that shows the elements when the user clicks a header (the actual elements that call these functions will be shown later):

```
09. function showone() {
10. if (LevelOneItem.style.visibility="hidden")
11. LevelOneItem.style.visibility="visible";
12. }
```

The *showone()* function itself is very straightforward. It simply checks to see if the element is already hidden, and if it is, displays the element by setting the visibility value to "visible." To hide the element, you can use the same function with the attributes reversed.

Next, you need to specify the text elements that are going to appear in the outline, name them, and set the style attributes for how the text will appear. This is a perfect application for the <DIV> tag because you want to combine several different properties so that you can treat them as one single entity. The final code does more with less:

```
45. <DIV id="LevelOneItem" STYLE="visibility: hidden; margin:10px
➡font-family: sans-serif; font-size: 3" onclick="showtwo()"
➡ondblclick="hidetwo()">
46. This is a first level item.</DIV>
```

This block of HTML establishes the ID for the Level One item (so you can refer to the ID later), and then sets *STYLE* properties that will affect its appearance, such as the font styles and the margin indent. You will also notice that it contains the two events *onclick* and *ondblclick*, which are used to modify the *next* element. This is important because clicking the current header reveals what is under it. Clicking one element, in this case a header, actually triggers a change in the properties of the next element in our outline.

That's really all there is to it—rinse-lather-repeat. You need to create the outline items and repeat the *show()* and *hide()* functions for each outline item. The code used to produce a three level sample outline is shown in listing 8.6.

Listing 8.6   A Collapsible Outline Example

```
01. <HTML>
02. <HEAD>
03. <TITLE>Outline Example</TITLE>
04. </HEAD>
05. <BODY>
06.
07. <SCRIPT LANGUAGE="JavaScript">
08.
09. function showone() {
10. if (LevelOneItem.style.visibility="hidden")
11. LevelOneItem.style.visibility="visible";
12. }
13.
14. function hideone() {
15. if (LevelOneItem.style.visibility="visible")
16.         LevelOneItem.style.visibility="hidden";
17. }
18.
19. function showtwo() {
20. if (LevelTwoItem.style.visibility="hidden")
21.     LevelTwoItem.style.visibility="visible";
22. }
23.
24. function hidetwo() {
25. if (LevelTwoItem.style.visibility="visible")
26.         LevelTwoItem.style.visibility="hidden";
27. }
28.
29. function showthree() {
30. if (LevelThreeItem.style.visibility="hidden")
31.     LevelThreeItem.style.visibility="visible";
32. }
33.
34. function hidethree() {
35. if (LevelThreeItem.style.visibility="visible")
36.         LevelThreeItem.style.visibility="hidden";
37. }
38.
39. </SCRIPT>
```

```
40.
41. <DIV id="Title" onclick="showone()" ondblclick="hideone()">
42. <FONT FACE=sans-serif SIZE=4>The Title Is Clickable</FONT>
43. </DIV>
44.
45. <DIV id="LevelOneItem" STYLE="visibility: hidden; margin:10px"
➥onclick="showtwo()" ondblclick="hidetwo()">
46. <FONT FACE=sans-serif SIZE=3>This is a first level item.</FONT>
47.
48. <DIV id="LevelTwoItem" STYLE="visibility: hidden; margin:20"
➥onclick="showthree()" ondblclick="hidethree()">
49. <FONT FACE=sans-serif SIZE=2>
50. This is a second level item.
51. </FONT>
52.
53. <DIV id="LevelThreeItem" STYLE="visibility: hidden; list-style: disc">
54. <FONT FACE=sans-serif SIZE=1>
55. This is a tiny little item
56. </FONT>
57.
58. </DIV>
59. </DIV>
60. </DIV>
61.
62. </BODY>
63. </HTML>
```

Figure 8.7 represents the final output for this listing.

FIG. 8.7
Dynamic HTML can be used to create text effects such as collapsible outlines.

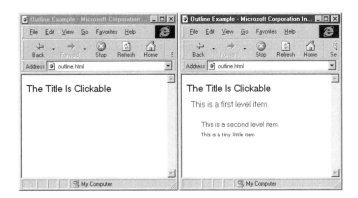

CSS Positioning

Before you learn how to position and manipulate elements with Dynamic HTML, it is important to understand the technology behind Cascading Style Sheets Positioning. This is the technology that Dynamic HTML positioning and layout is based on; to position elements with Dynamic HTML, you need to utilize it.

If you recall from Chapter 4, "Cascading Style Sheets Primer," the Cascading Style Sheets specification enables you to change the style characteristics for HTML elements to provide finer control over HTML page design. Dynamic HTML relies on CSS as the mechanism for changing styles, but it also relies on CSS Positioning to control the layout of elements on your web pages.

Cascading Style Sheets Positioning is not actually a portion of the original CSS specification. This means that not all browsers that support CSS will support positioning, nor is positioning bound to change if and when CSS does. CSS and CSS Positioning technologies are so closely related, however, that it is not likely to cause you a great deal of trouble if you decide to use CSS Positioning. How closely are the two related? Well, in previous examples in this chapter, you learned how to use the *visibility* property, which as fate would have it, is part of the CSS Positioning specification. So there you are, you were already using a CSS Positioning property without having to learn a new syntax. The sections that follow provide information about the intricacies of CSS Positioning and how to control the position of elements on your pages to enhance your presentation.

Position

When your web page is rendered in a browser window, the browser reads the elements in order and positions them in the window in the same order that they are specified in your document. You can use the <P> and <BR> tags to force new paragraphs to control layout and flow, or you can build complicated tables to try to create a layout. Neither of the solutions are very eloquent, nor graceful. The Position element enables you to specify the location of elements on your page, relative to the size of the browser window. There are three methods for establishing position: static positioning, absolute positioning, and relative positioning. Because static positioning is the same method of positioning that browsers use to render straight HTML pages, it won't be discussed here. Absolute and relative positioning are the methods of positioning of interest for the purposes of this chapter.

Absolute Positioning   Absolute positioning enables you to define a "container" on your web page into which you can place elements. Figure 8.8 shows how the page relates to the browser window:

FIGURE 8.8

Absolute positioning creates a container for HTML elements.

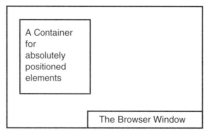

A Container for absolutely positioned elements

The Browser Window

By creating a smaller container, or canvas, on the page, designers can control how elements are established on the page. For example, listing 8.7 creates a column of text using absolute positioning:

Listing 8.7 Creating a Column of Text with Absolute Positioning

```
01. <HTML>
02. <HEAD>
03. <TITLE>Positioning</TITLE>
04. </HEAD>
05. <BODY>
06.
07.
08. <DIV id=AbPosition STYLE="position:absolute;left:10%;width:25%;top:10%">
09.
10. This is a paragraph of text that has been formatted with absolute
➥positioning.
11. </DIV>
12. <P>
13. </BODY>
14. </HTML>
```

The previous example uses the *STYLE* property to establish "*position:absolute*", which creates a container for the objects placed within the <DIV> element. You will also notice some other values: left, width, and top. These are the positioning values that specify where the container is located on the page. In this case, the absolute container location is defined as inset from the top and left, and only one fourth the width of the window. The result of this positioning example in listing 8.7 is shown in figure 8.9.

FIG. 8.9

Absolute positioning used to create columns in layout.

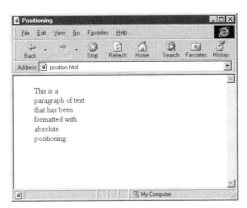

Relative Positioning   Relative positioning works similar to absolute positioning. You still need to define a style, and then create a container in which to place your elements. The key difference is that relative positioning enables you to move the container. That is, you create a position container with "*position:relative*" and then define the size of the container.

One of the other key differences between absolute and relative positioning is that elements defined with relative positioning can be altered with the scripting language. This enables the animation or movement of elements on the page, simply by altering the Position element. This type of animation is discussed more in Chapter 13, "Introducing Multimedia."

Float   The *float* property can be used to assign how an element attaches to the browser window. It could be considered analogous to aligning items left or right. In listing 8.8 for example, the image and text are aligned to the right side of the browser using the *float* property:

Listing 8.8   Using the *float* Property to Determine Element Alignment

```
01. <HTML>
02. <HEAD>
03. <TITLE>Positioning</TITLE>
04. </HEAD>
05. <BODY>
06.
07. <DIV id=bouy STYLE="float:right;left:10%;width:25%;top:10%">
08. <IMG SRC="picture.gif">
09. This image and text are aligned to the right side of the browser with float
10. </DIV>
11. <P>
12.
13. </BODY>
14. </HTML>
```

The *float* property in listing 8.8 aligns the elements to the right side of the browser window, as shown in figure 8.10.

Width and Height   The *width* and *height* properties specify the size of the positioning container with either absolute or relative positioning. You can use any of the accepted measurement values, such as inches, millimeters, centimeters, or pixels. In addition to values, you can specify percentages for the value. The percentages are always in relation to the browser window. So, "width: 50%; height: 75%" would create a position container that was half as wide as the current window, and three fourths as tall.

These properties are used to define the boundaries of the container, and then other elements may be placed within the container boundaries. The code in listing 8.9 demonstrates how to define the dimensions of the container.

FIG. 8.10

Aligning elements to
the right using the float
property.

Listing 8.9   Defining Container Boundaries with the *width* and *height* Properties

```
01. <HTML>
02. <HEAD>
03. <TITLE>Container Width and Height</TITLE>
04. </HEAD>
05. <BODY>
06.
07. <DIV id=AbPosition STYLE="position: relative; width: 100px; height: 100px;
➥background-color: black">
08. </DIV>
09. <P>
10. <DIV id=AbPosition STYLE="position: relative; width: 50%; height: 50%;
➥background-color: red">
11. </DIV>
12. <P>
13.
14. </BODY>
15. </HTML>
```

Figure 8.11 shows the output for listing 8.9.

FIG. 8.11

The *width* and *height* properties enable you to configure the dimensions of a Position container.

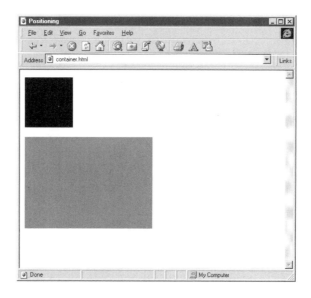

In line 7 in listing 8.9, *width* and *height* are used to create a container with dimensions of 100×100 pixels. The background is set to black so you can actually see the container. This demonstrates how you can define containers using specific measurements. Line 10 defines the dimensions of the container using percentages of the parent window. In this example, the container is created with dimensions that are 50 percent of the window size, with a red background to be able to see the container. Figure 8.11 shows both of the containers side by side to demonstrate the differences in methods for defining Position container dimensions.

Top and Left   Top and left specify the location of the container on the page. These two values are used to indicate the starting position of the upper-left corner of the container, and are always in relation to the top- and left-hand side of the browser window.

For example, "left: 50px; top:35px" would begin a style container 35 pixels from the top of the browser window, and 50 pixels from the window's left side.

The code in listing 8.10 demonstrates how you can specify the "position" of a Position container:

Listing 8.10   Positioning with the *top* and *left* Properties

```
01.  <HTML>
02.  <HEAD>
03.  <TITLE>Positioning Containers</TITLE>
04.  </HEAD>
05.  <BODY>
06.
```

```
07. <DIV id=AbPosition STYLE="position: absolute; width: 100px; height: 100px;
→top: 50px; left: 50px; background-color: black">
08. </DIV>
09. <P>
10. <DIV id=AbPosition STYLE="position: absolute; width: 100px; height: 100px;
→top: 50%; left: 50%; background-color: red">
11. </DIV>
12. <P>
13.
14. </BODY>
15. </HTML>
```

The results of listing 8.10 are displayed in figure 8.12.

FIG. 8.12

The *top* and *left* properties enable you to specify the location of a Positioning container with respect to the top left corner of the parent element.

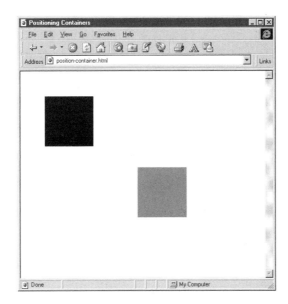

Lines 7–8 in listing 8.10 create a Position container that is 100×100 pixels, and then the *top* and *left* properties position the container 50 pixels from the top of the browser window, and 50 pixels from the left. Then, in lines 10–11 you take a similar container, but position it based on a percentage of the window size (in this case, 50 percent of the size of the window).

Overflow

Of course, it is not always possible to predict how wide or tall a position container will need to be when you are designing your page. Worse yet, the text may change, and a container that was adequate may become too small. For situations like this, the *overflow* property can be used to create a default for handling the extra information.

The *overflow* property accepts "clip" and "scroll" as values. The "clip" value will simply cut off the extra information so that is not displayed. This could be used to crop an image, for example.

For text, however, you will likely want to use the "scroll" value, which will enable the user to scroll the content container to view all the information. The HTML code in listing 8.11 demonstrates how the *overflow* property functions:

Listing 8.11   Handling Excess Text in the Container with the *overflow* Property

```
01. <HTML>
02. <HEAD>
03. <TITLE>Overflow</TITLE>
04. </HEAD>
05. <BODY>
06.
07. <DIV id=ScrollIt STYLE="position: absolute; width: 100px; height: 100px;
➥top: 25px; left: 25px; overflow: scroll">
08. This is some text that will appear in the container you have defined.
09. Because it won't fit, it will be overflowed. This example is scrolled.
10. </DIV>
11. <P>
12.
13. </BODY>
14. </HTML>
```

Figure 8.13 displays the results of listing 8.11.

FIG. 8.13

The *overflow* property enables you to specify how a container should deal with data that will not fit in the defined area.

Line 7 in listing 8.11 creates a container that is 100×100 pixels. However, the text that we are placing in the container is obviously going to be larger than 100×100 pixels. So at the end of line 7, the *overflow* property is used to specify that the container should have scroll bars that can be used to view all the data.

Z-Index

Z-index refers to the order in which elements are placed "on top" of one another, or in layers. The name derives from the Cartesian coordinate system (X,Y,Z), where Z refers to the axis that controls depth. Positioning enables the creation of layers by assigning a Z-index number to elements that determine their effective layer on the page.

This layering capability enables designers to specify how elements are to overlap, which can be used to create a variety of text effects, or to blend elements together. Z-indexing is discussed in greater detail in Chapter 9, "Layout and Positioning."

From Here...

This part of the book concentrates on the effects that Dynamic HTML can provide for the visual enhancement of your pages, and how to use these techniques to create new user interfaces and multimedia effects.

Now that you have seen some of the basic dynamic styles and effects that can be created by combining scripting and style sheets, you should be aware of how the Dynamic HTML Object Model is responsible for much of this functionality. These effects might be simple, but as you will see in later chapters, they will serve as the basis for more complex examples of how you can use Dynamic HTML to enhance your web presence. These techniques are covered in detail in the remaining chapters of this part of the book:

- Chapter 9, "Layout and Positioning"—This chapter discusses and demonstrates the importance of dynamic design through absolute positioning, relative positioning, the STYLE properties, and layering.

- Chapter 10, "Dynamic Content"—This chapter introduces the intricacies and usefulness of changing web page content at runtime, the dynamic capabilities provided by TextRange objects, as well as the Structured Object Model.

Layout and Positioning

Dynamic styles represent the first steps toward building new interfaces and designs with Dynamic HTML. One of the strongest aspects of this capability is the control provided by layout and positioning—an area that was long ignored in the early incarnations of web browsers that has since received a great deal of attention.

Chapter 8, "Dynamic Styles," provided you with a basic overview of positioning because it is a part of dynamic styles. Positioning and layout, however, are significant enough to warrant an entire chapter devoted to their coverage.

The layout and positioning mechanism utilized by Dynamic HTML is a combination of Cascading Style Sheets Positioning and JavaScript/VBScript. The combination of these two technologies provides you with the capability to create pages that have adaptable layout, provides a great deal of flexibility in positioning elements, and enables you to control element position after the page has loaded. Dynamic HTML does this by taking advantage of Cascading Style Sheets Positioning and the position property, which enables absolute and relative positioning of HTML objects. ■

CSS Positioning

The CSS Positioning working draft from the W3C is the foundation of positioning elements with Dynamic HTML.

Absolute Positioning

Absolute positioning enables designers to position elements on web pages, using a coordinate system.

Relative Positioning

Relative positioning enables designers to position elements on a page in relation to one another, or in relation to the default HTML positioning called static positioning.

CSS Properties

The CSS Positioning properties: to provide the means to specify coordinates, to handle overflow of data when a positioning container is too small, to layer elements, and to show and hide elements.

Layers

CSS Positioning and Dynamic HTML support layers through the *Z-index* property.

Layer Animations

Combining layers, positioning properties, and a scripting language you can create multimedia and interactive interfaces with CSS Positioning and Dynamic HTML.

CSS Positioning

Cascading Style Sheets Positioning is a mechanism for providing information about the location of elements on a page, either in relation to the overall browser window or in relation to other objects on the page.

The CSS Positioning specification is not actually a part of the Cascading Style Sheets specification, and therefore is subject to changes separate from CSS. For the most part, however, the CSS skills you've acquired from Chapter 4, "Cascading Style Sheets Primer," are applicable to CSS Positioning.

Absolute and relative positioning are actually types of positioning that can be implemented through the CSS Positioning *position* property. Each type of positioning offers different advantages, depending on the type of layout and elements with which you are working. As you continue to look at how Dynamic HTML uses positioning, those advantages will become more apparent.

Position Property

The capability to create diverse layouts with Dynamic HTML depends on the capability to describe to the browser where an element should be placed on a page. After an element has been placed on the page, there are mechanisms by which you can specify how the element should interact with other elements, such as the layering of elements.

When a browser parses the HTML that describes a page, the elements are laid out in the order they are read from the file. The beginning of an HTML file corresponds to the top of a completed web page, so as items are read sequentially from the beginning to the end of the file, the items are placed from the top to the bottom of the web page. This default positioning mechanism used by all browsers from Lynx to IE to Netscape is known as *static positioning*. Figure 9.1 demonstrates this default layout mechanism.

FIG. 9.1

The default layout mechanism for HTML, static positioning, results in a sequential layout of elements.

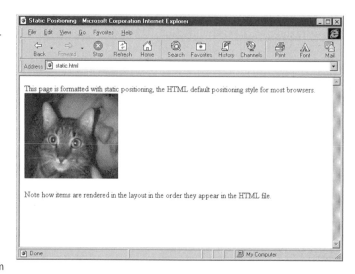

Unfortunately, static positioning found in browsers is quite limited. Without using tricks such as spacers or tables, it is nearly impossible to align elements properly, such as a caption with a photo, for example. It is also difficult to create any sort of columnar layout. Additionally, the elements cannot be layered, or provide for overlapping elements, leaving many layout styles and techniques out of reach for web designers.

To address these problems, CSS Positioning utilizes two additional types of positioning: absolute positioning and relative positioning. Whenever you refer to absolute and relative positioning in Dynamic HTML, you are really talking about CSS Positioning. Dynamic HTML makes the STYLE *position* property available for scripting via the Dynamic HTML Object Model, and uses absolute positioning and relative positioning for layout and position control.

Absolute Positioning

The first type of CSS Positioning discussed here is known as *absolute positioning*. Just as the name would imply, the special feature of absolute positioning is the capability to explicitly specify where layout elements will go on a page by using a coordinate system that is based on the top-left corner of the browser window (or the parent element).

N O T E   Coordinates for absolute positioning are always given with respect to the top-left corner of the parent element, which is usually the browser window. The X axis continues along the top of the parent element, for example, across the width of the browser window. What, however, would normally be thought of as the Y axis, actually continues "down: the element", for example, toward the bottom of the browser window. ■

The location of absolutely positioned elements remains constant, even if elements overlap with other elements, or if users resize their browser windows. The result is a number of new ways in which layouts can be created by placing elements on a page in precise locations.

You could use absolute positioning to overlap objects by placing them so that they would always have a portion of their areas shared, for example. You could also use absolute positioning to place a caption with an image, to make sure that the two elements are always rendered together. Suppose you want to have some text always appear next to a photo. Listing 9.1 shows how the positioning would work:

Listing 9.1   Aligning Images and Captions with Absolute Positioning

```
01. <HTML>
02. <HEAD>
03. <TITLE>Absolute Positioning</TITLE>
04. </HEAD>
05. <BODY>
06. <P>
07.
08. This page is formatted with absolute positioning, which places the
➥elements at specifically specified points on the page.
09.
```

continues

Listing 9.1   Continued

```
10. <DIV id="AbPosImage" STYLE="position: absolute; left: 50px; top:150px">
11. <IMG SRC="kitty.gif">
12. </DIV>
13.
14.
15. <DIV id="AbPosText" STYLE="position: absolute; left: 250px; top:150px;
➥width: 2in; color: blue">
16. Note how the second text block has been positioned beside the picture,
➥regardless of the window size.
17. </DIV>
18.
19. </BODY>
20. </HTML>
```

As you can see from line 10 in listing 9.1 using a new *STYLE* property called *position* with a value of "absolute" denotes that this element will be placed using absolute positioning.

In the same line, the location of the element on the page is given using the *left* and *top* STYLE properties. These properties accept values in pixels, centimeters, inches, points, and so on to place the element at a certain point on the page. These properties are discussed in more detail later. Figure 9.2 shows how the image is placed 50 pixels from the left side of the browser window, and 150 pixels from the top. Line 15 defines the values for the text then places the text next to the image, again using the *top* and *left* properties. The result of the code is that the text is always placed by the image, and both elements always remain in the same position, regardless of the size of the browser window.

FIG. 9.2

Absolute positioning enables designers to place elements at specific points on a page.

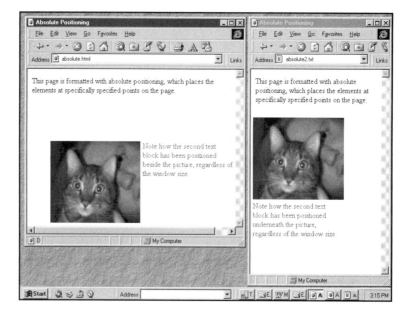

When the viewer is looking at this page, the image and the caption will always appear in exactly the same location, even if the viewer resizes the browser window. Also, you can change the position of the picture by changing the "*top*" and "*left*" property values, and nothing will happen to the location of the caption. With absolute positioning, each element is positioned explicitly and independently of the other elements.

Upon further examination of line 15 in listing 9.1, you will discover another property that is being used for the caption— "*width*." This property can be used to define how wide an element that is positioned absolutely can be. The result for listing 9.1 is that the width of the caption is limited to 2 inches. Upon breaching this 2-inch width limit, the text wraps to the next line.

Here are some other items to note about absolutely positioned elements:

- **Rectangular flow area**—Absolute positioning defines a rectangular flow area for the specified element that begins on the page at the top-left coordinates you specify. This flow area is also sometimes referred to as a *positioning container.*

- **Height and width specification**—The *height* and *width* properties can be used to define the total area of the flow rectangle. This gives you even greater control over the space an element occupies. For example:

```
#mystyle {position: absolute;top: 1in;left: 1in; height: 3in; width:
➥5in}
```

This code defines a flow rectangle that is placed one inch from the top and left-hand sides of the browser window and extends down the page 3 inches, and to the right 5 inches.

- **Elements can be nested**—If an element is positioned using the *mystyle* definition used in the preceding example, another absolutely positioned element could be nested within the element. For example:

```
    <DIV id="mystyle">
<SPAN STYLE="position: absolute;top: 50px;left: 50px>
Some Text
    </SPAN>
    </DIV>
```

This code could be used to place the words "Some Text" 50 pixels in from the top and bottom of the 3×5 area already specified in *mystyle.*

- **Positioning inside other elements by top and left**—Absolute positioned flow areas are always defined by the starting point from the top and left of the parent element, whether that parent is the browser window or another absolutely positioned element in which the new element is nested.

By exploiting these features of absolute positioning, it is possible to create some interesting layouts, and make sure that they are seen exactly as you want them to be.

Listing 9.2 incorporates some of the absolute positioning features to create an interesting layout. The output for this code is displayed in figure 9.3, which follows this listing:

Listing 9.2 Creating a Tight Layout with Overlapping Effects Through Use of Absolute Positioning

```
01. <HTML>
02. <HEAD>
03. <TITLE>Absolute Positioning Example</TITLE>
04. </HEAD>
05. <BODY>
06. <P>
07. <DIV id="Element1" STYLE="position: absolute; color: red; top: 2in; left
➥2in">
08. <H1>Absolute Positioning!</H1>
09. <SPAN STYLE="position: absolute; color: blue; top: 30px; left: 25px; width:
➥2in">This text is a nested element. Note that it is positioned within the
➥flow area defined by the DIV tag.</SPAN>
10. </DIV>
11.
12. <DIV id="Element2" STYLE="position: absolute; top:15px; left:25px">
13. <IMG SRC="kitty.gif">
14. </DIV>
15.
16. <SPAN STYLE="position: absolute; color: green; top:25px; left:35px">
17. <H2>Overlaping Text With Absolute Positioning</H2>
18. </SPAN>
19.
20. </BODY>
21. </HTML>
```

FIG. 9.3

An example layout with overlaps and nested elements using absolute positioning.

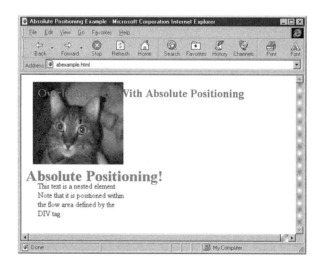

The code in listing 9.2 and the resulting output (refer to figure 9.3) demonstrate how elements can be positioned in the same space to create overlapping effects, and also how you can nest absolutely positioned objects for tighter layout control. First, in line 7, a flow area is created using the <DIV> tag and absolute positioning. This creates an area where we can actually position other nested elements, such as the <H1> and the <SPAN> tags that follow in lines 8 and 9. Finally, the image is placed on the page in line 12, and then line 16 places the text that overlaps the image.

Absolute positioning is best suited for placing elements on a page and leaving them there. After elements are positioned with absolute positioning, they do not move, regardless of page changes. Suppose you want to take advantage of CSS Positioning to animate page elements? This is where relative positioning is important.

Relative Positioning

Relative positioning is a hybrid between static positioning and absolute positioning. Like static positioning, elements positioned with relative positioning are flowed onto the page in the order in which they are parsed from the HTML file. This enables you to create pages in a more conventional way, without having to position each item explicitly.

In addition, relative positioning affords you the capability to specify the position of an element. For example,

```
<BODY>
This text would be positioned statically.
</BODY>
```

and

```
<SPAN STYLE="position: relative; color: green;">This text is just like static
➥text.
</SPAN>
```

are functionally equivalent. They will both place the text on the page in the same manner.

Using relative positioning offers some distinct advantages. Relative positioning enables you to specifically place elements on the page similar to absolute positioning. In addition, relative positioning enables you to place elements on the page relative to their parent elements. The advantages of relative positioning can also be found in the capability to treat relative positioned elements as objects, assigning them to layers with Z-indexing. Additionally, you can move relatively positioned elements with a scripting language, such as JavaScript or VBScript. Scripting relatively positioned objects will come into play in Chapter 13, "Introducing Multimedia."

Listing 9.3 shows an example of a layout put together through the use of relative positioning. The output for this listing is displayed in figure 9.4, which immediately follows this listing:

Listing 9.3   Laying Out a Page Using Relative Positioning

```
01. <HTML>
02. <HEAD>
```

continues

Listing 9.3 Continued

```
03. <TITLE>Relative Positioning</TITLE>
04. </HEAD>
05. <BODY>
06. <P>
07.
08. This page is formatted with relative positioning, which allows the
➥layout to flow naturally, while still affording some control.
09.
10. <DIV id="RelPosImage" STYLE="position: relative">
11. <IMG SRC="kitty.gif">
12. </DIV>
13.
14. <DIV id="RelPosText" STYLE="position: relative; width: 2in; color: blue">
15. Note the formatting that is applied to the 'caption' text below the image.
16. </DIV>
17.
18. </BODY>
19. </HTML>
```

FIG. 9.4

Relative positioning flows elements like static positioning, but allows greater control.

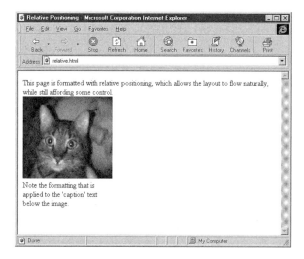

In the preceding example, lines 10 and 14 each define an element that is positioned on the page using relative positioning. When looking at the final page, it is laid out identically to the way it would be if positioning were not used at all. However, by using positioning for the object, you could now add a script to the page that would alter the position of the objects—something that is not possible with static positioning.

The sections that follow examine the mechanics of positioning elements on the page, and the attributes that can be tweaked to develop complex layouts.

position Property

The STYLE *position* property determines the type of positioning used by the browser to place an element. The default position value is static, which is the default for HTML. The *position* property is defined with the STYLE attribute, and uses the familiar CSS syntax:

```
<SOME_ELEMENT STYLE="position: value">
```

The values that are accepted are "absolute," "relative," and "static" as shown in the following lines:

```
<DIV STYLE="position: absolute">I'm Absolute</DIV>
<DIV STYLE="position: relative">I'm Relative</DIV>
<DIV STYLE="position: static">I'm Static</DIV>
```

N O T E   The static value for the *position* property is the default, and so it is not generally necessary to specify static positioning.

That is all there is to defining the type of positioning that is used by an element; however, you might have noticed some other properties used in the previous examples that are used to define where the elements are positioned.

left and *top* Properties

The *left* and *top* properties define where the placement of a positioned element begins. If you think of the browser window as a giant grid, then you need to be able to place an element on that grid by using some sort of coordinate system.

The *left* and *top* properties both accept three kinds of values:

- **length**—This is a unit of measurement, such as pixels (px) or inches (in), which are used to place the "top" of the element being positioned. Using a length can yield very precise control over element placement. The units of measurement can be found in table 4.2 in Chapter 4.
- **percentage**—This is a percentage that will result in the placement of the element in relation to the size of the parent element.

   If, for example, the parent element is the browser window (which it is most of the time), then a top value of "50%" would place the element halfway down the page. Another example could be a flow area (position container) that is 500×500 pixels. A value of 50% in this case would place the child element at 250 pixels, within the 500×500 flow area.
- **auto**—The auto value simply places the element where it would naturally fall if the page were being flowed in without positioning.

So, by determining the top and left coordinates, any element can be placed anywhere in the browser window; however, how absolute positioning and relative positioning determine the origin of the coordinates is different.

For absolute positioning, the origin of the top and left coordinates are in relation to the parent object. That is, if an item is placed within a browser window, then the top and left coordinates start from the top-left corner of the browser window. In fact, most of the time absolutely positioned elements will be in relation to the browser window; however, they can be nested inside other elements. It is also important to note that if absolutely positioned elements are placed with measurements, such as inches or pixels, then their position will not change if the browser window is resized. This can be used to make sure that the layout remains consistent proportionally by retaining the position of all the elements, regardless of the size to which the user sets the window. If you had a page that was a scale diagram, for example, you would not want the scale to change if the user resized the window.

Relative positioning functions slightly differently from absolute positioning. The origin for relative positioning is the default location of the element, which means that the top and left starting points begin with respect to where the element would be placed if it was flowed with no positioning. So relative positioning flows the page elements just like a normal, static-positioned page, with each element having a natural position based on how it is parsed from the HTML file. When an element is positioned with relative positioning, all the coordinates are given in relation to this natural position. Some other special characteristics of relative positioning are:

- When an element that is placed with relative positioning is moved, it will retain all the formatting characteristics, such as color or font-style, from its original position.

- When a relatively positioned element is moved, any child elements or elements positioned relative to it will also move.

- When a relatively positioned element is moved, the space in which it was originally rendered will not be cleared. Because of this, you will need to be conscious of layers and placement when animating relatively positioned elements.

The following code in listing 9.4 provides an example of how the different types of positioning are rendered when elements are placed by using *top* and *left*. Figure 9.5 shows the output for this code.

Listing 9.4   Rendering *top* and *left* Values with Absolute and Relative Positioning

```
01. <HTML>
02. <HEAD>
03. <TITLE>Positioning Examples</TITLE>
04. </HEAD>
05. <BODY>
06. <P>
07. This text is placed using static positioning.
08. <P>
09.
10. <DIV id="AB" STYLE="position: absolute; top: 50px; left: 50px; color: red">
11. This text is placed using absolute positioning.</DIV>
12.
13. <DIV id="REL" STYLE="position: relative; top: 50px; left: 50px; color:
➥blue">
14. This text is placed using relative positioning.</DIV>
15.
16. </BODY>
17. </HTML>
```

FIG. 9.5

Three elements with similar definitions placed with static, absolute, and relative positioning.

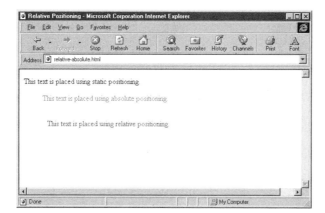

Listing 9.4 contains three text elements that are statically, absolutely, and relatively positioned. If you look closely at lines 10 and 13, you will note that the coordinates for placing the absolute and relative elements are exactly the same: *top:50; left:50;*. If you load the page, however, you will see that the elements are not rendered on top of each other, but are offset slightly instead.

In listing 9.4, the static line of text on line 7 is rendered normally at the top of the page. Next, the absolutely positioned element on lines 10 and 11 is rendered 50 pixels from the top of the window, and 50 pixels from the left side of the window. The same coordinates were used for the relative positioned element on lines 13 and 14.

Instead of being positioned in relation to the window, the relatively positioned element is aligned in relation to where the text would have been flowed automatically (as with static positioning). If the text were not positioned at all, it would have been placed along the left side of the window, underneath the absolutely positioned text. So the 50-pixel offset starts on near the left side, and below the absolutely positioned text, resulting in an even greater offset.

width and *height* Properties

In addition to being able to specify the position of elements, you can also specify the area that elements can occupy. If you think of positioning as creating a rectangular container for HTML elements, then the *top* and the *left* properties define where the rectangle starts. But how do you determine how big the rectangle is? By using the *width* and *height* properties.

The *width* property defines how wide the positioning container will be, and the *height* property determines how tall it will be. Keep in mind, however, that because you define the "top" of the rectangular container with positioning, the *height* property actually determines how far down the page your positioning container will extend.

Both of these properties can accept units of measurement or percentages as values. This enables you to define an area that is always a predefined size, or a size that changes with respect to the browser window. By using the *width* and *height* properties in combination, you can use positioning to create effects such as columns as demonstrated in listing 9.5 and its complementary figure (9.6).

Listing 9.5   Creating a Columnar Layout with *width* and *height* Properties

```
01. <HTML>
02. <HEAD>
03. <TITLE>Column Text</TITLE>
04. </HEAD>
05. <BODY>
06. <P>
07.
08. <DIV id="REL" STYLE="position: relative;
➡ top: 50px; left: 50px; width: 2in; color: blue">
09. This text is placed using relative positioning, but makes use of the
➡width tag to force the text into a 2 inch column. This effect can be
➡used to create columnar layouts or for greater control over the
➡page appearance</DIV>
10.
11. </BODY>
12. </HTML>
```

FIG. 9.6

You can use the width property to create columns.

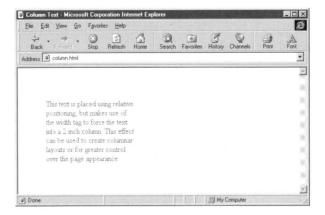

In this example on line 8, the *width* property defines a rectangle that has a width of 2 inches, so when text is inserted into the <DIV> tag, the result is a column of text.

This flexibility enables you to create some pretty complex layouts based on grids or columns; however, some important things to keep in mind are:

- The formatting defined in relative-positioned elements is retained when moving the elements. So, when you move a 2-inch column, it will remain a 2-inch column, complete with line breaks.

- Positioned containers defined with the *top*, *left*, *height*, and *width* properties are rectangular in shape. Although the area can contain elements that are not rectangular, the container itself is a rectangle.

So what happens when you define a container for positioning, but the content is too big for the area? This is where the *overflow* and *clip* properties come into play.

overflow Property

Although the *width* and *height* properties give you added flexibility, sometimes these attributes can work against you. Suppose you are trying to create a text area that is 2 inches wide, and 1 inch tall. No problem. What happens if you have more text to go in the text area than 2 square inches? Of course, you could use font attributes to make the text smaller, but then legibility would suffer. Instead, you can rely on the *overflow* property.

The *overflow* property enables you to instruct the browser how to handle the extra data if you have text that exceeds the specified height and width of the positioning container. The *overflow* property accepts three values:

- **none**—This value indicates that no overflow handling should be performed. The result will be the default handling based on the browser that you are using.

- **clip**—With the *overflow* property set to clip, any data that will not fit in the container will simply be left out.

- **scroll**—The scroll value instructs the browser to limit the display to the container area, but to add scroll bars to make the rest of the data accessible. This is generally the preferable method of handling overflow data.

Listing 9.6 demonstrates how to implement the *overflow* property. Figure 9.7 demonstrates the visual handling of data that exceeds the area constraints of the container defined in listing 9.6.

Part III

Ch 9

Listing 9.6 Handling Overflow Data

```
01. <HTML>
02. <HEAD>
03. <TITLE>Overflow</TITLE>
04. </HEAD>
05. <BODY>
06. <P>
07.
08. <DIV id="REL" STYLE="position: relative; top: 50px; left: 50px;
➥width: 2in; height: 1in; color: blue; overflow: scroll">
09. This text is placed using relative positioning, but makes use of the
➥width tag to force the text into a 2 inch column, and the height tag
➥to limit the column to 1 inch. Since there is an 'overflow' of text,
➥the scrollbars provide access to all of the text.</DIV>
10.
11.</BODY>
12.</HTML>
```

FIG. 9.7

The *overflow* property allows for handling data larger than a positioning container.

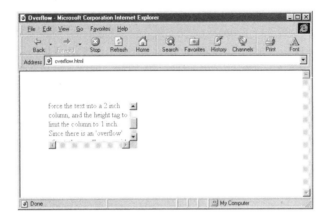

Line 8 in listing 9.6 specifies that the container area will be 2 inches by 1 inch, and that overflow should be handled with a scrollbar.

clip Property

The previous example of handling overflow (listing 9.6) dealt with handling too much text; however, what happens if the data that is too big for your positioning container is an image? In this scenario, you will need to make use of the clipping capability.

The *clip* property enables you to specify a clipping area for data and images—in effect, cropping the images in place. To use the *clip* property to crop an image, you need to follow these steps:

1. Define a container and use absolute positioning to position the element that will be clipped.
2. Use the *overflow* property to specify that overflowed data should clip.
3. Use the *clip* property to specify how the image should be clipped.

The *clip* property accepts two values:

- **auto**—With this value selected, the clipping area is the area of the container.
- **rect**—With this value selected, you can specify a clipping rectangle by giving it the coordinates for the top, right, bottom, and left sides of the rectangle, with respect to the container's origin.

The following line defines a clipping rectangle 3cm×2cm, with the rectangle defined by giving the coordinates for the top-left corner, and the bottom-right corner:

```
<DIV STYLE="position: absolute; overflow: clip; clip: rect(1cm 4cm 3cm 1cm)">
```

This clipping rectangle is defined in relation to whatever area would be defined with top, left, width, and height. Listing 9.7 demonstrates clipping using the 2cm×3cm container size. Figure 9.8 shows how the image is cropped using this clipping specification.

Listing 9.7 Cropping an Image with the *clip* Property

```
01. <HTML>
02. <HEAD>
03. <TITLE>Clipping</TITLE>
04. </HEAD>
05. <BODY>
06. <P>
07.
08. <DIV id="REL" STYLE="position: absolute; top: 5px; left: 250px; width: 5px;
➥height 5px; overflow: clip; clip: rect(1cm 4cm 3cm 1cm)">
09. <IMG SRC="toobig.gif">
10. </DIV>
11. <IMG SRC="toobig.gif">
12. </BODY>
13. </HTML>
```

FIG. 9.8

Clipping can be used to crop images in place.

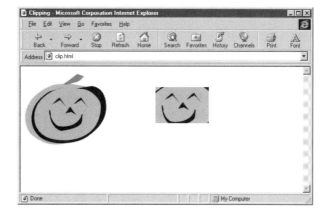

Layers

One of the most important features of CSS Positioning and Dynamic HTML is the capability to place HTML elements on different layers that can be manipulated. It is by exploiting layers that you can show and hide elements on a page, which is the basis for many Dynamic HTML effects, such as expanding and collapsing outlines.

The capability to specify which layers the elements appear on also contributes to the capability to overlap elements or create transitions between layers in response to user interaction. Without layers, overlapping elements would be nearly impossible, and it would be difficult to control which elements appeared in the foreground or background.

Layering elements with Dynamic HTML and CSS Positioning is very simple, and really only involves two concepts, Z-indexing and visibility.

z-index **Property**

If you think of the top and left positions as being the equivalent of Y and X coordinates, then it makes sense that layers would actually be defined by the Z coordinate, just as they would in a 3D world. Essentially, all you are doing with layers is determining which layer appears in the front from the successive layers working into the background.

CSS Positioning determines which layers appear in the foreground or background with the *z-index* property, which enables you to specify a numerical identifier for an element's layer. The Z-index values can be positive or negative integers. The default (foreground) layer is 0, and increasing numbers specify "deeper" layers. If you had two elements defined as

```
<DIV STYLE="position: absolute; z-index: 3">Front</DIV>
<DIV STYLE="position: absolute; z-index: 7">Back</DIV>
```

the element with a Z-index value of 3 would appear in front of the element with a Z-index value of 7. Layers can be specified with both positive and negative numbers. You can even place elements on the same layer by sharing Z-indexes:

```
<DIV STYLE="position: absolute; z-index: 5">I am</DIV>
<DIV STYLE="position: absolute; z-index: 5">With Him</DIV>
```

N O T E   Elements that have the same Z-index value will be stacked by the browser, and therefore have no pre-established layering order. This can be used to group objects that might not overlap with each other, but that you might want to have on the same layer. If, for example, you had an illustration of a pizza, the crust might be a layer, the sauce another, the cheese a third, but you might want to group both mushrooms and sausage together in a layer called "toppings." ▪

Listing 9.8 and its complementary figure (9.9) demonstrate the use of assigning *Z-index* values to layers.

Listing 9.8   Layering HTML Elements Through the Use of Z-Indexing

```
01. <HTML>
02. <HEAD>
03. <TITLE>Layers</TITLE>
04. </HEAD>
05. <BODY>
06. <P>
07.
08. <DIV id="Layer1" STYLE="position: absolute; top: 10px; left: 10px;">
➥<H1>Layer One</H1></DIV>
09. <DIV id="Layer2" STYLE="position: absolute; top: 20px; left: 20px;
➥color: blue;"> <H1>Layer Two</H1></DIV>
10. <DIV id="Layer3" STYLE="position: absolute; top: 30px; left: 30px;
➥color: red;"><H1>Layer Three</H1></DIV>
11. <DIV id="Layer4" STYLE="position: absolute; top: 40px; left: 40px;
➥color: green;"><H1>Layer Four</H1></DIV>
12.
13. <DIV id="Layer1" STYLE="position: absolute; top: 10px; left: 210px;
➥z-index: 4"><H1>Layer One</H1></DIV>
```

```
14. <DIV id="Layer2" STYLE="position: absolute; top: 20px; left: 220px;
➥color: blue; z-index: 3"><H1>Layer Two</H1></DIV>
15. <DIV id="Layer3" STYLE="position: absolute; top: 30px; left: 230px;
➥color: red; z-index: 2"><H1>Layer Three</H1></DIV>
16. <DIV id="Layer4" STYLE="position: absolute; top: 40px; left: 240px;
➥color: green; z-index: 1"><H1>Layer Four</H1></DIV>
17.
18. </BODY>
19. </HTML>
```

FIG. 9.9

Changing the z-index value enables you to manipulate an element's layering position.

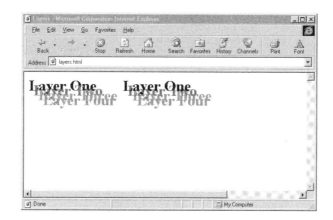

In listing 9.8, the first set of heads, defined in lines 8–11, are ordered naturally, with the first head on top, the next head below that, and so on until all the heads are displayed. In the second set of heads defined in lines 13–16, you can reverse how the headlines are rendered by assigning a different z-index value to each element.

visibility Property

Now that you can place elements on different layers, you are probably wondering what else can be done with layers. The capability to create layers is useful for overlapping and other layout effects. There is another feature of layers, however, that provides even greater flexibility for developing user interfaces—visibility.

The *visibility* property enables you to specify if a layer and its contents are visible on a rendered page. The *visibility* property accepts two values: "visible" and "hidden."

By changing these two values, you can essentially hide data from the user, so it does not appear on the page, although it is still loaded. You can show the user the data at an appropriate time, based on a user event or time span, with no further interaction with the server. This capability to hide and display data is a very handy feature, especially when used with expanding outlines as demonstrated in the example in Chapter 8, "Dynamic Styles."

CAUTION

Hiding elements on layers does not prevent them from being downloaded. Therefore, if you have large elements that are hidden, keep in mind that it will still take time for those elements to be downloaded when a viewer reaches your page, and that those elements will still consume memory.

Listing 9.9 provides a sample implementation of the *visibility* property:

Listing 9.9   Using the *visibility* Property to Hide and Display Element Layers

```
01. <HTML>
02. <HEAD>
03. <TITLE>Visibility</TITLE>
04. </HEAD>
05. <BODY>
06. <P>
07.
08. <DIV id="one" STYLE="position: absolute; top: 10px; left: 10px; color: red;
➥visibility: visible"><H1>Visible Text</H1></DIV>
09. <DIV id="two" STYLE="position: absolute; top: 20px; left: 20px; color: blue;
➥visibility: hidden"><H1>Hidden Text</H1></DIV>
10.
11. <DIV id="three" STYLE="position: absolute; top: 10px; left: 210px; color: red;
➥visibility: hidden"><H1>Visible Text</H1></DIV>
12. <DIV id="four" STYLE="position: absolute; top: 20px; left: 220px; color:
➥blue; visibility: visible"><H1>Hidden Text</H1></DIV>
13.
14. </BODY>
15. </HTML>
```

In this example, lines 8 and 9 establish the text elements, which make use of the *visibility* property to show one line of text and hide the other. The process is reversed in lines 11 and 12 to show how easy it is to alter the visibility of an element on the page. The result of swapping the *visibility* properties from lines 8–9 with lines 11–12 is shown in figure 9.10.

FIG. 9.10

Switching the visibility attributes makes the hidden text visible.

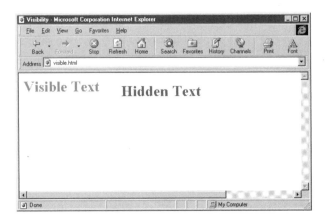

As you can see, the capability to hide and display the contents of layers is a very powerful feature. Part V of this book, "Multimedia and Dynamic HTML" makes extensive use of the visibility feature to make information available to viewers without re-loading data from the server.

Moving Elements

Now that you are familiar with CSS Positioning and the properties that are used to position elements on the page, this chapter will finish up with a demonstration of how you can use Dynamic HTML to animate those elements.

The process for animating elements with Dynamic HTML is pretty simple. You are simply going to employ JavaScript (or VBScript) functions to manipulate the parameters for defining element locations. The end result is the motion of those elements on the page. The lines in the code snippets that follow are numbered corresponding to their placement within the final code in listing 9.10.

First, you need to define an element that you are going to move:

```
43. <DIV id="CAT" STYLE="position: relative; top:-200; left:25px">
44. <IMG SRC="kitty.gif">
45. </DIV>
```

This code creates an element with an ID of "CAT" that is actually positioned off of the HTML page with the value for the top property specified as "–200". The element itself will not be rendered on the page when the page loads, but we are going to develop the script to animate it, so that it "flies" onto the page when the page is loaded.

Now that you have defined an element that you can move, it is time to write the script that will move the image. What you want to do is to manipulate the value of the *top* property to bring the image from off-screen until it is on-screen. This will be done by setting coordinates for the top value from a location off-screen to a location on-screen. This process starts with a simple function to increment the value of the *top* property:

```
07. function MoveThatCat() {
09.          CAT.style.posTop += 1;
12. }
```

The *MoveThatCat()* function is fine, except that now there is nothing to stop the image on the page. If you were to use the *MoveThatCat()* function by itself, the image would start at the coordinates off the viewable page, and continue to move off the page endlessly.

What you really want is to stop the image of the cat at the top of the page, say around 15. By adding an *if* statement, you instruct the *MoveThatCat()* function to stop when the value of the *top* property hits 15 pixels:

```
07. function MoveThatCat() {
08.          if (CAT.style.posTop < 15) {
09.          CAT.style.posTop += 1;
11.          }
12. }
```

Take a look at the code for this animation at this point and see how it functions:

```
01. <HTML>
02. <HEAD>
03. <TITLE>Move the Cat</TITLE>
04.
05. <SCRIPT>
06.
07. function MoveThatCat() {
08.         if (CAT.style.posTop < 15) {
09.             CAT.style.posTop += 1;
11.             }
12. }
13.
29. </SCRIPT>
30. </HEAD>
31.
32. <BODY onLoad="MoveThatCat();">
33.
43. <DIV id="CAT" STYLE="position: relative; top:-200; left:25px">
44. <IMG SRC="kitty.gif">
45. </DIV>
46.
47. </BODY>
48. </HTML>
```

Within this HTML code, a line has been added (line 32) within the <BODY> tag to invoke the *MoveThatCat()* function that moves the image.

This line binds the *MoveThatCat()* function to the *onLoad* event that is called when the page loads. If you view this page, you will see the image of the cat jump from off-screen to the final position when the page loads. But why doesn't it fly?

The problem is that the steps occur too rapidly for the eye to see. In order to create the illusion of flying, you need to add a JavaScript method called *window.setTimeout()* that slows down the *MoveThatCat()* function:

```
07. function MoveThatCat() {
08.         if (CAT.style.posTop < 15) {
09.             CAT.style.posTop += 1;
10.             window.setTimeout("MoveThatCat();", 1);
11.             }
12. }
```

The *window.setTimeout()* function takes two arguments, the function that is being timed out, and the value of the pause, in milliseconds. Here, the *setTimeout()* function is instructed to slow down *MoveThatCat()* by one millisecond before each step. This delay should be enough to fly our kitty.

The finished code in listing 9.10 adds a few more animated elements to create an entire page with moving images and text—some scrolling text and a text block that moves when it is clicked.

Listing 9.10   Animated Images and Text on a Page with Positioning and Scripting—Fly Kitty, Fly!

```
01. <HTML>
02. <HEAD>
03. <TITLE>Animation</TITLE>
04.
05. <SCRIPT>
06.
07. function MoveThatCat() {
08.     if (CAT.style.posTop < 15) {
09.         CAT.style.posTop += 1;
10.     window.setTimeout("MoveThatCat();", 1);
11.     }
12. }
13.
14. function ScrollText() {
15.     if (CAPTION.style.posLeft > 25) {
16.     CAPTION.style.posLeft -= 1;
17.         window.setTimeout("ScrollText();", 2);
18.     }
19. }
20.
21. function MoveTextBlock() {
22.     if (BLOCK.style.posLeft < 250) {
23.         BLOCK.style.posTop += 5;
24.     BLOCK.style.posLeft += 5;
25.     window.setTimeout("MoveTextBlock();", 1);
26.     }
27. }
28.
29. </SCRIPT>
30. </HEAD>
31.
32. <BODY onLoad="MoveThatCat();ScrollText();">
33.
34. <DIV id="BLOCK" STYLE="position: relative; top:10; left:25px; width: 2in;
➥color: blue; z-index: 2" onclick="MoveTextBlock();">
35. This is some text formatted into a column. If you click on this text, it
➥will move, but retain its formatting.
36. </DIV>
37.
38. <P>
39. <DIV id="CAPTION" STYLE="position: relative; color: red; top: 12; left:
➥250px; z-index: 1">
40. <H1>Scroll in Some Text</H1>
41. </DIV>
42.
43. <DIV id="CAT" STYLE="position: relative; top:-200; left:25px">
44. <IMG SRC="kitty.gif">
45. </DIV>
46.
47. </BODY>
48. </HTML>
```

Each of the elements in listing 9.10 has a JavaScript function that is responsible for moving it. The image of the cat will scroll in from the top, and the text will scroll in from the right. Finally, there is a paragraph of formatted text that will not move until the user clicks it. The motion for this element is actually called by a function bound to the element itself with the code in lines 34–36.

This code waits to receive a mouse click, and when it does, it calls the *MoveTextBlock()* function, which animates the text. Figure 9.11 shows the final page in action with the scrolling text and the flying cat. Figure 9.12 shows the path of the text block after it has been clicked.

FIG. 9.11

The position of the elements before any user interaction.

FIG. 9.12

The positions of the elements as they are moved on the screen.

As you can see, animating objects with Dynamic HTML is really a cross between CSS Positioning and scripting and additional methods accessed through the object model. As with many features of Dynamic HTML, it is simply through the Dynamic HTML Object Model exposing the elements that animation is possible. The end result can be more dynamic pages, or even new interfaces that can be used with technologies such as the Channel Definition Format to create new resources for the web.

From Here...

As you continue to learn about the features of Dynamic HTML, you will encounter more complex topics, from animation to full user interaction, and finally advanced multimedia with ActiveX Controls and data binding. As you have seen from this and previous chapters, there is a great deal of underlying technology that needs to be mastered to exploit Dynamic HTML to its fullest. In the end, the results can definitely be worth it.

As you continue on, please be sure that you are comfortable with each of the concepts in the chapter before progressing. Doing so will keep you armed and ready for the concepts that are discussed later, and help you build strong, interesting Dynamic HTML sites. For now, turn your attention to Chapter 10, "Dynamic Content," where you will explore topics such as replacing text, and manipulating elements on a page in real time. The capability to alter content dynamically, or on-the-fly, is one of the most powerful features of Dynamic HTML, enabling you to alter virtually the properties, style, even the meaning of any content on the web page.

CHAPTER 10

Dynamic Content

Previous chapters discussed the weaknesses of traditional HTML and the strengths of Dynamic HTML. You also learned about some of the merits of Microsoft's Dynamic HTML implementation versus that of other vendors such as Netscape. In both instances, one aspect of Dynamic HTML continues to set it apart as an important new technology—the capability to manipulate content on the page after the page has been loaded.

The capability to manipulate text, images, and even tags on a web page after it has been loaded is one of the primary advantages of Dynamic HTML. This feature, which is known as *dynamic content*, enables you to move images on a page, change styles, replace images, replace text, and even manipulate the actual HTML tags used to describe the page.

The advantage to this type of manipulation is that the content of web pages can be manipulated, by both the page author and the viewer, after the page has been fully loaded. Content can be altered through scripts that are timed to run after a set amount of time, or content could be altered by triggers in the user interface, creating a new graphical user interface for the web that is similar to actual applications. ■

Dynamic Content

Discover how to use Dynamic HTML to create web pages with content that changes after the page has been loaded, without recontacting the web server.

Runtime Content

Unlike traditional methods, such as cookies, Dyanmic HTML provides for content manipulation at runtime, after a page has been downloaded from the server.

Text Ranges

Text ranges provide a mechanism for selecting text on an HTML page, including HTML tags, and replacing the text and tags, all at runtime.

Object Model Properties

The object model properties: innerHTML, outerHTML, innerText, and outerText allow for very flexible manipulation of virtually any item on a web page.

Changing Content at Runtime

Prior to the release of Dynamic HTML and Internet Explorer 4.0, methods existed to manipulate the content of a page for an individual user. Cookies and other features could be used to pass information to the server about the user's environment and state. Pages then could be changed according to user parameters.

This is a very powerful feature for customizing the content of pages for users; however, you still had no means of altering the HTML on a page after the page had already been loaded without contacting the server.

The Dynamic HTML Object Model changes that by exposing all the elements on a page to manipulation through scripting. Specifically, the *TextRange* object enables you to alter any HTML tag, or the content of the tag, with a script. This enables you to make sweeping changes to an entire page, or to select a single tag to be changed. This type of manipulation enables complete content flexibility. Entire paragraphs can be replaced on a page, without ever recontacting the web server, speeding up content delivery for viewers while adding flexibility for designers.

Replacing Elements on an Existing Page

Dynamic HTML offers several mechanisms for changing the content on the page after the page has already been loaded. You have already seen several examples of this with dynamic styles. Dynamic styles affect the page layout after the page has already been loaded. Changing the fonts, colors, and layouts are all examples of dynamic styles and, in a sense, dynamic content.

The real power of dynamic content, however, actually lies in the capability to change the tags and text that make up a page. The process is not particularly difficult, but it is one of the more important aspects of Dynamic HTML. Dynamic content enables you to provide continuously updated information on a web page, which is useful for such applications as the dynamic content clock, shown in figure 10.1.

FIG. 10.1

The dynamic clock is an example of using dynamic content on a web page.

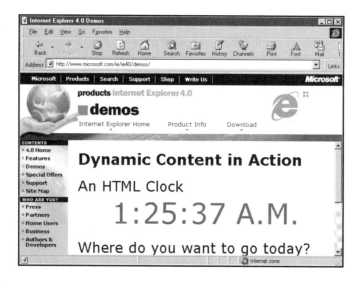

You also can use dynamic content to change the entire content of a page without contacting the server. The power to create dynamic content is all provided through the Dynamic HTML Object Model, and through two principle techniques: text ranges and the Structured Object Model.

NOTE In the text we will refer to the *TextRange* object as "TextRange" when we are discussing a specific aspect or usage of the object. When we are talking about generic "ranges" of text, they will be referred to as "text ranges." Although this might seem a little confusing, as you begin to understand more about the *TextRange* object, the distinction should become more clear. ■

Changing Text

The capability to change content dynamically at runtime allows for a number of different effects in relation to style and graphic elements on a page. You have already seen how you can use Dynamic HTML to change the information about styles on your pages in Chapter 8, "Dynamic Styles." These effects can be used to change fonts, colors, or other style characteristics on a page after the page has been loaded. But what about changing the actual content of the page itself? That is where *TextRange* objects come in.

TextRange Objects

HTML pages consist of HTML tags, scripts, other defining elements, and the text that makes up the content of the page. Take the following HTML code, for example:

```
<HTML>
<TITLE>Sample Page</TITLE>
<BODY>

<H2>This is a Sample Page.</H2>
<P>This is some sample text</P>
</HTML>
</BODY>
```

From a code standpoint, all the element tags are part of the document's structure, while the text is the part of the document known as the *stream*. In the preceding example, the stream would be "This is a Sample Page. This is some sample text". When defining the stream, there is no differentiating between what text is associated with what element in the stream. In other words, it doesn't matter whether the text is defined by the <H2> tag or the <P> tag—it's all text, regardless of the applied style.

The *TextRange* object enables you to select a stream of text, and then manipulate the stream to edit the text that appears on your page. *TextRange* objects are defined using the *createTextRange()* method as shown in the following line:

```
var someRange = document.body.createTextRange();
```

If this were called with the previous basic HTML example, the *TextRange* object would appear as:

```
Sample Page This is a Sample Page
```

After you select the text range, you can use a number of different methods to manipulate the resulting *TextRange* object. These methods can select various bits of text and replace it with new text, providing true dynamic content.

TextRange Object Properties and Methods

You can use a number of properties and methods with *TextRange* objects to provide the capability to change text and elements on the page. The following sections provide a rundown of the properties and methods available and how they function.

Properties   Two *TextRange* object properties can be used to access the data that is selected in a *TextRange* object. These properties are separated into the text and the HTML:

- **htmlText**—The *htmlText* property returns the HTML fragment for the selected text range. Use this property if you want to manipulate the tag. For example:

  ```
  <H2>This is the text</H2>
  ```

  The htmlText in the preceding code would be <H2></H2>.

- **text**—The *text* property returns only the text of the tag. Use this property if you want to alter the tag's content without changing the tag itself. For example:

  ```
  <H2>This is the text</H2>
  ```

  The text in the preceding code would be "This is the text".

Methods   A number of new methods exist that can be used to establish and select *TextRange* objects. The following list provides some descriptions of the methods and how they perform.

- **createTextRange()**—Call the *createTextRange()* method to select a text range. Creating a *TextRange* object with this method creates a text range for the selected element that is bound by the first and last items in the element. Later, when moving the start and ending points of the range, be aware that the boundaries cannot be moved beyond the initial boundaries of the range.

  The *createTextRange()* method is also limited in the number of elements on which it can be called. Currently, the *createTextRange()* method only supports the <BODY>, <INPUT TYPE=TEXT>, <TEXTAREA>, and <BUTTON> elements.

- **duplicate()**—Call this method to create a duplicate of the contents of the *TextRange* object.

- **parentElement()**—Calling this method returns the parent element for the selected range, which can be used to indicate the element that will be replaced or manipulated by other *TextRange* object methods.

■ **inRange()**—Use this method to compare two *TextRange* objects to see if one is contained within the other, or to see if the two ranges are equal. This can be used to assist in finding substrings within ranges.

■ **isEqual()**—Use this method to compare two selected *TextRange* objects to see if their content is the same. This can be useful for comparing copy.

■ **scrollIntoView()**—This method causes a selected *TextRange* object to scroll into view.

■ **setEndPoint()**—Use this method to select the endpoint of one *TextRange* object based on the endpoint of another text range.

■ **compareEndPoints()**—Use this method to determine if two *TextRange* objects share a common endpoint. The method returns a value of –1 (less than), 0 (equal), or 1 (greater than).

TextRange Object Movement Methods   After you select a *TextRange* object, you can move the starting and ending points of the range by using the range movement methods. When using these methods, understand that you are not actually moving any of the text on the page; you are actually moving the boundaries of the range itself, thereby affecting the text that is selected.

The following list contains some of the methods you can use to move *TextRange* objects:

■ **move()**—Use this method to move the text range—but not the text itself—a number of units.

■ **moveEnd()**—Use this method to move the ending point of the current *TextRange*. This is useful for truncating text within the text range on which this method is applied.

■ **moveStart()**—Use this method to change the starting point of a *TextRange*. Use this method in conjunction with the *moveEnd()* method to refine the text selected by a *TextRange*.

■ **pasteHTML()**—The *pasteHTML()* method is an orphan method that you can use to insert HTML text into a text range.

Part
III

Ch
10

Using *TextRange* Objects for Dynamic Content

The capability to manipulate *TextRange* objects is actually a very powerful feature of Dynamic HTML. The following sections provide some examples of the types of manipulations that can be performed on *TextRange* objects.

Changing an Entire Document

Perhaps the best demonstration of the power of *TextRange* objects is the capability to manipulate the entire content of the page in a few simple lines of code. This could be used to create a flip book effect or to reveal a solution to a puzzle, for example. The basic mechanism for these types of changes is to select the text range for the document, and then replace it with the text for a new document. The lines of code for these two processes are numbered to correspond with their placement in listing 10.1.

First, you need to define a page:

```
01. <HTML>
02. <HEAD>
13. <BODY onclick="replacePage()">
14.
15. <H1>Text Ranges</H1>
16. The entire text on this page can be selected and replaced
17. using text ranges.
18. </BODY>
19.
20. </HTML>
```

This creates a page that will call a function called *replacePage()* when the page is clicked. The page created before the *replacePage()* function is called is shown in figure 10.2.

FIG. 10.2

A straightforward web page.

Next you need to create the script that will replace the page:

```
06. <SCRIPT LANGUAGE=JAVASCRIPT>
07. function replacePage() {
08. var bRange = document.body.createTextRange();
09. bRange.pasteHTML("<H1>This text has replaced the page contents.</H1>");
10. }
11. </SCRIPT>
```

This script creates a simple *replacePage()* function that first creates a *TextRange* object that contains the entire page with the following line:

```
var bRange = document.body.createTextRange();
```

This line declares a *bRange* variable and then sets it to the text of the page which is the text contained within the BODY element. Then, you simply use the *pasteHTML()* function to replace the page's content:

```
bRange.pasteHTML("<H1>This text has replaced the page contents.</H1>");
```

Invoking this method replaces the *TextRange* object and modifies the appearance of the page. Listing 10.1 shows the final code, and the results of clicking on the page are shown in figure 10.3.

Listing 10.1   Replacing an Entire Document with TextRanges

```
01. <HTML>
02. <HEAD>
03. <TITLE>Text Ranges</TITLE>
04. </HEAD>
05.
06. <SCRIPT LANGUAGE="JAVASCRIPT">
07. function replacePage() {
08. var bRange = document.body.createTextRange();
09. bRange.pasteHTML("<H1>This text has replaced the page contents.</H1>");
10. }
11. </SCRIPT>
12.
13. <BODY onclick="replacePage()">
14.
15. <H1>Text Ranges</H1>
16. The entire text on this page can be selected and replaced
17. using text ranges.
18. </BODY>
19.
20. </HTML>
```

Part

III

Ch

10

FIG. 10.3

The new page after the *TextRange* object is changed.

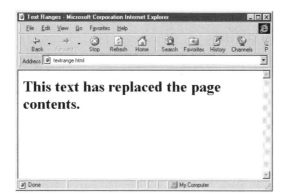

Deleting Page Contents

As you can see from listing 10.1, you can easily replace the entire page with new HTML; however, you can just as easily paste nothing onto the page, effectively deleting the entire page's content. This effect is shown in listing 10.2.

Listing 10.2   Deleting the Contents of a Web Page

```
01. <HTML>
02. <HEAD>
03. <TITLE>Text Ranges</TITLE>
04. </HEAD>
05.
```

continues

Listing 10.2   Continued

```
06. <SCRIPT LANGUAGE=JAVASCRIPT>
07. function replacePage() {
08. var bRange = document.body.createTextRange();
09. bRange.pasteHTML("");
10. }
11. </SCRIPT>
12.
13. <BODY onclick="replacePage()">
14.
15. <H1>Text Ranges</H1>
16. The entire text on this page can be selected and replaced
17. using text ranges.
18. </BODY>
19.
20. </HTML>
```

In listing 10.2, the *bRange.pasteHTML()* function shown in lines 7–10 selects and deletes the text on the page, as defined in lines 15–18. Line 8 uses the *createTextRange()* method to create the text range "bRange." Then, line 9 actually uses the *pasteHTML()* method to replace the content with an empty line, effectively deleting the page content.

Substituting Specified Text

Although some instances exist where it might be useful to replace the entire contents of a page, more often than not, it will be more useful to replace individual segments of text. To accomplish this, you can use the *TextRange* object movement methods to manipulate the starting and ending points of the text range, effectively narrowing down or selecting a limited portion of the text stream. Note that the progressive lines of code leading up to the final listing are numbered to correspond with their placement in listing 10.3.

The following code defines the page shown in figure 10.4:

```
01. <HTML>
14. <BODY onclick="replacePage()">
15.
16. <H1>Text Ranges</H1>
17. We can use TextRanges move methods to replace selected text.
18. </BODY>
19.
20. </HTML>
```

You can then define a function to replace the text, as performed in listings 10.1 and 10.2:

```
06. <SCRIPT LANGUAGE=JAVASCRIPT>
07. function replacePage() {
08. var bRange = document.body.createTextRange();
11. }
12. </SCRIPT>
```

FIG. 10.4

An unsuspecting web page.

At this point, if you call the *pasteHTML()* function as you did on line 9 of listing 10.2, you will replace the entire page, which is not the goal for this example. Instead, change the text on the page from "We can use TextRange's move methods to replace selected text" to "We can use TextRanges to manipulate text."

Your first task is to narrow the selection of the text range. The current *TextRange* object is:

```
Text Ranges We can use TextRange's move methods to replace selected text.
```

Now you can use the *moveStart()* method to move the starting point from the 0 element to the 7th word. The result of the following code

```
09. bRange.moveStart("Word", 7);
```

is that the text range will now be

```
move methods to replace selected text.
```

This is the text you are interested in replacing. Now all you have to do is use the *text* property to change the text as follows:

```
10. bRange.text="to manipulate text.";
```

Listing 10.3 shows the finished code, and figure 10.5 shows the resulting page.

Listing 10.3   Substituting Specific Text on a Page

```
01. <HTML>
02. <HEAD>
03. <TITLE>Text Ranges</TITLE>
04. </HEAD>
05.
06. <SCRIPT LANGUAGE=JAVASCRIPT>
07. function replacePage() {
08. var bRange = document.body.createTextRange();
09. bRange.moveStart("Word", 7);
10. bRange.text="to manipulate text.";
11. }
12. </SCRIPT>
```

continues

Part
III

Ch
10

Listing 10.3 Continued

```
13.
14. <BODY onclick="replacePage()">
15.
16. <H1>Text Ranges</H1>
17. We can use TextRanges move methods to replace selected text.
18. </BODY>
19.
20. </HTML>
```

FIG. 10.5
With *TextRange* object movement methods, a selected portion of the page can be replaced when a user clicks it.

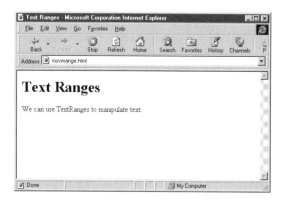

Structured Object Model

TextRange objects can be a very powerful, forceful technique for manipulating the text on a page. If you need to replace an entire page at once, *TextRange* objects will do the trick. At times, however, it might be necessary to change the contents of one tag. Likewise, if you want to change the tag itself, you will need to rely on the Object Model.

The Object Model provides four very important properties that give you a wide range of flexibility for manipulating HTML elements and text:

- innerText
- innerHTML
- outerText
- outerHTML

The following sections explore in detail how each of these properties work.

innerText

The *innerText* property defines or retrieves the text that can be found between the starting and ending tags of the current element. This property is used in the following manner:

```
element.innerText = "value";
```

Suppose, for example, that you had the following HTML code:

```
<H2 ID="MyHeadline">This is my headline</H2>
```

The *innerText* value of this would be "This is my headline". Writing the code:

```
MyHeadline.innerText="A New Headline";
```

would effectively change the <H2> tag to:

```
<H2 ID="MyHeadline">A New Headline</H2>
```

innerHTML

The *innerHTML* property defines the value of any HTML that is contained within a specified HTML element. It is used similarly to the *innerText* property:

```
element.innerHTML = "value";
```

Suppose, for example, that you had the following HTML code:

```
<P ID="MyText">This is <B>my</B> paragraph</P>
```

The *innerHTML* value of this would be "<B>my</B>". Writing the code:

```
MyText.innerHTML="<I>your</I>";
```

would effectively change the <P> tag to:

```
<P ID="MyText">This is <I>your</I> paragraph</P>
```

outerText

The *outerText* property simply defines the text value of the current element similarly to the *innerText* property; however, *outerText* also includes the element's HTML tags as text. This property is used in the following manner:

```
element.outerText = "value";
```

So, using our code from the *innerText* example:

```
<H2 ID="MyHeadline">This is my headline</H2>
```

The *outerText* value of this would be "<H2>This is my headline</H2>". The difference between inner and outer is that the outerText contains the HTML tags. Writing the code:

```
MyHeadline.outerText="<B>This is no longer a headline!</B>";
```

would effectively change the <H2> tag to:

```
<B ID="MyHeadline">This is no longer a headline!</B>
```

outerHTML

The *outerHTML* property sets the value of an HTML element's entire tag, including both the text and the HTML tag itself. The relationship between *innerHTML* and *outerHTML* is like that of *innerText* and *outerText*:

```
element.outerHTML = "value";
```

Suppose, for example, that you had the following HTML code:

```
<P ID="MyText">This is <B>my</B> paragraph</P>
```

The *outerHTML* value of this would be "<P>This is <B>my</B> paragraph</P>". Writing the code:

```
MyText.outerHTML="<H2>This is <I>your</I> healine</H2>";
```

would effectively change the <P> tag to:

```
<H2 ID="MyText">This is <I>your</I> headline</H2>
```

Using the Object Model for Dynamic Content

Now that you are familiar with the Object Model's properties, look at an example that will change the text in a tag when clicked, and then the entire tag when double-clicked. The progressive lines of code that follows are numbered to correspond with the placement in the final code in listing 10.4.

The first thing you need to do is design your basic page, as shown in figure 10.6, with the following code:

```
01. <HTML>
02. <HEAD>
17. </HEAD>
18. <BODY>
19. <P>
20. <H1 id="HEADLINE" STYLE="color: red" onclick="ChangeText()";
➥ondblclick="ChangeTag();">This is a Level One Headline</H1>
21. <P>
22. Click on the text above to watch it change.<BR>
23. Double click it for the magic.
24. </BODY>
25. </HTML>
```

FIG. 10,6

An innocent looking web page, waiting for interaction.

In this example, you want to first change the text in the tag when the headline is clicked, so you need to write a function that changes the text of the tag without altering the tag itself.

To change the text in a tag without altering the tag, the *innerText* property is perfect. If you call this property on the headline, you can replace the headline text while still keeping the tag a level one header. The function looks like this:

```
07. function ChangeText() {
08.     HEADLINE.innerText = "With a click the text is changed!";
09. }
```

Now when the *ChangeText()* function is called, the *innerText* property will change the headline, but leave the formatting intact, as shown in figure 10.7.

For the next step in this example, you will want to replace the text and the tag that is now the headline. Because you want to change the entire element and keep it HTML, you will use the *outerHTML* property to replace the entire tag as shown in figure 10.8. The second function looks like this:

```
11. function ChangeTag() {
12.     HEADLINE.outerHTML = "<H3>Now its a level three headline!!</H3>";
13. }
```

That's it! Now you have all the code you need to manipulate the individual tags in the document to create some dynamic content. Listing 10.4 shows the finished page code.

Listing 10.4 A Page Using the Structured Object Model

```
01. <HTML>
02. <HEAD>
03. <TITLE>Replacing Text</TITLE>
04.
05. <SCRIPT LANGUAGE=JavaScript>
06.
07. function ChangeText() {
08.     HEADLINE.innerText = "With a click the text is changed!";
09. }
10.
11. function ChangeTag() {
12.     HEADLINE.outerHTML = "<H3>Now its a level three headline!!</H3>";
13. }
14.
15. </SCRIPT>
16.
17. </HEAD>
18. <BODY>
19. <P>
20. <H1 id=HEADLINE STYLE="color: red" onclick="ChangeText()";
➥ondblclick="ChangeTag();">This is a Level One Headline</H1>
21. <P>
22. Click on the text above to watch it change.<BR>
23. Double click it for the magic.
24. </BODY>
25. </HTML>
```

Part
III

Ch
10

Figure 10.7 shows the results of changing the content of a tag with the *innerText* property. Conversely, figure 10.8 shows how you can actually change an HTML tag by making use of the outerHTML property.

FIG. 10.7

Changing the contents of a tag with the *innerText* property.

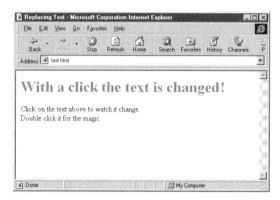

FIG. 10.8

Changing a tag with the *outerHTML* property.

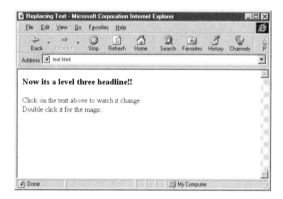

As you can see from the results in figures 10.7 and 10.8, the Structured Object Model provides a much finer control over manipulating individual page elements, enabling you to manipulate the content of virtually any tag on the page dynamically, exposing the power of Dynamic HTML.

From Here...

With dynamic styles and dynamic content at your disposal, you are probably wondering what more lies in store for Dynamic HMTL. Next, you will explore some of the advanced topics coming up in Part IV, "Data Awareness," which consists of the following coverage:

- Chapter 11, "Introduction to Data Binding"—Introduces the methods used to bind data to HTML objects, and how to create data integration with Dynamic HTML.

- Chapter 12, "Using Data Source Objects"—Discusses some of the advanced features of data awareness and using Data Source Objects to create fully functional database applications with Dynamic HTML.

PART IV

Data Awareness

Introduction to Data Binding

Data binding is one of the key features of Dynamic HTML. Why is this? Working with data stored remotely from the user is one of the most demanding and frustrating aspects of programming for the web. Dynamic HTML's facilities for data binding work to make this process much less demanding.

The first thing you need to know is exactly what is meant by the term data binding and why it is an important aspect of Dynamic HTML. ■

Server-Side Data Binding

Server-side data binding is not only quite complex to implement from the programmer's perspective, but also poses severe scalability problems. Learn the downsides of this commonly implemented dynamic content paradigm.

HTML Data Binding Extensions

Learn about the proposed HTML extensions for data binding presented by Dynamic HTML. These extensions consist of three attributes that enable you to specify where to get the data (DATASRC), what column of the data you are interested in (DATAFLD), and the format of the data that is being retrieved (DATAFORMATAS).

Data Consumers

Discover the various data consumers and their special capabilities as implemented by Dynamic HTML. A data consumer is the HTML element that the HTML data binding extensions are used on to allow data to be loaded into them dynamically.

Defining Data Binding

In a broad sense, *data binding* is the process of attaching data to an HTML page. This data does not come from the static HTML that makes up the page; instead it is provided by some sort of external data source. For instance, the data could be generated via a database or a data file on the server.

The data that is to be used for pieces of the web page that will display may come from many sources, including:

- A database server local to the web server
- A live data feed of some sort
- A remote database server
- A text file on the web server

When data binding is used, data is transferred from these data sources to the elements of the web page that are bound to that data. There are two general methods of accomplishing this. First, the work to do the data binding can be done completely on the server. Second, the data binding can be done by the client, off-loading work from the server to the client.

Server-Side Data Binding

The desire to dynamically retrieve data from the server has been strong in the web programming community for quite a while. In fact, this desire was one of the major contributors to the development of forms—the user interface items that have been present almost since the beginning of the web and CGI.

CGI (common gateway interface) scripts enable the user, usually through forms, to interact with the server machine to get data that the user wants to access. This process works quite well on the web, and many commercial and noncommercial sites use it on a daily basis to provide interactive content to web users.

This process of placing forms on the client side—within the browser that communicates to the web server via CGI scripts—can be referred to as *server-side data binding*. The name derives from the data retrieval workload on the server side.

Take a look at the following step-by-step list to see what goes on when data is communicated to the user through server-side binding:

1. The user connects to a remote site using a web browser running on his local machine.
2. The web page is downloaded to the user's browser.
3. The user, usually through a form, selects the data that he wants to be presented.
4. This form executes a CGI script on the server.
5. The server executes the CGI script as a separate process on the machine that it is running.
6. The CGI script fetches the subset of the data that it has the capability to access, which the user wants to access.

7. This data is communicated back to the user's machine as a new HTML document.

8. The user's browser displays the new web page.

Early Attempts at Client-Side Data Binding

With the addition of JavaScript to Netscape Navigator 2.0, Netscape added a new—if somewhat primitive—way to access data. JavaScript added the capability to download small scripts to the client that were executed as programs purely on the client side, without connecting to the server.

The trick to using this new programmatic capability to perform data binding is to embed the data that is to display into the JavaScript program itself. This method has many advantages, most importantly that it does not require any additional communication to the server after the initial contact.

Unfortunately, this method also has several large downsides, including the following:

- Increased script complexity
- Increased script maintenance
- Data maintenance
- Impracticality

Of these four issues, data maintenance and the impracticality of using this method are of the most concern.

When data is being embedded in the program itself, you really want a programmer updating the data that is contained inside the program. Using this early form of client-side scripting runs completely counter to the way things should be—the person responsible for the data should keep it up to date, not the person providing the script for presenting the data.

Regarding practicality, assume that you have several hundred kilobytes of information that you want to display dynamically. It doesn't make sense to force the user's web browser to download this data in its entirety just to see one small portion of it. It is important to take note of this downside due to the relatively slow connections most people have to the web.

Part

IV

Ch

11

Downsides to Server-Side Data Binding

It doesn't make much practical sense to use data embedded in JavaScript to provide the user with data because of the aforementioned reasons. It is a much more common practice to have the browser execute a CGI script to retrieve the data. As mentioned earlier, this can be referred to as server-side data binding.

Server-side binding has plenty of advantages; however, it also has many downsides. These downsides make server-side binding impractical as the web grows larger and the data that is being maintained expands and becomes more arduous with which to deal. The downsides of server-side binding include the following:

- Complexity
- Server scalability
- Round trip server transactions
- Partial data retrieval

The ramifications of these downsides to server-side data binding are covered in detail in the sections that follow.

Complexity of Server-Side Data Binding

The first problem with server-side data binding is the complexity that it entails. The first thing to realize is that basically no state is kept on the client itself.

N O T E The concept of state refers to the capability to keep track of changing conditions. Consider, for example, a user browsing through an online catalog. As the user travels from item to item, the current item that the user is viewing needs to be known. This sort of data is an example of keeping track of state.

Why is this? Think about the way that a web page is constructed. It basically is a static entity that represents a visual document, which is being presented to the user. When the user performs an action that is communicated to the server, the action is conveyed in one of two ways: via the URL that is requested or via the *POST/GET* method when using forms.

Therefore, the only state kept on the web page is the data for which the user is currently asking. Although this is certainly useful information, the client can't keep track of information that would be quite useful when searching through massive amounts of data. For instance, the web client has no idea how much of the database has currently been searched and cannot intelligently optimize the ways in which the data is found and displayed.

This means that all the logic for searching and retrieving this information must be done on the server, while the display must be done on the client. This causes a great deal of complexity in the programming process, because the programmer must keep track of remote browsers' state through the URLs for which they ask.

This also adds a layer of complexity if you want to save the user's search criteria across multiple sessions. Consider a real world example: a web-based search engine that does a very time- and computer-intensive search of medical data for a doctor. This search may take several minutes and a great deal of processor time on the server. In addition, doctors may well want to view this data over a period of several hours.

In this instance, you really do not want to do the search every time the doctor comes back to view the information. Therefore, you decide to cache the results of the query based on the URL of the search results —perhaps by assigning each search a unique ID number—and having the doctor bookmark it.

You can already see how this process can become quite complicated. How do you cache the information? How do you make sure that the correct cache is given to the correct doctor? What sort of data flow issues do you have to consider?

Perhaps most important of all considerations, if you are going to cache the data, you need to address a series of concerns: How long do you cache it? What do you do when the cache is cleared? How do you clear the cache? Do you have a separate "cleaner" program that goes through the search section of the web server?

This complexity affects multiple people throughout the process:

- **HTML Programmer(s)**—HTML programmer(s) must keep in mind while writing HTML code that only a subset of the data may be displayed currently. The HTML programmer(s) must also write complicated scripts to generate the unique URLs that will most likely be required to perform complicated searches.

- **CGI Programmer(s)**—The CGI programmers' lives are made more complicated by the fact that they have almost all segments of the process to consider. CGI programmers must decode a complicated URL into the arguments to derive the subset of data requested. Then the CGI script must retrieve that data from the data source, in many cases doing the search on the data itself. The CGI script must then dynamically convert the data into a form that is presentable on the client side—usually in HTML.

Server Scalabilty

Server-side data binding also introduces major problems related to the scalability of data access on the server. Why is this? Server-side data binding is quite memory and compute intensive on the server due to the many programs that are keeping track of many things at the same time.

N O T E Scalability refers to the server's capability to handle increasing amounts of traffic. If, for instance, the method of data binding you are using takes 25 percent of the server's CPU time it will work great only if a few people are using it at a time. If, however, 100 people try to use it at the same time it will run quite poorly. This is an example of a solution that is not scalable. In general, the less server resources and communications bandwidth used, the more scalable a solution is.

Consider the standard way in which CGI scripts are run. The most common programming language for CGI is Perl. Whenever a Perl CGI script is run on the server, an actual new instance of the Perl interpreter is executed on the server machine.

This may not seem that important until you realize that this process of starting a new interpreter occurs for *every* instance in which the CGI script is called. The Perl interpreter isn't an overwhelmingly huge program, but imagine what happens when thousands of copies of it are running at the same time. To put this in perspective, imagine starting up several hundred copies of Netscape on your machine.

Part
IV

Ch
11

This problem of starting up many copies of the environment that the CGI program is executing in has been recognized for a long time. In fact, to alleviate this problem, many web servers allow you to execute CGI programs through a method known as *in-process* that doesn't actually have to start up new copies of interpreters. Note, however, that by doing this, the process of coding and developing for these environments has become more complex.

Unfortunately, the problem of starting up the Perl interpreters themselves is not the only onerous problem regarding the amount of computing time that is takes to retrieve the proper data. There is also the issue of actually doing the searches themselves. To contemplate this, imagine doing several hundred "Find" processes on your machine at once.

Sadly, the problem of all this working being done on the server does not have a solution. One common method to alleviate this congestion on the server is by splitting up requests to multiple servers—making them all appear to be the same server. Note again, however, that this makes the process of programming and maintaining this environment much more complicated.

In addition to computational intensiveness, you should consider that because the server must keep track of all state, it may also need to have large amounts of storage space to store the state information—especially if the search that the user is doing needs to be maintained across sessions.

These scalability problems are not only problematic for the programmer, but also to the Webmasters and system administrators who are faced with the burdensome task of keeping these machines running at reasonable speeds, and keeping them from running out of disk space.

Round Trip Server Transactions

Another problem with server-side data binding is that a round trip to the server must be done for basically everything that the user requests. Take a look at the flow of information when a user does a search of a catalog that you have placed on your web site via server-side data binding.

Suppose, for example, that you have a stereo shop and the user wants to search for three different types of amplifiers: monaural, stereo, and surround.

1. The user enters the pertinent keywords at the stereo shop search screen to search for monaural amplifiers. The browser sends the search information to the server.
2. The data for monaural amplifiers is sent back to the browser.
3. The user enters the keywords to search for stereo amplifiers and executes the search. The browser again sends the search information to the server.
4. The data for stereo amplifiers is sent back to the browser.
5. The user enters the keywords to search for surround amplifiers and executes the search. The browser again sends the search information to the server.
6. The data for surround amplifiers is sent the browser.

By taking a close look at the process that occurs in the preceding example, you can see that three round trips to the server were required for these searches. In fact, a round trip is required every time a new search is executed.

In addition to the server scalability problems associated with this process, it is also important to consider the network implications. Because a round trip occurs for each search, the network becomes considerably more congested than it needs to be.

One possible solution to this problem is to do all the searches at once; however, this solution has multiple problems. The first problem to overcome is the display of multiple sets of data to the user if all the searches are done at once. Should all the data be intertwined within each other, or should the data be broken up into second pieces?

Secondly, and more importantly, the user may not know at the time of the first search that they want to do multiple searches. Why should the user be forced to think of ways to make his searches more resource friendly when the user is just there for the information?

Partial Data Retrieval

Many of the problems related to placing so much responsibility on the server have already been considered. High server responsibility causes network congestion problems, slows down the server, and forces the server to keep track of the state of the client.

The last point is more problematic than is immediately obvious. Quite often the entire results of the data that the user has asked for are not contained in the document.

The results are not contained in the document because browsers would be overwhelmed with data. Users would also be overwhelmed if 100 pages of results were shown at once, forcing them to scroll over a huge area.

To alleviate this problem, most web sites that deal with data retrieval break up the data that is delivered into sections. Here are a few examples:

- The most common sites that use the paradigm of dividing results into sections are web search engines. If you use your browser on one of the more common search engines that index the entire web to search for something common, the engine will return hundreds, if not thousands, of results. You don't get all the results at once, instead, a subset of the data that you are looking for—probably between 10 and 100 matches—displays.

- Another common set of sites that run into this situation are online catalogs. When you are searching for laptop computers, for instance, you might ask for all laptop computers that cost between one thousand and four thousand dollars. On most larger online catalogs, this would return over a hundred laptops, and usually only 25 or so are provided at once.

- A final example are news sites, where you can search through archived news stories using keywords to specify what you want to retrieve. If you do a search of common sorts of stories, you will most likely only receive a subset of the stories at a time.

Part
IV

Ch
11

This process of breaking up the data into chunks on the server causes all sorts of problems. First, it is more complex from the programming perspective. Second, it forces the server to keep track of even more user state. The server must remember which set of data the user is currently viewing.

Finally, this breaking up of data into sections causes problems for the user. Say you did a search on a site that produced matches pretty close to the item you wanted, but the server didn't let you do quite as fine a search as you wanted.

Perhaps you are only interested in laptops that use lithium-ion batteries but catalog search engines wouldn't let you add that to the search criteria. Instead, you want to use the find feature of your browser to go to each of the results on the page that contain the phrase "lithium-ion."

Unfortunately for the user, they will have to go through a long and arduous process to get at the data that they want, because they will have to get the subset, do a find, get the next subset, do a find, and so on.

Client-Side HTML Data Binding Solutions

Most of the problems that were discussed in the previous sections are related to the fact that everything is stored on the server. Wouldn't it be nice if large pieces of this process were off-loaded to the client?

Client-side data binding allows this off-loading to be done. In fact, client-side data binding provides several advantages that directly relieve the problems discussed over the last few sections:

- **Reduction in round trips to the server**—Because most or all the state is stored on the client, the only round trips to the server are for the retrieval of the data itself.

- **No need to divide data into sections**—Because the client only needs to download the data that is needed at any given time and can get new data easily, there is no need to divide the data into sections that are downloaded en masse.

- **Scalability**—Because the bulk of the work is done on the client side, much less work needs to be done on the server. This benefits the scalablity of the server a great deal.

Client-side HTML data binding enables you to do just that. It enables you to pick a source for the data that will be placed on the web page, and then automatically places the data from the data source on the web page.

A huge advantage of binding on the client side is that client-side binding only requires the new data that is to be placed on the page to be transmitted to the browser. This is because with client-side data binding, the data is bound only to certain elements on the page. With CGI, on the other hand, an entire new page must be downloaded when the data lookup is done.

The use of client-side binding is much less complex, because the web server needs only be used to send documents. The client can communicate directly to a database for the data it needs, use a middleware service such as ODBC, or load a file containing the data from the web server itself.

By reducing the workload on the web server, the entire process is much more scalable. The web server is much less inundated with work, because the process of figuring out what data is needed is computed somewhere else—perhaps on a relational database system or on the user's client machine. In any case, client-side binding enables the the web server to be used for its main purpose: serving web documents.

In addition, client-side data binding significantly reduces the number of round trips required to the server. The web page can, for instance, download the index to a catalog to the web browser. This index is not immediately displayed, but instead shown a bit at a time by the elements on the page, controlled by a script. This means that data can be dynamically viewed and navigated without ever contacting the server again. By reducing round trips to the server, the network impact of data binding is also reduced drastically.

By being able to download data, in a sense "caching" it locally to be viewed later, the web page can download all the data it needs, rather than breaking it down into sections. This means that the state of what is being viewed can be kept on the client rather than the server, saving precious server resources.

The server resources saved can be broad-ranging. Because the searching is not done on the server, that processor-intensive computation is off-loaded from the server. In addition, the server does not need to keep track of much state information of the client, and therefore does not need to cache data or spend processor time figuring out what subset the user needs to view next.

Because all the data is handled locally, the user also can (assuming the web page will let them) dynamically decide how much data to show at once. This means that, for the sake of easy viewing, the user can choose to have only 10 or 20 items viewed at the same time during most of their interactions with the data. Alternatively, the user could also have the option of showing all the data at the same time.

All these advantages are important, but the most obvious one is speed. One of the largest complaints about the web is how slow it is. If more of the intelligence for data retrieval and searching can be placed on the client, operations will tend to execute quicker, and the user will have a more pleasant browsing experience.

HTML Data Binding Extensions

HTML data binding enables you to semi-automatically present data to the user in various places on the document via data bound elements. This implementation is quite flexible and for the most part quite simple to program.

You, for example, can define a <SPAN> element on a page to be bound to the "Product Name" field in your data and another <SPAN> element to be bound to the "Price" field in your data. This would cause the Price and Product Name to automatically be placed into those elements via data binding.

HTML data binding has an important requirement, however, in addition to it being used on a client that supports it. The requirement is that the data being retrieved is available in tabular form.

Tabular form means that the data can be represented as columns and rows and that each column can be accessed one at a time. This form is used because it is easy to work with and maps naturally onto the types of data access normally done on the web.

N O T E It's important not to confuse the concept of data being in tabular form and the Tabular Data Control. Tabular form is a general term referring to the type of data that is being used, while the Tabular Data Control (which will be discussed in the next chapter) is a specific ActiveX Control that can be used with data binding.

This sounds a bit abstract, but if you look at the following concrete example, you'll gain a better understanding of tabular data. The following table contains data representing the prices of various types of furniture at a furniture shop, along with the item's price and color:

Table 11.1

Type	Color	Price
sofa	green	$600
bed	white	$250
desk	woodgrain	$350
chair	black	$75
table	red	$375
recliner	plaid	$425

The choice of using a table to represent this data is a good way to look at whether data is tabular. Note that each column can be read down and you can check the status of each item with respect to the type of data that is being stored. For instance, all the colors are stored in the color column.

Each of the columns represents what is known as a *field* of the database. A field indicates what is represented in each column of the table. Therefore, the first field of this data is the "type" field, the second is the "color" field, and finally, the third is the "price" field.

In much the same way, the entire status for one item can be read at once by grabbing a row from the table. Each row is often referred to by programmers as a *record*, because it defines a complete record of that item's data.

In general, if the data you are representing can fit into a table such as this one, it is a good candidate for tabular data. If, on the other hand, your data does not fit well into this paradigm, you might want to consider other options, such as reverting back to server-side data binding, or perhaps using an ActiveX object or Java applet to access the data.

The essence of HTML data binding can be broken down into two key concepts:

- **Data consumers**—The HTML elements that retrieve and display the desired data.
- **Data sources**—The origin of the data displayed by the data consumers.

A data source might be as complicated as fetching data via SQL calls to a relational database, or as simple as grabbing a text file that contains tabular data.

The process by which data consumers are attached to data sources is known as *binding*. This binding is specified in the HTML file that you write, by using special syntax developed specifically for HTML data binding.

Take a quick look at an example. The following code defines a data source and a data consumer:

```
<OBJECT id="furniture"
    classid="clsid:333C7BC4-460F-11D0-BC04-0080C7055A83"
    <PARAM name="DataURL" value="furniture.txt">
</OBJECT>

<SPAN DATASRC="#furniture" DATAFLD="type"></SPAN>
```

The data source is defined by the <OBJECT> element. In this case, the Tabular Data Control data source object is being used. Don't worry about understanding most of the parameters to the <OBJECT> right now—Data Source Objects will be considered in detail in the next chapter. The important thing to note at this point is that the <OBJECT> element is defining a data source and assigning it the ID "furniture."

For an HTML element to function as a data consumer and to bind to a data source, it must be able to specify two important aspects of its data-oriented nature. The HTML element must first be able to specify the data source that is attached to it. Second, the element must be able to specify which column of the data source to use. The HTML for specifying these properties is discussed in detail later in this chapter.

In the previous example, the data consumer is the <SPAN> element. In this case, the data source that is being attached to it is the "furniture" data source (ignore the "#" for now, it will be discussed later). The column of the data source that will be used is the "type" column. This process of data consumer binding will be covered in detail in the sections that follow.

Part

IV

Ch

11

Single- and Repeated-Table Valued Data Consumers

So far, this chapter has treated all data consumers (HTML elements that are set up to receive data from a data source) as entities of a singular type. It is true that all data consumers receive data, but two different types of data consumers exist: single-valued and repeated-table valued.

Single-valued data consumers retrieve one value at a time from the current row at which the data source is looking. This type of binding is known as *value binding*. The value retrieved represents the value of one field of the current row. So, if you were on the first row in table 11.1 and you were bound to the "type" field, the value would be "soft."

The second type of data consumer is the repeated-table type. This type of data consumer displays the *entire* contents of the tabular data at once. Each field does not need to be bound to a specific element, because the data that is retrieved is treated as a whole. This type of binding is known as *set binding*.

To bind HTML elements to data values, you need to have some way of specifying the data source and what column of that data source to use. The manner in which HTML elements are bound to data values is accomplished by setting HTML attributes of the elements that you want to be bound. There are three new attributes that enable this binding to be done:

- **DATASRC**—Specifies what data source to bind to.
- **DATAFLD**—Specifies what part of the data to bind to.
- **DATAPAGESIZE**—Specifies the number of rows to insert when using repeated-table binding.
- **DATAFORMATAS**—Specifies format for which the bound data is displayed (ASCII, HTML, raw).

The DATASRC Attribute

The DATASRC attribute enables you to specify the data source to which you want to bind. In other words, this attribute tells you where the data you will be binding to will come from. As previously discussed, the data can be bound to a single value (via value binding), or it can be bound to an entire table (via set binding).

The DATASRC attribute takes an id as its value. The id that it takes should be the id of a data source object that has been defined elsewhere in the HTML document. The id that is referenced must be unique on the page.

When you use the DATASRC attribute to specify set binding to bind to an entire table, you have no control over the rows that will display. All the subelements of the table are repeated until the entire data set from the data source displays.

Take a look at an example:

```
<TABLE DATASRC="#furniture">
</TABLE>
```

The DATASRC attribute binds this table to the data source object specified by the "#furniture" id. This data source object has been specified at some other point in the HTML file. Data Source Objects are explored in Chapter 12, "Using Data Source Objects."

The DATASRC attribute can be used with the following HTML elements: TABLE, SPAN, DIV, OBJECT, PARAM, INPUT, SELECT, TEXTAREA, IMG, MARQUEE, A, FRAME, IFRAME, and BUTTON.

DATAFLD

After you've specified where the data will be coming from via the DATASRC attribute, you must specify to what part of the data you want to bind. The DATAFLD attribute enables you to complete this task.

The DATAFLD attribute enables you to specify the column from the tabular data that you want to bind to the specified HTML element. This column represents a field that is then found in each row (or record).

The DATAFLD attribute cannot be set by itself. A DATASRC attribute must be specified. This makes sense, because it isn't very logical to try to bind to data without specifying from where it will be coming. The DATASRC attribute can be set either in the element that the DATAFLD attribute is contained in, or in its parents.

The value specified with the DATAFLD attribute is the name of the table column to which you will bind. Therefore, in the tabular data example in table 11.1, you would bind to the first column of the tabular data by setting the DATAFLD attribute to "type."

Take a look at an example by extending the code from the previous section on DATASRC attributes:

```
<TABLE DATASRC="#furniture">
    <TR>
        <TD>
            <SPAN DATAFLD="type"></SPAN>
        </TD>
    </TR>
</TABLE>
```

The additional code specifies the display of only one column from the tabular data being supplied from the data source object: the "type" column.

Because you are specifying this data field attribute within a table, it is going to be a set, or repeating type of data binding. By default, all the rows from the tabular data will be inserted into the table. The DATAPAGESIZE attribute (discussed in the next section), however, allows you to limit the number of rows to insert.

If you want to bind to a single column and a single value at a time, you would use the following syntax:

```
<SPAN DATASRC="#furniture" DATAFLD="type"></SPAN>
```

Instead of showing the entire contents of the tabular data at once, you now get only one field from one row at a time bound to one HTML element on the page. You can then move through the rows of the tabular data by accessing the methods of the Data Source Object (see Chapter 12).

The DATAFLD objects can be used with the following HTML elements: SPAN, DIV, OBJECT, PARAM, INPUT, SELECT, TEXTAREA, IMG, MARQUEE, A, FRAME, IFRAME, BUTTON, and LABEL.

DATAPAGESIZE

The DATAPAGESIZE attribute enables you to limit the number of rows that are inserted from the Data Source Object when repeated-table binding is used. If the DATAPAGESIZE attribute is not specified, all the rows available from the Data Source Object are inserted into the table.

The DATAPAGESIZE attribute is always used in conjunction with the DATASRC attribute. If, for example, you wanted to specify that 10 rows should be placed in the table from the "#furniture" data source, you would use the following code:

```
<TABLE DATASRC="#furniture" DATAPAGESIZE=10>
```

DATAFORMATAS

The final HTML data binding attribute that can be set is the DATAFORMATAS attribute. The DATAFORMATAS attribute enables you to specify just how the data that is coming from the Data Source Object will be represented.

The DATAFORMATAS attribute is optional. If it is not specified, the default data format is ASCII text. The importance of this attribute depends on whether you will be dealing with data that is in a special format or not. If you will just be working with standard ASCII text, you can ignore this attribute for the most part; however, it is worth keeping in mind in case you ever do need to work with data in one of the special formats.

The formats that can be specified by the DATAFORMATAS attribute are as follows:

- **text**—Specifies that the data is ASCII text. This type of data can be displayed with no conversions.
- **html**—Specifies that the data is in HTML. This informs the browser that the HTML data may need to be parsed before being displayed.
- **none**—Specifies that the data is in raw format. This might be used if you were bringing in data, such as long integers.

The DATAFORMATAS attribute is used with the following HTML elements: SPAN, DIV, MARQUEE, BUTTON, and LABEL.

Implementing the Data Binding Attributes

All the data binding attribute extensions to HTML have been covered. You've learned a lot of concepts and syntax, so now take a look at a real world example.

In this example, you'll take tabular data, previously discussed, and display it as a repeating table inside the web page. This example shows how straightforward it is to generate data dynamically via HTML data binding.

First, you'll need to define the data that will be used. For this example, data describing merchandise from a furniture store will be used. There are three aspects for each piece of furniture that will be provided: the type of furniture, its color, and its price. The format that is used to define this data is quite straightforward, but that is discussed in detail in the next chapter.

Here is the furniture file. Save this data as furniture.txt:

```
type,color,price:INT
sofa,green,300
bed,white,850
desk,woodgrain,350
chair,black,475
table,red, 175
recliner,plaid,425
```

Listing 11.1 shows the HTML document for the example (the file name is ch11ex01.htm):

Listing 11.1 Repeated-Table Binding

```
01. <HTML>
02. <HEAD>
03.    <TITLE>
04.       Chapter 11, Example 1
05.    </TITLE>
06. </HEAD>
07.
08. <BODY>
09.
10. <OBJECT id="furniture"
11.        classid="clsid:333C7BC4-460F-11D0-BC04-0080C7055A83"
12.        border="0"
13.        width="0"
14.        height="0">
15.    <PARAM name="DataURL" value="furniture.txt">
16.    <PARAM name="UseHeader" value="True">
17. </OBJECT>
18.
19. <TABLE DATASRC="#furniture" border=1>
20.    <TR>
21.       <TD>
22.          <SPAN DATAFLD="type"></SPAN>
23.       </TD>
24.       <TD>
25.          <SPAN DATAFLD="color"></SPAN>
26.       </TD>
27.       <TD>
28.          <SPAN DATAFLD="price"></SPAN>
29.       </TD>
30.
31.    </TR>
32. </TABLE>
33.
34. </BODY>
35. </HTML>
```

Part
IV

Ch

11

The output for the example in listing 11.1 is shown in figure 11.1.

FIG. 11.1

Output from repeated-table binding.

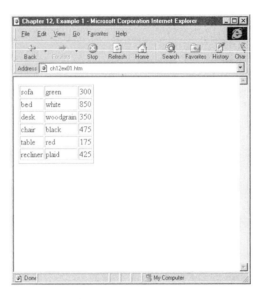

All the rows from the tabular data file supplied have automatically been inserted into the table. Note that you did not have to add anything else to the table definition to have it automatically filled in by repeated-table binding.

The table code that is used here with DATASRC (line 19) and DATAFLD (lines 22, 25, and 28) was discussed earlier in the chapter. The additional code is the <OBJECT> element on line 10. This element specifies the data source file that is used for data binding. (Data Source Objects are covered in detail in the next chapter.)

The <OBJECT> Data Source Object will contine to be used to keep things from getting too confusing. Just keep in mind that this data source object returns the furniture data in tabular form on a row by row basis.

One interesting thing to note that is a bit strange is that when the Data Source Object is defined it is named "furniture," but when it is referenced in the DATASRC attribute it is listed as "#furniture."

This may seem a bit strange, and in fact it is. The addition of the pound sign is just Dynamic HTML's syntactic way of saying, "This is special, this is a data source object." Like all technologies, Dynamic HTML has its quirks. Don't sweat it, just remember to put a pound sign ('#') in front of Data Source Objects when you're referring to them in DATASRC attributes.

Data Consumers

Now that you've learned the attributes that Dynamic HTML has added for data binding, you are ready to take a closer look at a few of the HTML elements with which these attributes can be used.

These elements are known as data consumers. Data consumers were discussed before. They are the HTML elements that can receive data from Data Source Objects via binding.

DIV

<DIV> tags are used in data binding to display a block of plain text or HTML code. If you do not specify the DATAFORMATAS attribute, the data always displays as pure ASCII text.

If, however, you want to display the data as HTML code, you must set the data format. This is done by setting the DATAFORMATAS attribute to "html."

If the underlying text changes in the Data Source Object to which the <DIV> element is bound, then the contents of the <DIV> element will change.

SPAN

The <SPAN> tag is used similar the <DIV> tag except that it is more limited in the content that it can show. It is best used for straightforward text.

The SPAN element is limited in that it cannot include HTML "block" tags. If you need to include this type of element, you should probably use a <DIV> element, because SPAN is meant mainly for limited amounts of text.

Much like the <DIV> tag, the <SPAN> tag can contain ASCII text or HTML code. If you are using HTML, set DATAFORMATAS to the value "html." Also similar to the <DIV> tag, when the Data Source Object's row value changes, the value of the text in the SPAN element changes.

SPAN binds data in a single-value manner. Listing 11.2 modifies the code from listing 11.1 to display only one value at a time by using just a SPAN element. Save this file as ch11ex02.htm:

Part
IV
Ch
11

Listing 11.2   Single-Value Binding

```
01. <HTML>
02. <HEAD>
03.    <TITLE>
04.        Chapter 11, Example 2
05.    </TITLE>
06. </HEAD>
07.
08. <BODY>
09.
10. <OBJECT id="furniture"
11.        classid="clsid:333C7BC4-460F-11D0-BC04-0080C7055A83"
```

continues

Listing 11.2 Continued

```
12.          border="0"
13.          width="0"
14.          height="0">
15.      <PARAM name="DataURL" value="furniture.txt">
16.      <PARAM name="UseHeader" value="True">
17. </OBJECT>
18.
19. <P><SPAN DATASRC="#furniture" DATAFLD="type"></SPAN>
20. <P><SPAN DATASRC="#furniture" DATAFLD="color"></SPAN>
21. <P><SPAN DATASRC="#furniture" DATAFLD="price"></SPAN>
22.
23. </BODY>
24. </HTML>
```

The output for the HTML code in listing 11.2 appears in figure 11.2.

FIG. 11.2

Output from single-value binding example (listing 11.2).

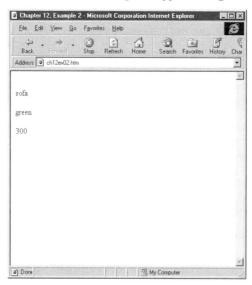

The main thing to pay attention to in this example is that the only lines of HTML displayed are contained within the SPAN element. This element is dynamically generated by loading the "type" column from the current row of the Data Source Object. In this instance, the Data Source Object is "furniture" and represents the tabular data from table 11.1 earlier in the chapter.

SELECT

The <SELECT> tag in HTML enables the user to make a choice. It is visually identical to a user interface element commonly referred to as a list box. The value of this SELECT element can be bound to a column value from a Data Source Object.

The syntax of the SELECT element is actually quite straightforward with respect to data binding. Just add the DATASRC and DATAFLD attributes to the SELECT element. Then add the options for the SELECT element, making sure that all the possible values that could be loaded from the data source are represented as valid options:

```
<SELECT DATASRC="#furniture" DATAFLD="type">
    <OPTION>sofa
    <OPTION>bed
    <OPTION>desk
    <OPTION>chair
    <OPTION>table
    <OPTION>recliner
</SELECT>
```

MARQUEE

A MARQUEE element is simply an area of text that scrolls by automatically. MARQUEE elements are often used for data that changes on a regular basis that the web author wants to provide to the user in an abbreviated form.

MARQUEE elements can have their value bound to a Data Source Object, which then provides the text that will be shown in a scrolling marquee.

Much like the <DIV> and <SPAN> tags, both raw ASCII text and HTML can be bound from a data source object into a MARQUEE element, depending on whether the DATAFORMATAS attribute is set to "html."

Normally when MARQUEE elements are used, text is placed between the <MARQUEE> and </MARQUEE> tags in the HTML file. This text is what then scrolls by in the marquee. If, however, data binding is being used, this text is ignored and the data from the Data Source Object is used instead.

IMG

Text isn't the only data that can be used with Dynamic HTML data binding. Images can also be bound to a data source. The actual image data, however, is not retrieved from the Data Source Object.

Instead of the actual image, an IMG element is used and bound to the Data Source Object. The value that it retrieves is used as an URL to seek out the image to be displayed. That image is then loaded via the URL and displayed in the browser.

For instance, say you wanted to associate an image with each piece of furniture in the example from the previous sections. You could do this by providing an URL that points to an image and bind this to an IMG tag on your page.

APPLET

The capability to load images dynamically via data binding is a pretty powerful concept; however, the capability to do data binding via the <APPLET> tag takes dynamic image loading one

Part
IV

Ch
11

step further by actually allowing parameters for executable program content to be dynamically specified via data binding.

Data binding with the <APPLET> tag is used by specifying DATASRC and DATAFLD attributes within the parameter definitions as defined in the following syntax:

```
<APPLET applet-info
    <PARAM NAME="login"
           VALUE=""
           DATASRC="#userinfo"
           DATAFLD="user_login"
    >
</APPLET>
```

This code causes the login parameter to be specified via data binding. The value of the "login" parameter is loaded from the "user_login" column of the row of the tabular data being provided by the "userinfo" Data Source Object.

You, for instance, might have a 3D applet that allowed the user to move around the piece of furniture they are looking at in three dimensions. Binding via the <APPLET> tag enables the parameters to that applet (such as which 3D model to view) to be retrieved from a Data Source Object.

From Here...

This chapter introduced you to the capabilities and the syntax of HTML data binding. The details of where that data comes from, however, have not been presented. You will learn about this in:

- Chapter 12, "Using Data Source Objects"—Here, you will learn about the use of data source objects and how they are used with the HTML data binding extensions.

Using Data Source Objects

Chapter 11, "Introduction to Data Binding," covered the aspects of Dynamic HTML that enable you to bind data information retrieved remotely to elements on an HTML page.

Because the data displayed is not included as part of the HTML code itself or the script associated with the page, nor is it generated by the web server, it must be generated by something other than these components.

The source of the data used in HTML data binding is accessed through what is known as a *Data Source Object*. A Data Source Object is an object that contains methods that enable the data bound control to retrieve data.

These Data Source Objects are, for the most part, generic ActiveX objects. What makes them special is that they support interfaces that the HTML data binding extensions look for to collect the data from them.

By the end of this chapter you should have a firm grasp on the fundamentals of the use of Data Source Objects, specifically the Tabular Data Control. ■

Understanding Data Source Objects

Learn the usage and capabilities of Data Source Objects and how they fit into Dynamic HTML.

Tabular Data Control

Explore the intricacies of the Tabular Data Control, which enables data binding using only data files stored on the server with no dedicated database server necessary.

Sorting

Learn how to implement one of the most fundamental operations of data—sorting. The Tabular Data Control includes simple, yet powerful, methods by which to sort data. It can sort in either ascending or descending order based on any column in the data.

Data Source Objects (DSOs)

When Microsoft was developing Dynamic HTML, an obvious addition to current HTML was client-side data binding. The first thing to consider was how the HTML elements would be extended to support data binding. Luckily, this was a fairly straightforward process.

Because the elements that would be bound to the data were already defined, the aspects of how to extend them came down to two decisions:

How to extend the elements

Which elements to extend with the data binding capability

The decisions related to how to supply that data were much more difficult, however. HTML is quite client-centric and does not lend itself easily to the supplying of data remotely. Therefore, Microsoft had to define a standard method of supplying this data from the server to the client.

Microsoft's solution to this dilemma was to introduce a new class of object to Dynamic HTML that supports the sending of data to data-bound HTML elements: the Data Source Object.

The Data Source Object is an embedded object in the HTML page that is given the parameters for where the data will be coming from and the method by which it should be retrieved.

Data Source Object Responsibilities

Data Source Objects are responsible for the specification of four major aspects of the data retrieval, as follows:

- The definition and implementation of the data transport mechanism
- The method used to retrieve requested data
- The manipulation of retrieved data
- The object model used for script access

Specifying the Data Transport Mechanism   The Data Source Object is responsible for the definition and implementation of the data transport mechanism by which the data will be sent to the browser. This transport mechanism may be completely independent of the transport by which the page was downloaded to the browser.

One common data transport mechanism is HTTP (Hypertext Transfer Protocol). HTTP provides a standard communication protocol that enables web browsers to request information (usually URL requests) and web servers to transfer information (usually HTML web pages) to each other.

Other common data transport mechanisms exist. NNTP (Network News Transfer Protocol), for instance, is the standard transport protocol for sending and receiving Usenet news. If you have a news reader on your PC, such as Microsoft's Internet News Reader, you will have to specify a news server through which to receive news. Your news reader then speaks to the news server through NNTP.

The sending and receiving of Internet e-mail has a standard data transport mechanism as well. The protocol that it uses is known as SMTP (Simple Mail Transfer Protocol). Whenever your PC-based e-mail client, such as Eudora, sends or receives e-mail, it uses SMTP.

Just like Usenet news or e-mail, there are protocols for sending tabular kinds of data over the web. The applications providing the data could range from desktop database programs to advanced SQL relational databases.

Unfortunately, most databases use a proprietary protocol to communicate over the network. The transport protocol used to communicate with an Oracle database, for example, will be completely different than the protocol used to communicate with a Microsoft SQL server database.

Due to these differences in communication protocols, Data Source Objects are given freedom to communicate with the data source via any method desired. For instance, the two DSOs that are included in IE 4.0 use completely different methods of retrieving data. The Tabular Data Control retrieves a text file containing data from the web server. On the other hand, the Remote Data Service uses ODBC to connect to database servers to retrieve data.

The capability to use wildly different transport protocols is a positive attribute because it does not lock Data Source Objects into communicating with only one class of data providers. No matter what the protocol, so long as it can be communicated over the Internet, Data Source Objects can deal with it.

This protocol independence means that Data Source Objects are not limited to the standard sorts of ways to retrieve data. Many programmers are accustomed to stores of data residing exclusively in databases and will expect all Data Source Objects to be associated with database programs.

However, this is not the case; the provider of the data can be almost anything. This flexibility is taken to an extreme with the Tabular Data Control (TDC), which does not deal with an actual running database program over the web. The TDC, instead, deals exclusively with raw files that it downloads via HTTP.

This may sound strange, but makes quite a bit of sense. If the data that you will be binding to is for the most part static, why do you need to have a separate database program providing it?

Specifying the Data Retrieval Method　　The Data Source Object is where the user specifies the method to retrieve the data that is being requested. This may sound suspiciously like the transport protocol (data transport mechanism) used, but there is an important and subtle difference.

The protocol used to transfer the data is usually transparent to the user. The protocol, for instance, used to transfer tables from a Sybase SQL Server is known as Tds; however, there is rarely any reason for the user of a Data Source Object that connects to a Sybase SQL Server to know that sort of information. From the user's perspective, the protocol used to transfer the data is all hidden behind the scenes and handled by the server and the driver.

Part
IV
Ch
12

On the other hand, the specification of the method to retrieve the data is the description from the client to the data source on exactly what data the client page is interested. The methods by which this is accomplished will vary widely from Data Source Object to Data Source Object. The Tabular Data Control, for example, accesses data through a text file on the web server, whereas the Remote Data Service accesses data via ODBC. The Tabular Data Control will be described later in this chapter. The Remote Data Service (usually used with SQL relational database servers) is beyond the scope of this book, but you can find information on RDS in the IE 4.0 documentation.

Suppose, for example, that you are connecting to the aforementioned Sybase SQL Server. You may have to supply many different pieces of information to the Data Source Object before you can retrieve information. Here's a list of the parameters that may be required:

- The name of the server
- The Internet address or qualified name of the remote machine that is running the server
- The TCP/IP port that the server is currently running on the remote machine
- The name of the database on the server on which you want to execute your query
- The SQL query to execute on the server

These data parameters are required due to the nature of relational database servers that process SQL queries. For robust, client-server applications, this kind of power and flexibility is required. Programmers who are accustomed to dealing with these types of servers will expect to have to provide this information.

Moreover, the syntax of an SQL query itself can be quite complicated. SQL syntax is a way to access fields from tabular data with a syntax that tries to approximate natural language—with varying degrees of success. The following query, for instance, selects all the "f_type" fields from an SQL table named "FURNITURE" where the furniture type has a price less than 500 dollars:

```
SELECT f_type FROM FURNITURE WHERE PRICE < 500
```

Even though this is a simple example of an SQL query, you can see how this method of specifying data to retrieve can become quite unwieldy. This is not a negative comment on SQL, just a realization that in some cases it will be the equivalent of using an industrial power tool when only a screwdriver is required.

Because Dynamic HTML does not require Data Source Objects to have one method of specifying the way to retrieve the desired data, it is much more flexible in this regard. Specifying the data, for instance, that you want by using the Tabular Data Control is much simpler than using a Data Source Object that connects to an SQL server.

To specify the source of the data for the Tabular Data Control, for example, you have to specify only one parameter. You must specify from where the data will be coming. This parameter is given as an URL and the file that contains the tabular data will be downloaded to the Data

Source Object on the client. For instance, you might use the following URL to point to the data file on your machine:

http://yourmachine.com/datafile.txt

The capability to retrieve this sort of tabular data with such simple syntax and without the necessity of having a database server is actually more important than it may seem at first. It is a great example of how simplicity can be quite powerful.

You might want to prototype a site using text file sample data and not worry about the vagaries associated with SQL servers, for instance. SQL servers usually require quite a bit of resources and expertise in their administration; however, often all that is required is to read rows of tabular data that may change on a regular basis. In this case, the Tabular Data Control can be used with files residing on the server, saving resources and programmer complexity. And, if you later move to a more powerful data access method, the only code you will need to change in your client is the specification of the Data Source Object itself.

Specifying the Manipulation of Requested Data   The Data Source Object is responsible for all *manipulations* that occur to the data. What is meant by manipulations? Quite often when accessing data, you might want to have it presented in a different form than it was delivered to you originally.

A good example of manipulating the data is doing a sort on the results returned by the Data Source Object. When you first receive the data it may or may not be sorted, depending on which Data Source Object you are using.

Most Data Source Objects will define methods that enable you to sort on various sections of the result that has been returned. Suppose, for example, that you have a database that contains types, colors, and prices of various tropical fish. The following table gives an example of the type of data that might appear in this database:

Part IV
Ch 12

Table 13.1   Tropical Fish Data from the Database

Type	Color	Price
Damsel	Red	6.95
Shark	Gray	22.95
Eel	Black	18.95
Rockfish	Blue	28.95
Ray	Gray	54.95

If you wanted to sort the data, you would use the methods of the Data Source Object relevant to sorting. Most Data Source Objects would, at the very least, enable you to sort in ascending and descending order based upon one of the fields in the result. Therefore, you would be able to sort based on the type, color, or price of the tropical fish.

In addition, Data Source Objects specify the filtering of any data they contain. Filtering is important if you want to specify a subset of the data based on certain criteria. You might filter the tropical fish data, for instance, by returning the subset of the fish types that all have the value gray for their color (for the example data, this would be the Shark and the Ray).

Specifying the Object Model for Script Access   The Data Source Object specifies the object model that is used for script access. The importance of object models is discussed in Chapter 6, "Dynamic HTML Object Model."

In a nutshell, the object model consists of the properties, methods, events, and objects that a scripting language can use to access the material it encapsulates.

For a Data Source Object, the object model specifies all the ways in which the user can interact with the DSO. All sorting and filtering capabilities, for instance, are usually exposed through properties that are set, followed by methods that execute the changes.

Much like the manipulations that can be done on the data via the Data Source Object, the object model that is exposed and supported by the Data Source Object is usually dependent on decisions made by the people who programmed the Data Source Object. This means that methods used for filtering and sorting may very well change from Data Source Object to Data Source Object.

A basic level of functionality, however, must be supported. This functionality is specified by Microsoft's OLE-DB API, which is a bare-bones API that requires Data Source Objects to provide a minimum level of functionality. You can find more information on the OLE-DB API at **http://www.microsoft.com/oledb/default.htm**.

The fact that Data Source Objects are required to implement the OLE-DB API specification shows an important and limiting aspect to the use of Data Source Objects. Data Source Objects are Microsoft Component Object Model (COM) objects, more commonly referred to as ActiveX objects.

Data Source Objects are ActiveX objects, which is both an advantage and a disadvantage depending on your perspective. If you are a proponent of ActiveX, or are not particularly concerned about cross-platform capabilities or security, the reliance on ActiveX may not be a stumbling block.

DSO Cross-Platform and Language Compatibility

Although Data Source Objects are ActiveX objects, Microsoft is certainly going out of its way to make sure that Data Source Objects can be written in a variety of languages.

Microsoft will be providing Data Source Objects written in Java using JavaBeans (which are automatically exposed as ActiveX objects) or through Visual Basic or Visual C++. Languages that can implement Data Source Objects have no restrictions other than that they must implement the required COM interface to create the ActiveX object.

If cross-platform capabilities are important to you, you should seriously consider using and implementing Data Source Objects with Java. Unfortunately, ActiveX objects written in C++ and Visual Basic are tied to the platform on which they were compiled.

ActiveX objects written in Java, however, can be used on any platform that supports ActiveX. Microsoft has currently announced plans for Internet Explorer 4.0 with ActiveX support for Windows, Macintosh, and many UNIX platforms. This support will cover most of the important current platforms, lessening the fears many have about cross-platform issues.

Tabular Data Control Basics

The Tabular Data Control (TDC) is a straightforward Data Source Object that ships with Internet Explorer 4.0. The TDC has the distinct advantage of not requiring a separate server (such as a relational database) to provide data to it.

Instead of using a remote server to perform queries, the Tabular Data Control downloads data files via HTTP (or directly if the file is on the local machine), then extracts the needed data itself. Several advantages to this method of data access are:

- It does not require a separate data access server.
- Because the file is transmitted via the web server via standard HTTP methods, no modifications to the web server are required.
- The processing time required to manipulate the data into forms necessary for displaying via data binding is done on the client instead of the server, resulting in a great reduction in server load.
- Fewer round trips over the network are necessary than if the data had been returned from a database server because the Tabular Data Control downloads the entire data file at once.

Tabular Data Control does have a few downsides.

- Because the entire file is downloaded to the client, more resources are required on the client side.
- Due to the loading of the entire file, more aggregate network bandwidth might be used than if the data searching was done on the server.
- The manipulations and queries that can be performed on the data are severely limited because the Tabular Data Control Data Source Object is not an advanced database engine.
- The Tabular Data Control is strictly a "read-only" form of data access. If you want to write data back to the server in a standard client/server type of process, the Tabular Data Control is not sufficient.

For these reasons, the choice of whether to use the Tabular Data Control depends on the simplicity of the actions that you want to perform with it. If your data access task falls into many of the following categories, you might want to seriously consider the Tabular Data Control:

- You only want to read remote data and foresee no need to write or replace remote data.

- The aggregate data you want to receive (all the rows put together) is relatively small, and downloading it will not be a problem either for the client or for network bandwidth, keeping in mind that many users might be connecting with 28.8K modems.

- The lookups that you need to do on the data are straightforward. In fact, if all you need to do is read the data a row at a time, this is the type of data access in which the Tabular Data Control excels.

- You are learning to work with Data Source Objects or want to refresh your knowledge of the peculiarities of working with Data Source Objects within a simple example.

For the purposes of this book, the Tabular Data Control provides an excellent way to learn how to work with Data Source Objects. In addition to being simple to work with, it is also guaranteed to work with all users' machines without concern for which software they are running because the Tabular Data Control can directly read the files containing the data.

Using the Tabular Data Control

The Tabular Data Control is quite straightforward to use. As previously mentioned, Data Source Objects are ActiveX objects. The methods for specifying the Tabular Data Control ActiveX object are similar to the methods discussed in Chapter 13, "Introducing Multimedia," when discussing the use of Multimedia Controls.

The basic syntax used in the HTML file for the Tabular Data Control consists of an <OBJECT> tag that specifies that an object will be present inside of this tag. Next, the CLASSID for the control is specified. In the case of the Tabular Data Control, the CLASSID is "333C7BC4-460F-11D0-BC04-0080C7055A83." Next, the HTML attributes that list the visual representation of the object are specified. In the case of a Data Source Object control, you don't want to have a visual representation, so you can set the attributes accordingly.

Setting an object to have no visual representation involves setting three attributes. The first attribute is the BORDER attribute, and it specifies the size of the border around the control. Because you don't want the user to see anything representing the object, this attribute is set to 0.

The next attribute is the WIDTH attribute, which specifies the width of the control in pixels. This attribute is set to 0. The HEIGHT attribute specifies the height of the control in pixels. In this case, it is also set to 0.

Each Data Source Object must also set its ID attribute. This provides the Data Source Object with an identifier that can be referenced via the DATASRC attribute of the Dynamic HTML data binding extensions, which can be referenced by elements that support data binding.

Take a look at the bare-bones OBJECT definition that has been described thus far:

```
<OBJECT id="cars"
        CLASSID="clsid:333C7BC4-460F-11D0-BC04-0080C7055A83"
        BORDER="0"
        WIDTH="0"
        HEIGHT="0">
</OBJECT>
```

This syntax defines the basic object reference for the Tabular Data Control. In addition to this basic reference, two parameters that you need to specify are "DataUrl" and "UseHeader."

The first parameter is the most important and specifies the URL that contains the data with which you want to retrieve and perform the data binding. This parameter is the "DataUrl" parameter and can contain either an absolute or relative URL. It is common to specify only the file name of the data file, which is automatically referred to as a relative URL:

```
<param name="DataURL" value="cars.txt">
```

The next parameter you need to specify is the "UseHeader" parameter. This parameter defines whether the data file has a header line containing the names of the fields that make up each row of the tabular data. The format of the data file is discussed further in the section called "Tabular Data Control File Properties." Normally you will want to set this to *true*, as follows:

```
<param name="UseHeader" value="True">
```

Now that you know the basics of how to use the Tabular Data Control, take a look at a basic example of the TDC in action. First, you need to specify the data file that will be used. This file is a standard text file with the name "cars.txt":

```
type,year:INT,price:INT
Chevy Nova,1986,1000
Infiniti Q45,1993,12000
Nissan Maxima,1989,4500
Ford Taurus, 1991, 6200
Toyota Camry, 1994, 8300
Honda Accord, 1995, 9200
Volkswagen Beetle, 1970, 800
```

The HTML file in listing 12.1 is named "ch12ex01.htm" and binds to one record (or row) at a time from the tabular data source, using the Tabular Data Control that has been constructed.

Part

IV

Ch

12

Listing 12.1   Basic Use of the Tabular Data Control

```
01. <HTML>
02. <HEAD>
03.    <TITLE>
04.       Chapter 12, Example 1
05.    </TITLE>
06. </HEAD>
07.
08. <BODY>
09.
```

continues

Listing 12.1   Continued

```
10. <OBJECT id="cars"
11.        CLASSID="clsid:333C7BC4-460F-11D0-BC04-0080C7055A83"
12.        BORDER="0"
13.        WIDTH="0"
14.        HEIGHT="0">
15.    <PARAM NAME="DataURL" value="cars.txt">
16.    <PARAM NAME="UseHeader" value="True">
17. </OBJECT>
18.
19. <H1>Car Type:</H1>
20. <INPUT TYPE=text
21.        DATASRC=#cars
22.        DATAFLD="type">
23.
24. <H1>Car Year:</H1>
25. <INPUT TYPE=text
26.        DATASRC=#cars
27.        DATAFLD="year">
28.
29. <H1>Car Price:</H1>
30. <INPUT TYPE=text
31.        DATASRC=#cars
32.        DATAFLD="price">
33.
34. </BODY>
35. </HTML>
```

The output of this example is shown in figure 12.1. This example provides a look at the use of the Tabular Data Control and will be the foundation of the rest of the examples throughout this chapter. The only code of significance added here, other than the object reference described earlier, is the data binding to the HTML elements, which was covered in detail in Chapter 11, "Introduction to Data Binding."

The Data Source Object is set up in lines 10–17. The Tabular Data Control is specified by the CLASSID in line 11, and its properties are defined in lines 15 and 16. After defining the Data Source Object, you need to perform the data binding.

In this case, three HTML INPUT fields are bound to the data. The first is bound to the "type" field (line 22), the second to the "year" field (line 27), and the third to the "price" field (line 32).

Navigating Data with the Tabular Data Control

Earlier in the chapter, you learned that Data Source Objects are responsible for manipulations on retrieved data. One such manipulation is the act of keeping track of where in the current set of tabular data the data binding is occurring.

FIG. 12.1

Output from basic Tabular Data Control example.

In Chapter 11, you learned about the concept of value binding versus set binding. When table binding is used, all the data from the data source is retrieved by the table-based data consumer and the entirety of that data is shown by default, but certain HTML attributes enable you to display a group at a time.

The situation with value binding is quite different. With value binding, only the current record (or row) is available at any given time. This means that when the page is first shown, only the fields from the first record returned by the Data Source Object are available.

This notion that only one record is available at a time is known as *current record binding*. When only the current record is bound, there must be a way to move around inside the Data Source for it to be truly useful.

The Tabular Data Control supports the standard methods for moving around in a data set required by Data Source Objects. The two important methods covered here are *MoveNext()* and *MovePrevious()*.

The *MoveNext()* method moves to the next row in the current Data Source Object. Conversely, the *MovePrevious()* method moves to the row that came before the current row in the Data Source Object.

These methods are not available via the main Data Source Object itself. Every Data Source Object, instead, contains an object called *recordset*. The methods for movement can be used through this *recordset* object.

So, to move forward a record in a Tabular Data Control named "parts," you would use the following JavaScript command:

```
parts.recordset.MoveNext();
```

Part
IV

Ch
12

To move backward a record to the previous record in the aforementioned Tabular Data Control, you would use this JavaScript code:

```
parts.recordset.MovePrevious()
```

To facilitate this type of movement, the Data Source Object keeps track of a pointer to the current row that is bound to the page. This pointer is also available to your scripting language programs.

This pointer is accessible through the Data Source Object you are using (in this case the Tabular Data Control) as the "*AbsolutePosition*" property of the *recordset* object contained in the relevant Data Source Object. One important thing to note is that the *AbsolutePosition* property starts counting records at 1. Therefore, the first record would be located at position 1.

Therefore, if you wanted to save the current position of the record pointer in the "part" Tabular Data Control into the JavaScript variable "curr_rec," you would use the following syntax:

```
var curr_rec = parts.recordset.AbsolutePosition;
```

When the pointer to the current record is moved via the *MoveNext()* or *MovePrevious()* method, the data bound HTML is automatically updated to the new row contents. All the fields with their DATASRC pointing to this Data Source Object will be updated.

In much the same manner as the *AbsolutePosition* property, the Data Source Object also keeps track of the number of records available. This information is contained in the "*RecordCount*" property, and is accessed as follows:

```
parts.recordset.RecordCount
```

Take a look at a concrete example. Use the data file from the previous example (cars.txt). Save the following HTML file in listing 12.2 as "ch12ex02.htm".

Listing 12.2   Moving Around in Recordsets

```
01. <HTML>
02. <HEAD>
03.    <TITLE>
04.       Chapter 12, Example 2
05.    </TITLE>
06. </HEAD>
07.
08. <BODY>
09.
10. <OBJECT id="cars"
11.        classid="clsid:333C7BC4-460F-11D0-BC04-0080C7055A83"
12.        border="0"
13.        width="0"
14.        height="0">
15.    <param name="DataURL" value="cars.txt">
16.    <param name="UseHeader" value="True">
17. </OBJECT>
18.
```

```
19. <SCRIPT LANGUAGE=JavaScript>
20.
21. function carsForward() {
22.
23.     if (cars.recordset.AbsolutePosition !=
24.                     cars.recordset.RecordCount) {
25.         cars.recordset.MoveNext();
26.     }
27. }
28.
29. function carsPrevious() {
30.
31.     if (cars.recordset.AbsolutePosition > 1) {
32.         cars.recordset.MovePrevious();
33.     }
34. }
35.
36. </SCRIPT>
37.
38.
39. <INPUT TYPE=BUTTON
40.         id=Next
41.         VALUE="  <—  "
42.         onclick="carsPrevious()">
43.
44. <INPUT TYPE=BUTTON
45.         id=Prev
46.         VALUE="  —>  "
47.         onclick="carsForward()">
48. <P>
49. <H1>Car Type:</H1>
50. <INPUT TYPE=text
51.         DATASRC=#cars
52.         DATAFLD="type">
53.
54. <H1>Car Year:</H1>
55. <INPUT TYPE=text
56.         DATASRC=#cars
57.         DATAFLD="year">
58.
59. <H1>Car Price:</H1>
60. <INPUT TYPE=text
61.         DATASRC=#cars
62.         DATAFLD="price">
63.
64. </BODY>
65. </HTML>
```

Part
IV

Ch
12

The output from this HTML code is shown in figure 12.2. Whenever the button with a left arrow on it is clicked, the previous record in the tabular data is shown. Whenever the right button is clicked, the next record is shown. The left arrow cannot move past the beginning of the records and the right arrow cannot move past the end.

FIG. 12.2

Output from moving around in recordsets example.

The first code addition to the previous example in listing 12.2 that you should focus on is the buttons that control the movement through the records. The following listing excerpt defines the left arrow button:

```
39. <INPUT TYPE=BUTTON
40.       id=Next
41.       VALUE="  ->  "
42.       onclick="carsForward()">
```

These four lines of code create an INPUT element that represents a button with a caption that makes it apparent that it causes forward movement. This code also sets up an event handler to execute when it is clicked.

The event handler that is called by the Next button is *"carsForward()"*:

```
21. function carsForward() {
22.
23.     if (cars.recordset.AbsolutePosition !=
24.                 cars.recordset.RecordCount) {
25.         cars.recordset.MoveNext();
26.     }
27. }
```

The *carsForward()* function first checks to see if the current position (AbsolutePosition) is equal to the number of records in this Tabular Data Control. If it is not, then you can move forward a record.

If you are currently at the last record in the Data Source Object, however, nothing is done. Why is this? You do not want to attempt to move past the end of the number of records that are available, so you do a check first. If you don't check first and try to move ahead when you're already at the end, a runtime error is generated.

The "*carsPrevious()*" function works similarly. It is bound to the Prev button that has the left arrow caption:

```
29. function carsPrevious() {
30.
31.     if (cars.recordset.AbsolutePosition > 1) {
32.         cars.recordset.MovePrevious();
33.     }
34. }
```

The *carsPrevious()* function checks first to see whether the current record is greater than 1. Records in Data Source Objects are referenced starting with "1," so first the current record is checked to make sure that it is greater than 1.

If the current record is greater than 1, the current record is set to the record that comes before it with the "*MovePrevious()*" method. If the current record is 1, however, nothing is done. You do nothing because you do not want to try to move to before the first record.

Tabular Data Control File Properties

Many of the properties supported by the Tabular Data Control are related to the file that it reads to retrieve the data to present to be bound. This file is parsed into columns and rows and is the representation of the desired tabular data.

CharSet Property   The first property supported by the Tabular Data Control is the character set used for the data file. It is represented by the property *Charset* (tdcObject represents a generic Tabular Data Control Object):

```
var cSet = tdcObject.Charset;
```

If you are running the scripting inside of Internet Explorer 4.0 in an English speaking language, the normal character set that will be returned by this property will be "-8859-1." If you are running with a language other than English, this property will return the character set type for that language.

Language Property   The *Language* property is similar to the *CharSet* property, except that instead of specifying the types of characters to use, it specifies the actual language with which the data file is written. This property is accessed as follows:

```
var Lang = tdcObject.Language;
```

Although English in the United States and in England use the same characters, for instance, the languages themselves are slightly different. For this reason, in the United States this property will be "eng-us."

UseHeader Property   The *UseHeader* property of the Tabular Data Control specifies whether the first line of the data file will contain a header line with the names of each column (and possibly the data type that the column represents).

The *UseHeader* property is a Boolean property and is accessed in the following manner:

```
tdcObject.UseHeader = boolean_value;
```

The header line is specified in much the same way as the data itself, with the same field delimiter (which is by default a comma) and row delimiter (which is by default a newline).

Take a look at a sample data file that represents the product line of a tool manufacturer:

```
PartName,InStock:Int,Price:Float
Hammer,20,6.99
Drill,150,49.99
Lathe,27,288.95
Press,10,1532.22
```

Assuming the *UseHeader* property has been set to true, the first line here will be interpreted as the header line. It defines three fields, as follows:

- **PartName**—A text string representing the name of the part in the company's database.
- **InStock**—The number of this item currently in inventory, represented as an integer value.
- **Price**—The price in dollars and cents for this item through the company, represented as a floating point value.

Note that the data type of each field is specified after the name of the field and is separated from the field name via a colon. The valid types available are as follows:

- **Boolean**—A logical value that can contain either true or false.
- **Date**—A value representing a day of the year.
- **Float**—A floating point number. Floating point numbers are those that can contain decimal points (for example, 25.624, 901.20, and so on).
- **Int**—A value that can hold any integer value. Integers are numbers that cannot contain decimal points.
- **String**—Any textual data that is representable as a string of characters. The sentences in this bullet point, for example, are strings themselves—*string* is the default data type for the field if none is specified.

The main reason you might want to specify the type of data that is contained in a field is for sorting reasons. This is because strings will sort differently than integers or numbers and may very well provide seemingly incorrect results.

DataURL Property   The *DataURL* property specifies the location of the data file that will be used for the actual tabular data in the Tabular Data Control. The value of this property can be any valid URL that the web browser can use to fetch the data file:

This property is normally specified in the <OBJECT> tag as follows:

```
<OBJECT id="cars"
   ...>

   <PARAM NAME="DataURL" value="cars.txt">

   ...
</OBJECT>
```

You can also specify this property dynamically later in your scripts, as follows:

```
tdcObject.DataURL = "boats.txt";
```

When you change the *DataURL* property in your scripts in this manner, the Tabular Data Control automatically drops the current tabular data and replaces it with the new file that you have specified.

This capability is useful if you want to reuse the same Tabular Data Control across multiple data files. If you have multiple data sets and will never need to access them at the same time, setting the *DataURL* property on one Tabular Data Control is certainly an efficient way to do so.

FieldDelim Property   The *FieldDelim* property specifies the character that is used to separate date fields from one another. This concept is known as field delimiting. The default character used is the comma (","); however, the field delimiting character can be any valid ASCII character. The following example specifies that the field delimiting character would be "|":

```
tdcObject.FieldDelim = "|"
```

If you were using this character for delimiting fields, the example data file from the "UseHeader Property" section would have to change to the following:

```
PartName|InStock:Int|Price:Float
Hammer|20|6.99
Drill|150|49.99
Lathe|27|288.95
Press|10|1532.22
```

RowDelim Property   The *RowDelim* property is much like the *FieldDelim* property, except that instead of specifying the delimiter between fields, it specifies the delimiter in between rows in the tabular data.

Take a look at how the *RowDelim* property is used. Suppose you wanted to change the row delimiter to "*". You would use the following syntax

```
tdcObject.RowDelim = "*";
```

Then (assuming you were also using the field delimiter that was used previously), your data file would look like the following:

```
PartName|InStock:Int|Price:Float*
Hammer|20|6.99*
Drill|150|49.99*
Lathe|27|288.95*
Press|10|1532.22*
```

Tabular Data Control Sorting

Sorting is one of the most common operations performed with data. You may remember from earlier in the chapter that the Data Source Object is responsible for all sorting performed on the data.

The Tabular Data Control supports two types of sorting: *ascending* and *descending*.

An ascending sort arranges the data from smallest to largest if a number is being used, and sorts by ASCII value (a comes before z) if a string is being used.

A descending sort arranges the data from largest to smallest if a number is being used, and sorts by ASCII value (z comes before a) if a string is being used.

Additionally, you may specify the column on which you want to sort. This means that you do not have to decide which column to put first in the data file because any column can be sorted.

The specification to sort can take place either in the <OBJECT> definition for the Data Source Object or in a script. The example in listing 12.3 places the sort specification in the <OBJECT> definition:

Here is the data file to use. Save this file as furniture.txt:

```
type,color,price:INT
sofa,green,300
bed,white,850
desk,woodgrain,350
chair,black,475
table,red, 175
recliner,plaid,425
```

Listing 12.3 shows the HTML document for specifying the data sort order. Save this file as "ch12ex03.htm". Figure 12.3 shows the output for this example.

Listing 12.3   Sorting Example

```
01. <HTML>
02. <HEAD>
03.    <TITLE>
04.       Chapter 12, Example 3
05.    </TITLE>
06. </HEAD>
07.
08. <BODY>
09.
10. <OBJECT id="furniture"
11.        CLASSID="clsid:333C7BC4-460F-11D0-BC04-0080C7055A83"
12.        BORDER="0"
13.        WIDTH="0"
14.        HEIGHT="0">
15.    <PARAM NAME="DataURL" VALUE="furniture.txt">
16.    <PARAM NAME="UseHeader" VALUE="True">
17.    <PARAM NAME="Sort" VALUE="price">
18. </OBJECT>
19.
20. <TABLE DATASRC="#furniture" BORDER=1>
21.    <TR>
22.       <TD>
23.          <SPAN DATAFLD="type"></SPAN>
24.       </TD>
```

```
25.        <TD>
26.            <SPAN DATAFLD="color"></SPAN>
27.        </TD>
28.        <TD>
29.            <SPAN DATAFLD="price"></SPAN>
30.        </TD>
31.
32.    </TR>
33. </TABLE>
34.
35. </BODY>
36. </HTML>
```

FIG. 12.3

Output from sorting example.

For the most part, this example should seem quite familiar to you because it uses many of the concepts discussed in detail in the previous two chapters.

The addition to this listing is related to the parameter for sorting. The "Sort" parameter specifies which column of the tabular data to sort upon. In this case, you want to generate a table that is sorted by the price of the item, so you specify the "price" column:

```
17.    <PARAM NAME="Sort" VALUE="price">
```

You can also specify whether to sort in ascending or descending order. By default, ascending order is used. If you want to use descending order instead, place a minus sign (–) before the name of the column in the "Sort" property. For instance, if you want to use descending order with the example, change line 17 to the following:

```
17.    <PARAM NAME="Sort" VALUE="-price">
```

From Here...

This chapter covered the use of Data Source Objects in Dynamic HTML in conjunction with the HTML data binding extensions. This chapter focused on the Tabular Data Control because it is the simplest Data Source Object to understand and can be guaranteed to run on any machine running Internet Explorer 4.0 because the Tabular Data Control does not require a separate server for data access.

The next section of the book will discuss the multimedia aspects of Dynamic HTML. These multimedia aspects are in many ways the most exciting aspect of Dynamic HTML because they enable you to include advanced visual effects in your web pages in a straightforward manner.

- Chapter 13, "Introducing Multimedia"— Introduces you to basic multimedia effects in Dynamic HTML like animating HTML elements on your web pages.

- Chapter 14, "Multimedia Transitions"— Gives you an overview of effects that can be used to transition from one HTML element to another.

- Chapter 15, "Multimedia Filters and ActiveX Controls"— Shows you how to use filters to specify interesting visual effects like blur on your HTML elements. In addition, using ActiveX multimedia controls with your documents will be discussed.

Multimedia and Dynamic HTML

CHAPTER 13

Introducing Multimedia

One of the Dynamic HTML features that has not been discussed much in earlier chapters is the multimedia effects supported with Internet Explorer 4.0. A number of new special effects can be achieved by exploiting various Dynamic HTML technologies, and in this chapter you begin to look at some of those features.

Implementing many of the multimedia controls is not trivial, so this chapter will provide in-depth coverage of some multimedia techniques that you can create without the ActiveX Multimedia Controls. Then you will be introduced to the effects that will be covered in greater detail in Chapter 14, "Multimedia Transitions," and Chapter 15, "Multimedia Filters and ActiveX Controls." ■

Multimedia with Scripting

Learn to use JavaScript methods to create multimedia effects without using ActiveX.

Rotating Text and Objects

The Dynamic HTML ActiveX Controls enable the manipulation of elements on the page, such as rotating objects.

Structured Graphics

The Structured Graphics Control enables you to create 2D line art and graphics primitives.

Path Animation Effects

In addition to animation through scripting, the Path Animation Control enables you to animate objects on a path.

Transitions

Dynamic HTML introduces a whole set of ActiveX Controls to provide multimedia transitions. In addition, some transition effects can be created using scripting.

Filters

Explore ActiveX Multimedia Controls that enable you to apply filters to objects on your pages to create a stunning array of multimedia effects.

Multimedia Effects with Dynamic HTML

Before discussing the types of multimedia effects, such as transitions and filters, that can be achieved by using ActiveX Controls, it is important that you understand what can be achieved with Dynamic HTML with scripting and positioning.

If you recall from the examples in Chapter 9, "Layout and Positioning," you already know that it is possible to manipulate images and text on the page by altering the CSS Positioning properties and attributes. You use JavaScript in conjunction with CSS Positioning to scroll images onto the screen and to move elements around on the page. The same techniques can be applied to other positioning properties to create effects such as scaling, transitions, and animations. These basic multimedia techniques implemented with positioning and scripting are described in the sections that follow.

Scaling Images

One simple effect you can create with Dynamic HTML and CSS Positioning is the *scaling of an image*. Scaling an image involves enlarging or shrinking the image from its original size. The progressive code that follows is numbered corresponding to its placement in the final code in listing 13.1.

The first thing you need to do is define the image that you are going to scale:

```
21. <IMG id="ScaleMe" STYLE="position: relative; top:25; left:25;
➥width: 195px; height: 171px;" onclick="scaleCat();" SRC="kitty.gif">
```

You can define the image using the <IMG> tag and the CSS Positioning elements. You place the image on the page with the *position* property, and then specify the width and height dimensions of the positioning container—in this case 195×171 pixels.

By specifying the width and height of the position container as the same size as the image, the image is shown normally. To scale the image, all you need to do is manipulate the *width* and the *height* property values. You can change the *width* and *height* property values by writing a JavaScript function to change these values:

```
07. function scaleCat() {
08.         if (ScaleMe.style.pixelWidth < 250) {
09.             ScaleMe.style.pixelWidth +=1;
10.         ScaleMe.style.pixelHeight += 1;
11.         window.setTimeout("scaleCat();", 1);
12.         }
13. }
```

The *scaleCat()* function uses an *if* statement to determine the stopping point for this scaling exercise, then increments the height and width each by a pixel. Incrementing both properties by the same amount will keep the proportions of the image in sync. If you want to stretch an image or squash an image, you could change one property, but not the other. Finally, you use the *window.setTimeout()* method to pause briefly between each step, so the animation is visible.

Listing 13.1 shows the final code to scale the image, and figure 13.1 shows the results of the exercise.

Listing 13.1   Scaling an Image

```
01. <HTML>
02. <HEAD>
03. <TITLE>Scale Image</TITLE>
04.
05. <SCRIPT>
06.
07. function scaleCat() {
08.     if (ScaleMe.style.pixelWidth < 250) {
09.         ScaleMe.style.pixelWidth +=1;
10.         ScaleMe.style.pixelHeight += 1;
11.         window.setTimeout("scaleCat();", 1);
12.         }
13. }
14.
15. </SCRIPT>
16.
17. <BODY>
18. <P>
19. <SPAN STYLE="position: absolute; top: 5; left: 5; color: red">
➥Click the image to adjust the scale.</SPAN>
20. <P>
21. <IMG id="ScaleMe" STYLE="position: relative; top:25; left:25;
➥width: 195px; height: 171px;" onclick="scaleCat();" SRC="kitty.gif">
22.
23. </BODY>
24. </HTML>
```

FIG. 13.1

Scaling an image with DHTML and CSS Positioning.

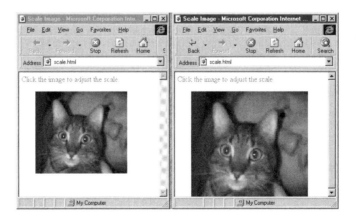

This scaling technique could be used to enlarge a photo for greater detail, such as a page of thumbnails for an art history lesson. Each image would be shown in miniature, and when the image is clicked, users would see the full-sized image. Also, later in this chapter you will take a look at how this technique can be used to create a multimedia transition without ActiveX.

Transitions

Microsoft provides a number of ActiveX-based Multimedia Controls that provide access to some pretty complex transitions; however, sometimes you might want a simple transition. Even more likely, there may be times when you do not feel like going through the hassle involved with ActiveX.

Using techniques such as the scale trick covered in the preceding section, you can build a number of transitions that are quick, look good, and are fairly straightforward to script.

Take a look, for example, at a modification you can make to the preceding scaling example. First, because it is possible to grow the image, it makes sense that the image can be shrunken as well. So why not shrink an image into oblivion? Then the image will no longer be on the page, creating a transition in effect.

To create this shrinking effect, you will make some small changes to the code in listing 13.1. First, you will need to modify the statements in the functions that increment the *width* and *height* properties so that the functions decrement these properties instead. Changing line 9 from listing 13.1 effectively causes the scaling function to operate in reverse:

```
09.     ScaleMe.style.pixelWidth +=1;
```

to

```
09.     ScaleMe.style.pixelWidth -=1;
```

Now all you need to do is ensure that the image disappears. You can accomplish this by implementing the *overflow* and *clip* properties.

If you recall from Chapter 9, "Layout and Positioning," the *overflow* property controls how to handle clipping when your image is too large for the area. The *clip* property enables you to define a clipping area. So you add these properties to the image object:

```
21. <IMG ID="ScaleMe" STYLE="position: relative; top:25; left:25;
➥width: 195px; height: 171px; overflow: clip; clip: auto;
➥" onclick="scaleCat();" SRC="kitty.gif">
```

This line ensures that the image will be clipped. Because the clipping value is *auto*, the image will be clipped according to the boundaries of the positioning container, so as you shrink the positioning container with the *width* and *height* property values, the image will shrink away into nothing. Listing 13.2 shows the final code used to create this effect.

Listing 13.2 A Shrinking Effect in Dynamic HTML

```
01. <HTML>
02. <HEAD>
03. <TITLE>Non ActiveX transition</TITLE>
04.
05. <SCRIPT>
06.
07. function scaleCat() {
08.     if (ScaleMe.style.pixelWidth > 0) {
```

```
09.         ScaleMe.style.pixelWidth -=1;
10.         ScaleMe.style.pixelHeight -= 1;
11.         window.setTimeout("scaleCat();", 1);
12.         }
13. }
14.
15. </SCRIPT>
16.
17. <BODY>
18. <P>
19. Click to shrink the cat.
20. <P>
21. <IMG id="ScaleMe" STYLE="position: relative; top:25; left:25;
➥width: 195px; height: 171px; overflow: clip; clip: auto;
➥" onclick="scaleCat();" SRC="kitty.gif">
22.
23. </BODY>
24. </HTML>
25. </HTML>
```

The results of the shrinking image script in listing 13.2 are shown in figure 13.2.

FIG. 13.2

Reversing the scaling process shrinks the image.

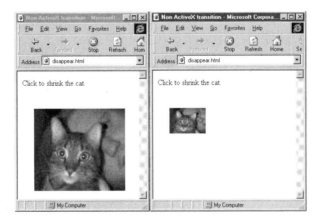

Although there are applications where scaling images might be necessary, there are also a number of transition techniques that could make use of scaling an image, such as a faux wipe.

Scaling Transitions

Now that you know how to scale images in either direction, it would be useful to create a transition using these techniques. For this transition the original image will shrink into a point; then the second image will grow out of the point. You might have seen a similar technique in old television shows or movies. Although similar transitions can be accomplished with ActiveX Controls, many users have disabled ActiveX Controls due to security concerns. Using pure Dynamic HTML transition assures that they will be visible to more users. Additionally, these types of transitions can also be easily adapted for use with CDF Channels, as means of transitions or user interface elements. The progressive code that follows is numbered according to its placement in the final code in listing 13.3.

Part
V

Ch
13

First, you must define the two elements to be used in the transition:

```
30. <IMG id="ScaleMe" STYLE="position: absolute; top:25; left:25; width: 195px;
➥height: 171px; overflow: clip; clip: auto;" onclick="scaleCat();
➥" SRC="kitty.gif">
31.
32. <IMG id="ScaleTwo" STYLE="position: absolute; top:25; left:25; width: 0px;
➥height: 0px; overflow: clip; clip: auto;" onclick="scaleCat();
➥" SRC="toobig.gif">
```

As with the scaling examples, these tags specify the following:

- The type of positioning
- The location of the element
- The position container parameters
- The overflow and clipping attributes
- The function to be called to start the transition
- The location of each image

Next, you create the function that will shrink the first image:

```
07. function scaleCat() {
08.       if (ScaleMe.style.pixelWidth > 0) {
09.           ScaleMe.style.pixelWidth -=1;
10.       ScaleMe.style.pixelHeight -= 1;
11.       window.setTimeout("scaleCat();", 1);
12.       scaleAnother();
13.       }
14. }
```

This function is identical to the shrinking function in listing 13.2 with only one exception: at the end of the function, *scaleAnother()* is called, which is the function you will use to grow the second image in place of the first. Here's the function that is called to grow the second image:

```
16. function scaleAnother() {
17.       if (ScaleMe.style.pixelWidth < 150) {
18.           ScaleTwo.style.pixelWidth +=1;
19.       ScaleTwo.style.pixelHeight += 1;
20.       }
21. }
```

That's all there is to it. With the *scaleCat()* and *scaleAnother()* functions in place and the elements defined accordingly, you have a transition that will zoom one image out, then zoom another image in to occupy its place. The final code is displayed in listing 13.3, and figure 13.3 shows the final results.

Listing 13.3   A Non-ActiveX Scaling Transition

```
01. <HTML>
02. <HEAD>
03. <TITLE>Non ActiveX transition</TITLE>
04.
05. <SCRIPT>
06.
```

```
07. function scaleCat() {
08.      if (ScaleMe.style.pixelWidth > 0) {
09.          ScaleMe.style.pixelWidth -=1;
10.      ScaleMe.style.pixelHeight -= 1;
11.      window.setTimeout("scaleCat();", 1);
12.      scaleAnother();
13.      }
14. }
15.
16. function scaleAnother() {
17.      if (ScaleMe.style.pixelWidth < 150) {
18.          ScaleTwo.style.pixelWidth +=1;
19.      ScaleTwo.style.pixelHeight += 1;
20.      }
21. }
22.
23. </SCRIPT>
24.
25. <BODY>
26. <P>
27. <SPAN STYLE="position: absolute; top: 210; left: 25; color: green;
➥">Click on the cat to turn it into a pumpkin.</SPAN>
28. <P>
29.
30. <IMG id="ScaleMe" STYLE="position: absolute; top:25; left:25; width: 195px;
➥height: 171px; overflow: clip; clip: auto;" onclick="scaleCat();
➥" SRC="kitty.gif">
31.
32. <IMG id="ScaleTwo" STYLE="position: absolute; top:25; left:25; width: 0px;
➥height: 0px; overflow: clip; clip: auto;" onclick="scaleCat();
➥" SRC="toobig.gif">
33. </BODY>
34. </HTML>
```

FIG. 13.3

The first image vanishes into nothing and a second image grows in its place.

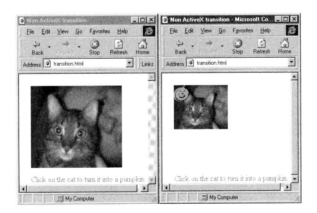

Part
V

Ch
13

Multimedia transitions like this one provide a more interesting way to flip between images. Perhaps, for example, you operate a garage that specializes in restoring antique cars. You could use this type of transition to flip between before-and-after photos of your work. Of course, if you were developing a CDF Channel, you could also use this type of transition to create a movie effect for the content of your channel.

Click and Drag Effects

In addition to the automated effects you can use to add more zip to your Dynamic HTML pages, you might want to take advantage of other types of multimedia devices on your site. Recall the Alien Head demo from earlier in the book, which was a game that functioned like Mr. Potato Head. In the Alien Head demo, users could click elements and drag them onto a head to create a face.

Dragging an element on a page, repositioning an element based on mouse events, and manipulating images are all useful effects for building new user interface designs. So how were these effects achieved in the Alien Head demo? The progressive code leading up to listing 13.4 examines the steps you need to take to create Dynamic HTML that can be used to reposition an image on the page. The progressive code snippets are numbered according to their final placement in listing 13.4.

In this example, you are going to create a function that enables the user to click an image and drag it around on a web page. You accomplish this type of interaction by designing a function that captures the mouse event when the image is clicked, then retrieves the coordinates of the mouse pointer. You will use these coordinates to reposition the images on the page.

First, you must define the two elements you are going to place on the page:

```
24. <IMG id="MONEY" STYLE="position: relative; top: 25px ; left: 25px;
⮑z-index: 2;" onmousemove="MoveObject();" SRC="money.gif">
26. <IMG id="CLIP" STYLE="position: relative; top: 50px; left: 25px;
⮑z-index: 1;" onmousemove="MoveObject();" SRC="paperclips.gif">
```

These image tags place the images on the page and set the layers so that the images overlap properly. These lines also use *onmousemove="MoveObject();"* to specify what function should be called when you move the element. The decision to use *onmousemove* is important, because the *mouseMove* event will enable you to access the window events objects that you can use for the coordinates.

That's all you have to do for the document itself, but now you need to write the function that is going to move the elements.

The *MoveObject()* function must perform several tasks. First, it needs to check to make sure the mouse button is pressed to move an object. Then, it needs to retrieve the coordinates of the mouse pointer and reapply these to coordinates the object. The *MoveObject()* function is defined in the following code:

```
07. function MoveObject() {
08.     if (window.event.button == 1) {
09.         var srcElement, newtop, newleft;
10.         srcElement = window.event.srcElement;
11.         newleft=window.event.x - (srcElement.width/2);
12.         newtop=window.event.y - (srcElement.height/2);
13.         srcElement.style.posTop = newtop;
14.         srcElement.style.posLeft = newleft;
15.         window.event.returnValue = false;
16.     }
17. }
```

A quick glance at the function also reveals that the ID of the images that are going to be moving are not listed anywhere on the page because you want to make sure that the function is not specific to any image. If you wrote a function that just moved one image, then you would have to repeat the function for each image on the page. This is not very scalable. With the function defined in lines 7–17, any image on the page could easily be moved without writing additional code. To help you understand what is going on in the preceding 11 lines of code, the following paragraphs dissect the function.

First, you need some mechanism to make sure that the actions of the "dragging" function are being performed only if the mouse button is clicked. Otherwise you would not be able to pick up and set down the image in between moving it. To accomplish this, you will use the *window.event.button* property that returns a value when mouse buttons are pressed. To determine if the left mouse button is clicked, you can use an *if* statement, which checks to see if the value for *window.event.button* is equal to 1:

```
07. function MoveObject() {
08.      if (window.event.button == 1) {
16.      }
17. }
```

Now you can be sure that whatever actions you include in the *if* statement will only be executed if the mouse button is pressed. Next, you are going to establish the variables you are going to use in the function to keep track of information:

```
09.      var srcElement, newtop, newleft;
```

Now that you have the variables, you must be able to do something with them. The first order of business is to assign a value to *srcElement*:

```
10.      srcElement = window.event.srcElement;
```

This assignment creates a handle that you can use to refer to the object that you are going to be moving. The value is set as being equal to the value that is passed to the function by the *window.event.srcElement* method. This method will pass along the ID of the element that you click, so you can then use *srcElement* as if it were the same as the object's ID.

The next two assignments might be somewhat confusing at first glance:

```
11.      newleft=window.event.x - (srcElement.width/2);
12.      newtop=window.event.y - (srcElement.height/2);
```

These are the variables that determine what the new value should be for the X and Y coordinates of the object being moved. To better understand this process, take a look at the following series of steps, which breaks down the entire transaction:

1. First, it might seem that you should just be able to use *window.event.x* to specify the X coordinate; however, this doesn't enable you to ensure that the X coordinate is always related to the image being moved. That is, after the mouse cursor left the image area, the image would stop moving, and the range of motion would be limited.

2. You also want to be able to move the element with respect to the center of the element, rather than its top or bottom. The way you accomplish this alignment is to take the width of the entire element, then divide it in half to put you in the center of the image.

3. Next, you subtract that coordinate from the X position of the cursor, which gives you a true new X coordinate based on the center of the image.

4. Repeat the previous three steps to determine the Y coordinate.

Now you are in the home stretch for the *MoveObject()* function. You now have values for the new X position (*newleft*) and the new Y position (*newtop*). All you need to do is to make the assignment to the *top* and *left* properties for the image you are moving:

```
13.      srcElement.style.posTop = newtop;
14.      srcElement.style.posLeft = newleft;
```

These lines use the *srcElement* variable to specify the element you are referencing. Next, you specify that you are modifying a style element (*posTop* and *posLeft*) and you assign the new values. Now the images are moving! There is, however, one last line:

```
15.      window.event.returnValue = false;
```

You can run the script without this line, but you might notice some strange behavior. The images animate with jerks and starts, or sometimes fail to move. This behavior is due to the features of Dynamic HTML event handling. Setting the *returnValue* property to false cancels the default event handling, resulting in a smooth transition. The script for the *MoveObject()* function appears in lines 5–19 in listing 13.4.

Now, if you assemble all the code snippets, the final code for clicking and dragging images is shown in listing 13.4.

Listing 13.4   Clicking and Dragging Images with Dynamic HTML

```
01. <HTML>
02. <HEAD>
03. <TITLE>Dynamic HTML Grabbing</TITLE>
04.
05. <SCRIPT>
06.
07. function MoveObject() {
08.      if (window.event.button == 1) {
09.      var srcElement, newtop, newleft;
10.      srcElement = window.event.srcElement;
11.      newleft=window.event.x - (srcElement.width/2);
12.      newtop=window.event.y - (srcElement.height/2);
13.      srcElement.style.posTop = newtop;
14.      srcElement.style.posLeft = newleft;
15.      window.event.returnValue = false;
16.      }
17. }
18.
19. </SCRIPT>
20. </HEAD>
21.
22. <BODY>
23.
24. <IMG id="MONEY" STYLE="position: relative; top: 25px ; left: 25px;
➡z-index: 2;" onmousemove="MoveObject();" SRC="money.gif">
```

```
25.
26. <IMG id="CLIP" STYLE="position: relative; top: 50px; left: 25px;
➥z-index: 1;" onmousemove="MoveObject();" SRC="paperclips.gif">
27.
28. </BODY>
29. </HTML>
```

Figure 13.4 shows the results of the this Dynamic HTML example. Each one of the elements can be clicked and the image repositioned by dragging it around the page.

FIG. 13.4
Click and drag animation is possible with Dynamic HTML.

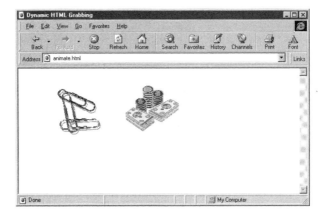

Introducing the ActiveX Multimedia Controls

Now that you have seen how you can use Dynamic HTML to create some multimedia effects on your pages, you probably are wondering how far the possibilities extend. In reality, given enough time, some very nice and compelling multimedia effects can be generated using positioning and scripting. Some effects, however, are not realistically possible using just positioning and scripting.

It would not be possible to perform complex transformations on images with just scripting, for example. What if you wanted to blur or invert an image? By the same token, you might want to have one image dissolve into another. These types of effects are all great uses of multimedia and could be useful on your pages; so, Microsoft has provided a mechanism called Multimedia Controls to create some stunning effects.

The Dynamic HTML Multimedia Controls are ActiveX Controls that you can use and manipulate in conjunction with Dynamic HTML to create multimedia effects in real time. The rest of this chapter introduces these controls and their functions. The usage of the controls is covered in Chapters 14 and 15.

Rotating Text and Objects

The first group of Multimedia Controls is designed to perform functions similar to positioning; however, they are slightly more advanced. Each of these controls can be applied to any type of element, and offer a number of highly customizable parameters.

Part
V

Ch
13

■ **Rotate**—The Rotate Control enables you to rotate an object in any direction. This control can be used to rotate images and text, as shown in figure 13.5.

FIG. 13.5
Multimedia Controls can be used to create effects such as rotated text.

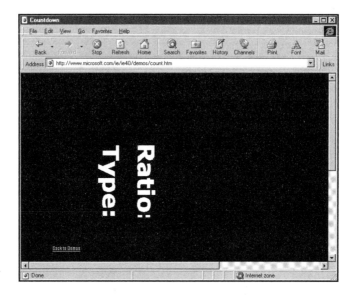

■ **Translate**—The Translate Control enables you to control the location of an element on the page. When used with a sequencer, this control can be used to create complex animation and flying effects that are machine independent and quite flexible.

■ **Scale**—The Scale Control enables you to scale elements. Although the effect can be achieved without ActiveX, the Scale Control offers some fine tuning and performance enhancements not possible when relying only on scripting.

Structured Graphics

Some of the most powerful Multimedia Controls are the Structured Graphics Controls. These controls enable you to render graphics on the screen using graphic primitives and techniques. This functionality enables you to create some complex vector graphic images and elements that are then easily manipulated by other Multimedia Controls.

The Structured Graphics Controls include several controls designed to perform the basic graphic functions needed to produce usable elements:

■ **Oval**—The Oval Control enables you to create an oval shape by providing the control with the proper coordinates. The oval can be constructed of lines or it can be a filled element. Circles can also be created with the Oval Control.

■ **Rect**—The Rect Control enables you to create a rectangle polygon by providing the control with the proper defining coordinates. The rectangle can be constructed of lines, or it can be a filled element. Users can also create squares with the Rect Control.

- **Fills**—The Fills Control enables you to create customized fills for various elements. The fills can be applied to elements constructed with the Oval and Rect Controls.
- **Lines**—In addition to polygon shapes, the Lines Control enables you to create lines that can be linked together to create a variety of different graphics.

Path Animation Effects

From earlier chapters and from the examples in this chapter, you have seen that it is possible to animate elements on a page using scripting and CSS Positioning. Using this methodology to get an object to follow a predefined path, however, can be quite difficult. It is also not easy to cause the object to loop on a path with this method.

With the Path Controls, you can actually create a path for an object to follow when it moves. This enables you to create some complex animations with great precision, and any object can be animated on a path. Here are the Path Controls:

- **pthRect**—The pthRect Control enables you to specify a rectangular shape that can be used as an element motion path.
- **pthOval**—The pthOval Control enables you to specify an oval shape that can act as the motion path for an object.
- **pthPolygon**—The pthPolygon Control enables you to create a polygon shape that will be used as the path for animating an object. This control could be used to create motion paths based on pentagons, octagons, and so on.
- **pthPolyline**—The pthPolyline Control enables you to describe a motion path that is constructed of multiple line segments. This enables you to create motion paths that are almost completely arbitrary and are not bound to a geometric shape as the other paths are.

Transitions

The list contained in this section is a brief description of the transitions available with Dynamic HTML by using the ActiveX Multimedia Controls. Each of these transitions and their implementations are covered in more detail in Chapter 14. All the transitions involve switching the image that is displayed between two images, using the method described. Instead of transitioning between two images, however, you could actually create a transition between an image and a black area or a white area to create the effect of a fade to black, or fade to white.

Visual Examples of each of these transitions can be found at **http://www.microsoft.com/ie/ ie40/demos/transall.htm**. The following are transitions provided by Dynamic HTML and Internet Explorer:

- **Box In**—Overlaps one image over another image from the center as a box until the original image is replaced with the second image.
- **Box Out**—Offers the same effect as Box In, only the box appears to shrink into the center of the image.
- **Circle In**—Similar to the Box In transition, only the image is replaced in a circular pattern instead of a box.
- **Circle Out**—Similar to Box Out, only with the shape of a circle.

Part
V

Ch
13

- **Wipe Up**—Switches between two images by scrolling the second image over the first from the bottom of the image to the top.
- **Wipe Down**—Switches between two images by scrolling the second image over the first from the top of the image to the bottom.
- **Wipe Right**—Switches between two images by scrolling the second image over the first from the right of the image to the left.
- **Wipe Left**—Switches between two images by scrolling the second image over the first from the left of the image to the right.
- **Vertical Blinds**—Creates stripes of the second image across the first, similar to opening vertical blinds, until the second image replaces the first.
- **Horizontal Blinds**—Creates stripes of the second image across the first, similar to opening horizontal blinds, until the second image replaces the first.
- **Checker Board Across**—Replaces the first image with the second image in the pattern of a checkerboard, starting on the left and moving toward the right.
- **Checker Board Down**—Replaces the first image with the second image in the pattern of a checkerboard, starting at the top and moving toward the bottom.
- **Random Dissolve**—Replaces the pixels of the first image with pixels from the second image in a random pattern until the image is entirely replaced. This effect can also be used with black or white images to create a "fade to black" effect.
- **Split Vertical In**—Switches from image one to image two by splitting the second image and wiping it from the right and the left sides simultaneously.
- **Split Vertical Out**—Switches from image one to image two by splitting the first image and scrolling the halves off the screen to reveal the second image.
- **Split Horizontal In**—Switches from image one to image two by splitting the second image and wiping it from the top and the bottom of the image simultaneously.
- **Split Horizontal Out**—Switches from image one to image two by splitting the first image and scrolling the halves off the top and bottom of the screen, leaving the second image.
- **Strips Left Down**—Reveals the second image in a series of two as a series of strips that progress from the upper-right corner of the screen, to the lower-left corner.
- **Strips Left Up**—Reveals the second image in a series of two as a series of strips that progress from the lower-right corner to the upper-left corner.
- **Strips Right Down**—Reveals the second image in a series of two as a series of strips that progress from the upper-left corner to the lower-right corner.
- **Strips Right Up**—Reveals the second image in a series of two as a series of strips that progress from the lower-left corner to the upper-right corner.
- **Random Bars Horizontal**—Replaces the first image by randomly displaying horizontal bars of the second image.
- **Random Bars Vertical**—Replaces the first image by randomly displaying vertical bars of the second image.

Filters

The transition effects offer alternatives for switching between several images. The Filter Controls also offer features for image manipulation, enabling designers to apply effects to images within the browser window, rather than having to load an entirely new image.

With standard HTML, for example, to blur an image you would need to have two versions of the image: one sharp and one blurry. Then you would need to somehow switch between the two images to give the impression that the image was blurred. With Filter Controls in Dynamic HTML, you can actually alter the image without loading a new image at all, similar to applying a filter to the image in an image editing tool such as Photoshop. The result is the capability to manipulate images in less time, while consuming less system resources, such as bandwidth and file space. These filters are covered in more detail in Chapter 15.

Dynamic HTML offers several Filter Controls through ActiveX. They include the following:

- **FlipH**—Enables an image to be flipped along the horizontal axis. The result is similar to turning a page over, but still being able to see the image on the other side.

- **FlipV**—Flips images along the vertical axis.

- **Gray**—Converts all the colored pixels in an image to a corresponding shade of gray. There are 256 levels of gray, and the result produces the same image with no color details.

- **Invert**—Causes the selected image to be inverted, or the color of each pixel in the image to be mapped to the opposite color of the original.

- **Xray**—Combines the effects of other Filters. It converts the image to a grayscale image and also flattens the color depth of the image, from 256 to 16 shades of gray.

- **Alpha**—Enables you to use Alpha Channel effects on images, such as specifying opacity for an image or enabling backgrounds or other images to be seen through the image.

- **Blur**—Enables you to apply a motion blur to an object, with parameters that enable you to specify the direction of motion and the strength of the blur.

- **Chroma**—Enables you to select a color in an image that will function as transparent. This is similar to the ChromaKey effect in television, which is often used to substitute backgrounds.

- **Drop Shadow**—Creates a drop shadow around the image or element. Parameters include the color of the shadow and the offset.

- **Glow**—Creates a glowing effect around the specified object.

- **Mask**—Causes any transparent pixels in an object to become solid, and any solid pixels to become transparent, effectively inverting the image and leaving a "hole" where the image previously was.

- **Shadow**—Creates a shadow of the image or object in a specified direction and color.

- **Wave**—Warps the image using a sine wave to create a rippled look over the image.

From Here...

By now the power of Dynamic HTML should be evident. The capability to manipulate content on a page, both during and after the page has been loaded, is compelling by itself. By using dynamic styles and content, pages can be changed and manipulated to create new user environments and experiences. You should now also have a feel for what is possible with Dynamic HTML through style sheets, positioning, and scripting. All these techniques have their value, and they make up the bulk of Dynamic HTML.

- Chapter 14, "Multimedia Transitions"—Provides an overview of multimedia technology incorporated into Dynamic HTML. Learn about creating multimedia effects with Dyanamic HTML, and some of the special features designed especially for multimedia, such as the ActiveX Multimedia Controls.

- Chapter 15, "Multimedia Filters and ActiveX Controls"—Provides detailed coverage of the filters and Multimedia Controls that bring ActiveX technology and Dynamic HTML together.

Multimedia Transitions

The aspects of Dynamic HTML covered thus far give you quite a bit of control over how and where visual elements are displayed on the screen. You can add and delete elements, show them or hide them, and you can even change their positions in real time.

Dynamic HTML, however, gives you a much wider range of multimedia effects than just the capability to manipulate the style and contents of an element. Examples of these expanded capabilities are transitions, filters, and path control.

All these expanded capabilities are implemented in Internet Explorer 4.0 as ActiveX objects. Most of these objects are accessed by embedding them with the <OBJECT> tag in your HTML document. Transitions and filters, however, are so important and common that Microsoft has added proprietary syntax to the style attribute of HTML elements to enable you to use them in a straightforward manner.

A *transition* is a control that enables you to show or hide a visual element over a specified period of time. Think of the last time you were watching a television show or a movie and the screen faded to black. This was a transition from the picture to black. Some of the other multimedia controls available to you will be discussed in the next chapter.

Why are these controls important? They give you unparalleled control over the visual presentation of HTML content, such as images. Previously, if you wanted to do a transition, your only option was to use either a server-side push or an animated GIF.

The capability to do this type of effect within HTML has several advantages from the server side. First, it means that only one copy of an image must be stored, instead of anticipating every possible circumstance.

Secondly, and possibly more important, no round trips to the server are required for this type of multimedia effect. All the work is done on the client side, minimizing both network traffic and server resources. ■

Using Transitions

As mentioned earlier, transitions enable you to specify how an object is shown or hidden over a predetermined time period. The transitions are similar to those you may have seen on television shows or movies: dissolves, wipes, boxing in or out, and so on.

To use a transition, you must specify where in the HTML document the transition will occur. The most common place to do this is inside of a container tag. Usually, you will want to transition between one element and another, and container tags such as the <DIV> tag are HTML's way of grouping elements.

The *FILTER* CSS property specifies which transition to use. This might seem a bit strange at first because there is a logical delineation between transitions and filters. As far as Dynamic HTML is concerned, however, a transition is a special case of a filter.

Why is this? Think of the <DIV> tag as its own visual element, with two elements on top of each other inside of it. Only one of these elements can be shown at any one time. A transition displays the hidden element, and simultaneously hides the currently displayed element. A filter, on the other hand, enables you to modify the appearance of a visual element.

In this way, a transition is a filter that works over a period of time. It is the lens through which the two elements that normally can be seen only independent of one another can now be seen at the same time.

Setting Up the HTML Document for a Transition

The *FILTER* property is set to *revealTrans()* to set the DIV element to use transitions. All the code excerpts within this section are numbered corresponding to their placement in the final code for this transition in listing 14.1. The following code excerpt starts building the DIV element by setting the *FILTER* property:

```
31. <DIV id="transEx"
35.    STYLE="FILTER:revealTrans()">
47. </DIV>
```

Because you'll be placing elements on top of one another, it makes sense to go ahead and use absolute positioning to ensure that the elements will indeed stack on top of each other. The width of this DIV element will be set to *500*, and the height will be set to *350*. The background will be set to *black*. Because the STYLE property of this element has already been set up, you just need to add this CSS information to the STYLE:

```
31. <DIV id="transEx"
33.    STYLE="POSITION:ABSOLUTE;WIDTH:500;HEIGHT:350;
34.           background-color:black;
35.           FILTER:revealTrans()">
47. </DIV>
```

Now that you've set up the DIV element, you need to decide what to place inside the element. The example in this chapter uses an image of a tiger (see figure 14.1) called "tiger.jpg."

FIG. 14.1

Using a simple image of a tiger for multimedia transitions.

To keep the images in the chapter as clear as possible, this example transitions to black instead of to another image. Begin by adding the tiger image and setting its positioning to *absolute*, with a width of *500*, a height of *350*, and a *black* background.

In addition, you need to ensure that the image is positioned at the top left of the DIV element, so that the *top* property is set to *0* and the *left* property to *0*:

```
37. <IMG id="ImageFrm"
38.    STYLE="POSITION:ABSOLUTE;WIDTH:500;HEIGHT:350;
39.           TOP:0;LEFT:0"
40.    SRC="tiger.jpg">
```

Now, because you want to transition to black, you need to have an element, which is just a place-holder, that happens to be black. The easiest way of doing this is to use another DIV element.

Begin by creating this DIV element and placing it as the *0* top and *0* left position in order to overlap the tiger image exactly. For this same reason, you want it to have a width of *500* and a height of *350* and a *black* background:

Part

V

Ch

14

```
42. <DIV id="FadeTo"
43.     STYLE="POSITION:ABSOLUTE;WIDTH:500;HEIGHT:350;
44.         TOP:0;LEFT:0;
45.         BACKGROUND:black">
47. </DIV>
```

Because this is the element that will be transitioned to, you want the element initially to not be visible. This is done by setting the VISIBILITY property of the element's CSS style to *hidden*:

```
42. <DIV id="FadeTo"
43.     STYLE="POSITION:ABSOLUTE;WIDTH:500;HEIGHT:350;
44.         TOP:0;LEFT:0;
45.         BACKGROUND:black
46.         VISIBILITY:hidden">
47. </DIV>
```

This almost completes the necessary work for the body of the document. The final thing you need is a trigger to start the transition. You can fulfill this need by defining a function called *startTrans()* that is called when the DIV element that contains the transition is clicked. The following code binds the *startTrans()* function to the DIV element and constructs the final version of the body of the document:

```
29. <BODY>
30.
31. <DIV id="transEx"
32.     onclick="startTrans()"
33.     STYLE="POSITION:ABSOLUTE;WIDTH:500;HEIGHT:350;
34.         background-color:black;
35.         FILTER:revealTrans()">
36.
37.     <IMG id="ImageFrm"
38.         STYLE="POSITION:ABSOLUTE;WIDTH:500;HEIGHT:350;
39.             TOP:0;LEFT:0"
40.         SRC="tiger.jpg">
41.
42.     <DIV id="FadeTo"
43.         STYLE="POSITION:ABSOLUTE;WIDTH:500;HEIGHT:350;
44.             TOP:0;LEFT:0;
45.             BACKGROUND:black
46.             VISIBILITY:hidden">
47.     </DIV>
48.
49. </DIV>
50.
51. </BODY>
```

Scripting the Transition

Now you want to build the *startTrans()* function that is evaluated when the encompassing <DIV> tag is clicked. When controlling transitions, you need to ensure that four aspects of their control are considered:

- The *Apply()* method of the transition must be called to start the transition.
- The type of transition to be executed must be set.

- The element that you want to transition to should be set to be visible and the element that you want to transition from should be set to be hidden.

- The *play()* method of the transition is called, with the speed of the transition passed as an argument.

To control these aspects of transitions, you need to have a reference to the transition object itself. This object can be returned from the element that contains the transition through the filters collection:

```
transEx.filters
```

Because only one transition is set in this case, you want the first element of this collection, which can be returned with *item (0)*:

```
transEx.filters.item(0)
```

As mentioned previously, the first thing that you must do in the script is call the *Apply()* method of the transition. This informs the browser not to update the contents of the containing element because a transition is about to take place.

The *startTrans()* function begins by calling the *Apply()* method of the transition:

```
09. function startTrans() {
10.
12.      transEx.filters.item(0).Apply();
13.
24. }
```

Next, you need to set the type of transition to execute. A property in the *transition* object called *Transition* is set depending on the transition desired. The *Transition* property can contain an integer in the range 0 to 23, with each number corresponding to a particular type of transition. The types of transitions are listed in table 14.1, and each will be discussed in detail later in this chapter:

Table 14.1 Transition Types

Transition Name	Integer ID
Box In	0
Box Out	1
Circle In	2
Circle Out	3
Wipe Up	4
Wipe Down	5
Wipe Right	6
Wipe Left	7
Vertical Blinds	8

Part

V

Ch

14

continues

Table 14.1 Continued

Transition Name	Integer ID
Horizontal Blinds	9
Checkerboard Across	10
Checkerboard Down	11
Random Dissolve	12
Split Vertical In	13
Split Vertical Out	14
Split Horizontal In	15
Split Horizontal Out	16
Strips Left Down	17
Strips Left Up	18
Strips Right Down	19
Strips Right Up	20
Random Bars Horizontal	21
Random Bars Vertical	22
Random	23

For this example, set the transition type to *12*, which will cause a Random Dissolve Transition to occur. The Random Dissolve Transition causes the element that is being transitioned from to disappear, pixel by pixel, in a random fashion as shown in figure 14.2. The syntax for setting the Random Dissolve Transition is as follows:

```
09. function startTrans() {
10.
12.     transEx.filters.item(0).Apply();
13.
14.     // Set the transition to Random Dissolve
15.     transEx.filters.item(0).Transition = 12;
16.
24. }
```

The next step is to switch the visibility of the two elements that will be transitioned between. This informs the transition control about which element to transition to and which element to transition from. In this case, you set the tiger image to be hidden and set the blank black area to be displayed (which is accomplished by setting its *visibility* property to the blank string):

```
09. function startTrans() {
10.
12.     transEx.filters.item(0).Apply();
15.     transEx.filters.item(0).Transition = 12;
16.
```

```
17.    // Prepare the elements for the transition
18.    ImageFrm.style.visibility = "hidden";
19.    FadeTo.style.visibility = "";
24. }
```

This may seem a bit disconcerting at first, because it seems to imply that the two images will be switched immediately. Why does this appear to be the case? In any other case, when you switch the visibility of an item, the change is executed immediately.

This is a special case because the *Apply()* method of the transition was previously called. This method causes the browser to temporarily suspend immediate changes to the visible state of the elements contained within the transitioned element. This is the trigger that signals that the transition has begun. Now all that needs to be done is to actually do the transition itself.

The final step in scripting the transition is to actually cause the transition to execute. This is accomplished with the *play()* method of the transition. One argument is passed to the *play()* method—*speed*.

The *speed* argument specifies the number of seconds over which to execute the transition. In this case, you set the number of seconds to *5*:

```
09. function startTrans() {
10.
12.    transEx.filters.item(0).Apply();
15.    transEx.filters.item(0).Transition = 12;
18.    ImageFrm.style.visibility = "hidden";
19.    FadeTo.style.visibility = "";
20.
21.    // Play the transition
22.    transEx.filters.item(0).play(5);
23.
24. }
```

This means that the transitions will occur over 5 seconds, after which the element transitioned from will have completely disappeared and the element transitioned to will be completely visible.

Implementing the Transition

Now that you've learned about the HTML and the scripting portions of transitions, take a look at a transition firsthand. Listing 14.1 places the body and scripting portions of the transition together in an example file (ch14ex01.htm):

Listing 14.1   Creating a Random Dissolve Transition Between Images

```
01. <HTML>
02. <HEAD>
03.    <TITLE>
04.       Chapter 14, Example 1
05.    </TITLE>
06.
07.    <SCRIPT LANGUAGE="JavaScript">
08.
```

Listing 14.1 Continued

```
09.    function startTrans() {
10.
11.       // Start the transition definition process
12.       transEx.filters.item(0).Apply();
13.
14.       // Set the transition to Random Dissolve
15.       transEx.filters.item(0).Transition = 12;
16.
17.       // Prepare the elements for the transition
18.       ImageFrm.style.visibility = "hidden";
19.       FadeTo.style.visibility = "";
20.
21.       // Play the transition
22.       transEx.filters.item(0).play(5);
23.
24.    }
25.    </SCRIPT>
26. </HEAD>
27.
28.
29. <BODY>
30.
31. <DIV id="transEx"
32.    onclick="startTrans()"
33.    STYLE="POSITION:ABSOLUTE;WIDTH:500;HEIGHT:350;
34.          background-color:black;
35.          FILTER:revealTrans()">
36.
37.       <IMG id="ImageFrm"
38.          STYLE="POSITION:ABSOLUTE;WIDTH:500;HEIGHT:350;
39.                TOP:0;LEFT:0"
40.          SRC="tiger.jpg">
41.
42.       <DIV id="FadeTo"
43.          STYLE="POSITION:ABSOLUTE;WIDTH:500;HEIGHT:350;
44.                TOP:0;LEFT:0;
45.                BACKGROUND:black;
46.                VISIBILITY:hidden">
47.       </DIV>
48.
49. </DIV>
50.
51. </BODY>
52. </HTML>
```

Figure 14.2 shows this transition in action. When the page is first loaded, only the image of the tiger is shown. As soon as the user clicks the tiger, however, the transition is triggered and the tiger slowly dissolves to black.

FIG. 14.2

The image of the tiger dissolves to black.

In this example, the transition starts when the user clicks the image; however, this is not the only way to trigger transitions.

Any event can be bound to the function to start the transition. You might want the transition to start whenever the user passes the mouse pointer over the element to be transitioned. You could also trigger the transition with a different element—perhaps a button that is identified as the controller for the transition. Refer back to Chapter 7, "Event Handling," for more examples of the types of events that could be bound to.

Transition Types

Many types of transitions are available to use in your Dynamic HTML documents. Choosing which one to use can be confusing. This section covers the different transitions available to you and gives an example of each one in action.

To make it easier to introduce these transitions into your own Dynamic HTML documents, an example <DIV> tag that can be placed directly into your Dynamic HTML documents will be provided with each example.

In addition to specifying the type of transition to be executed with the *Transition* property of the *transition* object externally, you can also specify the transition type as an argument to the *revealTrans()* function. To specify the transition type in this way, you still specify the transition by setting the *Transition* property to the transition required. However, instead of doing so in a script, you do this as an argument to the *revealTrans()* function:

```
revealTrans(Transition = <transition_id>)
```

Part

V

Ch

14

Therefore, if you wanted to set the transition type from listing 14.1 to *1* (causing a Box Out transition) inside the DIV element, you would use the following code:

```
<DIV id="transEx"
    onclick="startTrans()"
    STYLE="POSITION:ABSOLUTE;WIDTH:500;HEIGHT:350;
        background-color:black;
        FILTER:revealTrans(Transition=1)"> // Set the transition
```

The examples in the sections that follow on each of the transition types provide the appropriate version of this DIV element. These DIV elements can then be cut and pasted into the example in listing 14.1. The one additional modification that you will need to make to the example is the removal of the line that sets the transition in the *startTrans()* function, because you won't need it any longer. Therefore, remove line 15 from the example in listing 14.1 because the transition type is being set in *revealTrans()*:

```
transEx.filters.item(0).Transition = 12;
```

Box In

With the Box In Transition (see figure 14.3), the element that is being transitioned to replaces the element being transitioned from by starting from the outside going inward in a box. This causes the image being transitioned from to disappear, becoming a smaller and smaller box.

FIG. 14.3

Using the Box In Transition to hide the tiger.

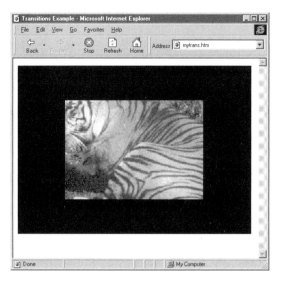

The Box In Transition has a transition ID of *0*, as shown in the following DIV element:

```
<DIV id="transEx"
    onclick="startTrans()"
    STYLE="POSITION:ABSOLUTE;WIDTH:500;HEIGHT:350;
        background-color:black;
        FILTER:revealTrans(Transition=0)">
```

Box Out

The Box Out Transition (see figure 14.4) is the exact opposite of the Box In Transition. When you run the Box Out Transition, the element being transitioned to starts out as a small box. This box grows larger and larger until it completely replaces the element being transitioned from.

FIG. 14.4
Using the Box Out Transition to hide the tiger.

The Box Out Transition has a transition value of 1, as shown in the following DIV element:

```
<DIV id="transEx"
   onclick="startTrans()"
   STYLE="POSITION:ABSOLUTE;WIDTH:500;HEIGHT:350;
      background-color:black;
      FILTER:revealTrans(Transition=1)">
```

Circle In

The Circle In Transition (see figure 14.5) causes the element being transitioned from to be seen in a smaller and smaller circular window until it completely disappears. While this is occurring, the image being transitioned to becomes the growing area that surrounds the disappearing circle.

Part
V

Ch
14

FIG. 14.5

Using the Circle In
Transition to hide the
tiger.

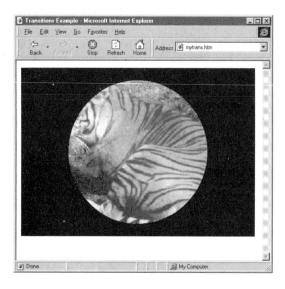

The Circle In Transition has a transition value of 2, as shown in the following DIV element:

```
<DIV id="transEx"
    onclick="startTrans()"
    STYLE="POSITION:ABSOLUTE;WIDTH:500;HEIGHT:350;
        background-color:black;
        FILTER:revealTrans(Transition=2)">
```

Circle Out

The Circle Out Transition (see figure 14.6) is the exact opposite of the Circle In Transition. When
the Circle In Transition is executed, the element being transitioned to starts out as a small circle.
This circle grows larger and larger until it completely replaces the element being transitioned from.

FIG. 14.6

Using the Circle Out
Transition to hide the
tiger.

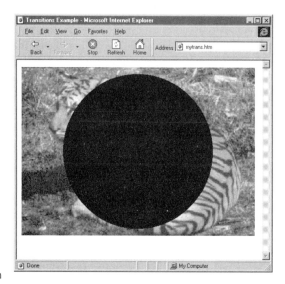

The Circle Out Transition has a transition value of 3, as shown in the following DIV element:

```
<DIV id="transEx"
    onclick="startTrans()"
    STYLE="POSITION:ABSOLUTE;WIDTH:500;HEIGHT:350;
        background-color:black;
        FILTER:revealTrans(Transition=3)">
```

Wipe Up

The Wipe Up Transition (see figure 14.7) causes the element being transitioned into to replace the element being transitioned from as if it were being wiped upward onto the screen. This is done by replacing the horizontal lines of the image being replaced one by one, starting at the bottom.

FIG. 14.7

Using the Wipe Up Transition to hide the tiger.

The Wipe Up Transition has a transition value of 4, as shown in the following DIV element:

```
<DIV id="transEx"
    onclick="startTrans()"
    STYLE="POSITION:ABSOLUTE;WIDTH:500;HEIGHT:350;
        background-color:black;
        FILTER:revealTrans(Transition=4)">
```

Wipe Down

The Wipe Down Transition (see figure 14.8) is the opposite of the Wipe In Transition. Instead of the element being replaced starting at the bottom and moving to the top, the element is replaced horizontally line by line, starting at the top of the element.

Part

V

Ch

14

FIG. 14.8

Using the Wipe Down Transition to hide the tiger.

The Wipe Down Transition has a transition value of 5, as shown in the following DIV element:

```
<DIV id="transEx"
    onclick="startTrans()"
    STYLE="POSITION:ABSOLUTE;WIDTH:500;HEIGHT:350;
        background-color:black;
        FILTER:revealTrans(Transition=5)">
```

Wipe Right

The Wipe Right Transition (see figure 14.9) is similar to the Wipe Up and Wipe Down Transitions, except that vertical lines are used. First, the leftmost vertical line of the element is replaced, then the rest are replaced vertical line by line moving to the right.

FIG. 14.9

Using the Wipe Right Transition to hide the tiger.

The Wipe Right Transition has a transition value of 6, as shown in the following DIV element:

```
<DIV id="transEx"
    onclick="startTrans()"
    STYLE="POSITION:ABSOLUTE;WIDTH:500;HEIGHT:350;
        background-color:black;
        FILTER:revealTrans(Transition=6)">
```

Wipe Left

The Wipe Left Transition (see figure 14.10) is the opposite of the Wipe Right Transition. Instead of the replacement of the vertical lines starting at the left side of the element, the lines of the element are replaced starting at the right side.

FIG. 14.10
Using the Wipe Left Transition to hide the tiger.

The Wipe Left Transition has a transition value of 7, as shown in the following DIV element:

```
<DIV id="transEx"
    onclick="startTrans()"
    STYLE="POSITION:ABSOLUTE;WIDTH:500;HEIGHT:350;
        background-color:black;
        FILTER:revealTrans(Transition=7)">
```

Vertical Blinds

The Vertical Blinds Transition (see figure 14.11) works much like a set of blinds that you may have on your window. Imagine that the element being transitioned from is painted on your blinds and the element being transitioned to is placed behind the blinds.

Now, imagine adjusting the blinds so that they cannot be seen, revealing what is behind them. This is similar to the process that is used by the Vertical Blinds Transition. The element transitioned from is broken into equal-sized vertical segments, then these segments are replaced one vertical line at a time by the element being transitioned to.

Part
V

Ch

FIG. 14.11

Using the Vertical Blinds Transition to hide the tiger.

The Vertical Blinds Transition has a transition value of 8, as shown in the following DIV element:

```
<DIV id="transEx"
   onclick="startTrans()"
   STYLE="POSITION:ABSOLUTE;WIDTH:500;HEIGHT:350;
       background-color:black;
       FILTER:revealTrans(Transition=8)">
```

Horizontal Blinds

The Horizontal Blinds Transition (see figure 14.12) is much like the Vertical Blinds Transition, except that the element transitioned from is broken into equal sized horizontal segments, then these segments are replaced a horizontal line at a time by the element being transitioned to.

FIG. 14.12

Using the Horizontal Blinds Transition to hide the tiger.

The Horizontal Blinds Transition has a transition value of 9, as shown in the following DIV element:

```
<DIV id="transEx"
    onclick="startTrans()"
    STYLE="POSITION:ABSOLUTE;WIDTH:500;HEIGHT:350;
        background-color:black;
        FILTER:revealTrans(Transition=9)">
```

Checkerboard Across

The Checkerboard Across Transition (see figure 14.13) breaks the transition into a checkerboard pattern with alternating squares containing pieces of the transitioned from and transitioned to elements. Then, the boxes containing pieces of the element being transitioned to grow horizontally until they completely replace the element being transitioned from.

FIG. 14.13

Using the Checkerboard Across Transition to hide the tiger.

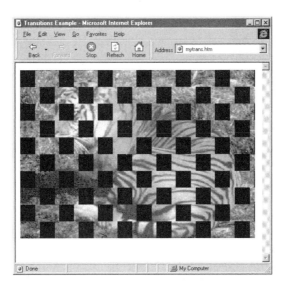

The Checkerboard Across Transition has a transition value of 10, as shown in the following DIV element:

```
<DIV id="transEx"
    onclick="startTrans()"
    STYLE="POSITION:ABSOLUTE;WIDTH:500;HEIGHT:350;
        background-color:black;
        FILTER:revealTrans(Transition=10)">
```

Part

V

Ch

14

Checkerboard Down

The Checkerboard Down Transition (see figure 14.14) is much like the Checkerboard Across Transition, except that the alternating squares containing the pieces of the element transitioned to grow vertically instead of horizontally, eventually replacing the element transitioned from.

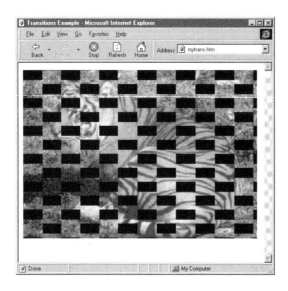

The Checkerboard Down Transition has a transition value of 11, as shown in the following DIV element:

```
<DIV id="transEx"
   onclick="startTrans()"
   STYLE="POSITION:ABSOLUTE;WIDTH:500;HEIGHT:350;
      background-color:black;
      FILTER:revealTrans(Transition=11)">
```

Random Dissolve

The Random Dissolve Transition (see figure 14.15) starts by randomly picking pixels in the element being transitioned from and replacing them with pixels from the element being transitioned to. This process is repeated until the entire image being transitioned from has been replaced.

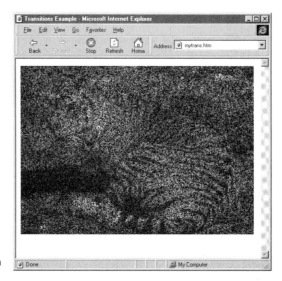

The Random Dissolve Transition has a transition value of 12, as shown in the following DIV element:

```
<DIV id="transEx"
    onclick="startTrans()"
    STYLE="POSITION:ABSOLUTE;WIDTH:500;HEIGHT:350;
        background-color:black;
        FILTER:revealTrans(Transition=12)">
```

Split Vertical In

The Split Vertical In Transition (see figure 14.16) is much like a combination of the Wipe Right and Wipe Left Transitions running at the same time. The transition starts by replacing a vertical line from both the left and right sides of the element being transitioned from and continues inward until the element is completely replaced.

FIG. 14.16

Using the Split Vertical In Transition to hide the tiger.

The Split Vertical In Transition has a transition value of 13, as shown in the following DIV element:

```
<DIV id="transEx"
    onclick="startTrans()"
    STYLE="POSITION:ABSOLUTE;WIDTH:500;HEIGHT:350;
        background-color:black;
        FILTER:revealTrans(Transition=13)">
```

Part
V

Ch
14

Split Vertical Out

The Split Vertical Out Transition (see figure 14.17) is the opposite of the Split Vertical In Transition. It starts by dividing the element in half vertically and replacing the two vertical lines in the center. It then moves outward, replacing more vertical lines toward the right and left edges of the screen until the element being transitioned from is replaced.

FIG. 14.17

Using the Split Vertical Out Transition to hide the tiger.

The Split Vertical Out Transition has a transition value of 14, as shown in the following DIV element:

```
<DIV id="transEx"
    onclick="startTrans()"
    STYLE="POSITION:ABSOLUTE;WIDTH:500;HEIGHT:350;
        background-color:black;
        FILTER:revealTrans(Transition=14)">
```

Split Horizontal In

The Split Horizontal In Transition (see figure 14.18) is like a combination of the Wipe Up and Wipe Down Transitions running at the same time. The transition starts by replacing a horizontal line from both the top and bottom of the element being transitioned from and continues inward until the element is completely replaced.

FIG. 14.18

Using the Split Horizontal In Transition to hide the tiger.

The Split Horizontal In Transition has a transition value of 15, as shown in the following DIV element:

```
<DIV id="transEx"
    onclick="startTrans()"
    STYLE="POSITION:ABSOLUTE;WIDTH:500;HEIGHT:350;
        background-color:black;
        FILTER:revealTrans(Transition=15)">
```

Split Horizontal Out

The Split Horizontal Out Transition (see figure 14.17) is the opposite of the Split Horizontal In Transition. It starts by dividing the element in half horizontally and replacing the two horizontal lines in the center. It then moves outward, replacing more horizontal lines toward the top and bottom edges of the screen until the element being transitioned from is replaced.

FIG. 14.19

Using the Split Horizontal Out Transition to hide the tiger.

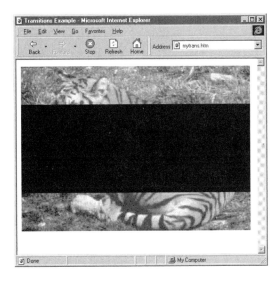

The Split Horizontal Out Transition has a transition value of 16, as shown in the following DIV element:

```
<DIV id="transEx"
    onclick="startTrans()"
    STYLE="POSITION:ABSOLUTE;WIDTH:500;HEIGHT:350;
        background-color:black;
        FILTER:revealTrans(Transition=16)">
```

Strips Left Down

A good way to think of a Strips Left Down Transition (see figure 14.20) is to imagine it as a wipe that starts at the upper-right corner of the element being transitioned from and wipes down and to the left diagonally, replacing the image transitioned from as it goes along.

Part

V

Ch

14

FIG. 14.20

Using the Strips Left
Down Transition to hide
the tiger.

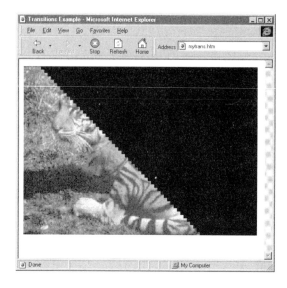

The Strips Left Down Transition has a transition value of 17, as shown in the following DIV element:

```
<DIV id="transEx"
    onclick="startTrans()"
    STYLE="POSITION:ABSOLUTE;WIDTH:500;HEIGHT:350;
        background-color:black;
        FILTER:revealTrans(Transition=17)">
```

Strips Left Up

The Strips Left Up Transition (see figure 14.21) is much like the Strips Left Down Transition, except that it starts at the lower-right corner of the element being replaced. It then replaces the element with the element being transitioned to by wiping up and to the left.

FIG. 14.21

Using the Strips Left Up
Transition to hide the
tiger.

The Strips Left Up Transition has a transition value of 18, as shown in the following DIV element:

```
<DIV id="transEx"
   onclick="startTrans()"
   STYLE="POSITION:ABSOLUTE;WIDTH:500;HEIGHT:350;
      background-color:black;
      FILTER:revealTrans(Transition=18)">
```

Strips Right Down

The Strips Right Down Transition (see figure 14.22) is much like the Strips Right Up Transition, except that it starts at the upper-left corner of the element being replaced. It then replaces the element with the element being transitioned to by wiping down and to the right.

FIG. 14.22

Using the Strips Right Down Transition to hide the tiger.

The Strips Right Down Transition has a transition value of 19, as shown in the following DIV element:

```
<DIV id="transEx"
   onclick="startTrans()"
   STYLE="POSITION:ABSOLUTE;WIDTH:500;HEIGHT:350;
      background-color:black;
      FILTER:revealTrans(Transition=19)">
```

Strips Right Up

The Strips Right Up Transition (see figure 14.23) is much like the Strips Right Down Transition, except that it starts at the lower-left corner of the element being replaced. It then replaces the element with the element being transitioned to by wiping up and to the right.

Part
V

Ch
14

FIG. 14.23

Using the Strips Right Up Transition to hide the tiger.

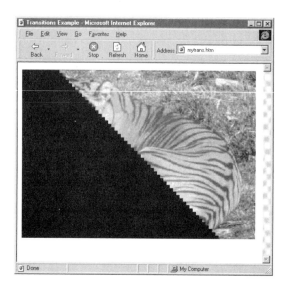

The Strips Right Up Transition has a transition value of 20, as shown in the following DIV element:

```
<DIV id="transEx"
    onclick="startTrans()"
    STYLE="POSITION:ABSOLUTE;WIDTH:500;HEIGHT:350;
        background-color:black;
        FILTER:revealTrans(Transition=20)">
```

Random Bars Horizontal

The Random Bars Horizontal Transition (see figure 14.24) is one of the more interesting transitions. It randomly selects horizontal lines of varying widths from the element being transitioned from and replaces them with equally sized lines from the element being transitioned to. It repeats this process until the transition between the two elements is complete.

FIG. 14.24

Using the Random Bars Horizontal Transition to hide the tiger.

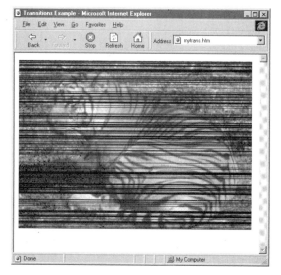

The Random Bars Horizontal Transition has a transition value of 21, as shown in the following DIV element:

```
<DIV id="transEx"
    onclick="startTrans()"
    STYLE="POSITION:ABSOLUTE;WIDTH:500;HEIGHT:350;
        background-color:black;
        FILTER:revealTrans(Transition=21)">
```

Random Bars Vertical

The Random Bars Vertical Transition (see figure 14.25) is much like the Random Bars Horizontal Transition, except with vertical lines instead of horizontal ones. It randomly selects vertical lines of varying widths from the element being transitioned from and replaces them with equally sized lines from the element being transitioned to. It repeats this process until the transition between the two elements is complete.

FIG. 14.25

Using the Random Bars Vertical Transition to hide the tiger.

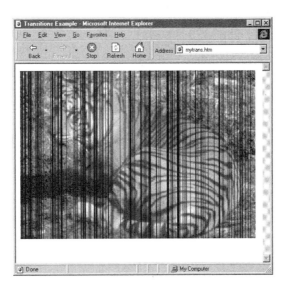

The Random Bars Vertical Transition has a transition value of 22, as shown in the following DIV element:

```
<DIV id="transEx"
    onclick="startTrans()"
    STYLE="POSITION:ABSOLUTE;WIDTH:500;HEIGHT:350;
        background-color:black;
        FILTER:revealTrans(Transition=22)">
```

Part

V

Ch

14

Random

The Random Transition randomly selects one of the other 23 transitions and executes it. If you're looking for an effect that changes every time it is executed, this is the one.

The Random Transition has a transition ID of 23, as shown in the following DIV element:

```
<DIV id="transEx"
   onclick="startTrans()"
   STYLE="POSITION:ABSOLUTE;WIDTH:500;HEIGHT:350;
      background-color:black;
      FILTER:revealTrans(Transition=23)">
```

From Here...

Transitions are arguably the most important multimedia controls that Dynamic HTML provides, but filters and the other multimedia controls aren't far behind in importance.

Chapter 15, "Multimedia Filters and Multimedia ActiveX Controls," discusses these multimedia controls and the ways they can further enhance your Dynamic HTML documents.

Multimedia Filters and ActiveX Controls

Differentiating Multimedia Objects

Differentiate between transitions, filters, and other multimedia objects.

Filters

Learn the motives behind, impact of, and techniques for setting up filters in your HTML documents.

Filter Types

Discover the intricacies of and how to implement all the multimedia filters offered by Dynamic HTML. Filters are one of the bedrock aspects of Dynamic HTML multimedia and knowing the types available can be quite helpful.

In addition to transitions, Dynamic HTML offers quite a few other multimedia effects that can be applied to your HTML elements.

These effects can be divided into two general classes, separated by how they are specified and controlled from within your Dynamic HTML documents.

The first class of multimedia effects is a Microsoft extension to CSS. These effects are specified in a style block or with the STYLE attribute for an element. You've already seen this type of effect in the last chapter with transitions. Filters are specified in much the same way and will be the first topic covered in this chapter.

The second class of multimedia effects must be added via an <OBJECT> tag. These Multimedia Controls are ActiveX objects and are treated as any other ActiveX object you might use, except you are guaranteed that they will be present in every instance of Internet Explorer 4.0 because they ship with it.

Although these controls are certainly no less powerful than the transitions and filters, they are more complicated to use because you must use quite a bit of syntax to work with them. This can be especially confusing if you have never worked with ActiveX objects. ■

> **N O T E** It is important to note that the transition and filter effects are ActiveX Controls as well.
> However, by making them accessible via the STYLE property of elements that use them,
> they are much simpler to specify and control. In addition, there is a much higher probability that their
> functionality may be duplicated in other browsers, even if those browsers do not support ActiveX. ■

Introducing Filters

A *filter* is a control that enables you to directly apply effects to the contents of an element. A blur filter, for instance, enables you to make an element blurry to the extent that you specify.

Many types of filters are available in Dynamic HTML. The following list presents the filters currently available, which will be discussed individually in detail throughout the rest of the chapter:

- X-Ray
- Drop Shadow
- Flip Horizontal
- Flip Vertical
- Grayscale
- Invert
- Lights
- Mask
- Motion Blur
- Opacity
- Shadow
- Wave
- Glow
- Chromakey

Much like transitions, the capability to apply filters on the client side is a great boon to HTML developers. Prior to Dynamic HTML, manipulating the way an image was displayed required performing the manipulation before load time (or in sophisticated situations possibly generated by a CGI script) when it was downloaded to the user.

Generating the image with the desired effect ahead of time causes a great deal of problems on the server side. For one thing, every conceivable effect that you want to perform must be thought of and generated before load time.

Placing all the effects that may be performed on the image on the server also causes server disk and scalability problems. Storage resources must be used to store all the varied images. Furthermore, a round trip is performed every time the next image effect is desired, congesting the network and limiting scalability.

Setting Up Filters in Your HTML

Adding filters to your Dynamic HTML document is actually quite straightforward. The first thing that you need to specify is a container for the element to which you will be applying the filter.

Usually, you will want to use a <DIV> element as the container for the element to be filtered because it is the most versatile container. You will want to give this container a unique ID that it can be referenced by because the filter will be associated with the container, not directly with the image that will be filtered. This is an important point. Think of the container that encapsulates the element to be filtered as a lens through which that element is filtered. This approach has one major advantage: You can apply the same filters to whatever you place inside the container, which can change whenever you please (see Chapter 10, "Dynamic Content"). The following example assigns the container ID as "filtEx."

To effectively see the difference before and after executing the filter, the following example delays the running of the filter until the user presses the mouse button down on the container. The function that will be called is *startFilter()*.

This example also uses absolute positioning to place the image in an arbitrary location on the screen. This is a good practice to get into in case you want to place multiple elements in the container because it enables you to stack them (see Chapter 9, "Layout and Positioning").

Given these requirements, the first thing you need to do is construct the required <DIV> element as follows:

```
<DIV id="filtEx"
    STYLE="POSITION:ABSOLUTE;TOP:100;LEFT:200; WIDTH:450;HEIGHT:300"
    onclick="startFilter()">
</DIV>
```

Next, the element you want to apply the filter to should be placed inside this <DIV> element. This chapter uses an image as the element to filter; however, you can use any type of element. You can even apply filters to raw text. The image of an eagle, *"eagle.jpg,"* is used consistently throughout this chapter so you can get a good idea of the effects achieved through filters (see fig. 15.1).

The following code excerpt from listing 15.1 (displayed in its entirety in the following section, "X-Ray Filter") adds an IMG element specifying the image of the eagle to the <DIV> element:

```
18. <DIV id="filtEx"
19.     STYLE="POSITION:ABSOLUTE;TOP:100;LEFT:200;WIDTH:450;HEIGHT:300"
20.     onclick="startFilter()">
21.
22.   <IMG id="theImg" SRC="eagle.jpg"
23.
24. </DIV>
```

Believe it or not, this is the extent of the HTML required to set up to use filters. Now that you've got a container through which to use the filter, you just need to write a JavaScript function that sets up the filter to be used.

FIG. 15.1

An image of an eagle waiting to be filtered.

Unlike transitions, specifying the filter to use is more involved than just setting a number from a list. You set a filter by specifying the filter via the *id.style.filter* property of the *container* object.

The set value of the *id.style.filter* property will vary from filter to filter. Now take a look at the next section, which builds an example around the X-Ray Filter that you will use throughout the rest of the chapter with each filter.

X-Ray Filter

The X-Ray Filter (see fig. 15.2) makes the element being filtered appear as if an x-ray were taken of it. This effect is achieved by converting the element to a very low color depth black-and-white visual representation and reversing the colors of the element (black becomes white, and so forth), giving it a photographic-negative feel.

FIG. 15.2

Applying the X-Ray Filter to the image of the eagle.

When the filter is set in Dynamic HTML with the *id.style.filter* property, the value that is passed is a string that contains the filter function.

A *filter function* is the name of the filter followed by any arguments it may contain as parameters to the function. You've already seen an example of this with transitions in Chapter 14, "Multimedia Transitions."

You specify the X-Ray Filter by setting the filter type to *xray()*. This filter function takes one argument, "enabled," which is set to *0* or *1* depending on whether you want the filter to take effect *(1)* or not *(0)*.

In this case, you want to enable the filter, so set the filter function to *1* as follows:

```
filtEx.style.filter = "xray(enabled = 1)";
```

Because you want this filter to be executed only when the mouse button is pressed on the container, you need to set the filter in the *startFilter()* event handler as follows (taken from the final syntax in listing 15.1):

```
09.    function startFilter() {
10.        filtEx.style.filter = "xray(enabled=1)";
11.    }
```

As soon as you set the filter type of the *container* object, the filter takes effect.

N O T E There is an important difference between working with transitions and working with filters: when working with transitions, you need to call methods of the transition object to let it know you will be executing a transition; but with filters, the mere act of setting the filter executes it. ■

Now that you've created all the pieces required to implement the X-Ray Filter, it's time to put them together into an example and take a look at the results. Save the following file as "ch15ex01.htm":

Listing 15.1   Implementing a Basic Filter

```
01. <HTML>
02. <HEAD>
03.    <TITLE>
04.       Chapter 15, Example 1
05.    </TITLE>
06.
07.    <SCRIPT LANGUAGE="JavaScript">
08.
09.    function startFilter() {
10.        filtEx.style.filter = "xray(enabled=1)";
11.    }
12.    </SCRIPT>
13.
14. </HEAD>
15.
16. <BODY>
17.
```

continues

Listing 15.1   Continued

```
18. <DIV id="filtEx"
19.     STYLE="POSITION:ABSOLUTE;TOP:100;LEFT:200;WIDTH:450;HEIGHT:300"
20.     onclick="startFilter()">
21.
22.     <IMG id="theImg" SRC="eagle.jpg">
23.
24. </DIV>
25.
26. </BODY>
27. </HTML>
```

Although listing 15.1 shows the code for the X-Ray in its entirety, the sections on the individual filters that follow will only provide the *startFilter()* function definition that occurs on lines 9–11 within the <SCRIPT> tags. The function definition provided with each filter can be cut-and-pasted into the code in listing 15.1 to generate the example figures provided with each filter.

Drop Shadow Filter

The Drop Shadow Filter (see fig. 15.3) places a colored, solid silhouette of the element being filtered behind the element. The filter function that is passed for the Drop Shadow Filter is *dropshadow()*.

FIG. 15.3

Applying the Drop Shadow Filter to the image of the eagle.

You can control the following aspects of the silhouette by changing the corresponding parameters to the filter function:

- **offx**—The number of pixels to set the shadow off on the x axis. If you specify a positive value, the shadow is offset to the right. If you specify a negative value, it is offset to the left.

■ **offy**—The number of pixels to set the shadow off on the y axis. If you specify a positive value, the shadow is offset to the bottom. If you specify a negative value, it is offset to the top.

■ **color**—The color of the shadow, expressed in the standard #RRGGBB HTML format.

■ **enabled**—*0* if the filter is disabled, *1* if enabled

Suppose, for example, that you wanted a drop shadow to appear as if a light were placed slightly above and to the left of your element. Note that the drop shadow does not affect the element that is being shadowed at all; it just places a shadow by it. So you need to make sure the container that the element is in is slightly larger than the element being shadowed.

For illustration purposes here, to keep the effect slight, you need to keep the offsets relatively small, say 10 pixels. Because the light would be shining from the upper left, the shadow should appear to the lower right. This means that you will want to make the *offx* and *offy* offsets positive. Therefore, you will want to set *offx* to *10* and *offy* to *10* as well.

The shadow can be painted in any color desired. This example applies a medium gray shadow. Medium gray in RGB format is #888888 (RGB and Hexadecimal color codes are referenced in Appendix F, "Browser-Safe Hexadecimal Chart"). The following code pulls this all together into the filter function:

```
dropshadow(offx=10,offy=10,color=#888888,enabled=1)
```

Finally, you need to place this filter function into the *startFilter()* function, ready to be pasted into the HTML code in listing 15.1 as lines 9–11. The results of running this filter on the eagle image are shown in figure 15.3.

```
function startFilter() {
    filtEx.style.filter = "dropshadow(offx=10,offy=10,color=#888888,enabled=1)";
}
```

Flip Horizontal Filter

The Flip Horizontal Filter (see fig. 15.4) takes the pixels that make up the element that the filter is applied to and reverses their order, giving the impression that the element has been flipped upon its horizontal axis.

This effect is created by taking the first vertical line in the image and making it the last vertical line, then taking the second and making it the second to last vertical line, repeated throughout the entire image.

The Flip Horizontal Filter function is represented by *fliph ()* and takes only one argument, "enabled," which is set to *0* if the filter is disabled and set to *1* if the filter is enabled.

The following line of code displays the standard version of this filter function:

```
fliph(enabled=1)
```

Finally, you need to place this filter function into the *startFilter()* function, ready to be pasted into the HTML code in listing 15.1 as lines 9–11. The results of running the Flip Horizontal Filter on the eagle image are shown in figure 15.4.

FIG. 15.4

Applying the Flip
Horizontal Filter to the
image of the eagle.

```
function startFilter() {
   filtEx.style.filter = "fliph(enabled=1)";
}
```

Flip Vertical Filter

The Flip Vertical Filter (see fig. 15.5) is much like the Flip Horizontal Filter, except that it mirrors the element along its vertical axis, giving the impression that the element has been flipped along this vertical axis.

This effect is achieved by taking the first horizontal line in the image and making it the last horizontal line, then taking the second and making it the second to last horizontal line, repeated throughout the entire image.

FIG. 15.5

Applying the Flip Vertical
Filter to the image of the
eagle.

The Flip Vertical Filter function is represented by *flipv ()* and takes only one argument, "enabled," which is set to *0* if the filter is disabled and set to *1* if the filter is enabled.

The following line of code displays the standard version of this filter function:

```
flipv(enabled=1)
```

Finally, you need to place this filter function into the *startFilter()* function, ready to be pasted into the HTML code in listing 15.1 as lines 9–11. The results of running the Flip Vertical Filter on the eagle image are shown in figure 15.5.

```
function startFilter() {
    filtEx.style.filter = "flipv(enabled=1)";
}
```

Grayscale Filter

The Grayscale Filter (see fig. 15.6) takes the element that the filter is being applied to and removes all color information that the element contains. This makes the element appear as if it were being viewed on a grayscale monitor.

It's important to note that rendering the element in grayscale is different from rendering it in black and white. With a black-and-white image, only two colors can be worked with, usually leading to a great deal of dithering. When the element is shown in grayscale, however, a shade of gray is chosen to represent the different color.

FIG. 15.6

Applying the Grayscale Filter to the image of the eagle.

The Grayscale Filter function is represented by *gray()* and takes only one argument, "enabled," which is set to *0* if the filter is disabled and set to *1* if the filter is enabled.

The following line of code displays the standard version of this filter function:

```
gray(enabled=1)
```

Finally, you need to place this filter function into the *startFilter()* function, ready to be pasted into the HTML code in listing 15.1 as lines 9–11. The results of running the Grayscale Filter on the eagle image are shown in figure 15.6.

```
function startFilter() {
    filtEx.style.filter = "gray(enabled=1)";
}
```

Invert Filter

The Invert Filter (see fig. 15.7) causes the element to appear as a photographic negative of the element. This effect is achieved by reversing the *hue*, *saturation*, and *brightness* values of the element.

FIG. 15.7

Applying the Invert Filter to the image of the eagle.

The Invert Filter function is represented by *invert()* and takes only one argument, "enabled," which is set to *0* if the filter is disabled and set to *1* if the filter is enabled.

The following line of code displays the standard version of the Invert Filter function:

```
invert(enabled=1)
```

Finally, you need to place the Invert Filter function into the *startFilter()* function, ready to be pasted into the HTML code in listing 15.1 as lines 9–11. The results of running the Invert Filter on the eagle image are shown in figure 15.7.

```
function startFilter() {
    filtEx.style.filter = "invert(enabled=1)";
}
```

Lights Filter

The Lights Filter (see fig. 15.8) is one of the most interesting and compelling filters that Dynamic HTML provides. Normally, one element displays with the same brightness as every other element on the page, as if a generic ambient light were shining on every element.

The Lights Filter enables you to change this by applying light sources to your element as if they were the only lights being shone on the element.

FIG. 15.8

Lights Filter with an ambient and point light source.

Setting up the Lights Filter function itself is quite straightforward. The filter function for the Lights Filter is *light()* and takes only one argument, "enabled," which is set to *0* if the filter is disabled and set to *1* if the filter is enabled.

The following line of code displays the standard version of the Lights Filter function:

```
light(enabled=1)
```

The Lights Filter becomes considerably more interesting when you consider that you have to add light sources to shine upon the element being filtered. The Lights Filter has several types of light that can be applied to your element, provided by variations of Ambient light and Point light.

Ambient light is added to the filter by calling the *addAmbient()* method of the filter. Ambient light is much like any diffused lighting that may be present in your home. It is light that illuminates an area, but does not appear to come from any one place. The *addAmbient()* method takes four arguments:

- **R**—The red value of the light, expressed in magnitude of saturation. The value can range from *0* being lowest to *255* being highest.
- **G**—The green value of the light, expressed in magnitude of saturation. The value can range from *0* being lowest to *255* being highest.

- **B**—The blue value of the light, expressed in magnitude of saturation. The value can range from *0* being lowest to *255* being highest.

- **strength**—The intensity of the light shining upon the element, expressed as an integer from *0* to *255*, with intensity increasing with the value of the integer.

When you add ambient light to your filter, not only can you specify the intensity of the light, but also the color of the light. Therefore, if you wanted to approximate sunlight instead of a pure white light, you could add a bit of yellow to the light. You could even approximate the effects of shining a pure red light on your element. This capability is not limited to ambient light, but can be used with all the light sources you generate.

The following example uses the *addAmbient()* method to create an Ambient light of fairly high intensity that is greyish blue:

```
addAmbient(200,200,255,150)
```

You can also apply a Point light source to your image. *Point light* is a light source that can be placed at a specified position in 3D space over your image; all the light it generates emanates from that point outward.

Point light enables interesting effects because its intensity is highest at the point of the light and decreases rapidly as it travels. A good way to imagine a point light source is to picture a small lamp in a very dark room. The areas that surround the lamp are brightly lit, but objects 15 feet away aren't illuminated very well, if at all.

Point lights are generated by the *addPoint()* method of the Lights Filter. The *addPoint()* method takes seven arguments:

- **x**—The x coordinate of the light source. The range of this coordinate is dependent upon the size of the element.

- **y**—The y coordinate of the light source. The range of this coordinate is dependent upon the size of the element.

- **z**—The z coordinate of the light source. This value corresponds to how far above the element you want the light source to be.

- **R**—The red value of the light, expressed in magnitude of saturation. The value can range from *0* being lowest and *255* being highest.

- **G**—The green value of the light, expressed in magnitude of saturation. The value can range from *0* being lowest and *255* being highest.

- **B**—The blue value of the light, expressed in magnitude of saturation. The value can range from *0* being lowest and *255* being highest.

- **strength**—The intensity of the light that is shining upon the element, expressed as an integer from *0* to *255*, with intensity increasing with the value of the integer.

The following example creates a Point light source at an x coordinate of *50* and a y coordinate of *50* on the element, with the light appearing 25 pixels "above" the element. The light will be a pure white light, with a fairly high intensity:

```
addPoint(50,50,25,255,255,255,250);
```

Finally, you need to place the Lights Filter function into the *startFilter()* function, ready to be pasted into the HTML code in listing 15.1 as lines 9–11. The results of running the Lights Filter on the eagle image were shown previously in figure 15.8.

```
function startFilter() {
   filtEx.style.filter = "light(enabled=1)";
   filtEx.filters.item(0).addAmbient(200,200,255,150);
   filtEx.filters.item(0).addPoint(50,50,25,255,255,255,250);
}
```

Motion Blur Filter

The Motion Blur Filter (see fig. 15.9) attempts to approximate what you might see if you took a snapshot as you were moving past the element at high speed. The image you saw would not only be blurry, but it would be blurry in a noticeable direction.

FIG. 15.9

Applying the Motion Blur Filter to the image of the eagle.

The Motion Blur Filter function is specified by *blur()* and takes four arguments:

- **direction**—The direction parameter specifies the direction of the motion of the blurred element. The default value of *0* specifies pointing straight up. The possible values are then specified in 45 degree increments clockwise around (*45,90,135,180,225,270,315*) with *90* being right, *180* being down, and *270* being left.

- **strength**—The strength parameter specifies how many pixels the image will blur. The larger this parameter, the more blurry the image.

- **add**—The add parameter can be set to either *0* or *1*. If it is set to *0*, the image is added to the motion-blurred image, if it is set to *1,* only the motion-blurred image is shown. The image will be more recognizable if you specify that the image should be added.

- **enabled**—*0* if the filter is disabled, *1* if enabled.

The following example constructs a Blur Filter that blurs up and to the right, with a relatively strong blur of 15 pixels. To see the effects of the blur clearly, you need to set the *add* parameter to not add the original image:

```
blur(direction=45,strength=15,add=0,enabled=1)
```

Finally, you need to place the Motion Blur Filter function into the *startFilter()* function, ready to be pasted into the HTML code in listing 15.1 as lines 9–11. The results of running the Motion Blur Filter on the eagle image were shown previously in figure 15.9.

```
function startFilter() {
    filtEx.style.filter = "blur(direction=45,strength=15,add=0,enabled=1)";
}
```

Opacity Filter

The Opacity Filter (see fig. 15.10) enables you to set the degree of transparency for your element. The more transparent your image is, the more ethereal it becomes, the harder it is to see, and the less opaque it is. As it becomes fainter to the naked eye, you can place things beneath the element and see them through it.

FIG. 15.10

Applying the Opacity Filter to the image of the eagle.

The Opacity Filter is specified by *alpha()*, which takes two arguments:

- **opacity**—The degree of transparency. *0* is completely transparent, whereas *100* is completely opaque.
- **enabled**—*0* if the filter is disabled, *1* if enabled.

The following code constructs an Opacity Filter that shows the element about halfway transparent:

```
alpha(opacity=50,enabled=1)
```

Finally, you need to place the Opacity Filter function into the *startFilter()* function, ready to be pasted into the HTML code in listing 15.1 as lines 9–11. The results of running the Opacity Filter on the eagle image were shown previously in figure 15.10.

```
function startFilter() {
    filtEx.style.filter = "alpha(opacity=50,enabled=1)";
}
```

Shadow Filter

The Shadow Filter (see fig. 15.11) renders a solid silhouette of the element along one edge of the element. The Shadow Filter is quite similar to the Drop Shadow Filter, except instead of rendering the shadow with an offset, it renders right from the edge and only in one direction.

FIG. 15.11

Applying the Shadow Filter to the image of the eagle.

The Shadow Filter is specified by *shadow()*, which takes three arguments:

- **color**—The color of the silhouette, given in HTML RGB format.
- **direction**—The direction parameter specifies the direction of the shadow that will be rendered. The default value of *0* specifies pointing straight up. The possible values are then specified in 45 degree increments clockwise around (*45,90,135,180,225,270,315*) with *90* being right, *180* being down, and *270* being left.
- **enabled**—*0* if the filter is disabled, *1* if enabled.

The following example constructs a Shadow Filter that renders a magenta shadow to the lower-right side of the element. Because the direction is given in counterclockwise degrees, you need to specify *135* as the direction:

```
shadow(color=#FF0088,direction=135,enabled=1)
```

Finally, you need to place the Shadow Filter function into the *startFilter()* function, ready to be pasted into the HTML code in listing 15.1 as lines 9–11. The results of running the Shadow Filter on the eagle image were shown previously in figure 15.11.

```
function startFilter() {
   filtEx.style.filter = "shadow(color=#FF0088,direction=135,
                          enabled=1)";
}
```

Wave Filter

The Wave Filter (see fig. 15.12) is one of the more interesting filters because it enables you to warp the image as if a wave had passed through it. The best way to visualize the effects of this filter is to imagine that you had placed a picture of the element you are filtering onto a flag, then placed that flag in a strong breeze. The element appears as if waves were traveling through it.

FIG. 15.12

Applying the Wave Filter to the image of the eagle.

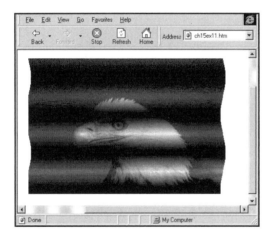

The Wave Filter is specified by *wave()*, which takes six arguments:

- **freq**—The freq is the number of waves you want to appear in the element when the filter is executed.

- **strength**—The strength is the intensity of the waves that will be applied to the image. The limits of the strength are dependent on the size of the element, but the range *0* to *10* tends to create interesting effects.

- **phase**—The wave that travels throughout the element is a sine wave. The phase enables you to set an offset for this sine wave. The values available are *0* to *100*, with *25* being an offset of 90 degrees.

- **lightstrength**—Enables you to specify the strength of the light on the waves as a percentage from 0 to 100.

■ **add**—The add parameter can be set to either *0* or *1*. If it is set to *0*, the image is added to the wave filtered image, if not only the wave filtered image is shown. If you specify that the image should be added, the image will be more recognizable.

■ **enabled**—*0* if the filter is disabled, *1* if enabled.

The following example creates a Wave Filter that contains two waves that are fairly strong. You will keep the wave in its normal phase and not apply any light to the wave (keeping the normal light intensity on the element). Finally, to accentuate the wave effect, you will not use the add parameter to add a copy of the original image to the filtered one:

```
wave(freq=2,strength=6,phase=0,lightstrength=0,add=0,enabled=1)
```

Finally, you need to place the Wave Filter function into the *startFilter()* function, ready to be pasted into the HTML code in listing 15.1 as lines 9–11. The results of running the Wave Filter on the eagle image were shown previously in figure 15.12.

```
function startFilter() {
    filtEx.style.filter = "wave(freq=2,strength=6,phase=0,lightstrength=0,add=0,
➥enabled=1)";
}
```

Glow Filter

The Glow Filter (see fig. 15.13) renders a radiant silhouette around the outside of the element along the right and bottom edges of the element. This radiant silhouette makes the element appear as if it is glowing.

FIG. 15.13

Applying the Glow Filter to the image of the eagle.

The Glow Filter is specified by *glow()*, which takes three arguments:

- **color**—The color of the silhouette, given in HTML RGB format.
- **strength**—The strength parameter specifies the intensity of the glow that is applied. This parameter can range from 0 (minimum glow) to 100 (maximum glow).
- **enabled**—*0* if the filter is disabled, *1* if enabled.

The following example constructs a Glow Filter that renders a red glow to the element at a strength of 50 (half the maximum strength):

```
glow(color=#FF0000,strength=50,enabled=1)
```

Finally, you need to place the Glow Filter function into the *startFilter()* function, ready to be pasted into the HTML code in listing 15.1 as lines 9–11. The results of running the Glow Filter on the eagle image were shown previously in figure 15.13.

```
function startFilter() {
    filtEx.style.filter = "glow(color=#FF0000,strength=50,enabled=1)";
}
```

Chromakey Filter

The Chromakey Filter is much like the "blue screen" effect you might have seen in documentaries of the making of special effects in movies. The Chromakey effect is also used during the TV weather reports. The weatherpersons appear to be standing in front of a weathermap, but they are actually standing in front of a blue screen or wall that a weather map is placed onto by the computer.

The way you achieve this effect in the Dynamic HTML color filter is by selecting a color that will be transparent in the filter. That color will be rendered transparently throughout the entire element and anything below pixels of that color will show through.

The Chromakey Filter is specified by the *chroma()*, which takes two arguments:

- **color**—The color that will be made transparent in the element. Specified in the standard HTML RGB format.
- **enabled**—*0* if the filter is disabled, *1* if enabled.

The following example shows a Chromakey Filter function that sets the Chromakey color to solid red:

```
chroma(color=#FF0000,enabled=1)
```

Finally, you need to place the Chromakey Filter function into the *startFilter()* function, ready to be pasted into the HTML code in listing 15.1 as lines 9–11.

```
function startFilter() {
    filtEx.style.filter = "chroma(color=#FF0000,enabled=1)";
}
```

The ActiveX Multimedia Objects

In addition to the Transitions and Filters available in HTML, several other multimedia controls are available to the Dynamic HTML programmer. These multimedia controls are grouped together into the Microsoft DirectAnimation API Controls, which is bundled with Internet Explorer 4.0.

Unlike the Transition and Filter controls, these DirectAnimation Controls are not integrated seamlessly into HTML as CSS properties. Instead, they are specified and controlled as generic ActiveX objects.

The use of ActiveX objects is a little tricky, so take a while to familiarize yourself with how ActiveX objects are used in Internet Explorer 4.0.

The tag to specify a control in Internet Explorer 4.0 is the <OBJECT> tag, and it normally takes three properties:

- **ID**—The unique identification that you want to give to the controls so it can be referenced from other HTML elements. This ID works in the same manner as the ID property in other elements.

- **CLASSID**—The CLASS ID property is the way in which you select the control being used. This is really the Achilles heel of using ActiveX Controls, because these identifiers can be quite complicated and hard to remember. An example of a Class ID is "CLDID:37992B41-F5E3-11CF-97DF-00A0C90FEE5".

- **PARAM**—The PARAM property is how properties are passed to the ActiveX Control. The name of the property is passed as the "NAME" attribute of the <PARAM> tag and the value that you want to use is passed as the "VALUE" property. So, if you wanted to pass the value *3* to the Tick property, you would use the following PARAM—<PARAM NAME=Tick VALUE=3>.

Although using ActiveX objects can be a bit confusing and complicated at times, they can be quite powerful. An added advantage is that the DirectAnimation API is built into Internet Explorer 4.0 so you can depend on its controls being available.

The DirectAnimation ActiveX Controls that ship with Internet Explorer 4.0 include the following:

- **Path Control**—Animates an element over a path.

- **Structured Graphics Control**—Provides an environment that enables the construction of relatively sophisticated line-art objects.

- **Sequencer Control**—Enables a list of actions to be performed on your HTML document over a period of time.

- **Sprite Control**—Animates an image according to the instructions you specify based upon the frames contained within the image.

Discussing the DirectAnimation Controls in detail is beyond the scope of this book, but if you plan on doing high-end multimedia development they may be worth investigating. Detailed

information on the DirectAnimation Controls is available on the Microsoft Web Site at:
http://www.microsoft.com/msdn/sdk/inetsdk/help/dxmedia/jaxa/default.htm.

From Here...

This chapter ends the discussion on the marriage of multimedia effects and Dynamic HTML. Although these advanced topics can be hard to grasp at first, they're definitely worth learning in detail because they can add a great deal to your Dynamic HTML programs.

The next part of the book will discuss applying the technologies you've learned over the course of this book in real-world situations. The process from design to implementation will be covered in detail.

- Chapter 16, "Pin the Tail on the Donkey"—Covers the construction of a simple game in a step-by-step manner. This game will use basic event handling, element positioning, and collision detection.

- Chapter 17, "Basketball Explained"—Takes a look at an interactive tutorial that explains some of basketball's finer points.

- Chapter 18, "Building an Online Catalog"—Takes a look at how Dynamic HTML can be used to create an online catalog with a variety of functionality.

- Chapter 19, "Building the Smashout Video Game"—Creates a fully functional version of a "breakout" style game, complete with collision detection, showcasing the power of Dynamic HTML.

Real World Dynamic HTML

CHAPTER 16

Pin the Tail on the Donkey

Layout

Apply positioning and layering to create a game board for play.

User Interfaces

Apply positioning and moving elements to create a game interface.

Counters

Learn how to create a counting mechanism to keep track of game events.

Detecting Element Location

Use positioning and scripting to detect the element positioning in an online game created with Dynamic HTML.

This section of the book presents you with a number of real world implementations of Dynamic HTML. These examples are designed to show you how the Dynamic HTML topics that you've learned about can be used to create new and exciting interfaces and applications for your web-based content.

This chapter begins by showing you how to design a lighthearted game of "Pin the Tail on the Donkey." The game shows how you can use Dynamic HTML to create an interface and to script functionality.

Without further delay, immerse yourself in building some actual applications that take advantage of Dynamic HTML's capabilities. ▓

Understanding the Game

In this chapter, you will develop a Dynamic HTML version of the classic children's game, "Pin the Tail on the Donkey," where a poor, hapless donkey has misplaced his tail. The goal of the game is to pin the tail back into the proper place on the donkey's rear. Of course, just grabbing a tail and sticking it on would be far too easy. So in the traditional game, the player is impaired through the use of a blindfold that prevents him from seeing where the donkey is while he is trying to pin on the tail. The usual process consists of a try or two, and then the player is out of the game.

The electronic version of the game also has a donkey who has lost his tail. The player is given three tails (three chances) to pin the tail back on the donkey, restoring the donkey's faith in humanity. Should the player fail, she is electronically admonished for her failure in animal care. Of course, to ask the player to blindfold herself before taking her turn might be a bit much, so instead, you will need to develop some electronic blindfolding mechanism. Besides, making the blindfolding automatic will remove any temptation to cheat. But you would never cheat, would you?

Now take a look at how you are going to lay out the game board, and then you will learn how to script the actual game play.

Laying Out the Game

The structure of the game is straightforward. You are basically going to construct a gameboard that will contain all the elements for the little game, and then position each element individually. The elements that you will need for your game include the following:

- A title
- The donkey
- Some rules
- A Tries counter
- A Reset button
- The tails

Now you need to lay out these elements. The following sections demonstrate how to do this.

Structuring the Document

The first step in creating the game is to establish a gameboard or a playing area. To accomplish this, you need to use the structure of the HTML document, and then create a single <DIV> tag that will serve as the gameboard, and also act as a positioning container for the other elements on the page.

Listing 16.1 shows the game's basic document structure, and the <DIV> tag that is used to define the game area.

Listing 16.1 Structuring the Gameboard and Document

```
01. <HTML>
02. <HEAD>
03. <TITLE>Pin the Tail on the Donkey</TITLE>
04. </HEAD>
05. <BODY>
06.
07. <EMBED STYLE="display: none" autostart="TRUE" loop="FALSE" SRC="donkey.wav">
08.
09. <DIV id="GameBoard" STYLE="position: absolute; top: 10; left: 10; width:
➥550; height: 400; border: solid; border-color: red; background: black; z-
➥index: -1;">
10. </DIV>
11.
12. </BODY>
13. </HTML>
```

Part

VI

Ch

16

Within this listing, you might also notice another special tag that creates the "haw-haw" donkey sound that is played when the game is first loaded in line 7. The <EMBED> tag invokes the Microsoft ActiveMovie player, but hides the actual sound element from the player's screen. With the board in place, you are ready to start adding game elements.

Positioning Static Elements

You may recall the discussions of layout in Chapter 9, "Layout and Positioning." Here you are going to put the principles discussed in that chapter into a practical, well, at least fun application. The first step in laying out the game is to position the elements that will be stationary and not subject to any interactivity. In this case, these elements are as follows:

- The donkey
- The rules
- The game title

Laying out these elements is simply a matter of defining an object for each element, using the <SPAN> tag, and then positioning the element by using absolute positioning. The results of this exercise are shown in listing 16.2.

Listing 16.2 Positioning Static Elements such as the Title, Donkey, and Rules

```
01. <SPAN id="GameTitle" STYLE="position: absolute; top: 25; left: 25;
➥color: red; font-family: sans-serif">
02. <H1>Pin the Tail on the Donkey!</H1>
03. </SPAN>
04.
05. <SPAN id="Donkey" STYLE="position: absolute; top: 75; left: 25">
06. <IMG SRC="poordonkey.jpg">
07. </SPAN>
08.
```

continues

Listing 16.2 Continued

```
09. <SPAN id="Rules" STYLE="position: absolute; top: 100; left: 300;
➥width: 200; color: red; font-family: sans-serif; visibility: visible">
10. Click on a tail to begin the game. When you click on a tail,
11.the screen will go black. Do your best to move the tail over
12.the Donkey's rear and restore his tail to its natural state!
13. <P>
14. Click on any tail to begin the game!
15. </SPAN>
```

In this listing, you can see that each of the elements is firmly rooted on the page, and if you contain these elements within the gameboard defined in line 1, you will never need to tinker with them again. Figure 16.1 shows these elements in their final resting place, and the game is beginning to take the form of a playable version of the classic children's game.

FIG. 16.1

The gameboard with static elements in place.

Positioning Dynamic Elements

Now that you have locked the static elements into position, it is time to add two of the elements that will receive user input. Later, these elements will be manipulated by the scripts that will give the game functionality. These two elements are as follows:

- The Tries counter
- The Reset button

Each of these elements serves an important function in the game. The Tries counter remains visible even when the player is blindfolded, so that the player is always aware of how many chances he has left to help out the poor donkey.

The Reset button also remains visible during the course of the game play, because after all, a frustrated user should always be allowed a chance to start over. Listing 16.3 shows how to code these two elements on the page.

Listing 16.3 Positioning Dynamic Content: the Counter, Blindfold, and Reset Button

```
01. <SPAN id="Counter" STYLE="position: absolute; top: 325; left: 325;
➥color: red; font-family: sans-serif; z-index: 1">
02. <H2>Tries = 3</H2>
03. </SPAN>
04.
05. <IMG id="Blindfold" STYLE="position: absolute; top: 25; left: 15;
➥display: none" SRC="blindfold.gif">
06.
07. <INPUT TYPE=BUTTON VALUE="Reset Game" STYLE="position: absolute;
➥top: 360; left: 330; z-index: 1" onclick="reset();">
```

As you can see, these elements are positioned in the same manner as the other elements—using CSS Positioning. You also have added a *z-index* property value for the elements to ensure that they stay on top no matter what happens during the game play. By doing this, you enable the player to always know his status, and he can always leave the game. You might also notice that you have added an element called "Blindfold" in line 5, which has been set to display "none." This element acts as the method for blindfolding the player during play. Basically, it is a large solid black area that will be placed over the gameboard, obscuring the donkey from the player's view. The tail elements will remain visible above the blindfold, as will the Reset button and the Tries counter. The user will then be able to drag and drop the tails to where he believes is the proper place. By using z-indexes and positioning, it is possible to make sure that the elements that need to remain visible do so to protect the functionality of the game. Figure 16.2 shows what the game looks like with the new dynamic elements added.

FIG. 16.2

The gameboard with dynamic elements added.

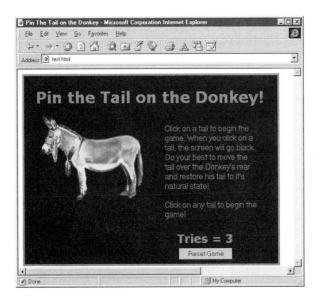

Positioning the Tails

Now you only have one set of dynamic elements left—the tails—to position on the gameboard before you are ready to start scripting the functionality of the game.

You will position the donkey tails exactly as you did the other elements, with CSS Positioning and z-indexing to make sure that they remain visible during game play. The code in listing 16.4 shows how you will position the tails.

Listing 16.4   Positioning the Tails

```
01. <IMG id="tail1" STYLE="position: relative; top: 275; left: 50;
➥visibility: visible; z-index: 1" onmousemove="MoveTail();" onclick="count();
➥" SRC="thetail.gif">
02.
03. <IMG id="tail2" STYLE="position: relative; top: 275; left: 100;
➥visibility: visible; z-index: 1" onmousemove="MoveTail();" onclick="count();
➥" SRC="thetail.gif">
04.
05. <IMG id="tail3" STYLE="position: relative; top: 275; left: 150;
➥visibility: visible; z-index: 1" onmousemove="MoveTail();"
➥onclick="count();" SRC="thetail.gif">
```

Up to this point, however, only the Reset button has dealt with event handling based on user interaction. Because the tails need to be able to move when clicked and dropped into position, they will need to have some events bound to them. In this case, two events are actually related to the tails, as shown in listing 16.4 on lines 1, 3, and 5:

```
onmousemove="MoveTail();" onclick="count();"
```

This code simply binds the *MoveTail()* function to the tail during the *onmousemove* event. So whenever the button is pressed on the tail, and the mouse is moving, the *MoveTail()* function will perform the work. This is also a good place to put in an event to decrement the Tries counter because each time you click a tail and move it, you are using a turn. By linking the *count()* function, which tracks the number of tries, to the mouse click, you can be sure that when a player clicks a tail to move it, he is using one of his turns. That's how to lay out the game! The final layout, complete with tails, is shown in figure 16.3.

FIG. 16.3

The complete Pin the Tail on the Donkey layout is shown.

Scripting Functionality

Now that you have completely laid out the gameboard, and all the elements that you are going to need for game play are in place, you are ready to start writing the script and functions that are needed to play the game. Table 16.1 lists the different elements of functionality you need in the game and the functions needed to implement them.

Table 16.1 Required Elements for Pin the Tail on the Donkey

Functionality Needed	Function to Implement
The capability to drag and drop the donkey tails.	MoveTail()
A mechanism for detecting when the tail is pinned correctly.	detect()
A mechanism for keeping track of the number of turns a player takes.	count()
A means of electronically blindfolding the player.	blindfold()
A way to remove the blindfold.	seeagain()
A message of sorrow for game losers.	sorry()
A message of congratulations for game winners.	winner()
A way to reset the game for the next player.	reset()

MoveTail( )

The first function that you need to create is the *MoveTail()* function. This function creates the means by which the donkey tails can be dragged and dropped on the gameboard.

To do this, you need to make use of the animation code that you wrote to move images in Chapter 13 (listing 13.4), "Introducing Multimedia." Listing 16.5 shows the code that accomplishes the motion.

Listing 16.5   Creating the Function to Drag and Drop the Tails

```
01. function MoveTail() {
02.          if (window.event.button == 1) {
03.          blindfold();
04.          var srcElement, newtop, newleft;
05.          srcElement = window.event.srcElement;
06.          newleft=window.event.x - (srcElement.width/2);
07.          newtop=window.event.y - (srcElement.height/2);
08.          srcElement.style.posTop = newtop;
09.          srcElement.style.posLeft = newleft;
10.          window.event.returnValue = false;
11.          window.event.cancelBubble = true;
12.          }
13. }
```

Basically, the *MoveTail()* function uses an *if* statement to make sure that the mouse button is pressed while you are moving the item. Then, the *srcElement* object property retrieves the X and the Y position coordinates for the tail. Finally, you calculate new values for the top and left positions based on the current location of the mouse, and then reassign those values to the tail, so that the tail moves with the mouse.

The end result is a tail that can be clicked, and while the mouse button is depressed, dragged anywhere on the gameboard.

detect( )

The next function that you need to construct is the *detect()* function. When the player places a tail on the gameboard at a location he believes is where the tail properly belongs, there needs to be some way for the game to check to see whether the player is correct. The *detect()* function accomplishes this as shown in listing 16.6.

Listing 16.6   The *detect()* Function that Determines Whether the Tail is on the Donkey

```
01. function detect() {
02.          var tail1x = tail1.style.posTop;
03.          var tail1y = tail1.style.posLeft;
04.          var tail2x = tail2.style.posTop;
05.          var tail2y = tail2.style.posLeft;
06.          var tail3x = tail3.style.posTop;
```

```
07.            var tail3y = tail3.style.posLeft;
08.
09.            if ((tail1x > 135) && (tail1x < 155) && (tail1y > 235) &&
➥(tail1y < 260))
10.                    winner();
11.            if ((tail2x > 135) && (tail2x < 155) && (tail2y > 210) &&
➥(tail2y < 235))
12.                    winner();
13.            if ((tail3x > 135) && (tail3x < 155) && (tail3y > 190) &&
➥(tail3y < 215))
14.                    winner();
15.            if (tries == 0)
16.                    sorry();
17. }
```

The *detect()* function first defines the variables that you are going to use to keep track of the location of each tail element—one, two, and three. Because each of the tail elements can be placed independently, they need to be monitored independently.

After you define the variables, and obtain their values from each of the tail objects, the next step is to see whether they are in the proper range to be on the donkey where they belong. You accomplish this with a series of *if* statements that look to see whether the X and Y coordinates of the tail fall between an acceptable range of coordinates on the donkey's behind. If, in fact, the tail is placed correctly, then the *detect()* function declares the player a winner, and the gameplay halts. If the value is not a winning value, however, then the function does nothing, and play continues until the player is out of turns.

count()

Because you are limiting players to only three chances to correctly pin the tail on the donkey, you need some mechanism for creating a counter to keep track of each player's turn. The code in listing 16.7 shows the *count()* function that is used for this purpose.

Listing 16.7   The count() Function Keeps Track of the Number of Tries

```
01. function count() {
02.         tries—;
03.         if (tries == 2) {
04.                 Counter.innerHTML = "<H2>Tries = 2</H2>";
05.                 detect();
06.         }
07.         if (tries == 1) {
08.                 Counter.innerHTML = "<H2>Tries = 1</H2>";
09.                 detect();
10.         }
11.         if (tries == 0) {
12.                 seeagain();
13.                 Counter.innerHTML = "<H2>Tries = 0</H2>";
14.                 detect();
15.         }
16. }
```

The *count()* function itself is quite simple. It uses the "tries" variable (which is initially set to 3) to keep track of the player's turns. Each time the user clicks a tail, the *count()* function is called and it subtracts a turn from the "tries" variable. The function then checks to see what turn it is, and alters the text for the Tries counter accordingly, by using the *innerHTML* object to manipulate the HTML on the page.

The result is a counter that not only keeps track of the turns a user has taken, but also updates the user of remaining attempts as the game progresses.

blindfold( )

As mentioned previously, this version of Pin the Tail on the Donkey would not be a very effective "cyber" game if you asked the player to put on a blindfold before each turn. So instead, you need to create an electronic blindfold that is placed "on" the user when he first selects a tail to initiate game play. Listing 16.8 shows the simple function that changes the value of the *display* property on the *blindfold* object, causing it to be displayed.

Listing 16.8 The blindfoldFunction

```
01. function blindfold() {
02.          Blindfold.style.display = "";
03. }
```

The result of calling this function is a "virtual" blindfold that allows the player to try to pin the tail on the donkey without being able to see the actual donkey image, as shown in figure 16.4.

FIG. 16.4

The game in action, with the blindfold applied.

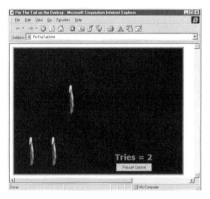

seeagain( )

Of course, even though you want the user blindfolded for the game play, you don't want them in the dark forever. Listing 16.9 shows the *seeagain()* function that removes the electronic blindfold, for example, if the player wins or loses, or if the game is reset.

Listing 16.9 The seeagain Function "Takes Off" the Blindfold

```
01. function seeagain() {
02.        Blindfold.style.display = "none";
03. }
```

sorry()

Of course, not everyone can be a winner. There will be times when even the most experienced veterinarian won't be able to properly pin the tail on the donkey. For those sad occasions, it is necessary to have a message of consolation, to lift the spirits of the broken player, and to let him know that he lost. Listing 16.10 shows the function that calls an *alert()* function to notify the player that he needs to start over.

Listing 16.10 The Function to Display a Message for Those Not Fortunate Enough to Win

```
01. function sorry() {
02.        alert("Sorry! Better Luck Next Time!");
03. }
```

The result of failing to pin on the tail is a message wishing you luck for next time, as shown in figure 16.5

FIG. 16.5
The sorry() function notifies players of disappointing results.

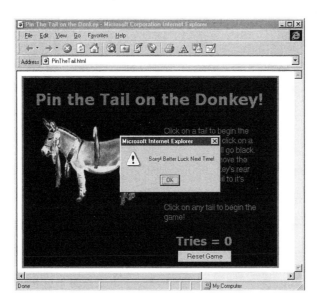

winner()

Because the game is not rocket science, most players will find some level of mastery with the game quite quickly. In these cases, you need to supply a function that will congratulate the player on his victory, as shown in listing 16.11.

Listing 16.11   The winner() Function, to Congratulate Victory

```
01. function winner() {
02.         seeagain();
03.         Donkey.innerHTML = "<IMG SRC=donkey.jpg>";
04.         tail1.style.visibility = "hidden";
05.         tail2.style.visibility = "hidden";
06.         tail3.style.visibility = "hidden";
07.         alert("You Win!!");
08. }
```

You will notice though that the *winner()* function does a little more than prompt the user with a congratulatory alert message. In addition to the congrats, the function hides the tails, because one has been correctly attached. The image of the poor donkey without his tail is also replaced with the image of the donkey that has his tail properly attached. Then, and only then is the alert message displayed for a job well done, as shown in figure 16.6.

FIG. 16.6

The winner() function congratulates winners.

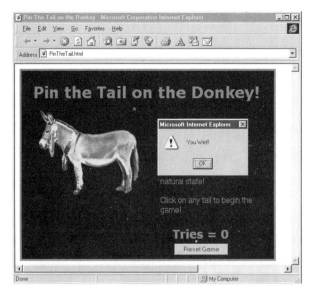

reset()

Now that you have the bulk of the functions written to provide functionality to the game, you still need a function to reset the game to its original state. This Reset button could be used by a player who has become frustrated with the game, or by a player who has finished his game and wants to reset the game for another player.

Listing 16.12 shows the *reset()* function, which changes all the values for the original elements back to their default values.

Listing 16.12   The reset() Function, to Play Again

```
01. function reset() {
02.
03.          tries = 3;
04.          seeagain();
05.          tail1.style.posTop = 275;
06.          tail1.style.posLeft = 50;
07.          tail1.style.visibility = "visible";
08.          tail2.style.posTop = 275;
09.          tail2.style.posLeft = 100;
10.          tail2.style.visibility = "visible";
11.          tail3.style.posTop = 275;
12.          tail3.style.posLeft = 150;
13.          tail3.style.visibility = "visible";
14.          Counter.innerHTML = "<H2>Tries = 3</H2>";
15.          Donkey.innerHTML = "<IMG SRC=poordonkey.jpg>";
16. }
```

First, the function resets the number of tries the player has to 3 (line 3), and then removes any blindfold that might be on (line 4). Next, the tails are each returned to their original positions and original visibility states (lines 5–13), so the game is ready for a new player to click and begin play. Finally, the on-screen Tries counter is reset so the player knows his current turn (line 14), and then the tail is ripped off the poor donkey (line 15). Voilà! The game is ready to play again.

The Final Page!

By combining all the functions and element layout into one file, you are ready to create the fully functional version of the Pin the Tail on the Donkey game. Listing 16.13 shows the final code for the game in its entirety.

Listing 16.13   The Complete Code for Pin the Tail on the Donkey

```
001. <HTML>
002. <HEAD>
003. <TITLE>Pin the Tail on the Donkey</TITLE>
004.
005. <SCRIPT LANGUAGE="JavaScript">
006. var tries = 3;
007.
008. function MoveTail() {
009.          if (window.event.button == 1) {
```

continues

Listing 16.13   Continued

```
010.          blindfold();
011.          var srcElement, newtop, newleft;
012.          srcElement = window.event.srcElement;
013.          newleft=window.event.x - (srcElement.width/2);
014.          newtop=window.event.y - (srcElement.height/2);
015.          srcElement.style.posTop = newtop;
016.          srcElement.style.posLeft = newleft;
017.          window.event.returnValue = false;
018.          window.event.cancelBubble = true;
019.          }
020. }
021.
022. function detect() {
023.          var tail1x = tail1.style.posTop;
024.          var tail1y = tail1.style.posLeft;
025.          var tail2x = tail2.style.posTop;
026.          var tail2y = tail2.style.posLeft;
027.          var tail3x = tail3.style.posTop;
028.          var tail3y = tail3.style.posLeft;
029.
030.          if ((tail1x > 135) && (tail1x < 155)
031. && (tail1y > 235) && (tail1y < 260))
032.                  winner();
033.          if ((tail2x > 135) && (tail2x < 155)
034. && (tail2y > 210) && (tail2y < 235))
035.                  winner();
036.          if ((tail3x > 135) && (tail3x < 155)
037. && (tail3y > 190) && (tail3y < 215))
038.                  winner();
039.          if (tries == 0)
040.                  sorry();
041. }
042.
043. function count() {
044.          tries—;
045.          if (tries == 2) {
046.                  Counter.innerHTML = "<H2>Tries = 2</H2>";
047.                  detect();
048.          }
049.          if (tries == 1) {
050.                  Counter.innerHTML = "<H2>Tries = 1</H2>";
051.                  detect();
052.          }
053.          if (tries == 0) {
054.                  seeagain();
055.                  Counter.innerHTML = "<H2>Tries = 0</H2>";
056.                  detect();
057.          }
058. }
059.
060. function blindfold() {
061.          Blindfold.style.display = "";
062. }
063.
```

```
064. function seeagain() {
065.          Blindfold.style.display = "none";
066.
067. }
068.
069. function sorry() {
070.          alert("Sorry! Better Luck Next Time!");
071. }
072.
073. function winner() {
074.          seeagain();
075.          Donkey.innerHTML = "<IMG SRC=donkey.jpg>";
076.          tail1.style.visibility = "hidden";
077.          tail2.style.visibility = "hidden";
078.          tail3.style.visibility = "hidden";
079.          alert("You Win!!");
080. }
081.
082. function reset() {
083.
084.          tries = 3;
085.          seeagain();
086.          tail1.style.posTop = 275;
087.          tail1.style.posLeft = 50;
088.          tail1.style.visibility = "visible";
089.          tail2.style.posTop = 275;
090.          tail2.style.posLeft = 100;
091.          tail2.style.visibility = "visible";
092.          tail3.style.posTop = 275;
093.          tail3.style.posLeft = 150;
094.          tail3.style.visibility = "visible";
095.          Counter.innerHTML = "<H2>Tries = 3</H2>";
096.          Donkey.innerHTML = "<IMG SRC=poordonkey.jpg>";
097. }
098.
099. </SCRIPT>
100. </HEAD>
101. <BODY>
102.
103. <EMBED STYLE="display: none" autostart="TRUE" loop="FALSE"
➥SRC="donkey.wav">
104.
105. <DIV id="GameBoard" STYLE="position: absolute; top: 10; left:10;
➥width: 550; height: 400; border: solid; border-color: red;
➥background: black; z-index: -1;">
106.
107. <SPAN id="GameTitle" STYLE="position: absolute; top: 25; left: 25;
➥color: red; font-family: sans-serif">
108. <H1>Pin the Tail on the Donkey!</H1>
109. </SPAN>
110.
111. <SPAN id="Donkey" STYLE="position: absolute; top: 75; left: 25">
112. <IMG SRC="poordonkey.jpg">
113. </SPAN>
114.
```

continues

Listing 16.13   Continued

```
115. <SPAN id="Rules" STYLE="position: absolute; top: 100; left: 300;
➥width: 200; color: red; font-family: sans-serif; visibility: visible">
116. Click on a tail to begin the game. When you click on a tail,
117. the screen will go black. Do your best to move the tail over
118. the Donkey's rear and restore his tail to its natural state!
119. <P>
120. Click on any tail to begin the game!
121. </SPAN>
122.
123. <SPAN id="Counter" STYLE="position: absolute; top: 325; left: 325;
➥color: red; font-family: sans-serif; z-index: 1">
124. <H2>Tries = 3</H2>
125. </SPAN>
126.
127. <IMG id="Blindfold" STYLE="position: absolute; top: 25; left: 15;
➥display: none" SRC="blindfold.gif">
128.
129. <INPUT TYPE=BUTTON VALUE="Reset Game" STYLE="position: absolute; top: 360;
➥left: 330; z-index: 1" onclick="reset();">
130.
131. </DIV>
132.
133. <IMG id="tail1" STYLE="position: relative; top: 275; left: 50;
➥visibility: visible; z-index: 1" onmousemove="MoveTail();
➥" onclick="count();" SRC="thetail.gif">
134.
135. <IMG id="tail2" STYLE="position: relative; top: 275; left: 100;
➥visibility: visible; z-index: 1" onmousemove="MoveTail();
➥" onclick="count();" SRC="thetail.gif">
136.
137. <IMG id="tail3" STYLE="position: relative; top: 275; left: 150;
➥visibility: visible; z-index: 1" onmousemove="MoveTail();
➥" onclick="count();" SRC="thetail.gif">
138.
139. </BODY>
140. </HTML>
```

With all the elements in place, the game is self-contained as an HTML file, yet provides a level of user interactivity that would not be possible with traditional HTML. Figure 16.7 shows the game after being played.

FIG. 16.7

The final game after a rousing round of Pin the Tail on the Donkey.

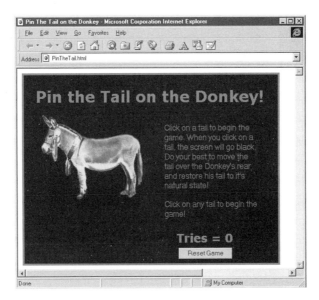

From Here...

Although it might not seem like a powerful application, Pin the Tail on the Donkey showcases some interface techniques that could be used to build much more advanced Dynamic HTML applications based on the same underlying principles. Instead of pinning the tail on our poor pal, for example, you could have been asked to simulate the repair of a nuclear reactor, with the "game" keeping track of the placement and order of the repairs you made. You could then check the work for safety without ever endangering the lives of anyone. Many users are also familiar with "virtual" dissections online for biology students. This type of application could easily be revised to incorporate Dynamic HTML to make the experience more interactive, more fun, and all around a better learning experience for students.

Now that you have seen how Dynamic HTML can function in a real life application, it's time to move on to look at some other examples.

- Chapter 17, "Basketball Explained," takes a look at an interactive tutorial that explains some of basketball's finer points.
- Chapter 18, "Building an Online Catalog," takes a look at how Dynamic HTML can be used to create an online catalog with a variety of functionality.
- Chapter 19, "Building the Smashout Video Game," caps it all off by creating a fully functional version of a "breakout" style game, complete with collision detection, showcasing the power of Dynamic HTML.

CHAPTER 17

Basketball Explained

Positioning Elements

Apply CSS Positioning and Dynamic HTML to create an interactive demonstration.

Controlling Visibility

Use layers and visibility to create graphic explanations.

Building a User Interface

Construct an intuitive user interface for a tutorial/demonstration.

There are many different applications for Dynamic HTML pages. Throughout the text you have been provided some smaller applications and ideas of how Dynamic HTML can be used. Now, take a look at how the technology might be used to create a tutorial and demonstration application that could be used as a sales tool or an educational tool.

One of the most frequent business activities is providing demonstrations. In fact, demonstrations are something we are familiar with from the earliest schooling. Learning is often achieved through some sort of presentation, and the more interesting, fun, and interactive a presentation is, the more the viewer is likely to take away from it.

This chapter puts Dynamic HTML to work in building a simple interactive explanation of basketball.

CAUTION

This demo is designed to showcase Dynamic HTML, and users who employ it to learn more about basketball do so at their own peril. Especially in any Big 10 state.

In this demo, you are going to create a simplified diagram of a basketball court with the correct markings, and then some images of various calls that a referee would make during a typical game. The user will then be able to pick and choose various elements, such as a three-point line, or a traveling call, to get an explanation of what the court marking or call means. Of course, the same type of instruction could be given in a static HTML format. The information would be the same, but the interaction with the user would not be as engaging, or as efficient. So now, take a look at how you can create a basketball tutorial. ■

Creating the Images

Although you might not think immediately of creating the images for your presentation when considering Dynamic HTML, it is an important part of designing the final product. In fact, in this example, you are going to need several images, and they will need to work together in layers, so it is only by carefully laying out and constructing the images that you will be able to make sure that they work together.

Creating the basketball court, for example, requires the following images:

- The court
- Half-court line
- Three-point line
- Top of the key
- The lane
- The basket

Each of these images needs to be in the same shape, with the exact same dimensions, so when layered, the elements actually line up as they would on a basketball court. As you can see in figure 17.1, these elements were first created in Photoshop, keeping the dimensions of each GIF at 432×288 pixels, so each element lines up correctly.

Next, you need to create the icons used to represent the various calls the referee might make during the course of the game. Although these images are not going to overlap, their size is also still important from an interface perspective. As you display several referee icons for the viewer to choose from, you will want to do so in a manner that allows easy access, while still providing a consistent layout. To do this, you again need images that have the same dimensions. Figure 17.2 shows how each of the referee images has been edited for consistency, keeping each icon at 120×105 pixels.

FIG. 17.1

Laying out the three-point line for the tutorial.

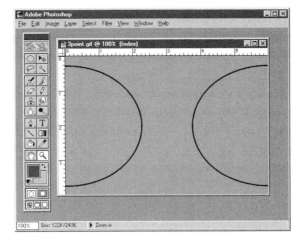

FIG. 17.2

Creating consistent icons for the referee interface.

Of course, before you can begin editing the images, you must have a rough idea of what the layout is going to look like. For this example, you want to start with the basketball court as the main element on the page, and build from there. This will help you to decide on relative size, and to determine how things will fit together.

Laying Out the Page

The first order of business in creating the tutorial is to layout the court elements. This is a pretty straightforward process, but there are a couple of things that you want to watch closely.

First, you need to create the layout of the court, and then add the layout for the icons next to that. The following sections show you how to accomplish this series of tasks.

Positioning the Initial Layout

The initial court layout is pretty straightforward. First, you need to employ absolute positioning to make sure that each of the court elements is in exactly the same position. If you leave it at this, however, you might not be able to see all the elements correctly.

To ensure that each of the elements functions correctly, you need to use z-indexing to place each element on its own layer, as shown in the following line of code:

```
<IMG id="Court" STYLE="position: absolute; top: 25px; left: 25; z-index: 0;
➥visibility: visible;" SRC="court.gif">
```

That's all there is to it. Listing 17.1 shows the code that creates the court layout, and figure 17.3 shows the court itself.

Listing 17.1 Laying Out the Basketball Court

```
01. <IMG id="Court" STYLE="position: absolute; top: 25px; left: 25; z-index: 0;
➥visibility: visible;" SRC="court.gif">
02. <IMG id="XPoint" STYLE="position: absolute; top: 25px; left: 25; z-index: 1;
➥visibility: visible;" SRC="3point.gif">
03. <IMG id="HalfCourt" STYLE="position: absolute; top: 25px; left: 25;
➥z-index: 2; visibility: visible;" SRC="halfcourt.gif">
04. <IMG id="Key" STYLE="position: absolute; top: 25px; left: 25; z-index: 3;
➥visibility: visible;" SRC="key.gif">
05. <IMG id="Lane" STYLE="position: absolute; top: 25px; left: 25; z-index: 4;
➥visibility: visible;" SRC="lane.gif">
06. <IMG id="Basket" STYLE="position: absolute; top: 25px; left: 25; z-index: 5;
➥visibility: visible;" SRC="basket.gif">
07. <IMG id="Screen" STYLE="position: absolute; top: 25px; left: 25; z-index: 0;
➥visibility: hidden;" SRC="court-screen.gif">
08.
09. <DIV id="Title" STYLE="position: absolute; top: 325; left: 50;
➥font-family: sans-serif; color: orange; visibility: visible;">
10. <H1>A Basketball Tutorial</H1>
11. </DIV>
```

In this code, lines 1–7 each specify the location of a different element, such as the basket or the lane. Lines 9–11 specify the location of the tutorial's title. These are straightforward uses of the <IMG> and <DIV> tags, but they will come into play later when you will hide and show these elements based on their *visibility* property values.

Creating the Scroll Box

With the court layout complete, you can move on to laying out the scroll box that contains the images of the referee and icons for the court elements. Later in the "Scripting the Functionality" section, you will add functionality that enables users to click an icon in this box to get an explanation of the call or court marking. For now, just format the icons.

FIG. 17.3
The finished basketball court layout.

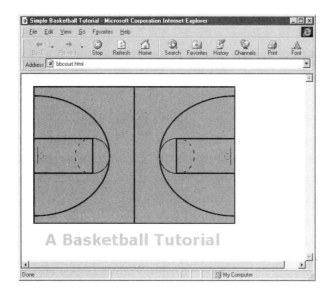

Because a number of icons are going to appear together, and you don't want to display them all on the screen at once, you need to create a scroll box to contain the icons. Users can then scroll through the icons, and click an icon to receive a detailed explanation.

Creating the scroll box exploits the <DIV> tag and OVERFLOW attribute. First, you will use the <DIV> tag to create an overall container element that will enclose all the icon images. If you recall from Chapter 9, "Layout and Positioning," with CSS Positioning, you can nest <DIV> tags, which enables you to treat each image as a separate element, all nested into a larger element called "Official" in this example, because it holds the referee icons:

```
<DIV id="Official" STYLE="position: absolute; top: 25; left: 475; height: 340;
➥width: 145; overflow: scroll">
</DIV>
```

Of course, all the icons will not fit in this 340×145 container; however, if you recall from Chapter 8, "Dynamic Styles," you can specify how container objects handle too much data using the *overflow* property. By setting the value of this property to "scroll" you can automatically create a scrolling home for the icons!

The only thing that remains is to format the icons themselves:

```
<IMG id="Ref1" STYLE="border: none; border-width: thin; border-color: orange;
➥" onclick="showObject(); highlight()"; ondblclick="reset()";
➥SRC="jumpball.gif">
```

You begin by naming each of the icons with a unique ID. This is important for keeping track of each of the images later. Next, you specify the STYLE elements for the icons, in this case some border information. Later, when users click the icon, you will want to highlight the icon with a border, so that you include the border information now and simply set the border to "none."

The result is that the border is not currently displayed, but the elements are in place to highlight the icon in the future.

You will also notice a couple of event handling items here. onclick="showObject(); highlight():" and ondblclick="reset()" are some functions that you will create in "Scripting the Functionality" section later to handle what happens when a user clicks an icon, and what happens when they double-click. When the user clicks an icon, you want to use the *showObject()* function to reveal the icon explanation, and the *highlight()* function to highlight the icon. When the user double-clicks, you want to reset the icon and court. Listing 17.2 shows what the layout of the icon scroll box looks like, and figure 17.4 shows the final layout of the icon scroll box.

Listing 17.2 Laying Out the Basketball Court

```
01. <DIV id="Official" STYLE="position: absolute; top: 25; left: 475;
➥height: 340; width: 145; overflow: scroll">
02. <IMG id="Ref1" STYLE="border: none; border-width: thin;
➥border-color: orange;" onclick="showObject(); highlight()";
➥ondblclick="reset()"; SRC="jumpball.gif">
03. <IMG id="Ref2" STYLE="border: none; border-width: thin;
➥border-color: orange;" onclick="showObject(); highlight()";
➥ondblclick="reset()"; SRC="3sec.gif">
04. <IMG id="Ref3" STYLE="border: none; border-width: thin;
➥border-color: orange;" onclick="showObject(); highlight()";
➥ondblclick="reset()"; SRC="travel.gif">
05. <IMG id="Ref4" STYLE="border: none; border-width: thin;
➥border-color: orange;" onclick="showObject(); highlight()";
➥ondblclick="reset()"; SRC="foul.gif">
06. <IMG id="Ref5" STYLE="border: none; border-width: thin;
➥border-color: orange;" onclick="showObject(); highlight()";
➥ondblclick="reset()"; SRC="one-in-one.gif">
07. <IMG id="Ref6" STYLE="border: none; border-width: thin;
➥border-color: orange;" onclick="showObject(); highlight()";
➥ondblclick="reset()"; SRC="timeout.gif">
08.
09. <IMG id="Court1" STYLE="border: none; border-width: thin;
➥border-color: orange;" onclick="showObject(); highlight()";
➥ondblclick="reset()"; SRC="basket-small.gif">
10. <IMG id="Court2" STYLE="border: none; border-width: thin;
➥border-color: orange;" onclick="showObject(); highlight()";
➥ondblclick="reset()"; SRC="halfcourt-small.gif">
11. <IMG id="Court3" STYLE="border: none; border-width: thin;
➥border-color: orange;" onclick="showObject(); highlight()";
➥ondblclick="reset()"; SRC="key-small.gif">
12. <IMG id="Court4" STYLE="border: none; border-width: thin;
➥border-color: orange;" onclick="showObject(); highlight()";
➥ondblclick="reset()"; SRC="lane-small.gif">
13. <IMG id="Court5" STYLE="border: none; border-width: thin;
➥border-color: orange;" onclick="showObject(); highlight()";
➥ondblclick="reset()"; SRC="3point-small.gif">
14. </DIV>
```

FIG. 17.4

The finished icon selection box.

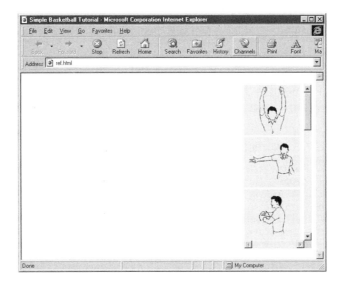

Combining the code from listings 17.1 and 17.2 results in the completion of the layout for this tutorial. The end result is the finished interface, ready to be scripted, as shown in figure 17.5.

FIG. 17.5

The final layout of the basketball tutorial.

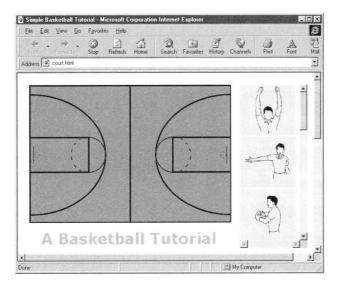

Formatting the Explanations

Now that the court and icons are laid out, you need to layout one final element: the explanations for the court markings and referee calls. To layout the explanations, once again you will make use of the <DIV> tag to create a single entity out of multiple tags.

To accomplish this, you first create an element that overlays the explanation on the court, creating a container element for the rest of the explanation text. Then you can format the actual text of the explanation, and a headline for the explanation so that they line up in the appropriate place in the tutorial.

You also need to use the *visibility* property to hide the explanations until the user selects the appropriate icon. Listing 17.3 shows an example of how each explanation is constructed.

Listing 17.3   Laying Out an Explanation

```
01. <DIV id="Court4Exp" STYLE="position: absolute; top: 25px; left: 25px;
➥height: 500px; width: 450px; font-family: sans-serif;
➥visibility: hidden" onclick="reset();">
02. <IMG id="Court4Img" STYLE="position: absolute; z-index: 1;
➥visibility: visible;" SRC="lane.gif">
03. <SPAN id="Court4Text" STYLE="position:absolute; top: 25px; left:75px">
04. The lane is the area underneath the basket.<br>
05. At the top of the lane is the foul line, and<br>
06. offensive players are only allowed to occupy<br>
07. the lane for three seconds at a time.
08. </SPAN>
09.
10. <SPAN id="Court4Head" STYLE="position: absolute; top: 300; left: 25;
➥font-family: sans-serif;">
11. <H1>The Lane</H1>
12. </SPAN>
13. </DIV>
```

Listing 17.3 uses the <DIV> tag in line 1 to create an overall container for one of the court marking explanations. In line 3, the <SPAN> tag is used to place the written explanation for the court marking. Line 10 uses the <SPAN> tag again to place the headline for the explanation.

You should note that the entire explanation is constructed of three separate elements: the explanation image, headline, and text. All these elements are grouped into a single element using the <DIV> tag. This enables you to add precision to the element's layout by positioning each element exactly where you want it, as shown in figure 17.6.

You will also notice that you are preparing the explanations to receive and process events as well. At the end of line 1, the event handler *onclick="reset();"* enables the explanation to be reset when the user clicks the explanation. Of course, right now it will not do anything, but it will soon enough.

FIG. 17.6
A fomatted
explanation.

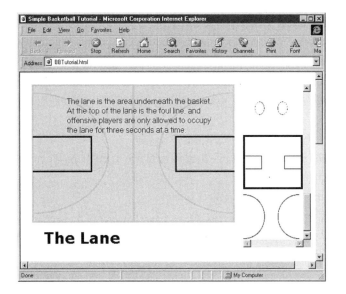

Scripting the Functionality

With all the elements in place, all that remains to make the basketball tutorial complete is to script the functionality. To accomplish this you will need to script a number of tasks. Table 17.1 lists the different elements of functionality you need in the game and the functions needed to implement them.

Table 17.1 Required Scripting Elements for the Basketball Tutorial

Functionality Needed	Function to Implement
Showing and Hiding Explanations	showObject() hideObject()
Graying Out the Court	showScreenCourt() hideScreenCourt()
Highlighting Selections	highlight() lowlight()
Resetting the Tutorial	reset()

The sections that follow show how to construct each one of these functions.

showObject() and hideObject()

The first task on the list is to write the functions that display and hide the explanations.

To show the explanation, the first thing you need to know is what element the user has clicked. You can accomplish this by exploiting the fact that the window will record events, such as a mouse click, and then make available the ID of the element that was clicked. So, the following code:

```
var srcElement;
```

declares the *srcElement* variable that you will use to track the element that has been clicked. Next, the line:

```
srcElement = window.event.srcElement;
```

assigns the ID obtained from *window.event.srcElement* to the *srcElement* variable. With the value of the element generating the event, you can use the *srcElement* variable to determine which of the icons has been clicked.

To determine which icon has been clicked, and what explanation to show, you need to use a series of if...then statements:

```
if (srcElement.id == "Ref1")
        Ref1Exp.style.visibility = "visible";
```

This code compares the ID of the element that has been clicked with the names that you have assigned to each element. From the IDs provided by *srcElement* and the names you have assigned your elements, you can then set the *visibility* property for the appropriate explanation to be visible. This will display the full explanations. Listing 17.4 shows a truncated version of the completed function.

Listing 17.4   The showObject() Function

```
01. function showObject() {
02.
03.        reset();
04.        showScreenCourt();
05.        var srcElement;
06.        srcElement = window.event.srcElement;
07.        if (srcElement.id == "Ref1")
08.            Ref1Exp.style.visibility = "visible";
09.        …
10.
11.        if (srcElement.id == "Court1")
12.            Court1Exp.style.visibility = "visible";
13.        …
14.        if (srcElement.id == "Court5")
15.            Court5Exp.style.visibility = "visible";
16.
17. }
```

You might notice that before the function determines which icon has been clicked and displays its explanation, it first calls the *reset()* and *showScreenCourt()* functions on lines 3 and 4.

The *reset()* function resets the application to make sure all elements are in order before displaying new information. The *showScreenCourt()* function grays out the elements on the court that are unnecessary. Both of these functions are covered in full detail in the next section in the chapter.

To hide explanations, you can use the exact same function from listing 17.4 with one small change. Instead of using the *if* statements to set the *visibility* property to "visible," you will set the *visibility* property to "hidden." In other words, all the lines in the form of:

```
Court1Exp.style.visibility = "visible";
```

become

```
Court1Exp.style.visibility = "hidden";
```

By changing one simple property, you alter the functionality of the entire function.

showScreenCourt() and hideScreenCourt()

When you display the explanations, you want the court elements to appear "grayed" out, so that they do not interfere with the readability of the explanation. This is similar to screening an image in graphics design so that it appears lighter on the page. Doing so simply enables you to retain the placement of the elements in the original for reference, but to place text over the elements and have it be readable. A similar technique is also used in many graphic user interfaces to signify that a button, control, or element is not available. A button that is "grayed out" in a dialog box, for example, cannot be clicked. To do this, you need to hide the court elements, and replace them with a screened image of the court.

N O T E As a challenge, try implementing a similar technique using a multimedia filter. ■

The function you write will hide all the court images, and then set the *visibility* property of the screened image to "visible." Listing 17.5 shows the full code for this functionality.

Listing 17.5 Graying Out the Court

```
01. function showScreenCourt() {
02.
03.       Title.style.visibility = "hidden";
04.       Court.style.visibility = "hidden";
05.       XPoint.style.visibility = "hidden";
06.       HalfCourt.style.visibility = "hidden";
07.       Key.style.visibility = "hidden";
08.       Lane.style.visibility = "hidden";
09.       Basket.style.visibility = "hidden";
10.       Screen.style.visibility = "visible";
11. }
```

Of course, *showScreenCourt()* is a fairly simple function, and one that you can duplicate to create the function that returns the court to its normal status. By simply reversing the statements from:

```
Basket.style.visibility = "hidden";
```

to

```
Basket.style.visibility = "visible";
```

where applicable, you can create a similar function to *showScreenCourt()* called *hideScreenCourt()*, which will essentially reset the court.

highlight() and lowlight()

As mentioned previously, when the user clicks an icon, you want that icon to be highlighted to reinforce the explanation that is given for that icon.

To accomplish this, you need to create two functions: one called *highlight()* that creates a border around the icon that has been clicked; and another called *lowlight()* that removes the border.

Listing 17.6 shows the *highlight()* function that makes use of the *srcElement* variable again.

Listing 17.6   The highlight() Function

```
01. function highlight() {
02.
03.       var srcElement;
04.       srcElement = window.event.srcElement;
05.       srcElement.style.border = "solid";
06.
07. }
```

The *highlight()* function uses the *srcElement* variable to track the ID of the element that has been clicked, which in this case is one of the icons. Then, because the border is already part of the icon's style definition, you can manipulate it directly with line 5, which takes the *border* property for the icon and changes it from "none" to "solid," effectively highlighting the icon. You can change this function into the *lowlight()* function by changing the *border* property again from line 5:

```
srcElement.style.border = "none";
```

Effectively, this line resets the border style to "none," removing the highlight from the icon.

reset()

In the course of displaying the various explanations for referee signals and court markings, there are times when it would be nice to reset the application to make sure everything is functioning correctly, and everything is ready to go for the next example. The *reset()* function serves this purpose.

As with all the previously covered functions, the functionality of the *reset()* function is very straightforward. It simply takes all the elements back to their original settings in one function, so it doesn't need to be done by hand. The first thing you need to do is hide the image of the grayed out court by calling the *hideScreenCourt()* function.

Then, you need to call the *lowlight()* function to make sure that the current highlighted element is no longer highlighted.

Next, you engage in a series of statements that reset the visibility of all the original elements to their original states. The process is simply repeated for all the elements on the page. Listing 17.7 shows the truncated final code for the *reset()* function.

Listing 17.7   The reset() Function

```
01. function reset() {
02.
03.        hideScreenCourt();
04.        lowlight();
05.        Title.style.visibility = "visible";
06.        Ref1Exp.style.visibility = "hidden";
07.        …
08.        Ref6Exp.style.visibility = "hidden";
09.        Ref1.style.border = "none";
10. …
11.        Ref6.style.border = "none";
12.
13.        Court1Exp.style.visibility = "hidden";
14.        …
15. Court5Exp.style.visibility = "hidden";
16.
17. Court1.style.border = "none";
18. …
19.        Court5.style.border = "none";
20. }
```

Part

VI

Ch

17

The Final Page!

Now that you have completed the functions for the basketball tutorial, it's time to assemble everything into the final code, as shown in listing 17.8. Within a typical Dynamic HTML document, you first list the functions, followed by all the layout details for the court elements, the icons, and finally the explanations. All the pieces fit together to create the final basketball tutorial code, shown in listing 17.8.

Listing 17.8   The Final Code for the Basketball Tutorial

```
001. <HTML>
002. <HEAD>
003. <TITLE>Simple Basketball Tutorial</TITLE>
004.
```

continues

Listing 17.8 Continued

```
005. <SCRIPT>
006.
007. function showObject() {
008.
009.     reset();
010.     showScreenCourt();
011.     var srcElement;
012.     srcElement = window.event.srcElement;
013.     if (srcElement.id == "Ref1")
014.         Ref1Exp.style.visibility = "visible";
015.     if (srcElement.id == "Ref2")
016.         Ref2Exp.style.visibility = "visible";
017.     if (srcElement.id == "Ref3")
018.         Ref3Exp.style.visibility = "visible";
019.     if (srcElement.id == "Ref4")
020.         Ref4Exp.style.visibility = "visible";
021.     if (srcElement.id == "Ref5")
022.         Ref5Exp.style.visibility = "visible";
023.     if (srcElement.id == "Ref6")
024.         Ref6Exp.style.visibility = "visible";
025.     if (srcElement.id == "Court1")
026.         Court1Exp.style.visibility = "visible";
027.     if (srcElement.id == "Court2")
028.         Court2Exp.style.visibility = "visible";
029.     if (srcElement.id == "Court3")
030.         Court3Exp.style.visibility = "visible";
031.     if (srcElement.id == "Court4")
032.         Court4Exp.style.visibility = "visible";
033.     if (srcElement.id == "Court5")
034.         Court5Exp.style.visibility = "visible";
035. }
036.
037. function hideObject() {
038.
039.     hideScreenCourt();
040.
041.     lowlight();
042.     var srcElement;
043.     srcElement = window.event.srcElement;
044.     if (srcElement.id == "Ref1")
045.         Ref1Exp.style.visibility = "hidden";
046.     if (srcElement.id == "Ref2")
047.         Ref2Exp.style.visibility = "hidden";
048.     if (srcElement.id == "Ref3")
049.         Ref3Exp.style.visibility = "hidden";
050.     if (srcElement.id == "Ref4")
051.         Ref4Exp.style.visibility = "hidden";
052.     if (srcElement.id == "Ref5")
053.         Ref5Exp.style.visibility = "hidden";
054.     if (srcElement.id == "Ref6")
055.         Ref6Exp.style.visibility = "hidden";
056.     if (srcElement.id == "Court1")
057.         Court1Exp.style.visibility = "hidden";
```

```
058.        if (srcElement.id == "Court2")
059.            Court2Exp.style.visibility = "hidden";
060.        if (srcElement.id == "Court3")
061.            Court3Exp.style.visibility = "hidden";
062.        if (srcElement.id == "Court4")
063.            Court4Exp.style.visibility = "hidden";
064.        if (srcElement.id == "Court5")
065.            Court5Exp.style.visibility = "hidden";
066. }
067.
068. function showScreenCourt() {
069.
070.        Title.style.visibility = "hidden";
071.        Court.style.visibility = "hidden";
072.        XPoint.style.visibility = "hidden";
073.        HalfCourt.style.visibility = "hidden";
074.        Key.style.visibility = "hidden";
075.        Lane.style.visibility = "hidden";
076.        Basket.style.visibility = "hidden";
077.        Screen.style.visibility = "visible";
078. }
079.
080. function hideScreenCourt() {
081.
082.        Title.style.visibility = "visible";
083.        Court.style.visibility = "visible";
084.        XPoint.style.visibility = "visible";
085.        HalfCourt.style.visibility = "visible";
086.        Key.style.visibility = "visible";
087.        Lane.style.visibility = "visible";
088.        Basket.style.visibility = "visible";
089.        Screen.style.visibility = "hidden";
090. }
091.
092. function reset() {
093.
094.        hideScreenCourt();
095.        lowlight();
096.        Title.style.visibility = "visible";
097.        Ref1Exp.style.visibility = "hidden";
098.        Ref2Exp.style.visibility = "hidden";
099.        Ref3Exp.style.visibility = "hidden";
100.        Ref4Exp.style.visibility = "hidden";
101.        Ref5Exp.style.visibility = "hidden";
102.        Ref6Exp.style.visibility = "hidden";
103.        Ref1.style.border = "none";
104.        Ref2.style.border = "none";
105.        Ref3.style.border = "none";
106.        Ref4.style.border = "none";
107.        Ref5.style.border = "none";
108.        Ref6.style.border = "none";
109.
110.        Court1Exp.style.visibility = "hidden";
111.        Court2Exp.style.visibility = "hidden";
112.        Court3Exp.style.visibility = "hidden";
113.        Court4Exp.style.visibility = "hidden";
```

Part

VI

Ch

17

continues

Listing 17.8 Continued

```
114.      Court5Exp.style.visibility = "hidden";
115.      Court1.style.border = "none";
116.      Court2.style.border = "none";
117.      Court3.style.border = "none";
118.      Court4.style.border = "none";
119.      Court5.style.border = "none";
120. }
121.
122. function highlight() {
123.
124.      var srcElement;
125.      srcElement = window.event.srcElement;
126.      srcElement.style.border = "solid";
127. }
128.
129. function lowlight() {
130.
131.      var srcElement;
132.      srcElement = window.event.srcElement;
133.      srcElement.style.border = "none";
134.
135. }
136.
137. </SCRIPT>
138. </HEAD>
139. <BODY>
140.
141. <IMG id="Court" STYLE="position: absolute; top: 25px; left: 25;
➥z-index: 0; visibility: visible;" SRC="court.gif">
142. <IMG id="XPoint" STYLE="position: absolute; top: 25px; left: 25;
➥z-index: 1; visibility: visible;" SRC="3point.gif">
143. <IMG id="HalfCourt" STYLE="position: absolute; top: 25px; left: 25;
➥z-index: 2; visibility: visible;" SRC="halfcourt.gif">
144. <IMG id="Key" STYLE="position: absolute; top: 25px; left: 25; z-index: 3;
➥visibility: visible;" SRC="key.gif">
145. <IMG id="Lane" STYLE="position: absolute; top: 25px; left: 25; z-index: 4;
➥visibility: visible;" SRC="lane.gif">
146. <IMG id="Basket" STYLE="position: absolute; top: 25px; left: 25;
➥z-index: 5; visibility: visible;" SRC="basket.gif">
147. <IMG id="Screen" STYLE="position: absolute; top: 25px; left: 25;
➥z-index: 0; visibility: hidden;" SRC="court-screen.gif">
148.
149. <DIV id="Title" STYLE="position: absolute; top: 325; left: 50;
➥font-family: sans-serif; color: orange; visibility: visible;">
150. <H1>A Basketball Tutorial</H1>
151. </DIV>
152.
153. <!— The following DIV tag specifies the scrolling box for
154.      official's signals. —>
155.
156. <DIV id="Official" STYLE="position: absolute; top: 25; left: 475;
➥height: 340; width: 145; overflow: scroll">
```

```
157. <IMG id="Ref1" STYLE="border: none; border-width: thin;
➥border-color: orange;" onclick="showObject(); highlight()";
➥ondblclick="reset()"; SRC="jumpball.gif">
158. <IMG id="Ref2" STYLE="border: none; border-width: thin;
➥border-color: orange;" onclick="showObject(); highlight()";
➥ondblclick="reset()"; SRC="3sec.gif">
159. <IMG id="Ref3" STYLE="border: none; border-width: thin;
➥border-color: orange;" onclick="showObject(); highlight()";
➥ondblclick="reset()"; SRC="travel.gif">
160. <IMG id="Ref4" STYLE="border: none; border-width: thin;
➥border-color: orange;" onclick="showObject(); highlight()";
➥ondblclick="reset()"; SRC="foul.gif">
161. <IMG id="Ref5" STYLE="border: none; border-width: thin;
➥border-color: orange;" onclick="showObject(); highlight()";
➥ondblclick="reset()"; SRC="one-in-one.gif">
162. <IMG id="Ref6" STYLE="border: none; border-width: thin;
➥border-color: orange;" onclick="showObject(); highlight()";
➥ondblclick="reset()"; SRC="timeout.gif">
163.
164. <IMG id="Court1" STYLE="border: none; border-width: thin;
➥border-color: orange;" onclick="showObject(); highlight()";
➥ondblclick="reset()"; SRC="basket-small.gif">
165. <IMG id="Court2" STYLE="border: none; border-width: thin;
➥border-color: orange;" onclick="showObject(); highlight()";
➥ondblclick="reset()"; SRC="halfcourt-small.gif">
166. <IMG id="Court3" STYLE="border: none; border-width: thin;
➥border-color: orange;" onclick="showObject(); highlight()";
➥ondblclick="reset()"; SRC="key-small.gif">
167. <IMG id="Court4" STYLE="border: none; border-width: thin;
➥border-color: orange;" onclick="showObject(); highlight()";
➥ondblclick="reset()"; SRC="lane-small.gif">
168. <IMG id="Court5" STYLE="border: none; border-width: thin;
➥border-color: orange;" onclick="showObject(); highlight()";
➥ondblclick="reset()"; SRC="3point-small.gif">
169. </DIV>
170.
171. <!— The following DIV tags define the location and text for
172.      explanations for the ref signals. —>
173.
174. <DIV id="Ref1Exp" STYLE="position: absolute; top: 75; left: 75;
➥height: 500; width: 450; font-family: sans-serif; visibility: hidden;"
➥onclick="reset();">
175.
176. <SPAN id="Ref1Text">
177. In the event of stopped play, some foul situations,<br>
178. and the start of the game, a Jump Ball is called. <br>
179. Two players compete to tip the ball to their side<br>
180. of the court and their teammates.
181. </SPAN>
182. <SPAN id="Ref1Head" STYLE="position: absolute; top: 250; left: 0;
➥font-family: sans-serif;">
183. <H1>Jump Ball</H1>
184. </SPAN>
185. </DIV>
186.
```

continues

Listing 17.8 Continued

```
187. <DIV id="Ref2Exp" STYLE="position: absolute; top: 75; left: 75;
➥height: 500; width: 450; font-family: sans-serif;
➥visibility: hidden" onclick="reset();">
188.
189. <SPAN id="Ref2Text">
190. A 3 Second Violation is called when a member of <br>
191. the offensive team is positioned in the 3 second<br>
192. lane for longer than 3 seconds.<br>
193. </SPAN>
194. <SPAN id="Ref2Head" STYLE="position: absolute; top: 250; left: 0;
➥font-family: sans-serif;">
195. <H1>3 Second Violation</H1>
196. </SPAN>
197. </DIV>
198.
199. <DIV id="Ref3Exp" STYLE="position: absolute; top: 75; left: 75;
➥height: 500; width: 450; font-family: sans-serif;
➥visibility: hidden" onclick="reset();">
200.
201. <SPAN id="Ref3Text">
202. Traveling is called when a player who has been <br>
203. dribbling the ball, stops dribbling but still moves<br>
204. forward. Once a player stops dribbling, they must<br>
205. pass the ball.
206. </SPAN>
207. <SPAN id="Ref3Head" STYLE="position: absolute; top: 250; left: 0;
➥font-family: sans-serif;">
208. <H1>Traveling</H1>
209. </SPAN>
210. </DIV>
211.
212. <DIV id="Ref4Exp" STYLE="position: absolute; top: 75; left: 75;
➥height: 500; width: 450; font-family: sans-serif;
➥visibility: hidden" onclick="reset();">
213.
214. <SPAN id="Ref4Text">
215. When one player makes physical contact with<br>
216. another player while the ball is in play, a foul<br>
217. is called. Other types of fouls include <br>
218. intentional and technical.
219. </SPAN>
220. <SPAN id="Ref4Head" STYLE="position: absolute; top: 250; left: 0;
➥font-family: sans-serif;">
221. <H1>Personal Foul</H1>
222. </SPAN>
223. </DIV>
224.
225.
226. <DIV id="Ref5Exp" STYLE="position: absolute; top: 75; left: 75;
➥height: 500; width: 450; font-family: sans-serif;
➥visibility: hidden" onclick="reset();">
227.
228. <SPAN id="Ref5Text">
229. A One-in-One shot is called for certain types<br>
```

```
230. of fouls. The player receives one penalty shot<br>
231. and if they make the basket, they are allowed<br>
232. one more.
233. </SPAN>
234. <SPAN id="Ref5Head" STYLE="position: absolute; top: 250; left: 0;
➥font-family: sans-serif;">
235. <H1>One-in-One Shot</H1>
236. </SPAN>
237. </DIV>
238.
239. <DIV id="Ref6Exp" STYLE="position: absolute; top: 75; left: 75;
➥height: 500; width: 450; font-family: sans-serif;
➥visibility: hidden" onclick="reset();">
240.
241. <SPAN id="Ref6Text">
242. This is called when a coach or member of one of the<br>
243. teams has called for a timeout. Officials may also<br>
244. call timeouts that do not count against the teams.
245. </SPAN>
246. <SPAN id="Ref6Head" STYLE="position: absolute; top: 250; left: 0;
➥font-family: sans-serif;">
247. <H1>Timeout Called</H1>
248. </SPAN>
249. </DIV>
250.
251. <DIV id="Court1Exp" STYLE="position: absolute; top: 25px; left: 25px;
➥height: 500px; width: 450px; font-family: sans-serif;
➥visibility: hidden" onclick="reset();">
252. <IMG id="Court1Img" STYLE="position: absolute; z-index: 1;
➥visibility: visible;" SRC="basket.gif">
253. <SPAN id="Court1Text" STYLE="position:absolute; top: 50px; left:75px">
254. Players score points for their teams by putting<br>
255. the ball through the basket. A basket is worth<br>
256. two points except in 3 point situations and<br>
257. certain fouls.
258. </SPAN>
259.
260. <SPAN id="Court1Head" STYLE="position: absolute; top: 300; left: 25;
➥font-family: sans-serif;">
261. <H1>The Basket</H1>
262. </SPAN>
263. </DIV>
264.
265. <DIV id="Court2Exp" STYLE="position: absolute; top: 25px; left: 25px;
➥height: 500px; width: 450px; font-family: sans-serif;
➥visibility: hidden" onclick="reset();">
266. <IMG id="Court2Img" STYLE="position: absolute; z-index: 1;
➥visibility: visible;" SRC="halfcourt.gif">
267. <SPAN id="Court2Text" STYLE="position:absolute; top: 40px; left:30px">
268. The half-court line divides <br>
269. the court into two halves.
270. </SPAN>
271.
272. <SPAN id="Court2Head" STYLE="position: absolute; top: 300; left: 25;
➥font-family: sans-serif;">
273. <H1>The Half-court Line</H1>
```

continues

Listing 17.8   Continued

```
274. </SPAN>
275. </DIV>
276.
277. <DIV id="Court3Exp" STYLE="position: absolute; top: 25px; left: 25px;
➥height: 500px; width: 450px; font-family: sans-serif;
➥visibility: hidden" onclick="reset();">
278. <IMG id="Court3Img" STYLE="position: absolute; z-index: 1;
➥visibility: visible;" SRC="key.gif">
279. <SPAN id="Court3Text" STYLE="position:absolute; top: 50px; left:75px">
280. The Top of the Key is used in jump ball<br>
281. situations and for foul shots.
282. </SPAN>
283.
284. <SPAN id="Court3Head" STYLE="position: absolute; top: 300; left: 25;
➥font-family: sans-serif;">
285. <H1>Top of the Key</H1>
286. </SPAN>
287. </DIV>
288.
289. <DIV id="Court4Exp" STYLE="position: absolute; top: 25px; left: 25px;
➥height: 500px; width: 450px; font-family: sans-serif;
➥visibility: hidden" onclick="reset();">
290. <IMG id="Court4Img" STYLE="position: absolute; z-index: 1;
➥visibility: visible;" SRC="lane.gif">
291. <SPAN id="Court4Text" STYLE="position:absolute; top: 25px; left:75px">
292. The lane is the area underneath the basket.<br>
293. At the top of the lane is the foul line, and<br>
294. offensive players are only allowed to occupy<br>
295. the lane for three seconds at a time.
296. </SPAN>
297.
298. <SPAN id="Court4Head" STYLE="position: absolute; top: 300; left: 25;
➥font-family: sans-serif;">
299. <H1>The Lane</H1>
300. </SPAN>
301. </DIV>
302.
303. <DIV id="Court5Exp" STYLE="position: absolute; top: 25px; left: 25px;
➥height: 500px; width: 450px; font-family: sans-serif;
➥visibility: hidden" onclick="reset();">
304. <IMG id="Court5Img" STYLE="position: absolute; z-index: 1;
➥visibility: visible;" SRC="3point.gif">
305. <SPAN id="Court5Text" style="position:absolute; top: 100px; left:75px">
306. Baskets made from behind the 3 point line<br>
307. count for 3 points, as opposed to a normal<br>
308. basket's 2 points.
309. </SPAN>
310.
311. <SPAN id="Court5Head" STYLE="position: absolute; top: 300; left: 25;
➥font-family: sans-serif;">
312. <H1>The 3 Point Line</H1>
313. </SPAN>
314. </DIV>
```

```
315.
316. </BODY>
317. </HTML>
```

When it all comes together, you have the final application, shown in figure 17.7.

FIG. 17.7
The final basketball tutorial in action. Clicking an icon shows an explanation of that aspect of the game.

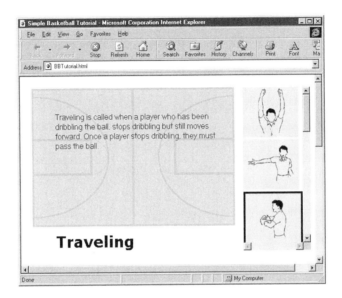

The tutorial now launches in the state shown in figure 17.5, and is ready for user interaction. By single-clicking any of the icons in the scroll box on the right, an explanation for the given referee signal, or court marking, is displayed. The user can reset the tutorial by clicking the explanation, or by clicking the selected icon again. Or the user can simply click another icon to learn more about the game.

Of course, the basketball tutorial might not help your selections in the next NBA draft; however, it is a pretty compelling example of how you can create an interactive tutorial, with application functionality in a simple Dynamic HTML page that downloads quickly and efficiently.

From Here...

Now you have some practical examples under your belt of how Dynamic HTML can be used to increase interactivity and add some multimedia excitement to presentations and explanations. So far you have looked at ways the Dynamic HTML can improve or revitalize applications that were still possible, even in a limited form, with static HTML. But before you jump in with both feet and redesign all your pages with Dynamic HTML, take a look at Chapters 18 and 19:

■ Chapter 18, "Building an Online Catalog," takes a look at how Dynamic HTML can be used to create an online catalog with a variety of functionality.

■ Chapter 19, "Building the Smashout Video Game," caps it all off by creating a fully functional version of a "breakout" style game, complete with collision detection, showcasing the power of Dynamic HTML.

Building an Online Catalog

Data binding is one of the most important real-world aspects of Dynamic HTML. This chapter puts data binding to work in an application that comes up quite often on the World Wide Web—an online catalog.

Over the course of this chapter, you will build an online catalog for a fictional musical instrument company called Burnham Brothers. Burnham Brothers builds a variety of musical instruments across several categories and over a broad price range.

For this application, you will assume that Burnham Brothers wants to create a catalog that provides several key features to its potential customers:

- Burnham Brothers wants customers to be able to get an overall feel for its product line by allowing the customer to see a "table of contents" containing its products.

- Because many of its customers will only be interested in a certain type of instrument, Burnham Brothers wants the customer to be able to select which types of instruments the table will show.

- Some customers will be constrained by price. Therefore, Burnham Brothers wants the customer to be able to limit the products they see based upon price.

- In addition to the table of their products, Burnham Brothers wants the customer to be able to navigate through a different view that shows one product at a time, with full information about each product.

This chapter builds the project in three steps. In the first step, you will build the basic foundation. This step includes setting up the data required for the application, building the basic HTML file, and showing a basic table containing the products.

In the second step, you will add more functionality to the table view of the products by providing the user with two advanced options. First, the user will be able to sort the products based upon selected criteria. Second, the user will be able to filter the products based upon product type and maximum cost.

Finally, you will add the product view. The product view shows only one product at a time and has navigation buttons to move through the product line. This feature also supports filtering from the table view. ■

Laying the Groundwork

When developing an application such as this, it's important at the outset to concentrate on the basics and get them working before moving on to more sophisticated features. This ensures that you don't get 80 percent of the way into the development process and find out that you have made a basic error at the beginning that precludes you from moving forward.

In addition to setting up the basic HTML in this section, you will learn three important foundation aspects for an online catalog:

- Determining which Data Source Object to use
- Setting up the structure of the data that will contain the products and the information about them
- Specifying the tabular form used to display the products

The Basic HTML

Because you will be using Dynamic HTML in this application, you need to start with the boilerplate code contained in any HTML document, specifying that this is the catalog application:

```
<HTML>
<HEAD>
    <TITLE>Catalog</TITLE>
```

```
</HEAD>
<BODY>
</BODY>
</HTML>
```

In addition, inside the body you need to add a basic header to indicate that this is the catalog application for the Burnham Brothers company:

```
<H1>Burnham Brothers</H1>
<H2>Product Catalog</H2>
```

Specifying the Data Source

One of the most important decisions you need to make in the development of a catalog is how to retrieve the data that contains the product descriptions or whatever data you're incorporating in your catalog. You can do this in a variety of ways.

You could use a CGI script on the server to retrieve the data. This is a common way of performing data retrieval on the web, and a great deal of example code is available showing how to accomplish this. As discussed in Chapter 11, "Introduction to Data Binding," this method has many drawbacks.

One of the great benefits of Dynamic HTML is its intrinsic capability to perform data binding through Data Source Objects along with the data binding HTML extensions. These aspects of Dynamic HTML are employed in this chapter's example where you will learn the straight-forward use of data binding constructs.

You will use a Data Source Object for the catalog. The next big decision is which Data Source Object to use. This decision is predicated on where your data is going to be stored.

If the data you will be retrieving will be stored in a relational database, such as Microsoft SQL Server or an Oracle RDBMS, you will probably want to use the Advanced Data Connector that is shipped with Internet Explorer 4.0.

However, the requirements in the Burnham Brothers' online catalog are much simpler. You want to have a list of products along with information about them that is easy to retrieve via data binding. The Tabular Data Control, which also ships with Internet Explorer 4.0, is just what you need.

The Tabular Data Control was discussed in some detail in Chapter 12, "Using Data Source Objects," so only aspects of the Tabular Data Control not previously covered are discussed here.

The Tabular Data Control will be a standard one. First, you need to place the products that will be displayed in a file called "items.txt". Because you will want to do sorting and filtering on the data, you will also specify that a header will be located in the data file. Call the data source "elem_list" because it will contain a list of the elements in the data file:

```
<OBJECT id=elem_list CLASSID="clsid:333C7BC4-460F-11D0-BC04-0080C7055A83">
    <PARAM NAME="DataURL" VALUE="items.txt">
    <PARAM NAME="UseHeader" VALUE="True">
</OBJECT>
```

Setting Up the Data File

Burnham Brothers decides that it wants to make five aspects of each product available in the catalog as follows:

- **Product**—The name of the product.
- **Type**—The type of the product. Burnham Brothers produces three types of products: horn, percussion, and string.
- **Price**—The price of the product.
- **Features**—Any special features of the product.
- **Image**—An image that represents the product.

Because you will be using a header for the data file, it makes sense to use names for each column that match each aspect. Because the structure of the data file for the Tabular Data Control is so straightforward, you could list the name for each column separated by commas and that would be enough, as shown in the following line:

```
Product,Type,Price,Features,Image
```

This is one place where looking ahead is a good idea, however. Because you will be sorting later on, you want to make sure that columns sort correctly. The default method of sorting is alphabetical, and in all cases but one, this method should be sufficient.

The one case where alphabetical sorting will not work correctly is "Price." Because the price will be represented by a number, you want it to sort as such. Additionally, the price could contain cents, so you need to take that into account.

The data type that you want to specify for "Price" to make it sort numerically is "FLOAT" because prices sort the same as floating point numbers due to the decimal point:

```
Product,Type,Price:FLOAT,Features,Image
```

Now that you have set up the header, it's time to specify some sample data. You want to ensure that you have products that vary widely in price and that each type of product (horn, percussion, and string) is represented. Create a file called "items.txt" that contains this data:

```
Product,Type,Price:FLOAT,Features,Image
Accordian,horn,249.95,Cherry Wood Case,<IMG SRC=images/accordian.gif>
Acoustic Guitar,string,149.95,Hand Carved,<IMG SRC=images/acoustic.gif>
Cymbals,percussion,79.95,Special Titanium/Brass Alloy,<IMG SRC=images/
➥cymbals.gif>
French Horn,horn,379.95,Oversize valves,<IMG SRC=images/frenchhorn.gif>
Grand Piano,string,4299.95,Includes Bench,<IMG SRC=images/grandpiano.gif>
Electric guitar,string,423.95,Automatically tunes itself,<IMG SRC=images/
➥guitar.gif>
Harp,string,799.95,Includes free stand,<IMG SRC=images/harp.gif>
Saxophone,horn,549.95,All brass construction,<IMG SRC=images/saxophone.gif>
Snare drum,percussion,455.95,brass rings,<IMG SRC=images/snare.gif>
Trumpet,horn,699.95,Includes free professional baffle,<IMG SRC=images/
➥trumpet.gif>
Tuba,horn,899.95,Special platinum alloy construction,<IMG SRC=images/tuba.gif>
Violin,string,1499.95,Special Austrian Strings,<IMG SRC=images/violin.gif>
```

Specifying the Table View

You know from the specification that Burnham Brothers wants the main view of the data to be via a table. In addition, they also want three aspects of each product to be contained in the table:

- Product Name
- Product Type
- Product Price

You have already set up the Data Source Object and the data file, now all you have to do is provide a way of viewing the data. This is a perfect place to use Dynamic HTML's repeated table binding, because it automatically generates a table row for every product in the data file.

Begin by specifying a table that consumes data from the Data Source Object (elem_list) and name it "elemtbl". In addition, you will want to specify a table column for the product name, bound to the "Product" column in the data set. You will want to bind a row to "Type" and "Price" as well, as demonstrated in the following code:

```
<TABLE ID=elemtbl datasrc=#elem_list>
   <TBODY>
     <TR>
       <TD><SPAN DATAFLD="Product"></SPAN></TD>
       <TD><SPAN DATAFLD="Type"></SPAN></TD>
       <TD><SPAN DATAFLD="Price"></SPAN></TD>
     </TR>
   </TBODY>
</TABLE>
</DIV>
```

Again, if these concepts are not clear to you, make sure you refer back to Chapters 11 and 12, which cover the basics of data binding and Data Source Objects.

This table definition has the effect of creating one table row for each row in the Data Source Object and displaying the Product, Type, and Price for each of those rows.

The Online Catalog Foundation

Now that you have enough code to get a basic version of the catalog application up and running, it's time to piece together the application thus far into a file called "catalog1.htm" as shown in listing 18.1:

Listing 18.1 The Foundations of the Online Catalog

```
01. <HTML>
02. <HEAD>
03.    <TITLE>Catalog</TITLE>
04. </HEAD>
05. <BODY>
06.
```

Part

VI

Ch

18

continues

Listing 18.1 Continued

```
07. <H1>Burnham Brothers</H1>
08. <H2>Product Catalog</H2>
09.
10. <OBJECT id=elem_list CLASSID="clsid:333C7BC4-460F-11D0-BC04-0080C7055A83">
11.     <PARAM NAME="DataURL" VALUE="items.txt">
12.     <PARAM NAME="UseHeader" VALUE="True">
13. </OBJECT>
14.
15. <TABLE id=elemtbl datasrc=#elem_list>
16.     <TBODY>
17.       <TR>
18.         <TD><SPAN DATAFLD="Product"></SPAN></TD>
19.         <TD><SPAN DATAFLD="Type"></SPAN></TD>
20.         <TD><SPAN DATAFLD="Price"></SPAN></TD>
21.       </TR>
22.     </TBODY>
23. </TABLE>
```

Figure 18.1 shows the output generated when you run the code in listing 18.1. Although you're nowhere near done yet, this code generates enough information so that you know you're on the right track.

FIG. 18.1
Output from online catalog foundation.

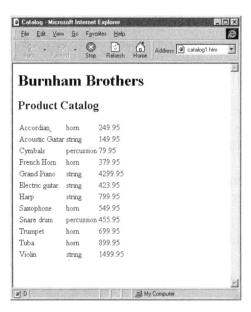

First, you know the Tabular Data Control Data Source Object is working because data is being generated. Second, you know that the data file is constructed correctly because all the rows of the data file are transferred to and displayed in the application.

Now you have all the products in the online catalog displayed in the table. The next step that you will want to add is the capability to filter and sort these products.

Providing Sort and Filter Capabilities

Now you've got the basic data binding aspects of the application up and running; however, the application isn't interactive at all. In many ways, you have the equivalent of a static web page that has a table with data hard-coded into it.

Even at this early stage, however, you're a large step ahead of hard-coding data. If you want to change the products displayed on this page, all you need to change are the product listings in "items.txt"; you do not need to touch the HTML page.

In this section you will add two methods of interacting with this table view of the products:

■ Sorting the table based upon product, type, or price

■ Filtering the table based on type or maximum price

By the end of this section you will be solidly into the kind of application capabilities that would be difficult to achieve with regular HTML. With Dynamic HTML, however, adding these capabilities becomes almost simple.

Sorting Data by Column

The first thing you need to do is set up a mechanism by which the user can sort the table of products based upon the product name, the type of product, or the price of the product.

Start this process by adding a table head to the repeated table and specify that this table head will contain one row:

```
<THEAD><TR>
</TR>
```

Now you need to create a column heading for each of the table columns. You may have noticed from looking at the results from the previous section that the columns were not quite wide enough to handle the data contained in them, resulting in a less than visually appealing display. You can correct this by making the first heading 150 pixels wide—more than wide enough to handle the product names:

```
<TD WIDTH=150>
```

Now you want to show the name of the column heading. Because this will be the name of the column and not actually a row in the dataset itself, you want to make sure that the column heading is definitely set apart from the other items that occur below it. You can do this by making the column heading bold and blue in a sans-serif font. In addition, because you want the user to be able to click the column heading to sort by that criteria, you will also underline it to give the user a visual cue to click it:

```
<B><U><FONT COLOR=BLUE FACE="ARIAL,HELVETICA">Product
</FONT></U></B>
```

Finally, because you want the user to be able to click the heading, you need a way to assign an event handler to this heading. The easiest way to do this is by using a <DIV> tag. Then give the heading an ID of "product" and have the function *product_onclick()* called whenever it is clicked:

```
<TD WIDTH=150><DIV id=product onclick="product_onclick()">
            <B><U><FONT COLOR=BLUE FACE="ARIAL,HELVETICA">
            Product</FONT></U></B></DIV></TD>
```

Next you need to repeat this process for the "Type" and "Price" headings. For the type heading, call the *type_onclick()* function, and for the price heading, call the *price_onclick()* function:

```
<TD WIDTH=150><DIV id=type onclick="type_onclick()">
            <B><U><FONT COLOR=BLUE FACE="ARIAL,HELVETICA">
            Type</FONT></U></B></DIV></TD>

<TD WIDTH=150><DIV id=price onclick="price_onclick()">
            <B><U><FONT COLOR=BLUE FACE="ARIAL,HELVETICA">
            Price</FONT></U></B></DIV></TD>
```

To perform sorting with the Tabular Data Control, you must do two things:

- Specify the column to sort upon by setting the *SortColumn* property of the Tabular Data Control.
- Execute the sort by calling the *Reset()* method of the Tabular Data Control.

Begin by building the *product_onclick()* function. First, you need to set the *SortColumn* property to be "Product":

```
function product_onclick() {
   elem_list.SortColumn = "Product"
   ...
}
```

Next, you need to call the *Reset()* method of the Tabular Data Control to actually run the sort:

```
function product_onclick() {
   elem_list.SortColumn = "Product"
   elem_list.Reset()
}
```

Believe it or not, that's all you need to do to set up and run the sort. Now you need to create the functions necessary to do the same thing with the *type_onclick()* and *price_onclick()* functions:

```
function type_onclick() {
  elem_list.SortColumn = "Type"
  elem_list.Reset()
}

function price_onclick() {
  elem_list.SortColumn = "Price"
  elem_list.Reset()
}
```

Now if you click any of the headings of the table, the product list is sorted based upon that criteria. If you click the "Price" heading, for instance, the products are sorted by price (see fig. 18.2).

FIG. 18.2
Setting up the online catalog data by category.

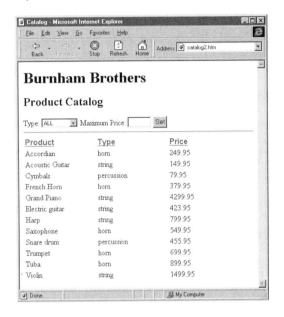

Specifying the User Interface Controls for Filtering

Next, you need to add the controls that will eventually enable the filtering of data based upon user criteria. The specification for this application states that those two criteria are the type of product and the price of the product.

Begin by creating the controls to filter by type. Call this control "Type." First, make a label for it that identifies it as the control for the type of product that is associated with the Type control:

```
<LABEL FOR=Type>Type: </LABEL>
```

Next, you need to create the control that enables the user to specify the type of product to show. The three types of product are horn, string, and percussion. In addition to showing these types, you also want the user to be able to specify the display of all the products.

Because the user is limited to four options, you will use a *SELECT control*. A SELECT control is a drop-down listbox that enables a user to select from the list.

Provide the user with four options: ALL, Horn, String, and Percussion. Because you want the product list to be filtered whenever the control is changed, set up the *ftype_onchange()* function to be called whenever the user selects an item:

```
<SELECT id=Type onchange="ftype_onchange()">
  <OPTION SELECTED>ALL
  <OPTION>Horn
```

```
   <OPTION>String
   <OPTION>Percussion
</SELECT>
```

Now you will go through a similar process to specify the controls to set the filter for the maximum price. Set the name of the control that enables the user to set the price "Max." Again, you need to specify a label for this control:

```
<LABEL FOR=Max>Maximum Price: </LABEL>
```

Next, you need the control that enables the user to specify a price. Unlike the *Type* control, the user is not limited to a set number of choices. The user might want to set the maximum amount, for instance, to an arbitrary number such as $723. Because of this unpredictability factor, you need to use a text input HTML control, with the width set to *50* to allow any number into the tens of thousands of dollars:

```
<INPUT id=Max TYPE=TEXT value="" STYLE="width:50">
```

Finally, after the user enters the maximum dollar amount, you need to provide a way for the user to inform the application to run that filter. Add a button with the label "Set" that calls the *max_onchange()* function whenever it is clicked:

```
<INPUT TYPE=BUTTON id=Go value="Set" onclick="max_onchange()">
```

Filtering Based on Product Type

Now that you have built the controls that enable the user to specify the filter to use, you need to build the functions that actually run the filter.

Filtering is much like sorting, except that four things must be done to set the filter to use:

- Set the criteria that will apply to the filter via the *FilterCriterion* property of the Tabular Data Control. This criteria is based upon comparison operators. So, for equals you use "=", for not equals you use "<>", and so on.

- Set the column that will be filtered via the *FilterColumn* property of the Tabular Data Control.

- Set the *FilterValue* property containing the data that will be filtered against. If you do not want to filter the data, set this to "no data."

- Call the *Reset()* method of the Tabular Data Control, which is called to run the filter.

Begin by building the *ftype_onchange()* function. You can start by setting the filter column to "Type" because you know you will want to filter against the type of product:

```
function ftype_onchange() {
    elem_list.FilterColumn = "Type"
}
```

Next, you need to set the filter based upon the option that the user chooses. SELECT controls are zero-based, so if the user chooses the first option, it will be 0. The index of the selected option is available with the *selectedIndex* property of the control.

Begin with the 0 index, which corresponds to the ALL choice. When ALL is chosen, the user wants to see all the types, so you need to set the *FilterCriterion* property to "<>" (not equals) and the *FilterValue* property to "no value", which ensures that all the products are shown:

```
if (Type.selectedIndex == 0) {
  elem_list.FilterCriterion = "<>"
  elem_list.FilterValue = "no value"
}
```

Next, if the user selects the Horn option, the index returned is 1. You need to set the *FilterCriterion* to "=" and the *FilterValue* to "horn":

```
else if (Type.selectedIndex == 1) {
  elem_list.FilterCriterion = "="
  elem_list.FilterValue = "horn"
}
```

If the user selects the String option, the index returned is 2. You need to set the *FilterCriterion* to "=" and the *FilterValue* to "string":

```
else if (Type.selectedIndex == 2) {
  elem_list.FilterCriterion = "="
  elem_list.FilterValue = "string"
}
```

Finally, if the user selects the Percussion option, the index returned is 3. You need to set the *FilterCriterion* to "=" and the *FilterValue* to "percussion":

```
else {
  elem_list.FilterCriterion = "="
  elem_list.FilterValue = "percussion"
}
```

After you have set all the properties for the filter, you need to actually execute the filter. You execute the filter with the *Reset()* method:

```
elem_list.Reset()
```

The results of choosing the "Horn" option to filter the products are shown in figure 18.3.

Filtering Data Based on Maximum Cost

Now you will create the *max_onchange()* function that is called whenever the user sets the maximum price for the products.

This function needs to do four things to filter the products based upon the price entered:

- Set the *FilterColumn* to "Price" because you are filtering on price.
- Set the *FilterCriterion* to less than (<) because you want to show all the products below a certain price.
- Set the *FilterValue* to the value to be filtered against, which is contained in the *value* property of the "Max" control.
- Call the *Reset()* method of the Tabular Data Control to execute the filter.

The following function accomplishes these four objectives:

Part
VI

Ch
18

FIG. 18.3

Filtering by type with the "Horn" option.

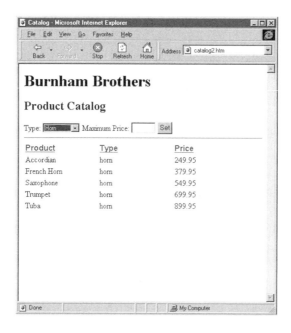

```
function max_onchange() {
   elem_list.FilterColumn="Price"
   elem_list.FilterCriterion="<"
   elem_list.FilterValue=Max.value;

   elem_list.Reset()
}
```

Examining the Online Catalog Foundation

This is a good point to stop and take a look at what you have accomplished so far. Listing 18.2 shows the code for the online catalog application up to this point (save this file as catalog2.htm):

Listing 18.2   The Online Catalog with Data Sorting Mechanisms in Place (catalog2.htm)

```
01. <HTML>
02. <HEAD>
03.    <TITLE>Catalog</TITLE>
04. </HEAD>
05. <BODY>
06.
07. <SCRIPT LANGUAGE=JavaScript>
08. function product_onclick() {
09.    elem_list.SortColumn = "Product"
10.    elem_list.Reset()
11. }
```

```
12.
13. function type_onclick() {
14.    elem_list.SortColumn = "Type"
15.    elem_list.Reset()
16. }
17.
18. function price_onclick() {
19.    elem_list.SortColumn = "Price"
20.    elem_list.Reset()
21. }
22.
23.
24. function ftype_onchange() {
25.    elem_list.FilterColumn = "Type"
26.    if (Type.selectedIndex == 0) {
27.      elem_list.FilterCriterion = "<>"
28.      elem_list.FilterValue = "no value"
29.    } else if (Type.selectedIndex == 1) {
30.       elem_list.FilterCriterion = "="
31.       elem_list.FilterValue = "horn"
32.    } else if (Type.selectedIndex == 2) {
33.       elem_list.FilterCriterion = "="
34.       elem_list.FilterValue = "string"
35.    } else {
36.       elem_list.FilterCriterion = "="
37.       elem_list.FilterValue = "percussion"
38.    }
39.
40.    elem_list.Reset()
41. }
42.
43. function max_onchange() {
44.    elem_list.FilterColumn="Price"
45.    elem_list.FilterCriterion="<"
46.    elem_list.FilterValue=Max.value;
47.
48.    elem_list.Reset()
49. }
50.
51.
52. </SCRIPT>
53.
54. <H1>Burnham Brothers</H1>
55. <H2>Product Catalog</H2>
56.
57. <OBJECT id=elem_list CLASSID="clsid:333C7BC4-460F-11D0-BC04-0080C7055A83">
58.      <PARAM NAME="DataURL" VALUE="items.txt">
59.      <PARAM NAME="UseHeader" VALUE="True">
60. </OBJECT>
61.
62. <LABEL FOR=Type>Type: </LABEL>
63.
64. <SELECT ID=Type onchange="ftype_onchange()">
65.    <OPTION SELECTED>ALL
66.    <OPTION>Horn
```

continues

Listing 18.2 Continued

```
67.    <OPTION>String
68.    <OPTION>Percussion
69. </SELECT>
70.
71. <LABEL FOR=Max>Maximum Price: </LABEL>
72.
73. <INPUT id=Max TYPE=TEXT value="" STYLE="width:50">
74.
75. <INPUT type=BUTTON id=Go value="Set" onclick="max_onchange()">
76. <HR>
77.
78.
79. <TABLE id=elemtbl datasrc=#elem_list>
80.    <THEAD><TR>
81.      <TD WIDTH=150><DIV ID=product onclick="product_onclick()">
82.                   <B><U><FONT COLOR=BLUE FACE="ARIAL,HELVETICA">
83.                   Product</FONT></U></B></DIV></TD>
84.      <TD WIDTH=150><DIV ID=type onclick="type_onclick()">
85.                   <B><U><FONT COLOR=BLUE FACE="ARIAL,HELVETICA">
86.                   Type</FONT></U></B></DIV></TD>
87.      <TD WIDTH=150><DIV ID=price onclick="price_onclick()">
88.                   <B><U><FONT COLOR=BLUE FACE="ARIAL,HELVETICA">
89.                   Price</FONT></U></B></DIV></TD>
90.    </TR></THEAD>
91.    <TBODY>
92.      <TR>
93.        <TD><SPAN DATAFLD="Product"></SPAN></TD>
94.        <TD><SPAN DATAFLD="Type"></SPAN></TD>
95.        <TD><SPAN DATAFLD="Price"></SPAN></TD>
96.      </TR>
97.    </TBODY>
98. </TABLE>
99. </DIV>
```

You have come quite a way from the basic version earlier in the chapter. What was formerly a static web page with no user interaction can now be modified by the user in several ways:

- The user can sort based upon any of the table columns.
- The user can filter the products based upon product type.
- The user can filter the products based upon maximum price.

Figure 18.4 shows the results of using the maximum price filter to set the maximum cost to $600.

FIG. 18.4
Filtering with a
maximum price of 600
dollars.

Providing Detailed Product Information

Part
VI

Ch
18

Now you have completed almost all the functionality required for the user to view Burnham Brothers' products via a table. The next thing you need to tackle is the other view that Burnham Brothers requested—the product view.

You need to add the functionality related to the product view in several steps:

1. Set up a mechanism to switch between the product and table views.
2. Add the actual product view of the data.
3. Navigate within the product view.

Switching Between Table View and Product View

The first aspect of the product view that you will tackle is switching between the table view and the product view. You can achieve this in several ways.

The first method you could use is to make the table view one HTML page and the product view another HTML page. This has the advantage of making a clean division between the views. By making them separate pages, each page is smaller.

Making the pages separate, however, has two disadvantages. One reason that using Dynamic HTML with data binding is so powerful is that you can reduce the amount of round trips to the server. But requiring a server round trip for switching between what is essentially two views of one set of data defeats this benefit.

The other disadvantage to using two separate pages is that information needs to be communicated between the two views. You want the current filter to remain the same in the product and table views. To accomplish this using two pages, for instance, you would need to provide some external method (via the server or passing parameters via the URL) for keeping track of this.

It is much simpler and more efficient to make both views part of the same page and have only one view shown at a time. This approach enables you to use the same Tabular Data Control for both views and much of the same HTML.

Begin by defining two buttons that will switch between the two views. The first button will show the table view by calling the *showTable()* function, and the second will show the product view by calling the *showCurr()* function:

```
<INPUT TYPE=BUTTON VALUE="Table View" onclick="showTable()">
<INPUT TYPE=BUTTON VALUE="Item View" onclick="showCurr()">
```

Because you will be showing and hiding the table and product view, you need to wrap them inside a tag that will enable its entire contents to be shown or hidden. The <DIV> tag works perfectly for this purpose. Place the table view code inside a <DIV> element with the ID of "Table_View":

```
<DIV id="Table_View">

   ... The code for the table view ...

</DIV>
```

When you create the product view, you will also create a DIV element to contain the product view. The name of the ID for the product view will be "Curr_View," which stands for the view of the current product.

Armed with this knowledge, it's time to build the functions to show each view. At first glance you may think that the property you will want to set here to show and hide each view is the *visibility* CSS property.

The *visibility* property is not sufficient for purposes here, however. The *visibility* property states whether an element is shown or not, but does not affect its position. If you were to use it here, one of the views would always be above the other, and when hidden, a large blank spot would reside where it was.

Instead, you want to use the CSS *display* property, which enables an element to be completely removed from rendering in the HTML page when it is set to *none*.

Therefore, you can create the *showTable()* function by setting the table view to be displayed and the product view to not be displayed as follows:

```
function showTable() {
   Table_View.style.display="";
   Curr_View.style.display="none";
}
```

Conversely, you can create the *showCurr()* function by setting the table view to not be displayed and the product view to be displayed as follows:

```
function showCurr() {
   Table_View.style.display="none";
   Curr_View.style.display="";
}
```

Adding the Product View

The product view needs to show one product at a time. It needs to include all available information about the product. Five different aspects of each product need to be shown:

- An image representing the product
- The name of the product
- The type of the product
- The price of the product
- The features of the product

You need to start by specifying a <DIV> element that wraps the product view so the *showCurr()* function can show and hide it. Give this <DIV> element the ID "Curr_View." In addition, because you want the application to start with the table view, you need to set the CSS STYLE *display* property to "none":

```
<DIV id="Curr_View" STYLE="display:none">

   ... The code for the current product view

</DIV>
```

Next, you want to start displaying the different aspects of the product. Begin with the image representing the product. If you look back at the data file for the products, you will note that the fields for the "Image" column are HTML IMG elements.

By structuring the data in this way, you can use the DATAFORMATAS property of HTML data binding to tell the browser to render the HTML associated with the data element. Therefore, those IMG elements specified in "items.txt" will cause an actual image to be displayed.

The way this is accomplished is with a <DIV> tag specifying that the source of the data (DATASRC) will be the *#elem_list*, that the data field (DATAFLD) that you want is "Image," and finally that the data format (DATAFORMATAS) is "html":

```
<DIV DATASRC=#elem_list DATAFLD="Image"
     DATAFORMATAS="html"></DIV><br>
```

Next, you want to show the name of the product. Provide a label next to the name of the product to let the user know what that particular line represents. Accentuate this label with the <STRONG> tag to differentiate it from the actual name of the product.

You need to use a <SPAN> tag instead of a <DIV> tag because only text data will be loaded. Finally, the DATASRC will be the *#elem_list* and the DATAFLD will be "Product":

```
<STRONG>Product:   </STRONG><SPAN DATASRC=#elem_list
                            DATAFLD="Product"></SPAN><br>
```

Perform this same process for the "Type," "Price," and "Features" columns of the data source:

```
<STRONG>Type:      </STRONG><SPAN DATASRC=#elem_list
                            DATAFLD="Type"></SPAN><br>

<STRONG>Price:     </STRONG><SPAN DATASRC=#elem_list
                            DATAFLD="Price"></SPAN><br>

<STRONG>Features:  </STRONG><SPAN DATASRC=#elem_list
                            DATAFLD="Features"></SPAN><br>
```

Navigating through the Product View

Because only one product is shown at a time in the product view, you will want a method of moving throughout the products in this view.

Use a straightforward method of navigating that uses two buttons, "Prev Item" and "Next Item," to move to the previous and next items respectively. Begin by defining the two buttons. The "Prev Item" button will call the *prev()* function and the "Next Item" button will call the *next()* function:

```
<INPUT TYPE=BUTTON VALUE="Prev Item" onclick="prev()">
<INPUT TYPE=BUTTON VALUE="Next Item" onclick="next()">
```

Then, you need to define the *next()* function. The first thing to be aware of when working with Data Source Objects a record at a time is the concept of a *recordset*. This recordset contains the information representing the current state of the Data Source Object.

For instance, the recordset contains the number of records contained in this Data Source Object at this time. Note that the number of records is not necessarily the number of records that were originally loaded because the current number of records can be modified by setting filters on your data.

The first thing you need to do in the *next()* function is get the recordset for the Tabular Data Control Data Source Object. Each Data Source Object has a *recordset* property that contains the recordset. Set this property to the variable "*rs*":

```
function next() {
  var rs = elem_list.recordset;

  ... The rest of the next() function

}
```

Now you want to move to the next record in the Tabular Data Control; however, first you want to check to make sure that you are not at the end of the available records.

Check this by making sure the current position (represented by the *AbsolutePosition* property of the recordset) is not equal to the last position (represented by the *RecordCount* property of the recordset).

If you are not at the end of the records, you will use the *MoveNext()* method of the recordset to move to the next record. If you are at the last record, however, an alert box will be generated informing the user of this occurrence:

```
if (rs.AbsolutePosition != rs.RecordCount)
        rs.MoveNext()
  else
     alert("At the End")
```

You want to follow a similar process with the *prev()* function. You will move to the previous record (with the *MovePrevious()* method of the recordset) unless you are at the first position. Positions in recordsets start at 1, so you just need to make sure the current *AbsolutePosition* is not 1 before you call *MovePrevious()*:

```
function prev() {
  var rs = elem_list.recordset;
  if (rs.AbsolutePosition != 1)
     rs.MovePrevious()
  else
     alert("At the beginning")
}
```

The Final Page!

Now you have finished the catalog, meeting all the specifications supplied by Burnham Brothers. Listing 18.3 shows the final version of the code for the online catalog with data sorting and detailed information capabilities (save this file as "catalog.htm"):

Listing 18.3   The Final Burnham Brothers Online Catalog

```
001. <HTML>
002. <HEAD>
003.    <TITLE>Catalog</TITLE>
004. </HEAD>
005. <BODY>
006.
007. <SCRIPT LANGUAGE=JavaScript>
008. function product_onclick() {
009.    elem_list.SortColumn = "Product"
010.    elem_list.Reset()
011. }
012.
013. function type_onclick() {
014.    elem_list.SortColumn = "Type"
015.    elem_list.Reset()
016. }
017.
```

Part

VI

Ch

18

continues

Listing 18.3   Continued

```
018. function price_onclick() {
019.    elem_list.SortColumn = "Price"
020.    elem_list.Reset()
021. }
022.
023.
024. function ftype_onchange() {
025.     elem_list.FilterColumn = "Type"
026.     if (Type.selectedIndex == 0) {
027.        elem_list.FilterCriterion = "<>"
028.        elem_list.FilterValue = "no value"
029.     } else if (Type.selectedIndex == 1) {
030.         elem_list.FilterCriterion = "="
031.         elem_list.FilterValue = "horn"
032.     } else if (Type.selectedIndex == 2) {
033.         elem_list.FilterCriterion = "="
034.         elem_list.FilterValue = "string"
035.     } else {
036.         elem_list.FilterCriterion = "="
037.         elem_list.FilterValue = "percussion"
038.     }
039.
040.     elem_list.Reset()
041. }
042.
043. function max_onchange() {
044.     elem_list.FilterColumn="Price"
045.     elem_list.FilterCriterion="<"
046.     elem_list.FilterValue=Max.value;
047.
048.     elem_list.Reset()
049. }
050.
051. function showTable() {
052.     Table_View.style.display="";
053.     Curr_View.style.display="none";
054. }
055.
056. function showCurr() {
057.     Table_View.style.display="none";
058.     Curr_View.style.display="";
059. }
060.
061. function next() {
062.    var rs = elem_list.recordset;
063.    if (rs.AbsolutePosition != rs.RecordCount)
064.              rs.MoveNext()
065.    else
066.       alert("At the End")
067. }
068.
069. function prev() {
070.    var rs = elem_list.recordset;
```

```
071.   if (rs.AbsolutePosition != 1)
072.       rs.MovePrevious()
073.   else
074.       alert("At the beginning")
075. }
076.
077.
078. </SCRIPT>
079.
080. <H1>Burnham Brothers</H1>
081. <H2>Product Catalog</H2>
082. <INPUT TYPE=BUTTON VALUE="Table View" onclick="showTable()">
083. <INPUT TYPE=BUTTON VALUE="Item View" onclick="showCurr()">
084. <BR><BR>
085.
086. <OBJECT id=elem_list CLASSID="clsid:333C7BC4-460F-11D0-BC04-0080C7055A83">
087.       <PARAM NAME="DataURL" VALUE="items.txt">
088.       <PARAM NAME="UseHeader" VALUE="True">
089. </OBJECT>
090.
091.     <LABEL FOR=Type>Type: </LABEL>
092.
093.     <SELECT id=Type onchange="ftype_onchange()">
094.       <OPTION SELECTED>ALL
095.       <OPTION>Horn
096.       <OPTION>String
097.       <OPTION>Percussion
098.     </SELECT>
099.
100.     <LABEL FOR=Max>Maximum Price: </LABEL>
101.
102.     <INPUT id=Max TYPE=TEXT value="" STYLE="width:50">
103.
104.     <INPUT TYPE=BUTTON id=Go value="Set" onclick="max_onchange()">
105. <HR>
106.
107. <DIV id="Table_View">
108. <TABLE id=elemtbl datasrc=#elem_list>
109.     <THEAD><TR>
110.       <TD WIDTH=150><DIV ID=product onclick="product_onclick()">
111.                    <B><U><FONT COLOR=BLUE FACE="ARIAL,HELVETICA">
112.                    Product</FONT></U></B></DIV></TD>
113.       <TD WIDTH=150><DIV ID=type onclick="type_onclick()">
114.                    <B><U><FONT COLOR=BLUE FACE="ARIAL,HELVETICA">
115.                    Type</FONT></U></B></DIV></TD>
116.       <TD WIDTH=150><DIV ID=price onclick="price_onclick()">
117.                    <B><U><FONT COLOR=BLUE FACE="ARIAL,HELVETICA">
118.                    Price</FONT></U></B></DIV></TD>
119.     </TR></THEAD>
120.     <TBODY>
121.       <TR>
122.         <TD><SPAN DATAFLD="Product"></SPAN></TD>
123.         <TD><SPAN DATAFLD="Type"></SPAN></TD>
124.         <TD><SPAN DATAFLD="Price"></SPAN></TD>
125.       </TR>
```

continues

Listing 18.3   Continued

```
126.     </TBODY>
127. </TABLE>
128. </DIV>
129.
130. <DIV id="Curr_View" STYLE="display:none">
131.
132. <DIV DATASRC=#elem_list DATAFLD="Image" DATAFORMATAS="html"></DIV><br>
133. <STRONG>Product:  </STRONG><SPAN DATASRC=#elem_list DATAFLD="Product">
➡</SPAN><br>
134. <STRONG>Type:      </STRONG><SPAN DATASRC=#elem_list DATAFLD="Type">
➡</SPAN><br>
135. <STRONG>Price:     </STRONG><SPAN DATASRC=#elem_list DATAFLD="Price">
➡</SPAN><br>
136. <STRONG>Features: </STRONG><SPAN DATASRC=#elem_list DATAFLD="Features">
➡</SPAN><br>
137. <BR>
138.
139. <INPUT TYPE=BUTTON VALUE="Prev Item" onclick="prev()">
140. <INPUT TYPE=BUTTON VALUE="Next Item" onclick="next()">
141. </DIV>
142. </BODY></HTML>
```

The result of reviewing a specific product in the current product view is shown in figure 18.5.

FIG. 18.5

Viewing product information from the final Burnham Brothers online catalog.

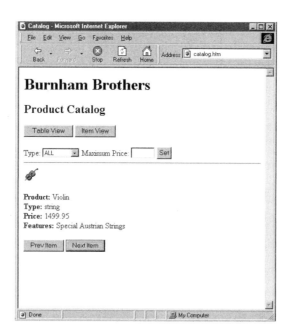

From Here...

This chapter demonstrated how to build an online catalog from the ground up. All the basic requirements are there, but you might want to try adding new features to the catalog for experience. Here are a few ideas to try adding to the catalog application:

- The capability to select an item in the table view and bring it up in the product view.
- Building a "shopping basket" that enables the user to make selections from the catalog.
- Adding more sophisticated filters to the catalog. You could, for instance, let the user set a minimum price for an item.

This chapter demonstrated the sophisticated kinds of applications you can create with surprisingly little code with Dynamic HTML. You can use this as a launchpad to create your own interesting and useful Dynamic HTML data binding applications.

Now that you've created a practical real-world application in Dynamic HTML, it's time to have a little fun. Chapter 19, "Building the Smashout Video Game," builds a video game in Dynamic HTML from the ground up with very little code. The video game features how to use event handling, absolute positioning, and collision detection with Dynamic HTML.

Building the Smashout Video Game

Designing

Learn the process that goes into designing a video game.

The Arena

Explore the steps necessary to build the arena in which the game will take place.

Animating

Learn how to start the game in motion through animation.

Keeping Track

Explore how to keep track of different aspects of the game, such as the number of lives the player has left.

Programming video games is one of the most challenging projects you can attempt in the field of programming. It requires not only keeping track of the state of what's going on, but strict attention to timing and movement.

In short, programming a video game is just about the last thing you'd expect to be able to do with only HTML and JavaScript; however, that's exactly what you're going to do in this chapter.

Over the course of this chapter, you will develop a video game called *Smashout*. Smashout is a relatively straight-forward game that involves bouncing a ball off a paddle while trying to hit targets, without letting the ball escape off the bottom of the screen.

Although video game programming can become quite involved and complicated, the concepts and code in this chapter are kept as simple as possible to make them understandable. In fact, the entire Smashout game requires less than two pages of code! ▪

The Rules of the Game

The Smashout game takes place in a rectangular arena. Inside this arena are three classes of objects:

- **The Player**—The player is represented by a paddle 60 pixels wide and 15 pixels tall (see fig. 19.1) placed near the bottom of the arena. This paddle can be moved left and right to the edges of the arena.

FIG. 19.1

The player as repre-sented by a paddle.

- **The Targets**—Sixteen rectangular targets (see fig. 19.2) are placed at the top of the screen. These targets are 75 pixels wide and 15 pixels tall. These targets disappear when hit by the ball.

FIG. 19.2

The target.

- **The Ball**—The ball is placed in the center of the arena (see fig. 19.3). The ball is 13 pixels wide and 12 pixels tall. When the game starts, the ball begins moving toward the top of the screen.

FIG. 19.3

The ball.

The objective of the game is to destroy all 16 targets at the top of the screen without letting the ball escape off the bottom of the arena. The ball is kept from escaping by the player hitting the ball with the paddle, keeping it in play.

The player is given three "lives" in which to destroy all 16 targets. Whenever the ball escapes off the bottom of the screen, the player loses a life. When all three lives are lost, the game is over.

If the player manages to hit all 16 targets before losing all three lives, however, the player wins the game. If the player wants to play again, hitting the Start button regenerates all 16 targets, and play begins again.

Challenges of Video Game Programming

Several challenges come up in video game programming that you need to consider:

- **Timing**—The first and most important aspect of video game programming is timing. For the user to feel as if the experience is a natural and fluid one, all animation and user interaction has to appear as if it were happening in real time. The ball must appear to be moving, for instance, and when it strikes a target, that target must immediately disappear.

- **Monitoring Game State**—The second aspect of video game programming to keep in mind is that the state of the game must be monitored exactly. It would be disconcerting if two balls were to appear on the screen or if targets randomly disappeared and reappeared.

- **Game Speed**—Finally, you need to consider the speed of the game. If at all possible, the speed of the game should be the same on all computers. If this is not possible, the program should be tested on as many computers as possible, and you should settle on a compromise speed.

Part
VI

Ch
19

All these aspects will come up during the development of Smashout. Although none of them are insurmountable, they do point out why game programming can be one of the harder programming disciplines to master.

Building the Arena

You will begin by building the arena itself and placing the game objects inside of it. All the components in the game will be images represented by IMG elements.

You have already covered the *target*, *ball*, and *player* objects. Now you need to consider the other objects present in the game:

- Left wall
- Right wall
- Top wall
- Bottom wall

The Left and Right walls are represented by side.gif (see fig. 19.4). The Top and Bottom walls are represented by top.gif (see fig. 19.5). All the walls will be ten pixels thick.

FIG. 19.4

The Side wall.

FIG. 19.5

The Top wall.

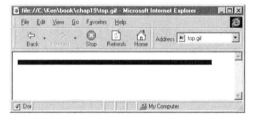

Positioning Game Objects

Now that you've got the object images that you will be using in the game, you need to decide where to place these images. You want to build an arena that is 400 pixels wide and 450 pixels tall and place it 10 pixels from the top and 10 pixels from the right side of the screen, so the arena is slightly inset from the left and top sides of the browser.

Positioning the Top, Left, Right, and Bottom Sides   Begin by placing the top side of the arena at the 10 left and 10 top position. This insets the arena 10 pixels into the browser. Assign the ID "top" to the *top* object:

```
<IMG ID=top    SRC="top.gif"
               STYLE="position:absolute;top:10;left:10">
```

Next, you need to place the bottom side of the arena, which uses the same GIF as the *top* object. Because you want the arena to be 450 pixels tall, you will place this GIF 460 pixels from the top. The GIF is placed at 460 pixels rather than 450 pixels to take into account the 10 pixels that make up the top part of the arena.

```
<IMG ID=bottom SRC="top.gif"
           STYLE="position:absolute;top:460;left:10">
```

Now you will start placing the side. First, you will place the left side of the arena 10 pixels from the left side of the screen to inset it. You will also want to place the left side of the arena 20 pixels from the top of the screen to adjust for the width of the top:

```
<IMG ID=left    SRC="side.gif"
           STYLE="position:absolute;top:20;left:10">
```

Perform a similar placement with the right side of the arena, which should be 20 pixels from the top of the screen and 400 pixels from the left side of the screen:

```
<IMG ID=right   SRC="side.gif"
           STYLE="position:absolute;top:20;left:400">
```

Positioning the Targets   Now that you have built the arena, you can place the targets for which the player will be aiming. You need to create four rows of four targets, for which you will use the "bar.gif" image. Each target will be 75 pixels wide and 15 pixels high. Begin by placing the targets 40 pixels down from the top of the screen.

You will be creating 16 separate IMG elements, one for each target. Each target will have an ID starting with "bar" and ending with the number of the target—the first target will be "bar1" and the last will be "bar16."

To position the first target, place it 40 pixels from the top of the screen. You will want to fit four of these targets horizontally across the screen, so place the first target near the left side of the arena at the horizontal position of 35:

```
<IMG id=bar1    SRC="bar.gif"
           STYLE="position:absolute;top:40;left:35">
```

To position the second target, place it 90 pixels to the right of the first target to provide some space between targets:

```
<IMG id=bar2    SRC="bar.gif"
           STYLE="position:absolute;top:40;left:125">
```

Positioning the third target involves the same process, adding 90 pixels to the right position of the second target:

```
<IMG id=bar3    SRC="bar.gif"
           STYLE="position:absolute;top:40;left:215">
```

Finally, apply this same logic to the fourth target, placing it 90 pixels to the right of the third target.

```
<IMG id=bar4    SRC="bar.gif"
           STYLE="position:absolute;top:40;left:305">
```

Apply this same process to the second, third, and fourth rows of targets. The second row is placed 70 pixels from the top, the third row 100 pixels from the top, and the fourth row 130 pixels from the top. The actual code for the second, third, and fourth rows is shown in the following section, "The Smashout Game Foundation." The first target on the second row, for example, would be placed with the following code:

```
<IMG id=bar5   SRC="bar.gif"
               STYLE="position:absolute;top:70;left:35">
```

Positioning the Player   The next step in building the arena components is to place the player paddle on the screen. You will want to place the paddle near the bottom of the arena. It also makes sense to place the default position of the player paddle halfway into the arena on the horizontal axis:

```
<IMG id=player
    SRC="player.gif" STYLE="position:absolute;top:410;left:210">
```

Positioning the Ball   Finally, you need to place the image for the ball the player will be trying to hit. Place it about halfway between the player paddle and the targets and halfway across the horizontal axis of the arena. Assign the ball a z-index of *-1* to make sure that it always shows up behind other objects in the game:

```
<IMG id=ball SRC="ball.gif"
     STYLE="position:absolute;z-index:-1;top:235;left:210">
</DIV>
```

The Smashout Game Foundation

At this point, you have constructed the entire arena and placed all the visual components that make up the game. Now is a good time to stop and take a look at what you have accomplished so far. Save the following file as "smashout1.htm":

Listing 19.1   Building the Arena

```
01. <HTML>
02. <HEAD>
03. <TITLE>Smashout</TITLE>
04.
05. <BODY>
06.
07. <DIV>
08. <IMG id=top     SRC="top.gif"
09.                 STYLE="position:absolute;top:10;left:10">
10. <IMG id=bottom SRC="top.gif"
11.                 STYLE="position:absolute;top:460;left:10">
12. <IMG id=left    SRC="side.gif"
13.                 STYLE="position:absolute;top:20;left:10">
14. <IMG id=right   SRC="side.gif"
15.                 STYLE="position:absolute;top:20;left:400">
16.
```

```
17. <IMG id=bar1     SRC="bar.gif"
18.                  STYLE="position:absolute;top:40;left:35">
19. <IMG id=bar2     SRC="bar.gif"
20.                  STYLE="position:absolute;top:40;left:125">
21. <IMG id=bar3     SRC="bar.gif"
22.                  STYLE="position:absolute;top:40;left:215">
23. <IMG id=bar4     SRC="bar.gif"
24.                  STYLE="position:absolute;top:40;left:305">
25.
26. <IMG id=bar5     SRC="bar.gif"
27.                  STYLE="position:absolute;top:70;left:35">
28. <IMG id=bar6     SRC="bar.gif"
29.                  STYLE="position:absolute;top:70;left:125">
30. <IMG id=bar7     SRC="bar.gif"
31.                  STYLE="position:absolute;top:70;left:215">
32. <IMG id=bar8     SRC="bar.gif"
33.                  STYLE="position:absolute;top:70;left:305">
34.
35. <IMG id=bar9     SRC="bar.gif"
36.                  STYLE="position:absolute;top:100;left:35">
37. <IMG id=bar10    SRC="bar.gif"
38.                  STYLE="position:absolute;top:100;left:125">
39. <IMG id=bar11    SRC="bar.gif"
40.                  STYLE="position:absolute;top:100;left:215">
41. <IMG id=bar12    SRC="bar.gif"
42.                  STYLE="position:absolute;top:100;left:305">
43.
44. <IMG id=bar13    SRC="bar.gif"
45.                  STYLE="position:absolute;top:130;left:35">
46. <IMG id=bar14    SRC="bar.gif"
47.                  STYLE="position:absolute;top:130;left:125">
48. <IMG id=bar15    SRC="bar.gif"
49.                  STYLE="position:absolute;top:130;left:215">
50. <IMG id=bar16    SRC="bar.gif"
51.                  STYLE="position:absolute;top:130;left:305">
52.
53.
54. <IMG id=player
55.      SRC="player.gif" STYLE="position:absolute;top:410;left:210">
56.
57. <IMG id=ball SRC="ball.gif" STYLE="position:absolute;z-index:
➥-1;top:235;left:210">
58. </DIV>
59.
60. </BODY>
61. </HTML>
```

Part
VI

Ch
19

Figure 19.6 shows the output from smashout1.htm. Although you haven't yet started any animation or logic for the game, you now know exactly what the game is going to look like, and you can see all the core components that make it up.

FIG. 19.6
The Smashout game
arena.

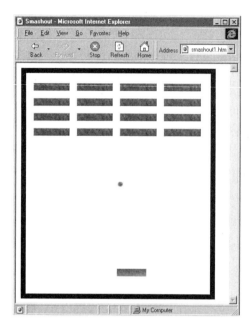

Animating the Smashout Game

Now that you have built the arena and added the player paddle, targets, and ball, it's time to start making the game interactive. You will begin by enabling the user to interact with the player paddle.

Animating the Player Paddle with Mouse Events

To move the paddle whenever the player moves the mouse, you need to incorporate mouse events. To do this, you need to capture mouse events over the entire arena. What is the one element that surrounds the entire arena? The BODY element.

You want the player paddle to move whenever the mouse moves, so you need to capture the *onmousemove* event from the BODY element. You want several things to occur when the mouse is moved, so you need to abstract the code for these actions into a function called *movePlayer()*:

```
<BODY onmousemove="movePlayer()">
```

Now you need to write the *movePlayer()* function. You want the paddle to follow the mouse, but you only want it to follow the mouse along the X axis because the paddle should only move horizontally. To accomplish this, you need to retrieve the X position of the mouse when it moves. This position is available from the *x* property of the *window.event* object available inside the event handler:

```
function movePlayer() {
   var xpos = window.event.x;
   ... The rest of the movePlayer() function ...
}
```

The next thing you need to do is move the player paddle to the X position to where the mouse moves. You can accomplish this by setting the *player.style.posLeft* position to the *xpos* position you receive from the *window.event* object.

You cannot blindly set the X position of the player paddle, however. Why is this? Because you're getting the mouse events from the BODY element, which reports mouse movement across the entire body of the browser window. If you placed the paddle to whatever position is received, the player paddle would move outside of the boundary of the arena.

To prevent this from happening, you want to check first to make sure that the X position you will use to set the player paddle positioning is inside the boundary of the arena:

```
if ((xpos >= 20) && (xpos <= 350))
   player.style.posLeft = xpos;
```

Starting the Game

Because the game will involve animation that the user must respond to, a mechanism is needed for the user to start the game. Without this functionality, the user would be caught off guard because the game would start without player involvement.

To the right of the arena, create a "Start Game" button that actually starts the game. By pressing this button, the user calls the *initialize()* function that starts the code that sets the game in motion:

```
<INPUT TYPE=BUTTON VALUE="Start Game" STYLE="position:absolute;top:10;left:450"
      onclick="initialize()">
```

The next step is to write the *initialize* function. The first thing you will want to do is make sure that the ball is in the correct starting position:

```
function initialize() {

   ball.style.posTop = 235;
   ball.style.posLeft = 210;

}
```

Next, you need to start the ball in motion. Abstract this functionality into a function called *moveBall()* (this function is defined in the next section):

```
moveBall();
```

Getting the Ball Moving

Unlike the movement of the player paddle, the movement of the ball must be controlled entirely by the scripts that make up the Smashout program. You need to pay careful attention to several aspects of the movement of the ball, including:

- Keeping track of the speed and direction of the ball
- Changing the position of the ball to give the illusion of movement
- Having a mechanism that enables the animation of the ball to occur at regularly scheduled intervals, making the animation smooth

First you need a mechanism for keeping track of the speed and direction of the ball. The movement of the ball occurs in two dimensions, so whenever the ball moves, it moves a certain amount in the X direction and a certain amount in the Y direction. Create variables called "dx" and "dy" to hold the amount that the ball moves each time the *moveBall()* function is called:

```
var dx;
var dy;
```

A positive "dx" means that the ball is moving to the right, and a negative "dx" means it is moving to the left. In much the same way, a positive "dy" means that the ball is moving downward, and a negative "dy" means that the ball is moving upward.

Whenever a user starts the game, you want the ball to start moving up and to the left to give the player some time to get ready before the ball starts coming. In addition, you want the ball to move only a few pixels at a time to give the illusion of smooth movement. Therefore, you need to set the "dx" value to −4, causing the ball to move slowly to the left, and the "dy" value to −4, causing the ball to move slowly upward.

Because you want these movement values at the beginning of the game, you need to place them in the *initialize()* function:

```
function initialize() {

   ...

   dx = -4;
   dy = -4;

}
```

Now you're ready to start writing the *moveBall()* function. The main purpose of this function is to move the ball, so start the function by adding the "dy" value to the *posTop* property of the ball, and the "dx" value to the *posLeft* property of the ball:

```
function moveBall() {

   ball.style.posTop  += dy;
   ball.style.posLeft += dx;

}
```

Now, whenever the *moveBall()* function is called, the ball moves slightly in the direction specified by "dx" and "dy." Note that as the code currently stands, however, the *moveBall()* function is called only once.

You could call the *moveBall()* function again inside of the *moveBall()* function itself and this would cause the ball to animate; however, you would have absolutely no control over how often the ball is moved. On a fast machine, the ball would move so quickly you would never see it.

Fortunately, JavaScript provides an alternative in the *setTimeout()* method of the *window* object. The *setTimeout()* method takes three arguments:

- The function to be called
- The amount of time in milliseconds to wait before calling it
- The language in which the function is written

In this case, you want the *moveBall()* function to be called. The amount of time to wait is a little trickier. Testing has shown that the amount of time to wait in *setTimeout()* to get smooth animation is somewhere between 5 and 20 milliseconds.

For this game, select a value midway between this range—13 milliseconds. If you want to speed up the game, lower this value. Conversely, if you want to slow it down, raise the value.

Finally, you want to set the name of the language that the *moveBall()* function is written in to "JavaScript" because that is the scripting language used in the Smashout example. Place this call to *setTimeout()* at the end of the *moveBall()* function:

```
window.setTimeout("moveBall()", 13, "JavaScript");
```

Checking to See if the Ball Hit a Wall

Now you've got the ball moving, but unfortunately, nothing stops it from moving. If you executed the code as it stands right now, the ball would just drift off the upper-left side of the arena and move off the edge of the browser.

To prevent this from happening, you need to have some type of process to make sure the ball is kept in the arena. You can do this by adding code to the *moveBall()* function before the position of the ball is updated.

The first set of circumstances you need to watch out for involves the ball hitting the edges of the arena. You need to check for four occurrences:

- The ball hitting the left side of the arena
- The ball hitting the right side of the arena
- The ball hitting the top of the arena
- The ball hitting the bottom of the arena

To check for these occurrences, you need to have the current X and Y positions of the ball. Create local variables in the *moveBall()* function to retrieve this data:

```
var xp = ball.style.posLeft;
var yp = ball.style.posTop;
```

First, check to see if the ball has hit the left or right side of the screen. In either case, you want to reverse the X direction of the ball. If this doesn't make sense to you, think about it for a moment.

If the ball is traveling to the right and hits the right wall, it then starts moving to the left. Conversely, if the ball travels to the left and hits the left wall, you want it to start traveling to the right. If the ball is to the left of the X position of 20, it has hit the left wall; if it is to the right of the X position of 392, it has hit the right wall, as dictated by the following lines of code:

```
if ((xp < 20) || (xp > 392)) {
    dx = -dx;
}
```

For the second check you will want to see if the ball has hit the top of the screen. You can accomplish this by seeing if the ball's Y position is less than 10. If the ball hits the top of the screen, you will want to reverse its Y direction:

```
else if (yp < 10) {
    dy = -dy;
}
```

Finally, if the ball hits the bottom of the screen, the player loses a life. You will add the logic for keeping track of lives in the next part of the chapter; so for now, you will stop the animation by returning from the function, and making sure that the *moveBall()* function doesn't call the *setTimeout()* method again.

```
else if (yp > 450) {
    return;
}
```

Checking to See if the Ball Hit the Paddle or a Target

At this point, the ball can bounce around the inside of the arena until it hits the bottom of the arena, at which point it stops. The next step is to check to see if the ball has hit an object inside the arena.

You need to check two objects to see if the ball has hit them:

- The player paddle
- A target

The process of checking if a moving object has collided with another object is called *collision detection,* and it can be one of the trickier aspects of game programming. You can use various algorithms to check if two objects are intersecting, but they can get quite complicated. In fact, if you had to do collision detection by hand, programming the Smashout game would be beyond the scope of this book.

Luckily, Dynamic HTML comes to the rescue here with a method contained in the document object called *elementFromPoint()*. This method enables you to find out which HTML element is present at any given point. By using the X and Y positions of the ball as arguments to the *elementFromPoint()* method, you can then find out with what element the ball is intersecting.

At this time, you may be thinking that the element residing at the point where the ball is located is the ball itself. Remember, however, that you set the z-index of the ball to *–1*, making sure it is behind all other elements. Therefore, the element returned by *elementFromPoint()*

will be the element with which the ball collides. You will use the "xp" and "yp" variables that you have already defined in the *moveBall()* function to pass to the *elementFromPoint()* method:

```
var hit = document.elementFromPoint(xp,yp);
```

First, you want to check to make sure that an element was returned into the "hit" variable. You can check this by seeing if the contents of "hit" are null:

```
if (hit != null) {
```

Next, you will want to do the next check, which is to see if the player paddle was hit. If the ID of the element the ball has hit is the player paddle, the Y direction of the ball is reversed:

```
    if (hit.id == "player") {
        dy = -dy;
    }
```

Next, you want to check to see if the ball hit one of the targets. The most straightforward method of checking this is to see if the ID of the element the ball has hit is one of the target IDs. This method, however, has one big disadvantage: checking all 16 IDs would be relatively slow, and it's important to keep the amount of code in the *moveBall()* function as small as possible because it will be repeated many times a second.

Instead, you can do something a bit trickier. The ID is not the only aspect of the target that is different from all the other elements in the arena. The target is the only element on the page that is 75 pixels wide. Therefore, you can check to see if the width of the element hit is 75 pixels. If it is, you know that a target has been hit.

If a target has been hit, you want to do two things. First, the target should be removed from the screen by setting its display attribute to "none." Second, the Y direction of the ball should be reversed:

```
else if (hit.width == 75) {
        hit.style.display = "none";
        dy = -dy;
    }
```

The Foundation for Animating the Smashout Game

At this point, you have enough code that the game is actually playable. Save the following code as "smashout2.htm":

Listing 19.2   Animating the Smashout Game

```
001. <HTML>
002. <HEAD>
003. <TITLE>Smashout</TITLE>
004.
005. <SCRIPT LANGUAGE="JavaScript">
006. var dx;
007. var dy;
```

continues

Part

VI

Ch

19

Listing 19.2   Continued

```
008.
009. function initialize() {
010.
011.     dx = -4;
012.     dy = -4;
013.     ball.style.posTop = 235;
014.     ball.style.posLeft = 210;
015.     moveBall();
016.
017. }
018.
019. function moveBall() {
020.     var xp = ball.style.posLeft;
021.     var yp = ball.style.posTop;
022.     var hit = document.elementFromPoint(xp,yp);
023.
024.     if ((xp < 20) || (xp > 392)) {
025.         dx = -dx;
026.     } else if (yp < 10) {
027.         dy = -dy;
028.     } else if (yp > 450) {
029.         return;
030.     }
031.
032.     if (hit != null) {
033.         if (hit.id == "player") {
034.             dy = -dy;
035.         } else if (hit.width == 75) {
036.             hit.style.display = "none";
037.             dy = -dy;
038.         }
039.     }
040.
041.     ball.style.posTop  += dy;
042.     ball.style.posLeft += dx;
043.
044.     window.setTimeout("moveBall()", 13, "JavaScript");
045. }
046.
047. function movePlayer() {
048.     var xpos = window.event.x;
049.     if ((xpos >= 20) && (xpos <= 350))
050.         player.style.posLeft = xpos;
051. }
052.
053. </SCRIPT>
054. </HEAD>
055. <BODY onmousemove="movePlayer()">
056.
057. <DIV>
058. <IMG id=top     SRC="top.gif"
059.                 STYLE="position:absolute;top:10;left:10">
060. <IMG id=bottom SRC="top.gif"
```

```
061.                     STYLE="position:absolute;top:460;left:10">
062. <IMG id=left   SRC="side.gif"
063.                     STYLE="position:absolute;top:20;left:10">
064. <IMG id=right  SRC="side.gif"
065.                     STYLE="position:absolute;top:20;left:400">
066.
067. <IMG id=bar1   SRC="bar.gif"
068.                     STYLE="position:absolute;top:40;left:35">
069. <IMG id=bar2   SRC="bar.gif"
070.                     STYLE="position:absolute;top:40;left:125">
071. <IMG id=bar3   SRC="bar.gif"
072.                     STYLE="position:absolute;top:40;left:215">
073. <IMG id=bar4   SRC="bar.gif"
074.                     STYLE="position:absolute;top:40;left:305">
075.
076. <IMG id=bar5   SRC="bar.gif"
077.                     STYLE="position:absolute;top:70;left:35">
078. <IMG id=bar6   SRC="bar.gif"
079.                     STYLE="position:absolute;top:70;left:125">
080. <IMG id=bar7   SRC="bar.gif"
081.                     STYLE="position:absolute;top:70;left:215">
082. <IMG id=bar8   SRC="bar.gif"
083.                     STYLE="position:absolute;top:70;left:305">
084.
085. <IMG id=bar9   SRC="bar.gif"
086.                     STYLE="position:absolute;top:100;left:35">
087. <IMG id=bar10  SRC="bar.gif"
088.                     STYLE="position:absolute;top:100;left:125">
089. <IMG id=bar11  SRC="bar.gif"
090.                     STYLE="position:absolute;top:100;left:215">
091. <IMG id=bar12  SRC="bar.gif"
092.                     STYLE="position:absolute;top:100;left:305">
093.
094. <IMG id=bar13  SRC="bar.gif"
095.                     STYLE="position:absolute;top:130;left:35">
096. <IMG id=bar14  SRC="bar.gif"
097.                     STYLE="position:absolute;top:130;left:125">
098. <IMG id=bar15  SRC="bar.gif"
099.                     STYLE="position:absolute;top:130;left:215">
100. <IMG id=bar16  SRC="bar.gif"
101.                     STYLE="position:absolute;top:130;left:305">
102.
103.
104. <IMG id=player
105.      SRC="player.gif" STYLE="position:absolute;top:410;left:210">
106.
107. <IMG id=ball SRC="ball.gif" STYLE="position:absolute;z-index:
➥-1;top:235;left:210">
108. </DIV>
109.
110. <INPUT TYPE=BUTTON VALUE="Start Game"
➥STYLE="position:absolute;top:10;left:450"
111.        onclick="initialize()">
112.
113. </BODY>
114. </HTML>
```

Try playing the game for a while. Start the game by pressing the Start Game button. Most of the mechanics for the game are present, but notice what happens when the ball hits the bottom of the screen—the game stops (see fig. 19.7). You will add the logic to take care of this type of occurrence in the next section of the chapter.

FIG. 19.7
Smashout stops when the ball hits the bottom of the arena.

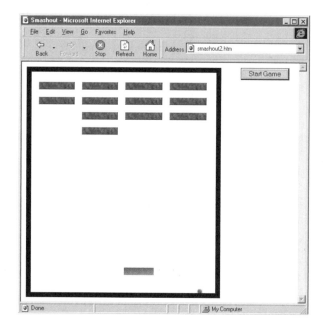

Adding Game Logic

Now that you've got the basic functionality of the game implemented, you need to add more logic to the game to tell the program what to do in the following circumstances:

- When the player loses a life
- When the player wins the game

Losing a Life and Possibly the Game

For convention's sake, the player will start with 3 lives. To keep track of the number of player lives, you will use a global variable in the script called "lives":

```
var lives;
```

Next, you want the player to know how many lives they have at any given time. Therefore, you need to place a SPAN of text listing the number of lives to the right of the arena. This span will be given the ID of "show_lives" so you'll be able to change it dynamically:

```
<B><SPAN id=show_lives STYLE="position:absolute;top:50;left:450">
➥Lives:</SPAN></B><BR>
```

When will you want to set the number of lives that the player has? Whenever the player starts the game. The game started by calling the *initialize()* function, so you will set the value of lives to 3 there:

```
lives = 3;
```

You will want to let the player know he has 3 lives at the beginning of the game, so you need to set the *innerHTML* property of the *show_lives* element to *"Lives: 3"* in the *initialize()* function as well. This is done by appending the number of lives to the "Lives: " string with the '+' operator:

```
show_lives.innerHTML = "Lives: " + lives;
```

Now, how does the player lose a life? Whenever the ball hits the bottom of the arena. To add this functionality, have the *moveBall()* function call a function called *loseLife()* whenever the ball drifts off the bottom of the arena:

```
if (yp > 450) {
   loseLife(); // Call loseLife()
   return;
}
```

Now you need to define the *loseLife()* function. The first thing you need to do is reduce the "lives" variable by 1. Next, you will want to update the "Lives" indicator:

```
function loseLife() {

   lives—;
   show_lives.innerHTML = "Lives: " + lives;

}
```

Now the player starts with a new life. What needs to be done? First, reset the position of the ball to its original starting place as follows:

```
ball.style.posTop = 235;
ball.style.posLeft = 210;
```

Next, you need to check to see if the player has any lives left. If he does, you will want to start the ball moving again with a call to the *moveBall()* function. If the player has exhausted his lives, however, the game should inform the player that the game is over. The ball should not start moving again (see fig. 19.8):

```
if (lives > 0) {
   moveBall();
} else {
   alert("Game Over");
}
```

Part

VI

Ch

19

FIG. 19.8

Alerting the player that the game is over.

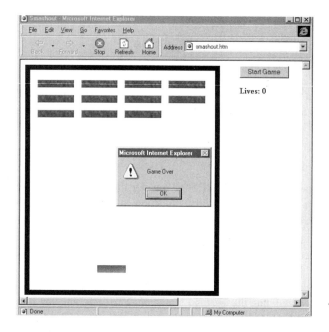

Winning the Game

The player wins the game by eliminating all the targets. Therefore, you need to provide a mechanism that keeps track of the number of targets left in the game. Begin by defining a global variable called "targets":

```
var targets;
```

Next, in the *initialize()* function, set the number of targets to 16 because 16 targets are always used at the beginning of any game:

```
targets = 16;
```

Next, you need to subtract 1 from "targets" in the *moveBall()* function if a target has been hit. In addition, if no targets remain, a message box should pop up telling the user, "You win!" (see fig. 19.9):

```
} else if (hit.width == 75) {

    .... The rest of the code for hitting a target ...

    targets—;
    if (targets == 0) {
        alert("You Win!");
        return;
    }

}
```

FIG. 19.9

Winning the game.

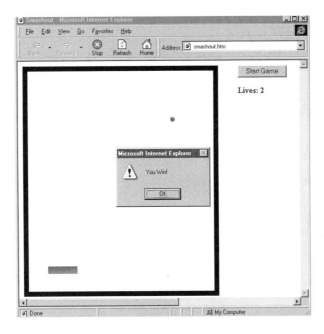

Finally, when the game is restarted, you need to make sure that all the targets are shown. You can accomplish this by adding a call to *showTargets()* inside the *initialize()* function:

```
showTargets();
```

To define the *showTargets()* function, all you need to do is set the STYLE *display* property of each of the targets to "", which tells the browser to make them visible:

Part

VI

Ch

19

Listing 19.3   Making the Targets Visible Again

```
01. function showTargets() {
02.
03.     bar1.style.display = "";
04.     bar2.style.display = "";
05.     bar3.style.display = "";
06.     bar4.style.display = "";
07.     bar5.style.display = "";
08.     bar6.style.display = "";
09.     bar7.style.display = "";
10.     bar8.style.display = "";
11.     bar9.style.display = "";
12.     bar10.style.display = "";
13.     bar11.style.display = "";
14.     bar12.style.display = "";
15.     bar13.style.display = "";
16.     bar14.style.display = "";
17.     bar15.style.display = "";
18.     bar16.style.display = "";
19.
20. }
```

The Final Page!

Believe it or not, you're done programming Smashout! Here's the final version of the code (save this file as "smashout.htm"):

Listing 19.4   The Final Code for Smashout

```
001. <HTML>
002. <HEAD>
003. <TITLE>Smashout</TITLE>
004.
005. <SCRIPT LANGUAGE="JavaScript">
006. var targets;
007. var lives;
008. var dx;
009. var dy;
010.
011. function initialize() {
012.
013.    targets = 16;
014.    lives = 3;
015.    dx = -4;
016.    dy = -4;
017.    showTargets();
018.    ball.style.posTop = 235;
019.    ball.style.posLeft = 210;
020.    show_lives.innerHTML = "Lives: " + lives;
021.    moveBall();
022.
023. }
024.
025. function showTargets() {
026.
027.    bar1.style.display = "";
028.    bar2.style.display = "";
029.    bar3.style.display = "";
030.    bar4.style.display = "";
031.    bar5.style.display = "";
032.    bar6.style.display = "";
033.    bar7.style.display = "";
034.    bar8.style.display = "";
035.    bar9.style.display = "";
036.    bar10.style.display = "";
037.    bar11.style.display = "";
038.    bar12.style.display = "";
039.    bar13.style.display = "";
040.    bar14.style.display = "";
041.    bar15.style.display = "";
042.    bar16.style.display = "";
043.
044. }
045.
046. function moveBall() {
047.    var xp = ball.style.posLeft;
```

```
048.     var yp = ball.style.posTop;
049.     var hit = document.elementFromPoint(xp,yp);
050.
051.     if ((xp < 20) || (xp > 392)) {
052.         dx = -dx;
053.     } else if (yp < 10) {
054.         dy = -dy;
055.     } else if (yp > 450) {
056.         loseLife();
057.         return;
058.     }
059.
060.     if (hit != null) {
061.         if (hit.id == "player") {
062.             dy = -dy;
063.         } else if (hit.width == 75) {
064.             hit.style.display = "none";
065.             dy = -dy;
066.             targets--;
067.             if (targets == 0) {
068.                 alert("You Win!");
069.                 return;
070.             }
071.         }
072.     }
073.     ball.style.posTop  += dy;
074.     ball.style.posLeft += dx;
075.
076.     window.setTimeout("moveBall()", 13, "JavaScript");
077. }
078.
079. function loseLife() {
080.
081.     lives--;
082.     show_lives.innerHTML = "Lives: " + lives;
083.
084.     ball.style.posTop = 235;
085.     ball.style.posLeft = 210;
086.
087.     if (lives > 0) {
088.         moveBall();
089.     } else {
090.         alert("Game Over");
091.     }
092. }
093.
094. function movePlayer() {
095.     var xpos = window.event.x;
096.     if ((xpos >= 20) && (xpos <= 350))
097.         player.style.posLeft = xpos;
098. }
099.
100. </SCRIPT>
101. </HEAD>
102. <BODY onmousemove="movePlayer()">
```

Part
VI

Ch
19

continues

Listing 19.4   Continued

```
103.
104. <DIV>
105. <IMG id=top     SRC="top.gif"
106.                  STYLE="position:absolute;top:10;left:10">
107. <IMG id=bottom SRC="top.gif"
108.                  STYLE="position:absolute;top:460;left:10">
109. <IMG id=left    SRC="side.gif"
110.                  STYLE="position:absolute;top:20;left:10">
111. <IMG id=right   SRC="side.gif"
112.                  STYLE="position:absolute;top:20;left:400">
113.
114. <IMG id=bar1    SRC="bar.gif"
115.                  STYLE="position:absolute;top:40;left:35">
116. <IMG id=bar2    SRC="bar.gif"
117.                  STYLE="position:absolute;top:40;left:125">
118. <IMG id=bar3    SRC="bar.gif"
119.                  STYLE="position:absolute;top:40;left:215">
120. <IMG id=bar4    SRC="bar.gif"
121.                  STYLE="position:absolute;top:40;left:305">
122.
123. <IMG id=bar5    SRC="bar.gif"
124.                  STYLE="position:absolute;top:70;left:35">
125. <IMG id=bar6    SRC="bar.gif"
126.                  STYLE="position:absolute;top:70;left:125">
127. <IMG id=bar7    SRC="bar.gif"
128.                  STYLE="position:absolute;top:70;left:215">
129. <IMG id=bar8    SRC="bar.gif"
130.                  STYLE="position:absolute;top:70;left:305">
131.
132. <IMG id=bar9    SRC="bar.gif"
133.                  STYLE="position:absolute;top:100;left:35">
134. <IMG id=bar10   SRC="bar.gif"
135.                  STYLE="position:absolute;top:100;left:125">
136. <IMG id=bar11   SRC="bar.gif"
137.                  STYLE="position:absolute;top:100;left:215">
138. <IMG id=bar12   SRC="bar.gif"
139.                  STYLE="position:absolute;top:100;left:305">
140.
141. <IMG id=bar13   SRC="bar.gif"
142.                  STYLE="position:absolute;top:130;left:35">
143. <IMG id=bar14   SRC="bar.gif"
144.                  STYLE="position:absolute;top:130;left:125">
145. <IMG id=bar15   SRC="bar.gif"
146.                  STYLE="position:absolute;top:130;left:215">
147. <IMG id=bar16   SRC="bar.gif"
148.                  STYLE="position:absolute;top:130;left:305">
149.
150.
151. <IMG id=player
152.     SRC="player.gif" STYLE="position:absolute;top:410;left:210">
153.
154. <IMG id=ball SRC="ball.gif" STYLE="position:absolute;z-index:
➡-1;top:235;left:210">
```

```
155. </DIV>
156.
157. <INPUT TYPE=BUTTON VALUE="Start Game"
➥STYLE="position:absolute;top:10;left:450"
158.       onclick="initialize()">
159. <B><SPAN id=show_lives STYLE="position:absolute;top:50;left:450">Lives:
➥</SPAN></B><BR>
160.
161. </BODY>
162. </HTML>
```

From Here...

This chapter demonstrated how to build a relatively complex video game from the ground up. All the basic requirements are there, but you might want to try adding new features to the game for experience. Here are a few ideas to try adding to the Smashout game:

- Keep track of the number of targets the player has hit during the game through a scoring algorithm.

- Increase the speed of the ball every time the player finishes a level.

- Use an animated GIF for either the ball or some of the targets, which would enhance the visual appeal of the game.

- Add special targets that do different things when the player hits them. For instance, create a target that when hit causes a second ball to appear.

- Improve the bounce algorithm. In the current game the movement of the ball is predictable. Add some randomness to the bouncing of the ball to make its movement more erratic.

You certainly have come a long way throughout this book. You started by learning the basics of programming and layout in Dynamic HTML. Along the way you learned many of the important aspects of Dynamic HTML, such as dynamic style, dynamic content, multimedia, and data binding.

Hopefully the last few chapters have given you insights into how you can use the Dynamic HTML concepts you have learned to make your web pages much more appealing, effective, and interactive. Here's hoping you're able to go a long way with Dynamic HTML. A whole new world is waiting to be explored.

Now that you've taken an in-depth look at Dynamic HTML, you probably want to start building Dynamic HTML programs of your own. Appendix G, "Plug-and-Play Dynamic HTML" will make this easier by presenting a great deal of code that you can easily cut-and-paste into your own Dynamic HTML programs.

Appendixes

HTML Elements and Attributes

There are a number of HTML tags that are used in conjunction with Dynamic HTML to create interactive pages and applications. The sections that follow give a complete rundown of the HTML tags that can be used with Dynamic HTML, their functionality, the values they take (if any), and a brief code example to show how they are implemented.

<!-- -->

The <!-- and --> are the beginning and closing markers for HTML comments. Comments are preceded with <!--, which instructs the browser to ignore any text until it reaches the terminating -->.

```
<!-- This is an HTML comment
this <B>tag</B> will be ignored -->
```

<!DOCTYPE>

The <!DOCTYPE> tag specifies the type of information enclosed in a document, including the markup language and the version number. Because the HTML specification is constantly being updated (with version 4.0 now in the works), it's a good idea to use this tag so that the browser will always render your pages correctly.

```
<!DOCTYPE HTML PUBLIC "-//W3C//DTD HTML 3.2//EN">
```

<A>

The anchor tag, <A>, denotes a hypertext link. It requires the specification of a NAME or HREF location. The anchor tag accepts the following attributes and values:

ACCESSKEY=*key*

CLASS=*classname*

DATAFLD=*colname*

DATASRC=*#ID*

HREF=*url*

ID=*value*

LANG=*language*

LANGUAGE=JAVASCRIPT | JSCRIPT | VBSCRIPT | VBS

METHODS=*http-method*

NAME=*name*

REL="stylesheet"

REV="stylesheet"

STYLE=*css1-properties*

TARGET=*window_name* | **_blank** | **_parent** | **_self** | **_top**

TITLE=*text*

URL=*url*

```
<A HREF="http://www.myserver.com">
```

<ADDRESS>

The <ADDRESS> tag specifies the address of a page's author or party responsible for the page's management. Text enclosed in the tag will be italic. The <ADDRESS> tag accepts the following attributes and values:

>**CLASS**=*classname*
>
>**ID**=*value*
>
>**LANG**=*language*
>
>**LANGUAGE**=**JAVASCRIPT** | **JSCRIPT** | **VBSCRIPT** | **VBS**
>
>**STYLE**=*css1-properties*
>
>**TITLE**=*text*

```
<ADDRESS>dgublran@bluemarble.net</ADDRESS>
```

<APPLET>

The <APPLET> tag places an executable on a web page. These executables may currently be in the form of ActiveX or Java applets; however, the tag is not limited to these forms. The <APPLET> tag accepts the following attributes and values:

>**ALIGN**=**ABSBOTTOM** | **ABSMIDDLE** | **BASELINE** | **BOTTOM** | **LEFT** | **MIDDLE** | **RIGHT** | **TEXTTOP** | **TOP**
>
>**ALT**=*text*
>
>**CLASS**=*classname*
>
>**CODE**=*filename*
>
>**CODEBASE**=*url*
>
>**DATAFLD**=*colname*
>
>**DATASRC**=*#ID*
>
>**HEIGHT**=*n*
>
>**HSPACE**=*n*
>
>**ID**=*value*
>
>**NAME**=*name*
>
>**SRC**=*url*
>
>**STYLE**=*css1-properties*
>
>**TITLE**=*text*
>
>**VSPACE**=*n*
>
>**WIDTH**=*n*

```
<APPLET CODE="myjava.class"
NAME="myApplet"
```

```
        WIDTH=500
        HEIGHT=500>
</APPLET>
```

<AREA>

The <AREA> tag specifies the shape of a "target" area on a client-side image map.

The <AREA> tag accepts the following attributes and values:

ALT=*text*

CLASS=*classname*

COORDS=*coordinates*

HREF=*url*

ID=*value*

LANG=*language*

LANGUAGE=JAVASCRIPT | JSCRIPT | VBSCRIPT | VBS

NOHREF

SHAPE=CIRC | CIRCLE | POLY | POLYGON | RECT | RECTANGLE

STYLE=*css1-properties*

TARGET=*window_name* | **_blank** | **_parent** | **_self** | **_top**

TITLE=*text*

```
<AREA SHAPE="RECT" COORDS="0, 0, 75, 125" HREF="http://www.myserver.com">
```

<B>

The <B> tag denotes bold text.

```
<B>This type will be displayed in boldface</B>
```

<BASE>

The <BASE> tag specifies the base URL for a document. The <BASE> tag accepts the following attributes and values:

CLASS=*classname*

HREF=*url*

ID=*value*

LANG=*language*

TARGET=*window_name* | **_blank** | **_parent** | **_self** | **_top**

TITLE=*text*

```
<BASE HREF="http://www.myserver.com/thisdoc.html">
```

<BASEFONT>

The <BASEFONT> tag specifies a default typeface for rendering a document. The
<BASEFONT> tag accepts the following attributes and values:

> **CLASS**=*classname*
>
> **COLOR**=*color*
>
> **FACE**=*font*
>
> **ID**=*value*
>
> **LANG**=*language*
>
> **SIZE**=*n*
>
> **TITLE**=*text*

```
<BASEFONT FACE="Times" SIZE=3>
```

<BGSOUND>

The <BGSOUND> tag enables you to specify a background soundtrack for a page. The
<BGSOUND> tag accepts the following attributes and values:

> **BALANCE**=*n*
>
> **CLASS**=*classname*
>
> **ID**=*value*
>
> **LANG**=*language*
>
> **LOOP**=*n*
>
> **SRC**=*url*
>
> **TITLE**=*text*
>
> **VOLUME**=*n*

```
<BGSOUND SRC="http://www.myserver.com/mysound.loud">
```

<BIG>

The <BIG> tag specifies that the font should be displayed "bigger" in relation to the current
font. The <BIG> tag accepts the following attributes and values:

> **CLASS**=*classname*
>
> **ID**=*value*
>
> **LANG**=*language*
>
> **LANGUAGE=JAVASCRIPT | JSCRIPT | VBSCRIPT | VBS**
>
> **STYLE**=*css1-properties*
>
> **TITLE**=*text*

```
If this text is normal, then <BIG>this text is bigger!</BIG>
```

<BLOCKQUOTE>

The <BLOCKQUOTE> tag enables you to specify a quotation that will be offset from the regular text. The <BLOCKQUOTE> tag accepts the following attributes and values:

CLASS=*classname*

ID=*value*

LANG=*language*

LANGUAGE=**JAVASCRIPT** | **JSCRIPT** | **VBSCRIPT** | **VBS**

STYLE=*css1-properties*

TITLE=*text*

Shakespeare didn't write:

```
<BLOCKQUOTE>To code or not to code,
That is never a question.</BLOCKQUOTE>
```

<BODY>

The <BODY> tag specifies the beginning and ending of the main body section of an HTML document. The <BODY> tag accepts the following attributes and values:

ACCESSKEY=*string*

ALINK=*color*

BACKGROUND=*url*

BGCOLOR=*color*

BGPROPERTIES=FIXED

BOTTOMMARGIN=*pixels*

CLASS=*classname*

ID=*value*

LANG=*language*

LANGUAGE=**JAVASCRIPT** | **JSCRIPT** | **VBSCRIPT** | **VBS**

LEFTMARGIN=*pixels*

LINK=*color*

RIGHTMARGIN=*pixels*

SCROLL=**YES** | **NO**

STYLE=*css1-properties*

TEXT=*color*

TITLE=*string*

TOPMARGIN=*n*

VLINK=*color*

```
<HTML>
<BODY BACKGROUND="mybkgd.gif">
</BODY>
</HTML>
```


The <BR> tag forces a line break.

```
This is<BR>
an abnormal line break.
```

<BUTTON>

The <BUTTON> tag displays a button on the page with the label specified between the start and end tags. The <BUTTON> tag accepts the following attributes and values:

ACCESSKEY=*string*

CLASS=*classname*

DATAFLD=*colname*

DATAFORMATAS=HTML | TEXT

DATASRC=#*ID*

DISABLED

ID=*value*

LANG=*language*

LANGUAGE=JAVASCRIPT | JSCRIPT | VBSCRIPT | VBS

STYLE=*css1-properties*

TITLE=*text*

TYPE=BUTTON | RESET | SUBMIT

```
<BUTTON TYPE="RESET">Reset me!</BUTTON>
```

<CAPTION>

The <CAPTION> tag specifies a caption for a TABLE element. The <CAPTION> tag accepts the following attributes and values:

ALIGN=BOTTOM | CENTER | LEFT | RIGHT | TOP

CLASS=*classname*

ID=*value*

LANG=*language*

LANGUAGE=JAVASCRIPT | JSCRIPT | VBSCRIPT | VBS

STYLE=*css1-properties*

TITLE=*text*

VALIGN=BOTTOM | TOP

```
<TABLE>
<CAPTION VALIGN=BOTTOM>
The table above shows HTML tags.
</CAPTION>
...
</TABLE>
```

<CENTER>

The <CENTER> tag aligns enclosed text and elements on the center of the page.

```
<CENTER>This text will be centered.</CENTER>
```

<CITE>

The <CITE> tag specifies a citation to reference material. The text is displayed italic.

```
Everyone will be using DHTML soon.
<CITE>Where did you go today?</CITE> By Gil Bates
```

<CODE>

The <CODE> tag specifies that the enclosed text is a code listing or code fragment. The text is displayed in a small, fixed-width font.

```
<CODE>
    myfunction(){
        var foo, bar;
        bar= foo*1;
        alert("This doesn't do anything!");
    }
</CODE>
```

<COL>

The <COL> tag specifies the column parameters for TABLE elements. The <COL> tag accepts the following attributes and values:

ALIGN=CENTER | LEFT | RIGHT

CLASS=*classname*

ID=*value*

> **SPAN**=*n*
> **STYLE**=*css1-properties*
> **TITLE**=*text*
> **VALIGN=BASELINE | BOTTOM | MIDDLE | TOP**
> **WIDTH**=*n*

```
<TABLE>
<COL ALIGN=CENTER>
<TR>
<TD>This is centered</TD>
</TR>
</TABLE>
```

<COLGROUP>

The <COLGROUP> tag groups together mulitple <COL> definitions. The <COLGROUP> tag accepts the following attributes and values:

> **ALIGN=CENTER | LEFT | RIGHT**
> **CLASS**=*classname*
> **ID**=*value*
> **SPAN**=*n*
> **STYLE**=*css1-properties*
> **TITLE**=*text*
> **VALIGN=BASELINE**

```
<TABLE>
<COLGROUP SPAN=2 ALIGN=CENTER>
<TR>
<TD>Column One</TD>
<TD>Column Two</TD>
</TR>
</TABLE>
```

<DD>

The <DD> tag denotes the definition in a definition list. It is usually indented from the definition list. Refer to the sections on the <DT> and <DL> tags for an HTML code example.

<DFN>

The <DFN> tag marks the first instance of a term's definition, to be referenced later in the text.

```
<DFN>DHTML is Dynamic HTML, a variant of HTML</DFN>
```

<DIR>

The <DIR> tag denotes a directory listing. Items are specified with the <LI> tag.

```
<DIR>
<LI>Item One
<LI>Item Two
</DIR>
```

<DIV>

The <DIV> tag creates container elements that can be treated as a single entity with Dynamic HTML or CSS. The <DIV> tag accepts the following attributes and values:

ALIGN=CENTER | LEFT | RIGHT

CLASS=classname

DATAFLD=colname

DATAFORMATAS=HTML | TEXT

DATASRC=#ID

ID=value

LANG=language

LANGUAGE=JAVASCRIPT | JSCRIPT | VBSCRIPT | VBS

STYLE=css1-properties

TITLE=text

```
<DIV id="Container1" STYLE="color: red">
All of the tags.
<B>and text</B>
Within the <PRE>DIV</PRE> tag are<BR>
treated as one element.
</DIV>
```

<DL>

The <DL> tag denotes a definition list, or a list of terms and their accompanying definitions. The <DL> tag accepts the following attributes and values:

```
<DL>
<DT>Dynamic HTML
<DD>A mixture of HTML and scripting.
<DT>Microsoft
<DD>One company creating versions of Dynamic HTML
</DL>
```

<DT>

The <DT> tag denotes a definition term for inclusion in a definition list. Refer to the previous section on the <DL> tag for an HTML code example featuring the <DT> tag.

<EM>

The <EM> tag specifies emphasis. Most browsers render the emphasis tag in italic.

```
<EM>This will be italicized.</EM>
```

<EMBED>

The <EMBED> tag embeds documents or applications of any type into a web page. If the embedded element requires a separate viewer, the user must have that viewer installed to correctly view the document. The <EMBED> tag accepts the following attributes and values:

ALIGN=ABSBOTTOM | ABSMIDDLE | BASELINE | BOTTOM | LEFT | MIDDLE | RIGHT | TEXTTOP | TOP

ALT=*text*

CLASS=*classname*

CODE=*filename*

CODEBASE=*url*

HEIGHT=*n*

HSPACE=*n*

ID=*value*

NAME=*name*

SRC=*url*

STYLE=*css1-properties*

TITLE=*text*

VSPACE=*n*

WIDTH=*n*

```
<EMBED CODE="myjava.class"
NAME="myApplet"
     WIDTH=500
     HEIGHT=500
     ALT="Your browser doesn't support the EMBED tag">
</EMBED>
```

<FONT>

The <FONT> tag specifies font information in a document. The <FONT> tag accepts the following attributes and values:

CLASS=*classname*

COLOR=*color*

FACE=*font*

ID=*value*

LANG=*language*

LANGUAGE=JAVASCRIPT | JSCRIPT | VBSCRIPT | VBS

SIZE=*n*

STYLE=*css1-properties*

TITLE=*text*

```
<FONT SIZE=4 COLOR=RED>
This text is small and red.
</FONT>
```

<FORM>

The <FORM> tag specifies the information to construct forms on the HTML page. The <FORM> tag accepts the following attributes and values:

ACTION=*url*

CLASS=*classname*

ENCTYPE=*encoding*

ID=*value*

LANG=*language*

LANGUAGE=JAVASCRIPT | JSCRIPT | VBSCRIPT | VBS

METHOD=GET | POST

NAME=*name*

STYLE=*css1-properties*

TARGET=*window_name* | **_blank** | **_parent** | **_self** | **_top**

TITLE=*text*

```
<FORM ACTION="http://www.myserver.com/find.cgi" METHOD="POST">
The form definition would appear here.
</FORM>
```

<FRAME>

The <FRAME> tag defines an individual FRAME element within a FRAMESET. The <FRAME> tag accepts the following attributes and values:

> **BORDERCOLOR**=*color*
>
> **CLASS**=*classname*
>
> **DATAFLD**=*colname*
>
> **DATASRC**=*#ID*
>
> **FRAMEBORDER**=**NO | YES | 0 | 1**
>
> **HEIGHT**=*n*
>
> **ID**=*value*
>
> **LANG**=*language*
>
> **LANGUAGE**=**JAVASCRIPT | JSCRIPT | VBSCRIPT | VBS**
>
> **MARGINHEIGHT**=*pixels*
>
> **MARGINWIDTH**=*pixels*
>
> **NAME**=*window_name* | **_blank** | **_parent** | **_self** | **_top**
>
> **NORESIZE**=**NORESIZE | RESIZE**
>
> **SCROLLING**=**AUTO | NO | YES**
>
> **SRC**=*url*
>
> **TITLE**=*text*
>
> **WIDTH**=*n*

```
<FRAME FRAMEBORDER=2 SRC="http://www.myserver.com/myframe.html">
```

<FRAMESET>

The <FRAMESET> tag specifies information about the number and type of frames in a document. The <FRAMESET> tag can also be used to create frames within frames. The <FRAMESET> tag accepts the following attributes and values:

> **BORDER**=*pixels*
>
> **BORDERCOLOR**=*color*
>
> **CLASS**=*classname*
>
> **COLS**=*col-widths*
>
> **FRAMEBORDER**=**NO | YES | 0 | 1**
>
> **FRAMESPACING**=*spacing*
>
> **ID**=*value*
>
> **LANG**=*language*

App

A

LANGUAGE=JAVASCRIPT | JSCRIPT | VBSCRIPT | VBS

ROWS=*row-heights*

TITLE=*text*

```
<FRAMESET COLS="50%, 50%">
<FRAME SRC="http://www.myserver.com/frameone.html">
<FRAME SRC="http://www.myserver.com/frametwo.html">
</FRAMESET>
```

<HEAD>

The <HEAD> tag specifies the header section of an HTML document. Scripts are often placed in the header to ensure they are loaded before the remainder of the page content.

```
<HTML>
<HEAD>
<TITLE>My Page</TITLE>
</HEAD>
<BODY>
Page info
</BODY>
</HTML>
```

<H1>, <H2>, <H3>, <H4>, <H5>, <H6>

The <H1>…<H6> tags specify headlines ranging from the largest size, <H1>, to the smallest, <H6>. The headlines also include a default carriage return.

```
<H1>Level One is the largest headline</H1>
<H3>This is a level 3 headline, and is smaller</H3>
```

<HR>

The <HR> tag draws a horizontal rule line on the page, and can be varied in alignment, width, and thickness. An URL can also be used to specify an image as the rule line. The <HR> tag accepts the following attributes and values:

ALIGN=CENTER | LEFT | RIGHT

CLASS=*classname*

COLOR=*color*

ID=*value*

LANG=*language*

LANGUAGE=JAVASCRIPT | JSCRIPT | VBSCRIPT | VBS

NOSHADE

SIZE=*n*

SRC=*url*

STYLE=*css1-properties*

TITLE=*text*

WIDTH=*n*

```
<HR ALIGN=CENTER WIDTH="75%">
The above line is 75% of the window and centered.
```

<HTML>

The <HTML> tag specifies that the document contents are defined using the Hypertext Markup Language.

```
<HTML>
This is an HTML Document.
</HTML>
```

<I>

The <I> tag specifies italicized text.

```
<I>This text is italicized</I>
```

<IMG>

The <IMG> tag inserts a graphic element on the page. The <IMG> tag accepts the following attributes and values:

ALIGN=ABSBOTTOM | ABSMIDDLE | BASELINE | BOTTOM | LEFT | MIDDLE | RIGHT | TEXTTOP | TOP

ALT=*text*

BORDER=*n*

CLASS=*classname*

DATAFLD=*colname*

DATASRC=*#ID*

DYNSRC=*url*

HEIGHT=*n*

ISMAP

LANG=*language*

LANGUAGE=JAVASCRIPT | JSCRIPT | VBSCRIPT | VBS

LOOP=*n*

LOWSRC=*url*

NAME=*name*

SRC=*url*

STYLE=*css1-properties*

TITLE=*text*

```
<IMG SRC="some-picture.gif">
```

<INPUT>

The <INPUT> tag defines an input area on a form to accept user data entry. The <INPUT> tag accepts the following attributes and values:

ACCESSKEY=*key*

CLASS=*classname*

DISABLED

ID=*value*

LANG=*language*

LANGUAGE=JAVASCRIPT | JSCRIPT | VBSCRIPT | VBS

MAXLENGTH=*n*

NAME=*name*

READONLY

SIZE=*n*

SRC=*url*

STYLE=*css1-properties*

TABINDEX=*n*

TITLE=*text*

TYPE=BUTTON | CHECKBOX | FILE | HIDDEN | IMAGE | PASSWORD | RADIO | RESET | SUBMIT | TEXT

VALUE=*value*

```
<FORM>
<INPUT NAME="UserName" TYPE=TEXT VALUE="Your Login ID:">
</FORM>
```

<LABEL>

The <LABEL> tag defines a label for elements that accept events, such as user buttons. The <LABEL> tag accepts the following attributes and values:

ACCESSKEY=*key*

CLASS=*classname*

DATAFLD=*colname*

DATAFORMATAS=**HTML** | **TEXT**

DATASRC=*#ID*

FOR=*ID*

ID=*value*

LANG=*language*

LANGUAGE=**JAVASCRIPT** | **JSCRIPT** | **VBSCRIPT** | **VBS**

STYLE=*css1-properties*

TITLE=*text*

<LI>

The <LI> tag specifies a list item in any number of list types including numbered lists, ordered lists, and unordered lists.

```
<UL>
<LI>List Item One
<LI>List Item Two
</UL>
```

<LINK>

The <LINK> tag links two documents together, such as when using a global CSS style sheet. The <LINK> tag accepts the following attributes and values:

DISABLED

HREF=*url*

ID=*value*

REL=*stylesheet*

TITLE=*text*

TYPE="*text/css*"

```
<LINK REL=stylesheet HREF="mystyle.css" TYPE="text/css">
```

<MAP>

The <MAP> tag defines the "target" areas for a client-side image map. The <MAP> tag accepts the following attributes and values:

DISABLED

HREF=*url*

ID=*value*

REL=*stylesheet*

TITLE=*text*

TYPE="*text/css*"

```
<MAP HREF="http://www.myserver.com/mymap.gif">
<AREA SHAPE="RECT" COORDS="0, 0, 75, 125">
</MAP>
```

<MARQUEE>

The <MARQUEE> tag creates a special text marquee for a page. The <MARQUEE> tag accepts the following attributes and values:

BEHAVIOR=ALTERNATE | SCROLL | SLIDE

BGCOLOR=*color*

CLASS=*classname*

DATAFLD=*colname*

DATAFORMATAS=HTML | TEXT

DATASRC=*#ID*

DIRECTION=DOWN | LEFT | RIGHT | UP

HEIGHT=*n*

HSPACE=*n*

ID=*value*

LANG=*language*

LANGUAGE=JAVASCRIPT | JSCRIPT | VBSCRIPT | VBS

LOOP=*n*

SCROLLAMOUNT=*n*

SCROLLDELAY=*milliseconds*

STYLE=*css1-properties*

TITLE=*text*

TRUESPEED

VSPACE=*n*

WIDTH=*n*

```
<MARQUEE BEHAVIOR=SCROLL LOOP=4 SCROLLDELAY=500>
What an annoying tag!
</MARQUEE>
```

<META>

The <META> tag provides extraneous document information, such as keywords for search engines. You can also use this tag to provide a rudimentary level of document control, such as forcing the browser to reload the page contents at a certain interval. The <META> tag accepts the following attributes and values:

CONTENT=*description*

HTTP-EQUIV=*response*

NAME=*name*

TITLE=*text*

URL=*url*

```
<META HTTP-EQUIV="REFRESH" CONTENT=10>
```

<NOBR>

The <NOBR> tag forces text to be rendered with no line breaks.

```
<NOBR>This text would be shown as one line, even if we added the entire alphabet
a...z to it.</NOBR>
```

<NOSCRIPT>

The <NOSCRIPT> tag displays alternate information for browsers that do not support a scripting language.

```
<NOSCRIPT>Why are you reading about DHTML if your
browser doesn't support scripting!</NOSCRIPT>
```

<OBJECT>

The <OBJECT> tag enables you to construct an HTML object by combining different HTML tags. The object is then available to scripting methods under the Dynamic HTML Object Model, in a fashion similar to creating objects using <DIV> or <SPAN>. The <OBJECT> tag accepts the following attributes and values:

ACCESSKEY=*key*

ALIGN=ABSBOTTOM | ABSMIDDLE | BASELINE | BOTTOM | LEFT | MIDDLE | RIGHT | TEXTTOP | TOP

CLASS=*classname*

CLASSID=*id*

CODE=*url*

CODEBASE=*url*

CODETYPE=*media-type*

DATA=*url*

DATAFLD=*colname*

DATASRC=*#ID*

HEIGHT=*n*

ID=*value*

LANG=*language*

LANGUAGE=JAVASCRIPT | JSCRIPT | VBSCRIPT | VBS

NAME=*name*

STYLE=*css1-properties*

TABINDEX=*n*

TITLE=*text*

TYPE=*MIME-type*

WIDTH=*n*

```
<OBJECT ID="MyObject">
<H1>An Object</H1>
<IMG SRC="object.gif">
<HR>
</OBJECT>
```

<OL>

The <OL> tag creates an ordered list with items specified using the <LI> tag.

```
<OL>
<LI>Ordered List Item One
<LI>Ordered List Item Two
</OL>
```

<OPTION>

The <OPTION> tag creates choices for selection in forms when used in conjunction with the SELECT element. The <OPTION> tag accepts the following attributes and values:

CLASS=*classname*

ID=*value*

LANGUAGE=JAVASCRIPT | JSCRIPT | VBSCRIPT | VBS

SELECTED

TITLE=*text*

VALUE=*value*

Refer to the <SELECT> tag section for an HTML example that shows the <OPTION> tag as implemented in HTML.

<P>

The <P> tag denotes the beginning of a new paragraph.

```
<P>This is a paragraph
<P>This is a new paragraph
```

<PARAM>

The <PARAM> tag specifies <APPLET> or <EMBED> tag parameters. The <PARAM> tag accepts the following attributes and values:

DATAFLD=*colname*

DATAFORMATAS=HTML | TEXT

DATASRC=*#ID*

NAME=*name*

VALUE=*value*

```
<APPLET CODE="MyApplet.class" WIDTH=500 HEIGHT=500>
<PARAM NAME=LOCATION VALUE="USA">
<PARAM NAME=SKILL VALUE="EXPERT">
<PARAM NAME=SPEED VALUE="FAST">
</APPLET>
```

<PRE>

The <PRE> tag specifies preformatted text. The text will be rendered with the same spacing and line breaks in a fixed-width font.

```
<PRE>
The PRE tag
    Would
    be
    good
    for formatting
    poetry.
</PRE>
```

<S>

The <S> tag specifies strikethrough text.

```
<S>This text is strikethrough</S>
```

<SCRIPT>

The <SCRIPT> tag defines scripting elements in a page. When using Dynamic HTML, the scripts can be JavaScript or VBScript. The <SCRIPT> tag accepts the following attributes and values:

> **CLASS**=*classname*
>
> **EVENT**=*eventname*
>
> **FOR**=*element*
>
> **ID**=*value*
>
> **LANGUAGE=JAVASCRIPT | JSCRIPT | VBSCRIPT | VBS**
>
> **SRC**=*url*
>
> **TITLE**=*text*

```
<SCRIPT LANGUAGE=JAVASCRIPT>
      function scaleCat() {
            if (ScaleMe.style.pixelWidth > 0) {
                ScaleMe.style.pixelWidth -=1;
            ScaleMe.style.pixelHeight -= 1;
            window.setTimeout("scaleCat();", 1);
            scaleAnother();
            }
}
</SCRIPT>
```

<SELECT>

The <SELECT> tag enables you create a drop-down list box, with various items to choose from, which are denoted by the <OPTION> tag. The <SELECT> tag accepts the following attributes and values:

> **ACCESSKEY**=*key*
>
> **ALIGN=ABSBOTTOM | ABSMIDDLE | BASELINE | BOTTOM | LEFT | MIDDLE | RIGHT | TEXTTOP | TOP**
>
> **CLASS**=*classname*
>
> **DATAFLD**=*colname*
>
> **DATASRC**=*#ID*
>
> **DISABLED**
>
> **ID**=*value*
>
> **LANG**=*language*
>
> **LANGUAGE=JAVASCRIPT | JSCRIPT | VBSCRIPT | VBS**
>
> **MULTIPLE**
>
> **NAME**=*name*

SIZE=*n*

    STYLE=*css1-properties*

    TABINDEX=*n*

    TITLE=*text*

```
<SELECT NAME="Meals" SIZE=1>
<OPTION VALUE="1">Chicken
<OPTION VALUE="2">Beef
<OPTION VALUE="3" SELECTED>Vegetarian
</SELECT>
```

<SMALL>

The <SMALL> tag specifies text that will appear smaller in relation to the normal page text size.

```
If this is normal text...<SMALL>then this is small text</SMALL>
```

<SPAN>

The <SPAN> tag creates an object similar to the <DIV> tag. The <SPAN> tag accepts the following attributes and values:

    CLASS=*classname*

    DATAFLD=*colname*

    DATAFORMATAS=HTML | TEXT

    DATASRC=*#ID*

    ID=*value*

    LANG=*language*

    LANGUAGE=JAVASCRIPT | JSCRIPT | VBSCRIPT | VBS

    STYLE=*css1-properties*

    TITLE=*text*

```
<SPAN ID="RefSpec"><IMG SRC="schematic.gif"></SPAN>
```

<STRONG>

The <STRONG> tag places emphasis on text. Most browsers display strong as boldface.

```
<STRONG>This is bold!</STRONG>
```

\<STYLE\>

The \<STYLE\> tag is used with Cascading Style Sheets to establish style parameters for elements. The \<STYLE\> tag accepts the following attributes and values:

DISABLED

TITLE=*text*

TYPE=*"text/css"*

```
<STYLE>
P {color: red; font-family: sans-serif}
H3 {color: blue}
</STYLE>
```

\<SUB\>

The \<SUB\> tag creates subscript text.

```
<SUB>This text is subscript</SUB>
```

\<SUP\>

The \<SUP\> tag creates superscript text.

```
The 2<SUP>nd</SUP> example.
```

\<TABLE\>

The \<TABLE\>tag enables you to organize HTML and text into tables. The \<TABLE\> tag accepts the following attributes and values:

ALIGN=CENTER | LEFT | RIGHT

BACKGROUND=*url*

BGCOLOR=*color*

BORDER=*n*

BORDERCOLOR=*color*

BORDERCOLORDARK=*color*

BORDERCOLORLIGHT=*color*

CELLPADDING=*n*

CELLSPACING=*n*

CLASS=*classname*

COLS=*n*

DATAPAGESIZE=*n*

DATASRC=*#ID*

    **FRAME=ABOVE | BELOW | BORDER | BOX | INSIDES | LHS | RHS | VOID |
VSIDES**

    HEIGHT=*n*

    ID=*value*

    LANG=*language*

    LANGUAGE=JAVASCRIPT | JSCRIPT | VBSCRIPT | VBS

    RULES=ALL | COLS | GROUPS | NONE | ROWS

    STYLE=*css1-properties*

    TITLE=*text*

    WIDTH=*n*

```
<TABLE>
<TR>
<TD>This is Row One, Entry One.</TD>
<TD>This is Row One, Entry Two.</TD>
</TR>
<TR>
<TD>This is Row Two, Entry One</TD>
<TD>This is Row Two, Entry Two</TD>
</TR>
</TABLE>
```

<TD>

The <TD> tag specifies a single table entry. The <TD> tag accepts the following attributes and values:

    ALIGN=CENTER | LEFT | RIGHT

    BACKGROUND=*url*

    BGCOLOR=*color*

    BORDERCOLOR=*color*

    BORDERCOLORDARK=*color*

    BORDERCOLORLIGHT=*color*

    CLASS=*classname*

    COLSPAN=*n*

    ID=*value*

    LANG=*language*

    LANGUAGE=JAVASCRIPT | JSCRIPT | VBSCRIPT | VBS

    NOWRAP

    ROWSPAN=*n*

> **STYLE**=*css1-properties*
>
> **TITLE**=*text*
>
> **VALIGN=BASELINE | BOTTOM | CENTER | TOP**

Refer to the section on the <TABLE> tag to see how <TD> is implemented in HTML code.

<TEXTAREA>

The <TEXTAREA> tag creates an area for users to enter text data in a form (such as a "comments" box). The <TEXTAREA> tag accepts the following attributes and values:

> **ACCESSKEY**=*key*
>
> **ALIGN=ABSBOTTOM | ABSMIDDLE | BASELINE | BOTTOM | LEFT | MIDDLE | RIGHT | TEXTTOP | TOP**
>
> **CLASS**=*classname*
>
> **COLS**=*n*
>
> **DATAFLD**=*colname*
>
> **DATASRC**=*#ID*
>
> **DISABLED**
>
> **ID**=*value*
>
> **LANG**=*language*
>
> **LANGUAGE=JAVASCRIPT | JSCRIPT | VBSCRIPT | VBS**
>
> **NAME**=*name*
>
> **READONLY**
>
> **ROWS**=*n*
>
> **STYLE**=*css1-properties*
>
> **TABINDEX**=*n*
>
> **TITLE**=*text*
>
> **WRAP=OFF | PHYSICAL | VIRTUAL**

```
<FORM METHOD="POST">
<TEXTAREA NAME=COMMENTS ROWS=10>
</TEXTAREA>
</FORMS>
```

<TITLE>

The <TITLE> tag specifies a title for an HTML page.

```
<HTML>
<TITLE>Some Generic Page</TITLE>
</HTML>
```

<TR>

The <TR> tag specifies a new table row. The <TR> tag accepts the following attributes and values:

ALIGN=CENTER | LEFT | RIGHT
BGCOLOR=_color_
BORDERCOLOR=_color_
BORDERCOLORDARK=_color_
BORDERCOLORLIGHT=_color_
CLASS=_classname_
ID=_value_
LANG=_language_
LANGUAGE=JAVASCRIPT | JSCRIPT | VBSCRIPT | VBS
STYLE=_css1-properties_
TITLE=_text_
VALIGN=BASELINE | BOTTOM | CENTER | TOP

Refer to the section on the <TABLE> tag to see how <TR> is implemented in HTML code.

<TT>

The <TT> tag specifies "teletype" text, which is rendered as plain text in a fixed-width font.

```
<TT>This text is plain text!</TT>
```

<U>

The <U> tag specifies text that is to be displayed underlined.

```
<U>This text is underlined</U>
```

<UL>

The <UL> tag creates an unordered list.

```
<UL>
<LI>Item One on the List
<LI>Item Two
</UL>
```

CSS and CSS Positioning Attributes

This appendix provides an overview of the Cascading Style Sheets and Cascading Style Sheets Positioning attributes and properties at your disposal for Dynamic HTML. For further reading about CSS and CSS Positioning, consult the following:

W3C Recommendation (REC-CSS1-961217)
Cascading Style Sheets, Level 1
http://www.w3.org/pub/WWW/TR/REC-CSS1

W3C Working Draft (WD-positioning-970131)
Positioning HTML Elements with Cascading Style Sheets
http://www.w3.org/TR/WD-positioning

CSS Properties

The following properties can be used in any browser that supports the CSS-1 Specification, including Internet Explorer versions 3.x or higher, and Netscape Communicator versions 4.x and higher. Each of the CSS Properties is listed and accompanied by the values it accepts.

Fonts

The CSS Font Properties enable the manipulation of the fonts rendered in a web page. These properties enable complete customization of the fonts used, ranging from the size of the fonts to the style and the face of the fonts. Browser support for font features is quite robust; however, keep in mind that when specifying font faces, that face must still be installed on a user's machine in order to be rendered properly by the browser.

font   The *font* property enables you to specify the characteristic of the font to be used in a style. It accepts the following values: *font-family, font-weight, font-style, font-size, font-variant, line-height.* Each of the values can be set independently, but the *font* property provides a shortcut for specifying many properties in one declaration.

Usage:

```
font: font-family | font-weight | font-style | font-size | font-variant |
line-height
```

Example:

```
font:  times-roman bold italic small
```

font-family   The *font-family* property enables you to specify the name of the font family that will be used to render the text of a style. The family name can be either a specific font face (such as Times, Ariel) or a generic family name (such as Serif, Cursive). Keep in mind that not all machines will have all families installed; therefore, you can provide alternate font families by separating entries with a comma. The accepted generic family names are as follows:

- Serif
- Sans-serif
- Monospace
- Cursive
- Fantasy

Usage:

```
font-family: family-name | generic-family
```

Example:

```
font-family: Times, serif
```

font-weight   The *font-weight* property enables you to specify the weight of the rendered font. It accepts keywords and a numeric value. The accepted values are as follows (Note: Normal = 400, Bold =700):

- 100, 200, 300, 400, 500, 600, 700, 800, 900
- normal
- bold
- bolder
- lighter

Usage:

```
font-weight: value
```

Examples:

```
font-weight: bold
font-weight: 400
```

font-style The *font-style* property enables you to specify the style with which the font is rendered. The accepted values of this property are as follows:

- normal
- italic
- oblique

Usage:

```
font-style: style
```

Example:

```
font-style: italic
```

font-size The *font-size* property enables you to specify the size of the rendered font. It accepts values as an absolute size specified with a keyword, a length, a relative size, or a percentage. Keywords for absolute size are as follows:

- xx-small
- x-small
- small
- medium
- large
- x-large
- xx-large

The length represents the length of a character expressed in units, such as point size. The relative and percentage values are context dependent, with the size of the font being set in relation to the size of either a previous font or the container (such as the browser window). Relative size can be set with the following keywords:

- smaller
- larger

Usage:

```
font-size: absolute-size | relative-size | length | percentage
```

Examples:

```
font-size: x-large
font-size: 24pt
font-size: 120%
```

font-variant The *font-variant* property enables you to specify a small-caps version of the font face. This property accepts only two values: normal and small-caps.

Usage:

```
font-variant: normal | small-caps
```

Example:

```
font-variant: small-caps
```

line-height The *line-height* property enables you to specify the height for a line of text. It accepts three types of values:

- **normal**—This is a keyword value and the default, specifying that the line-height should be normal for the font.
- **number**—This is a unit value specifying a line-height.
- **percentage**—This sets the line-height in relation to the window size.

Usage:

```
font-height: normal | number | percentage
```

Example:

```
font-height: 20%
```

Backgrounds

CSS Style Sheets are capable of manipulating background information. This can be used to specify different background characteristics, including colors and images.

background The *background* property enables you to specify the characteristics of a page's background. The *background* property itself represents a shorthand method to specify all values in one tag; or attributes can be set with the individual properties. The *background* property accepts the following values: *color, url, repeat, scroll, position,* and the keyword "transparent."

Usage:

```
background: transparent | color | url | repeat | scroll | position
```

Example:

```
background: red http://www.images.com/monkey.gif
```

background-color   The *background-color* property enables you to specify a color value for the background of a page. This property accepts a value of *color* and also accepts a keyword of "transparent."

Usage:

```
background-color: transparent | color
```

Example:

```
background-color: red
```

background-image   The *background-image* property enables you to specify an image for use as a page's background. It accepts an image location as an URL, and the default value is *none*.

Usage:

```
background-image: none | url
```

Example:

```
background-image: myface.gif
```

background-repeat   The *background-repeat* property enables you to specify how a background image will repeat. The property accepts several keyword values of *repeat*, *repeat-x*, *repeat-y*, and *no-repeat*.

Usage:

```
background-repeat: repeat | repeat-x | repeat-y | no-repeat
```

Example:

```
background-repeat: repeat-x
```

background-attachment   The *background-attachment* property enables you to specify how a background attachment is treated. It accepts the keyword values of *scroll* and *fixed*.

Usage:

```
background-attachment: scroll | fixed
```

Example:

```
background-attachment: fixed
```

background-position   The *background-position* property enables you to specify the position of a background element on the page.

Usage:

```
background-position: percentage | length | top | center | bottom | left | right
```

Example:

```
background-position: 75%
```

App
B

Borders

Element borders can be manipulated with the following CSS attributes. Borders in CSS are similar to borders for any HTML element that accepts a border parameter, such as images or tables.

border   The *border* property enables you to specify various border attributes with one property. The *border* property accepts several types of keyword values for *border-width* and *border-style.*

Usage:

```
border: border-width | border-style | color
```

Examples:

```
border: 75% solid red
```

border-top, border-bottom, border-left, border-right   These border properties enable you to specify different values for each of the different border edges, resulting in a variety of different border techniques.

Usage:

```
border-location: border-width | border-style | color
```

Examples:

```
border-top: 50px solid blue
border-left: 100px dashed green
```

border-color   The *border-color* property enables you to specify a color value for the border. The *border-color* property accepts all the standard color keywords or specifications.

Usage:

```
border-color: color
```

Example:

```
border-color: green
```

border-style   The *border-style* property enables you to choose a rendering style for the border. Keyword values for this property include *none, dotted, dashed, solid, double, groove, ridge, inset,* and *outset.*

Usage:

```
border-style: keyword
```

Example:

```
border-style: dashed
```

border-width, border-top-width, border-bottom-width, border-left-width, border-right-width   The *border-width* properties enable you to specify the width of the entire border or individual border segments. You can specify the border width with units of measurement, percentages, or keywords. Keyword values include *thin*, *medium*, and *thick*.

Usage:

```
border-width: length | keyword
```

Examples:

```
border-width: 50%
border-width: thin
```

Text Formatting

The text formatting properties enable you to specify how to format different aspects of text on your pages. Attributes such as letter-spacing and line-spacing can be manipulated to create special looks.

word-spacing   The *word-spacing* property enables you to change the amount of whitespace that appears between words. The values for this property can be specified as *normal*, for no deviation, or as any acceptable CSS unit of measurement.

Usage:

```
word-spacing: normal | length
```

Example:

```
word-spacing: .5in
```

letter-spacing   The *letter-spacing* property enables you to specify the amount of whitespace that appears between letters on the page. As with the *word-spacing* property, the value can be specified as *normal* or as a CSS unit of measurement.

Usage:

```
letter-spacing: normal | length
```

Example:

```
letter-spacing: 3px
```

text-decoration   The *text-decoration* property enables you to specify any special styles that need to be applied to the text. It accepts several keyword values, including *none*, *underline*, *overline*, and *line-through*.

Usage:

```
text-decoration: keyword
```

Example:

```
text-decoration: underline
```

vertical-align   The *vertical-align* property enables you to specify how to align elements vertically, in relation to the baseline of the text. The value of this property can be specified as a percentage or as a keyword. Keywords include *baseline, sub, super, top, text-top, middle, bottom,* and *text-bottom.*

Usage:

```
vertical-align: keyword | percentage
```

Example:

```
vertical-align: baseline
```

text-transform   The *text-transform* property enables you to specify transformations that can be performed on text, manipulating the capitalization. The keyword values include *capitalize, uppercase, lowercase,* and *none.*

Usage:

```
text-transform: keyword
```

Example:

```
text-transform: capitalize
```

text-align   The *text-align* property enables you to specify how to align text elements on a page. Keyword values include *left, right, center,* and *justify.*

Usage:

```
text-align: left | right | center | justify
```

Example:

```
text-align: justify
```

text-indent   The *text-indent* property enables you to specify how elements are indented on a page. The value can be given as a percentage value of the page width or as a CSS unit of measurement.

Usage:

```
text-indent: length | percentage
```

Example:

```
text-indent: 1in
```

margin   The *margin* property enables you to set all the margin values on a page if uniform margins are desired. Values can be specified as a percentage of the window (or parent element) or as a CSS unit of measurement.

Usage:

```
margin: length | percentage | auto
```

Example:

```
margin: 1in
```

margin-top, margin-bottom, margin-left, margin-right   These *margin* properties enable the same control over margins as offered by the <MARGIN> tag, but enable more control over each margin. Values can be given as percentages or as CSS units of measurement.

Usage:

```
margin-top: length | percentage | auto
```

Example:

```
margin-top: auto
```

The *padding* property enables you to specify the amount of padding space between an element and the margin or a border. The padding can be specified as a percentage of the window (or parent element) width or as a CSS unit of measurement.

Usage:

```
padding: length | percentage
```

Example:

```
padding: 25%
```

padding-top, padding-bottom, padding-left, padding-right   These *padding* properties offer the same functionality of the *padding* property, but enable more flexibility. Values also can be specified as percentages or as CSS units of measurement.

Usage:

```
padding-top: length | percentage
```

Example:

```
padding-top: 15px
```

Layout Formatting

The *layout formatting* properties enable you to specify values for layout elements, such as a positioning container. This provides you with the flexibility to design complicated layouts that will be reproduced faithfully on different browsers.

width   The *width* property enables you to specify the width of an element or positioning container. The width can be set to any valid CSS unit of measurement, a percentage value of the window (or parent element), or *auto*.

Usage:

```
width: measurement | percentage | auto
```

Example:

```
width: 250px
```

App

B

height   The *height* property enables you to define the height of an element or positioning container. The height can be specified in any valid CSS unit of measurement or set to *auto*.

Usage:

```
height: measurement | auto
```

Example:

```
height: 100px
```

float   The *float* property enables you to specify elements that are to be "floated" next to other elements. Floating an image right, for example, will cause text to wrap around the left side of the image. Keywords include *none*, *left*, and *right.*

Usage:

```
float: none | left | right
```

Example:

```
float: left
```

clear   The *clear* property enables you to specify where floating elements may or may not be floated. This property enables the designer to specify an area to be kept clear. Keywords include *none*, *left*, *right,* and *both*.

Usage:

```
clear: none | left | right | both
```

Example:

```
clear: both
```

display   The *display* property enables you to specify how to display an element on the page. Keyword values include *block, inline, list-item,* and *none*. Choosing a display value of block causes the element to appear in a new box, typical of elements such as head tags, (for example, <H2>) inline also results in the creation of a new box, however, keeps the element on the same line, with no forced carriage return. List-item results in the item being treated as if it were in a list, similar to using the <LI> tag. Users should note that the *none* keyword causes the item not to be displayed at all.

Usage:

```
display: block | inline | list-item | none
```

Example:

```
display: none
```

white-space   The *white-space* property enables you to determine how to treat whitespace on a page. This property only accepts three keyword values: *normal, pre,* or *nowrap.*

Usage:

```
white-space: normal | pre | nowrap
```

Example:

```
white-space: normal
```

List Formatting

The list formatting values enable you to specify the appearance of lists and how the labels of list items appear.

list-style   The *list-style* property enables you to specify all the attributes for list styles in one property tag. It accepts the keyword values for *type, image,* and *position.*

Usage:

```
list-style: keyword | position | url
```

Example:

```
list-style: disc inside
```

list-style-type   The *list-style-type* property enables you to specify the type of bullet point to use for list items. The value is given as a keyword. Keywords include *disc, circle, square, decimal, lower-roman, upper-roman, lower-alpha, upper-alpha,* and *none.*

Usage:

```
list-style-type: keyword
```

Example:

```
list-style-type: square
```

list-style-image   The *list-style-image* property enables you to specify an image file that will be used as the list bullet. This enables you to create customized bullet points for designs and to specify the image by using an URL.

Usage:

```
list-style-image: url
```

Example:

```
list-style-image: mydot.gif
```

list-style-position   The *list-style-position* property enables you to specify how the bullet points are aligned next to list items. Keywords are *inside* and *outside.*

Usage:

```
list-style-position: keyword
```

Example:

```
list-style-position: inside
```

Pseudo Classes

CSS provides several pseudo classes, which are classes that are automatically defined by the browser environment. You can use the pseudo classes to specify styles for the link, active, and visited psuedoelements; then the classes are automatically applied to the elements in the appropriate document. Here are the currently defined pseudo classes and their usage:

- *:link*—The *:link* pseudo class represents a link.
- *:active*—The *:active* pseudo class represents an active link or a link that is in the process of being clicked. This can be used to create special effects when a user follows a link.
- *:visited*—The *:visited* pseudo class represents a link that has already been visited.

Currently, only the Anchor tag <A> makes use of the pseudo classes.

Usage:

```
ELEMENT:link {style definition}
```

Examples:

```
A:link {color: red}
A:visited {color: gray}
```

Pseudo Elements

The pseudo elements are similar to the pseudo classes in that they represent a short-hand way of setting styles for elements already defined by the browser. Currently, the two pseudo elements are as follows:

- *:first-line*—The *:first-line* pseudo element represents the first line in a block of text, such as a paragraph.
- *:first-letter*—The *:first-letter* pseudo element represents the first letter in a text element.

These pseudo elements can be used to create text effects such as drop-caps and lead-ins.

Usage:

```
ELEMENT:first-line {style definition}
```

Examples:

```
P:first-line {text-transform: uppercase}
P:first-letter {font-size:200%; color: red}
```

Colors

The *color* property can be applied to a number of different CSS attributes. The color property accepts 128 different colors, which are listed in Appendix F, "Browser-Safe Hexadecimal Chart."

Colors can also be controlled more subtly by using hex color values or RGB color values. This gives designers more control over the precise colors rendered on the screen.

Table B.1 RGB and Hexadecimal Color Codes

Color Specifiers	Value Code
Hex Color	#RGB
Hex Color	#RRGGBB
RGB Color	rgb(R, G, B)
RGB Percentage	rgb(r%, g%, b%)

Usage:

```
color: keyword | #RGB | #RRGGBB | rbg(R, G, B) | rgb(r%, g%, b%)
```

Examples:

```
color: red
color: #550000
color: rgb(100%, 5%, 5%)
```

Units

For CSS attributes that require a physical value, it is useful, if not absolutely necessary, to apply a measurement unit to the value for more explicit control. CSS provides a wide range of measurement units:

Table B.2 CSS Measurement Units

Unit	Symbol	Equivalent
Points	pt	1/72 inch
Picas	pc	12 points
Ems	em	
X-Height	ex	
Pixels	px	
Millimeters	mm	
Centimeters	cm	
Inches	in	2.54 cm

CSS Positioning Attributes

The syntax for specifying CSS Positioning attributes and values is identical to that of CSS-1. The following properties can be used with the STYLE attribute to specify the location of elements on a page layout. Using CSS Positioning is covered in detail in Chapter 9, "Layout and Positioning."

position Property

The *position* property enables you to specify the style of positioning that the browser will use when positioning an element. The default HTML position value is "static"; however, two values are accepted:

- **absolute**—Absolute positioning renders the element on the page according to the location specified by coordinates.

- **relative**—Relative positioning flows like static positioning; however, coordinates can be given. The placement of the element is then relative to its normally flowed position.

Usage:

```
position: value
```

Example:

```
position: absolute
```

top and left Properties   The *top* and *left* properties enable you to specify the location of a positioned element. These properties refer to the measurement from the top and the left of the parent element, such as a browser window. The values accept unit measurements or percentage values.

Usage:

```
top: value
left: value
```

Examples :

```
top: 1cm
left: 20%
```

width and height Properties   The *width* and *height* properties enable you to specify the width and height of a position container element. The width and height are always specified with respect to the origin of the element, as specified by the *top* and *left* properties. The *width* and *height* properties also accept unit measurements or percentages.

Usage:

```
width: value
height: value
```

Examples:

```
width: 15pc
height: 75%
```

overflow

The *overflow* property enables you to specify how excess data is handled for position containers that have width and height values set. The *overflow* property accepts three values:

- **none**—This enables all the data to be shown, effectively ignoring the width and height restrictions.
- **clip**—This causes the data to be truncated according to the parameters defined by the *clip* property.
- **scroll**—This value adds scroll bars to the container, enabling all the data to be seen by scrolling.

Usage:

```
overflow: value
```

Example:

```
overflow: scroll
```

clip

The *clip* property enables you to define a clipping area if the *overflow* property is set to *clip*. The *clip* property accepts a shape value, or a value of "auto." If the value is set to "auto," then the clipping area is defined as the area of the container. Otherwise a "rect" may be specified for the shape, along with the coordinates in relation to the origin, defining the clipping rectangle:

```
rect(top right bottom left)
```

Usage:

```
clip: value
```

Example:

```
clip: rect(1cm 3cm 4cm 1cm)
```

z-index

The *z-index* property enables you to specify a layer for a positioned element to occupy. The default layer is 0, with increasing integers being placed in the foreground. Negative integers are also acceptable values. The layering of elements that share a z-index is determined by the browser.

Usage:

```
z-index: value
```

Example:

```
z-index: 1
```

visibility

The *visibility* property enables you to specify if an element or layer is currently visible or not. It accepts two values: *visible* and *hidden*.

N O T E   It is important to note that hidden elements are still downloaded and occupy space in the layout, but are rendered transparently.

Usage:

```
visibility: value
```

Example:

```
visibility: hidden
```

Using VBScript Instead of JavaScript

As you may have noticed, this book focuses almost exclusively on JavaScript; however, scripting in VBScript is definitely a viable alternative to JavaScript in Internet Explorer 4.0.

This appendix provides a short introduction to the features and syntax of VBScript. We have attempted to keep the structure and examples as close as possible to those in Chapter 5, "JavaScript Primer," so that you can flip back and forth easily to compare differences between the two scripting languages. ■

Introduction to VBScript

VBScript was developed by Microsoft as an alternative to JavaScript for browser scripting. It is descended from Microsoft's Visual Basic and shares much of the same syntax.

Throughout the book, the scripts have been programmed in JavaScript. Letting the browser know that the script is going to use VBScript instead requires setting the LANGUAGE parameter to "VBScript" in the <SCRIPT> tag:

```
<SCRIPT LANGUAGE="VBScript">
    ... Your Script ...
</SCRIPT>
```

The following Hello World script is a good starting point for learning VBScript:

```
<HTML>
<HEAD>
   <TITLE>
   Hello World in VBScript
   </TITLE>
</HEAD>
<BODY>

   <SCRIPT LANGUAGE="VBScript">

      document.write("Hello, world")

   </SCRIPT>

</BODY>
</HTML>
```

If the <SCRIPT> tag is new to you, take a look at Chapter 5, which discusses it in more detail. Take a look at the only line in the document that contains VBScript code:

```
document.write("Hello World")
```

You can use VBScript to output any HTML you like, not just plain text. Try replacing the VBScript from the previous example with the following:

```
<SCRIPT LANGUAGE="VBScript">

   document.write("<H1>Hello, world</H1>")

</SCRIPT>
```

Make sure you reload the HTML page to ensure the script is updated. Note that now "Hello World" has been shown as an HTML heading rather than regular text.

Comments

Comments in VBScript are specified on a line-by-line basis. When you want to start a comment, use the quote (') character; then everything you enter until the end of the line is not executed by the VBScript Interpreter.

Add a comment to the Hello World example script:

```
<SCRIPT LANGUAGE="VBScript">

   'Write "Hello World" as a level 1 heading to the document
   document.write("<H1>Hello, world</H1>")

</SCRIPT>
```

Operators

VBScript provides a full range of operators to work with your data. You use operators to build expressions. The standard types of operators used in VBScript are Arithmetic, Comparison, and Logical Operators.

Arithmetic Operators

You use Arithmetic Operators to perform the standard types of mathematical operations that you have been working with since childhood, but written in their full form. For instance, this is the numerical expression for "2 plus 3":

```
2 + 3
```

Table C.1 lists the common available operations that can be used on numbers in VBScript.

Table C.1   VBScript Arithmetic Operators

Operator	Example	Definition
+	3 + 3	Addition
–	12 – 4	Subtraction
*	22 * 3	Multiplication
/	18 / 4	Division
Mod	18 Mod 4	Modulo: The remainder after division. The result here would be 2 because 4 goes into 18 four times with a remainder of 2.
–	–(12 * 3)	Unary Negation: The negative of the expression that follows. For example, the result here would be –36. The negative of a negative is a positive.

If you have an expression that contains more than one set of operations, you can group them together with parentheses('(' and ')'). This makes explicit the order in which the expressions are evaluated. The following arithmetic expression uses parentheses to make the precedence:

```
((36 * 12) % 15) - (32 * 12) /3))
```

App

C

Logical and Comparison Operators

A logical (or Boolean) expression is an expression that, when evaluated, returns a result of either true or false. Several ways can be used to generate Boolean expressions, but the most common is to use logical or comparison operators (see table C.2). Take a look at a few Boolean expressions:

```
True And False
```

This expression evaluates to false because one of the sides is not true, and the *And* operator requires both sides to be true for the expression to evaluate to true.

```
26 < 50
```

The preceding expression, however, evaluates to true because 26 is indeed less than 50.

```
(26 < 50) Or False
```

Using the *Or* operator makes this expression a little less restrictive than *And*, needing only one side to be true, so this expression evaluates to true.

Finally,

```
Not (10 <> 4)
```

evaluates to false. This type of expression required a little bit of thought—10 doesn't equal 4, which is true, but the NOT operator gives the opposite, which is false. Table C.2 lists the logical and comparison operators used by VBScript.

Table C.2   Logical and Comparison Operators

Operator	Usage
And	(exp1 And exp2) returns true if both exp1 and exp2 are true, otherwise returns false
Or	(exp1 Or exp2) returns true only if either exp1 or exp2 are true
Not	(Not exp) returns false only if exp1 is true, or true if exp is false
=	(exp1 = exp2) returns true only if the if exp1 is equal to exp2
<>	(exp1 <> exp2) returns true only if exp1 is not equal to exp2
>	(exp1 > exp2) returns true only if exp1 is greater than exp2
>=	(exp1 >= exp2) returns true only if exp1 is greater than or equal to exp2
<	(exp1 < exp2) returns true only if exp1 is less than exp2
<=	(exp1 < exp2) returns true only if exp1 is less than or equal to exp2

Variables

When working with data, it is often advantageous to have a place to store your data temporarily. VBScript enables you to use variables to store data during the duration the program is running. A variable has a name and a value. The value of a variable can change over time.

Defining and Naming Variables

Defining variables in VBScript is quite straightforward. You use the "Dim" keyword before the name of the variable you want to define. So, if you wanted to declare a variable named "position," you would use the following code:

```
Dim position
```

You can name a variable just about anything, as long as you follow these rules:

1. The variable name must begin with an alphabetic character.
2. The name cannot contain an embedded period.
3. The name cannot exceed 255 characters.
4. There cannot be another variable with the same name.

Here are a few examples of valid variable names:

```
Dim x_location
Dim_loc
Dim choice32
Dim answer_42
```

Here are a few examples of variable names that are not valid:

```
Dim 99balloons    'violates the first rule
Dim eggs.bacon    'violates the second rule
```

Unlike JavaScript, VBScript is not case-sensitive. This means that two variables can appear to be different, but be the same variable. The following two statements, for example, would create the same variable.

```
Dim testResult
Dim TestResult
```

Changing the Value of a Variable

To give a variable a new value after it is created, you need to use the assignment operator (=). The variable name is listed on the left side of the statement. The expression containing the value to be assigned to the variable is listed on the right side of the statement. Consider the following simple example (assuming that the variable "currPosition" has already been created):

```
currPosition = 10
```

This changes the value of "currPosition" to 10. Variables can hold any type of data that you want. Unlike JavaScript, there is no variable-type definition in VBScript. All the variables you define in VBScript are automatically of type *Variant*. A *Variant* is a data type that automatically adjusts itself to whatever data you ask it to hold.

From the programmers perspective there is only one data type, but internally the *Variant* data type can hold many different types of data. These data types are known as the subtypes of the *Variant* and it is often useful to know the ranges of the values that your variables can hold. Table C.3 lists the subtypes of the *Variant* data type:

Table C.3   Variant Subtypes

Subtype	Description
Boolean	Contains either True or False.
Byte	Contains integer in the range 0 to 255.
Integer	Contains integer in the range –32768 to 32767.
Currency	–922337203685477.5808 to 922337203685477.5807.
Long	Contains integer in the range –2147483648 to 2147483647.
Single	Contains a single-precision floating-point number in the range –3.402823E38 to –1.401298E-45 for negative values; 1.401298E-45 to 3.402823E38 for positive values.
Double	Contains a double-precision floating-point number in the range –1.79769313486232E308 to –4.94065645841247E-324 for negative values; 4.94065645841247E-324 to 1.79769313486232E308 for positive values.
Date	(Time) Contains a number that represents a date between January 1st 100 to December 31 9999.
String	Contains a variable-length string that can be up to approximately two billion characters in length.
Object	Contains an object.

Because variables are all the *Variant* type and the *Variant* type can hold different types of values, you can put different types of data into a variable at different times:

```
currPosition = True
currPosition = "foobar"
```

All the expressions you have seen so far are made up of constant data, but there's no reason you couldn't use a variable in the expression as well. The interpreter just substitutes the value of the variable into the expression. Therefore, assuming "currPosition" has the value 10, the statement

```
currPosition = currPosition + 10
```

sets the value of currPosition to 20, adding 10 to the current value of the variable.

Procedures

It is often helpful to collect sections of code in a group that can be called again and again. Much like a variable, you can name this grouping of code. These groups of code that can be called are referred to as *procedures*.

VBScript has two different types of procedures: *Sub procedures* and *functions*. The difference between the two is that Sub procedures cannot return values, but functions can.

Sub procedures and functions are called using their names, immediately followed by parentheses that enclose any arguments they may take. If a procedure exists named *foo ()* that takes one argument named "bar", for instance, you would use the following syntax to call the procedure:

```
foo(bar)
```

Writing Your Own Sub Procedures

Writing your own Sub procedures is pretty straightforward. You start with the "Sub" keyword followed by the name of the procedure, followed by any arguments that it takes in parentheses.

Next, you enclose any code you want to execute whenever the procedure is called. Finally, you place "End Sub" on a line by itself to signify that the Sub procedure definition is complete.

Start by defining a Sub procedure called *printIt*:

```
Sub printIt(theText)
End Sub
```

This is a valid procedure definition, although admittedly it doesn't do very much. Now, what do you want to do inside the Sub procedure? Suppose that you want to print out the string "theText" to the document:

```
Sub printIt(theText)

    document.write(theText)

End Sub
```

Now, whenever you want to call the procedure, you just use the keyword "Call" followed by the name of the procedure, followed by a comma-delimited list of the arguments inside of parentheses. Therefore, if you wanted to use *printIt* to print "Hi There" to the document, you would use the following code:

```
Call printIt("Hi There")
```

Returning Values via Functions

Although Sub procedures are quite useful, they have one major downfall: they cannot return values. When you want to return values, you need to use a function. Functions are quite similar to procedures except that they use the keyword "Function" and return a value.

The way functions return values is a little tricky. To return values, you need to use the name of the function as if it were a variable and set it to the return value. The following code shows a simple function that takes a number and returns the square of that number to the calling expression:

```
Function square(inNum)
    square = inNum * inNum
End Function
```

You are not limited to returning numbers via functions. In fact, any data that a *Variant* type can hold can be returned via a user-defined function.

Flow Control

With the VBScript presented up to this point, any program you might write is *linear*. That is, the program starts at the first statement, goes to the next, and so on.

Programming is, in many ways, about making decisions. What you do in one circumstance may not be what you do in another. Also, you may want to do something over and over and over, but up to this point the only way to do that would be to place the statements you want to repeat in a function, then call that function over and over (or worse, cut and paste the statements you want to call repeatedly).

The concept of diverting what the program does at a given point based upon differing conditions is called *flow control*. VBScript gives you quite a bit of control over the flow program through conditional statements such as *if...else* and repetition statements, such as *for* and *while* loops.

Conditional statements like *if...else* enable you to make choices regarding which multiple paths to take in your programs. On the other hand, repetition statements, such as *for* and *while*, give you the option of executing a section of code over and over.

If...Then...Else

The most basic concept in flow control is branching based upon a conditional expression. That sounds complicated, but all it means is to use a logical expression (remember those from earlier in this appendix?) to decide whether to follow one path or another.

You construct an *if* statement by using the keyword "If" followed by a logical expression (the "Then" keyword) followed by the statements to execute if that logical expression is true. Finally, the line *End If* indicates that the *if* statement is complete. Take a look at a few concrete examples:

```
Dim x
x = 10
Dim y
y = 25;

If x < y Then
    document.write("x less than y")
End If
```

```
If x <> y Then
    document.write("x doesn't equal y")
End If

If x >= y Then
    document.write("x greater than or equal to y")
End If

If x = y Then
    document.write("y equals y")
End If
```

In the first case, "x less than y" is printed to the page because 10 is less than 25, which is true, so the statement included in the *if* statement is executed. By the same logic, the second *if* statement causes "x doesn't equal y" to be printed to the screen. For the final two *if* statements, nothing is printed, because their logical expressions are false, so the statement that follows is not executed.

An *if* statement can be followed by more than one line of code; therefore, the *End If* construct is used. All the code between the *Then* and the *End If* is executed if the logical expression returns true. Take a look at the following example of this (assuming the same x and y variables from the previous example):

```
If (x = y) Or (x < y) Then
    document.write("x less than y ")
    document.write("or x equals y")
End If
```

In this case, "x less than y or x equals y" is printed because the logical expression is true (work it out in your head if it isn't immediately obvious, because it's this sort of thinking that acclimates you to quickly understanding conditionals), and the block that follows the *if* contains two statements that are then executed in order.

You can also construct an *If...Then...Else* conditional statement by adding the "Else" keyword to the end of an *if* statement. In this case, the program will execute the statements following the logical expression if the expression is true, or the statements following the "Else" keyword if the expression is false. Take a look at another example (assuming again that x and y have the values from the first example):

```
If x = y Then
    document.write("y equals y")
Else
    document.write("x doesn't equal y")
End If
```

In this case "x doesn't equal y" is printed. Why? The logical expression is false (because 10 doesn't equal 25) so the statement following the expression isn't executed. Because the expression was false, however, the statement following the "Else" keyword is executed, which prints "x doesn't equal y".

For..Next loops

The *For..Next* loop is the most basic of looping statements. This looping statement enables you to execute a statement (or block) a set number of times, based upon a counter and expression to compare that counter against.

A *For* loop is constructed by starting with the keyword "For" followed by the name of a counter variable, followed by the range that the variable will follow. If you wanted the loop to execute 10 times, for instance, you would use the range "1 to 10". Finally come the statements to execute. You specify the end of the *For* loop with the keyword "Next."

This sounds a bit complicated, so try constructing a simple *for* loop. Suppose that you want to print out every number from 1 to 10. This is the *for* loop you might use to do so:

```
Dim count
For count = 1 to 10
    document.write(count)
    document.write("<br>")   'Print a break to separate lines
Next
```

Although this *for* loop is pretty simple, you could certainly get more complicated in the logic of the loop by using the "Step" keyword, which states the amount the loop counter will be incremented each time it is executed. You could have the loop start at 64, for instance, and then subtract 1 from the counter until the counter variable equals 1:

```
For count = 64 To 1 Step -1
```

While..Wend loops

A *While..Wend* loop is much like a *For..Next* loop, except it only has a test case. Therefore, you must make sure that conditions change over the execution of the *while* loop to ensure the test case eventually fails (returns false).

You construct a *While..Wend* loop by using the "While" keyword, followed by a logical expression as a test case, then the statement(s) to execute each time, and finally the "Wend" keyword to signify the end of the loop. The test case is checked before each time the statement(s) of the *while* loop is executed.

You will want to initialize the counter variable outside the *While..Wend* loop (assuming you are using a counter variable and not some other means of testing for completion), and somewhere inside the *While..Wend* loop, you will want to make sure that the counter variable is updated.

The following code constructs a *while* loop that behaves the same way as the first *for* loop example:

```
Dim count
count = 1
```

```
While count <= 10

    document.write(count)
    document.write("<br>")   // Print a break to separate lines
    count = count + 1
Wend
```

First, before getting to the *while* loop itself, the counter variable is created and initialized to 1 because no section in the *while* loop itself is set aside for creating and initializing the counter variable. Next, the test case is checked inside the *while* loop. Then, if the test case is true, the body of the loop (the statement or block that follows) is executed. Note that 1 is added to count at the end of the body, making sure that the condition in the test case will change after each run through the loop.

Constants

VBScript enables you to define names for values that you will use often. Suppose, for instance, you knew that the width of the image that you were going to work with in your VBScript program was 350 pixels. You could continually add 350 throughout your code whenever you wanted to use the width.

It would be much more readable and simpler to understand, however, if you could refer to that width as "imgWidth". VBScript provides you with this capability through *constants*.

A constant is defined much like a variable, except that instead of using the "Dim" keyword, you use the "Const" keyword. Therefore, if you wanted to use the previous example and define a constant "imgWidth" that had the value 350, you would use the following code:

```
Const imgWidth = 350
```

Four types of VBScript constants will be discussed in this appendix:

- Color constants
- Date/Time constants
- Date Format constants
- String constants

Color Constants

VBScript provides quite a few built-in constants that you can use in your programs. These are quite helpful because you can refer to things by name instead of a more confusing value. You can specify the color black, for instance, by "vbBlack" instead of "&h00". Table C.4 lists the built-in color constants employed in VBScript.

Table C.4   Color Constants

Constant	Value	Description
vbBlack	&h00	Black
vbBlue	&hFF0000	Blue
vbCyan	&hFFFF00	Cyan
vbGreen	&hFF00	Green
vbMagenta	&hFF00FF	Magenta
vbRed	&hFF	Red
vbWhite	&hFFFFFF	White
vbYellow	&hFFFF	Yellow

Date/Time Constants

You can use the date/time constants whenever working with VBScript's data functions instead of using the numbers associated with the values. Table C.5 lists the built-in date/time constants employed in VBScript.

Table C.5   Date/Time Constants

Constant	Value	Description
vbSunday	1	Sunday
vbMonday	2	Monday
vbTuesday	3	Tuesday
vbWednesday	4	Wednesday
vbThursday	5	Thursday
vbFriday	6	Friday
vbSaturday	7	Saturday
vbFirstJan1	1	The week in which January 1 occurs (default) is used.
vbFirstFourDays	2	The first week that has at least four days in the new year is used.
vbFirstFullWeek	3	The first full week of the year is used.

Constant	Value	Description
vbUseSystem	0	The date format contained in the regional settings for your computer is used.
vbUseSystemDayOfWeek	0	The day of the week specified in your system settings for the first day of the week is used.

Date Format Constants

You can use the date format constants wherever date formats or conversions are needed instead of the values. Table C.6 lists the built-in date format constants employed in VBScript.

Table C.6   Date Format Constants

Constant	Value	Description
vbGeneralDate	0	Display a date or a time. If the number is a real number, display the date and time. If there is not a fractional part, then only the date is displayed. If there is not an integer part, only the time is displayed. The date and time display is determined by your system settings.
vbLongDate	1	Display a date using the long date format specified in your computer's regional settings.
vbShortDate	2	Display a date using the short date format specified in your computer's regional settings.
vbLongTime	3	Display a time using the long time format specified in your computer's regional settings.
vbShortTime	4	Display a time using the short time format specified in your computer's regional settings.

App
C

String Constants

String constants can be useful when building strings or writing to the document. Table C.7 lists the built-in string constants employed in VBScript.

Table C.7   String Constants

Constant	Value	Description
vbCr	Chr(13)	Carriage return
vbCrLf	Chr(13) + Chr(10)	Carriage return & line feed combination
vbFormFeed	Chr(12)	Form feed; useful on platforms other than MS Windows
vbLf	Chr(10)	Line feed
vbNewLine	Chr(13) & Chr(10) or Chr(10)	Platform-specific newline character; whatever is appropriate for the platform
vbNullChar	Chr(0)	Character having the value 0
vbNullString	String having value 0	Useful to call external procedures
vbTab	Chr(9)	Horizontal tab
vbVerticalTab	Chr(11)	Vertical tab; Useful on platforms other than MS Windows

From Here...

With VBScript, Microsoft provides a viable and competent competitor to JavaScript. Although JavaScript is currently more popular among web programmers, VBScript enables the millions of programmers with Visual Basic experience to leverage their skills on the web.

If you want to learn more about VBScript, the best place to start is at Microsoft's Visual Basic, Scripting Edition web site. This site is available at **http://www.microsoft.com/vbscript** and provides extensive tutorials and documentation along with a great deal of sample VBScript code.

Scripting Objects, Collections, Methods, and Properties

This appendix will cover the objects, methods, and properties of the Dynamic HTML Object Model. The Dynamic HTML Object Model enables the current HTML page and even the browser window itself to be accessed as a large collection of objects.

These objects are available via the Dynamic HTML Object hierarchy. This hierarchy is shown in figure D.1. The Dynamic HTML Object Model and its object hierarchy are explored in Chapter 6, "Dynamic HTML Object Model." ■

FIG. D.1
The Dynamic HTML
Object hierarchy.

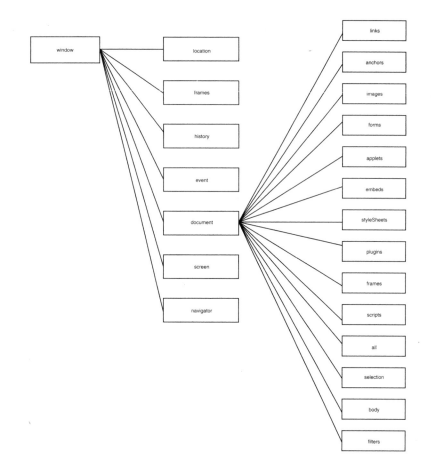

window object

The *window* object represents an open window in the browser. You can use it to access the rest of the document, navigate throughout the browser, execute scripts, and perform many other functions that are represented by the browser window itself.

The *window* object contains the following properties:

- **client**—The *navigator* object.
- **closed**—True if the window is closed, false if open.
- **defaultStatus**—The default message in the status bar.
- **dialogArguments**—The value passed to a modal dialog.
- **dialogHeight**—The height of the current modal dialog.
- **dialogLeft**—The left position of the current modal dialog.
- **dialogTop**—The top position of the current modal dialog.

- **dialogWidth**—The width of the current modal dialog.
- **document**—The *document* object for the window.
- **event**—The *event* object for the window.
- **history**—The *history* object for the window.
- **length**—The number of elements in the window collection.
- **location**—The *location* object for the window.
- **name**—The name of the window.
- **navigator**—The *navigator* object for the window.
- **offscreenBuffering**—Boolean reporting true if off-screen buffering is enabled, false if otherwise.
- **opener**—A reference to the window that opened this window.
- **parent**—The *parent* object of the window.
- **returnValue**—The return value from the current modal dialog.
- **self**—A self reference to the *window* object itself.
- **status**—The status message at the bottom of the window.
- **top**—The topmost window.
- **window**—A window that is the child of this window, such as a frame.

The *window* object contains the following methods:

App

D

- **alert()**—Opens an alert box that contains an OK button and a programmatically supplied message.
- **blur()**—Causes the current browser window to lose focus and fire the onblur() event.
- **clearInterval()**—Cancels an interval previously set with setInterval.
- **clearTimeout()**—Clears a timeout previously set by setTimeout.
- **close()**—Closes the browser window.
- **confirm()**—Opens a confirm dialog box with a programmatically supplied message and an OK box.
- **execScript()**—Executes a script (default is JavaScript).
- **focus()**—Causes the browser window to receive mouse and keyboard focus.
- **navigate()**—Displays the URL passed as an argument.
- **open()**—Opens a new window with the URL passed as an argument.
- **prompt()**—Displays a prompt dialog box with a user-editable input field and a message.
- **scroll()**—Scrolls the window to the X and Y position supplied as arguments.
- **setInterval()**—Repeatedly evaluates the supplied expression after a number of milliseconds specified as an argument.
- **setTimeout()**—Evaluates the supplied expression after a number of milliseconds specified as an argument.

- **showHelp()**—Shows a help file located at the specified URL.
- **showModalDialog()**—Creates a modal dialog box at the specified URL.

location object

The *location* object contains all the information on the location that the window is currently displaying and all the details on that location (the port, the protocol, and so on). The *location* object contains the following properties:

- **hash**—The section of the href following the # symbol.
- **host**—The hostname:port part of the URL.
- **hostname**—The hostname part of the URL.
- **href**—The entire URL.
- **pathname**—The file (or possibly object) path following the third slash.
- **port**—The port part of the URL.
- **protocol**—The protocol portion of the URL.
- **search**—The search portion of the URL following the ? symbol.

The *location* object contains the following methods:

- **assign()**—Sets the current URL to the supplied argument.
- **reload()**—Reloads the current URL.
- **replace()**—Replaces the current document with the URL given as an argument.

frames collection

The *frames* collection contains all the frame windows contained in the current window that is being displayed in the browser. It is important to note that what is contained in the *frames* collection is not the frame elements themselves, but the window objects associated with those frames.

history object

The *history* object contains information on all the URLs that the browser has recently visited.

The *history* object contains only one property, *length*, which indicates the number of URLs currently saved in the *history* object.

The *history* object contains the following methods:

- **back()**—Causes the browser to move back one into the history. This is the same as hitting the Back button in the browser.
- **forward()**—Causes the browser to move forward one into the history. This is the same as hitting the Forward button in the browser.
- **go()**—Causes the browser to go to a specified point in the history based upon a partial URL passed as an argument.

screen object

The *screen* object enables you to find the capabilities and size of the screen on which the content will be displayed. It, for instance, is often advantageous to know the size of the screen ahead of time to know whether your content will fit on the screen or not. The *screen* object's properties enable you to find out this sort of information.

The screen object contains the following properties:

- **height**—The height of the screen in pixels.
- **width**—The width of the screen in pixels.
- **colorDepth**—The color depth contains the number of color bits per pixel for the screen.
- **bufferDepth**—Specifies whether or not there is an off-screen basket.
- **updateInterval**—The updateInterval property specifies how often, in milliseconds, the screen is updated.

navigator object

The *navigator* object contains information about the capabilities of the browser itself.

The *navigator* object contains the following properties:

- **appCodeName**—The code name of the browser.
- **appName**—The name of the browser.
- **appVersion**—The version of the browser.
- **cookieEnabled**—Boolean representing whether the browser is enabled for cookies on the client side.
- **userAgent**—The user agent string sent by the browser to the server via HTTP when a connection is made.

The *navigator* object contains the following methods:

- **javaEnabled()**—Returns true if Java is enabled in the current browser, false if Java is not enabled.
- **taintEnabled()**—Returns true if data tainting is available, false if it is not. This method always returns false in Internet Explorer 4.0.

event object

The *event* object contains a great deal of information about the state of the browser that can be useful to programs when the event was fired.

The *event* object contains the following properties:

- **altKey**—True if the Alt key is pressed when the event was fired, false if otherwise.
- **button**—The mouse button that has been pressed: 0 if no button was pressed, 1 if the left button was pressed, 2 if the right button was pressed, and 4 if the middle button was pressed.

App

D

- **cancelBubble**—True if the current event should bubble up the event hierarchy, false if otherwise.

- **clientX**—The X position of the mouse relative to the client area of the window.

- **clientY**—The Y position of the mouse relative to the client area of the window.

- **ctrlKey**—True if the Ctrl key was pressed when the event was fired, false if otherwise.

- **fromElement**—The last element the mouse was over before it was over this one.

- **keyCode**—The code of the key that was pressed when the event was fired.

- **offsetX**—The X position of the mouse when the event was fired relative to the container that received the event.

- **offsetY**—The Y position of the mouse when the event was fired relative to the container that received the event.

- **reason**—The current condition of the data transfer object. Can be one of three states: 0—the data was transferred successfully, 1—the data transfer was aborted, and 2—there was an error in the data transmission.

- **returnValue**—The return value from the event.

- **screenX**—The X position of the mouse relative to the size of the screen rather than the browser window.

- **screenY**—The Y position of the mouse relative to the size of the screen rather than the browser window.

- **shiftKey**—The state of the Shift key when the event was fired. The value is true if it was pressed, false if otherwise.

- **srcElement**—The element that originally fired the event that is now being handled.

- **srcFilter**—The *filter* object that fired the *onfilterchange* event.

- **toElement**—The element that the mouse moved to after it left the current one.

- **type**—The name of the event as a string. The name of the event is retrieved without the "on" prefix. Therefore, "onmouseover" would just be "mouseover."

- **X**—The X position of the *mouse* object when the event was fired relative to the nearest *parent* object that was positioned with CSS Positioning.

- **Y**—The Y position of the *mouse* object when the event was fired relative to the nearest *parent* object that was positioned with CSS Positioning.

document object

The *document* object represents the current HTML document displayed in the browser window. You can use the *document* object to get information about the document and change the document's contents.

The *document* object contains the following properties:

- **activeElement**—The element that has the focus.

- **alinkColor**—The color of the active link.
- **bgColor**—The background color of the page.
- **body**—The *body* object for this document.
- **cookie**—The string value of the current cookie.
- **domain**—The security domain of the document.
- **fgColor**—The text color of the document.
- **lastModified**—The last modified date of the document.
- **linkColor**—The color of links on the document.
- **location**—The *location* object for this document.
- **parentWindow**—The window that contains this document.
- **readyState**—The current state of the document. Possible values are as follows:
  - **complete**—if the document is loaded
  - **interactive**—if the document is not completely loaded but the user can interact with it
  - **loading**—if the document is in the process of loading
  - **uninitialized**—when the document is in the process of downloading but not loaded on the browser window yet
- **referrer**—The URL of the location viewed previously to this one.
- **selection**—The *selection* object for this document.
- **title**—The title of this document.
- **URL**—This document's URL.
- **vlinkColor**—The color of visited links in this document.

The *document* object contains the following methods:

- **clear()**—Clears the document output stream and transmits the data that was in the stream to the document.
- **close()**—Closes the current output stream.
- **createElement()**—Creates a new IMG or OPTION element.
- **elementFromPoint()**—Given an X and Y position as arguments, this method returns the element present at that point.
- **execCommand()**—Executes a command over a selection or a text range.
- **open()**—Opens a stream that collects output from write or *writeln* methods.
- **queryCommandEnabled()**—Returns true if the command passed as an argument is enabled, false if otherwise.
- **queryCommandIndeterm()**—Returns true if the command passed is in an indeterminate state.
- **queryCommandState()**—Returns true if the command passed has been carried out.

- **queryCommandSupported()**—Returns true if the command passed is supported in the browser.
- **queryCommandText()**—Returns the string associated with the command passed as an argument.
- **queryCommandValue()**—Returns the value of the command passed as an argument.
- **write()**—Writes the HTML expression passed as an argument to the document.
- **writeln()**—Writes the HTML expression passed as an argument to the document followed by a carriage return.

selection object   The *selection* object enables scripts to access the information that the user has currently highlighted with the mouse.

The *selection* object contains one property, *type*, which indicates the type of selection. The type property can be one of two values—0, if there is no selection insertion point, or 1, if the selection is a text selection and there is in fact an insertion point.

The *selection* object contains the following methods:

- **clear()**—Clears the contents of the selection.
- **createRange()**—Creates a text range over the selection.
- **empty()**—Deselects the current selection.

body object   The *body* object contains information about the HTML elements that make up the visible part of the HTML document in the current browser window.

The *body* object contains the following properties:

- **accessKey**—The accelerator for the body.
- **background**—The picture in the background of the body.
- **bgColor**—The background color for the body.
- **bgProperties**—The properties for the background picture, such as whether the picture scrolls on the page.
- **bottomMargin**—The bottom margin in pixels for the body of the page.
- **className**—The CSS class name associated with the body of the page.
- **clientHeight**—The height of the body in pixels.
- **clientWidth**—The width of the body in pixels.
- **document**—The *document* object for the body.
- **id**—The CSS Identifier for the body.
- **innerHTML**—The HTML code between the start and end tags of the body.
- **innerText**—The HTML code between the start and end tags of the body represented purely as text.

- **isTextEdit**—Whether the text range can be edited. True if it can, false if otherwise.
- **lang**—The ISO code for the language being used. Note that this is not the scripting language, but the actual written language being used.
- **language**—Specifies the computer scripting language in which the current script is written.
- **leftMargin**—The left margin for the entire page represented in pixels.
- **offsetHeight**—The height of the body in pixels, relative to the parent.
- **offsetLeft**—The left position of the body in pixels, relative to the parent.
- **offsetParent**—The object that contains the body and provides the offset.
- **offsetTop**—The top position of the body in pixels, relative to the parent.
- **offsetWidth**—The width of the body in pixels, relative to the parent.
- **parentElement**—The parent element of the body.
- **parentTextEdit**—The next element in the object hierarchy on which a text range can be created.
- **rightMargin**—The right margin for the entire page represented in pixels.
- **scroll**—Whether the scroll bars are on or off. If "yes," they are on; if "no," they are off.
- **scrollHeight**—The scrolling height of the body in pixels, including content that is not visible.
- **scrollLeft**—The amount in pixels between the left edge of the body and the left edge that is currently visible to the user in the browser.
- **scrollTop**—The amount in pixels between the top edge of the body and the left edge that is currently visible to the user in the browser.
- **scrollWidth**—The scrolling height of the body in pixels, including content that is not visible.
- **sourceIndex**—The position of the body in the document's source index.
- **style**—The inline style sheet for the body.
- **tabIndex**—The tab index for the body.
- **tagName**—The tag for the current element (the body tag).
- **text**—The text color for the body.
- **title**—A Tooltip for the body.
- **topMargin**—The top margin for the entire page represented in pixels.

The *body* object contains the following methods:

- **blur()**—Causes the *body* object to lose mouse and keyboard focus.
- **click()**—Simulates the user clicking the mouse button.
- **contains()**—Returns true if the element passed as an argument is contained in the body, false if otherwise.
- **createTextRange()**—Creates a text range over the body.

- **focus()**—Causes the body to receive mouse and keyboard focus.
- **getAttribute()**—Returns the value for the attribute passed as an argument.
- **insertAdjacentHTML()**—Inserts HTML code passed as an argument into the body.
- **insertAdjacentText()**—Inserts text passed as an argument into the body.
- **removeAttribute()**—Removes the attribute passed as an argument from the body.
- **scrollIntoView()**—Scrolls the body into view.
- **setAttribute()**—Sets the attribute passed as an argument.

***anchors* collection**   The *anchors* collection contains all the elements that contain an <A> tag in them. Anchors are normally used in documents to specify hyperlinks, as in the following example:

```
<A HREF="http://www.microsoft.com">The Microsoft Site</A>
```

***links* collection**   The *links* collection contains all the hyperlinks in the document. This collection contains all the elements in the anchors collection, plus all the elements that use the <AREA> tag.

***images* collection**   The *images* collection contains all the images in the document. An image is defined as an element that used the IMG HTML tag. Images that are produced without an IMG tag, such as from a Java applet or ActiveX Control will not be present in this collection. All these images are also contained in the applets collection.

***forms* collection**   The *forms* collection contains all the forms present in the document. A form is defined as an element that uses the FORM HTML tag. Dynamic HTML will enable you to place user interface controls outside of a form, but it is important to note that these controls will not be present in the forms collection.

***applets* collection**   It may appear from the use of the term *applets* in this collection that the applets collection only contains Java applets. In fact, the applets collection contains all the "objects" in the document.

Microsoft defines the following elements as "objects" that will appear in the applets collection:

- **applets**—Elements with the <APPLET> tag.
- **embeds**—Elements with the <EMBED> tag.
- **images**—All images in the document, usually specified with the <IMG> tag.
- **objects**—Any element that uses the <OBJECT> tag.
- **intrinsic controls**—These are the controls that are built into Internet Explorer 4.0 by default.

***embeds* collection**   The *embeds* collection contains all the embedded content (plugins) in the document. Plugins are programs that have been integrated into the browser to increase its functionality. The Real Audio Player is a good example of a plugin.

styleSheets collection The *styleSheets* collection contains all the style sheets for this document. A style sheet is contained for each occurrence of a LINK or STYLE element present in the document.

plugins collection The *plugins* collection is an alias for the embeds collection.

frames collection The *frames* collection contains all the frames in the document. Frames are considered windows themselves in HTML, so this collection contains window objects instead of the actual frame element objects.

scripts collection The *scripts* collection contains all the scripts in the document. The scripts themselves are represented by pure text and can be retrieved as pure text.

all collection The *all* collection encompasses the entire content of the page. It does this by containing all the HTML elements that make up the document.

filters collection The *filters* collection contains all the Dynamic HTML multimedia filters for the document. A filter enables the visible aspect of any element to be modified on-the-fly. For instance, a blur filter causes the content of an element to become blurry.

From Here...

The scripting object, methods, properties, and collections form the foundation of Dynamic HTML and are well worth exploring in more detail. Chapter 6 presents these objects, methods, properties, and collections and explores how they fit into the rest of Dynamic HTML.

App

D

Special Edition Using Dynamic HTML Web Site

The *Special Edition Using Dynamic HTML* web site can be found at **http://www.quecorp.com/**. The site is designed to provide you with links to references cited within the text, as well as being a source for the code and examples used in this book. All the sample pages used in this book can be found on the site, and the source code for the examples can also be downloaded in the form of a zip file. ▪

Using the Web Site

To take advantage of the *Special Edition Using Dynamic HTML* web site, it is important that you use the latest version of Microsoft's Internet Explorer 4.0 or higher. Because Dynamic HTML is not currently an accepted Internet standard, most of the features and techniques on this site apply only to Internet Explorer, although some of the techniques may work with Netscape Navigator, the Netscape implementation of Dynamic HTML is not nearly as robust as Microsoft's, so Netscape users should proceed with caution. The site is divided into three sections:

- Online resources
- Dynamic HTML chapter examples
- Code zip files

Online Resources

The online resources section of the site contains links to popular Dynamic HTML sites, reference materials, and other tutorials that can be found online. These links are divided into three sections:

- **Dynamic HTML**—This section contain links to Dynamic HTML specific sites, and reference materials for Dynamic HTML.
- **Cascading Style Sheets**—This section contains links to reference materials for Cascading Style Sheets and CSS Positioning.
- **Scripting Languages**—This section contains links to reference materials for JavaScript and VBScript.

Dynamic HTML

Dynamic HTML is both a collection of technologies and a new technology, designed to increase the functionality of the browser. Because there is no Dynamic HTML standard yet, it is important to be aware of changes in the various vendor's versions of Dynamic HTML. Keeping on top of the latest implementations of Dynamic HTML will help you keep your pages current, so that your site can always look its best.

In the following sections you will find some links to the more important Dynamic HTML web sites currently available. Check these sites frequently for reference material and late breaking news about Dynamic HTML.

Microsoft Dynamic HTML Main Page   The Microsoft Dynamic HTML Main Page is a part of the Microsoft Site Builder Network. On this page you can find tutorials, FAQs, news, and links to other Dynamic HTML resources. This is one of the most comprehensive Dynamic HTML pages on the net.

http://www.microsoft.com/workshop/author/dhtml/

Microsoft Dynamic HTML Gallery   The Micrsoft Dynamic HTML Gallery is a showcase of what can, and is, being done with Dynamic HTML. This page is a great resource for seeing how things are done, and for generating ideas on how Dynamic HTML can enhance your site.

http://microsoft.com/gallery/files/html/

Microsoft Internet Client SDK   The Microsoft Internet Client SDK is a comprehensive developer's resource for all aspects of site development. Consider this site the ultimate reference and final authority for Dynamic HTML.

http://microsoft.com/msdn/sdk/inetsdk/help/default.htm

Microsoft Data Source Object Gallery   The Microsoft Data Source Object Gallery contains examples of how you can integrate database information into your web site. If you are exploring the data awareness and data binding features of Dynamic HTML, this site is a valuable resource.

http://microsoft.com/gallery/files/datasrc/

The DHTMLZone   The DHTMLZone is a Macromedia site devoted to tracking Dynamic HTML. It contains articles, news, examples, and showcases for Dynamic HTML on the net, including Netscape's implementation.

http://www.dhtmlzone.com/

W3C Document Object Model   The W3C Document Object Model page points to the technical specifications for the object model on which Dynamic HTML is based. This site is an excellent technical reference.

http://www.microsoft.com/workshop/prog/ie4/dom.htm

Cascading Style Sheets

App
E

The Cascading Style Sheets technology is an integral part of Dynamic HTML. Because style sheets are so fundamentally important to DHTML, you should also be aware of trends and changes in the CSS and CSS Positioning recommendations.

The following sites can provide you with news, information, and reference materials related to Cascading Style Sheets.

W3C Cascading Style Sheets Home Page   The World Wide Web Consortium's Style Sheets Home Page contains links to all kinds of materials related to Cascading Style Sheets, including technical references, tutorials, and press clippings.

http://www.w3.org/Style/

W3C Cascading Style Sheets Level 1 Recommendation   This is the official recommendation for Cascading Style Sheets, as determined by the W3C. The authoritative technical reference for CSS.

http://www.w3.org/pub/WWW/TR/WD-css1

W3C CSS Positioning Proposal   Here you will find the current working proposal for the Cascading Style Sheets Positioning recommendation. Because this is still a working draft, you might want to check here periodically to keep up with changes.

http://www.w3.org/TR/WD-positioning

Microsoft Guide to Style Sheets   The Microsoft Guide to Style Sheets contains tutorials and information that are specific to Microsoft's implementation of style sheets in Internet Explorer.

http://www.microsoft.com/workshop/author/css/css-f.htm

Microsoft Style Sheets Gallery   The Microsoft Style Sheets Gallery is part of the Site Builder Network, and showcases what designers are doing with Style Sheets. This is a good place for idea generation and to see "how it's done."

http://www.microsoft.com/gallery/files/styles/default.htm

Microsoft Typography Style Sheet Demo Pages   Another "gallery" style site from Microsoft that showcases what can be done with CSS, particularly in regard to typography and typesetting.

http://www.microsoft.com/truetype/css/gallery/entrance.htm

Scripting Languages

Dynamic HTML makes extensive use of scripting languages, both JavaScript and VBScript. Because VBScript and JavaScript are not exclusive to Dynamic HTML, changes might be made to the scripting languages that could affect your DHTML pages. Keeping on top of the scripting language you choose to use could prevent problems. The pages in the following sections provide reference points for both languages.

Netscape JavaScript Guide   The Netscape JavaScript Guide provides information and tutorials on JavaScript, the scripting language featured in this book. This site is a good place for learning JavaScript and for looking at examples.

http://home.netscape.com/eng/mozilla/3.0/handbook/javascript/index.html

Netscape JavaScript Reference   The Netscape JavaScript Reference is a comprehensive reference for JavaScript. It is technical in nature, but a valuable resource when coding JavaScript.

http://developer.netscape.com/library/documentation/communicator/jsref/index.htm

Microsoft JScript Home   The Microsoft JScript Home is the Microsoft guide to JavaScript. Although the Netscape sites tend to be more comprehensive, this site can be useful for seeing which JavaScript versions and/or features are implemented in Microsoft products.

http://www.microsoft.com/jscript

Microsoft VBScript Home   The Microsoft VBScript Home is a great jumping point for VBScript resources. The site contains links to tutorials, examples, and reference materials.

http://www.microsoft.com/vbscript

Cool DHTML Sites

In addition to all the resources that are available for Dynamic HTML, there are also some advantages to seeing what other sites are doing. Following is a list of sites that are "cool" Dynamic HTML sites. What makes them cool? The fact that they are using Dynamic HTML for starters! But these sites also showcase new and innovative ways that you can use Dynamic HTML to enhance your site.

Project Cool   Project Cool is a site that features resources and tools for Internet developers. The site contains lessons for Dynamic HTML, and a host of examples.

http://www.projectcool.com/developer/

ActiveIE   ActiveIE is more than just a Dynamic HTML page. Because Dynamic HTML is just one of the many new features of Internet Explorer 4.0, this site showcases new features and contains links to documentation, FAQs, and so on.

http://www.activeIE.com

IE4 Globe   The IE4 Globe is another web site that showcases new Internet Explorer 4.0 features. A large section is dedicated to Dynamic HTML, featuring news clips, examples, and references.

http://www.pconline.com/~mf5/ie4/

App

E

Code Examples

The following examples from *Special Edition Using Dynamic HTML* can be viewed on the site, and correspond to the numbered code listings found in the text.

Chapter 4: Cascading Style Sheets Primer

▓ A Global Style Sheet Example (global.css)

▓ A Local Style Sheet Example (local.css)

▓ 4.1 An Example of Conflicting Style Definitions (ch04ex01.htm)

▓ 4.2 Nesting Styles (ch04ex02.htm)

▓ 4.3 More Nesting Styles (ch04ex03.htm)

Chapter 5: JavaScript Primer

▓ 5.1 Hello World in JavaScript (ch05ex01.htm)

▓ 5.2 Changing Variable Contents (ch05ex02.htm)

▓ 5.3 Using the Eval Function (ch05ex03.htm)

▓ 5.4 Building Your Own Function (ch05ex04.htm)

▓ 5.5 A JavaScript Date Program (ch05ex05.htm)

Chapter 6: Dynamic HTML Object Model

▓ 6.1 Counting Paragraphs with the document.all Collection (ch06ex01.htm)

▓ 6.2 Looking at the Properties of an Element (ch06ex02.htm)

Chapter 7: Event Handling

▓ 7.1 Basic JavaScript Event Handling (ch07ex01.htm)

▓ 7.2 Event Handling on Arbitrary HTML Elements (ch07ex02.htm)

Chapter 8: Dynamic Styles

▓ 8.1 Changing a Font Style (ch08ex01.htm)

▓ 8.2 Changing Font Size (ch08ex02.htm)

▓ 8.3 Changing Font Color (ch08ex03.htm)

▓ 8.4 Hiding an Element with Visibility (ch08ex04.htm)

▓ 8.5 Peek-A-Boo Example (peekaboo.html)

▓ 8.6 An Expanding Outline (outline.html)

Chapter 9: Layout and Positioning

Chapter 10: Dynamic Content

Chapter 11: Introduction to Data Binding

Chapter 12: Using Data Source Objects

Chapter 13: Introducing Multimedia

Chapter 14: Multimedia Transitions

App
E

G.7   ArcDegrees (appGex07.htm)

G.8   Page Analyzer (appGex08.htm)

Source Code Zip File

The complete source code and graphic image files for the examples used in *Special Edition Using Dynamic HTML* can be found in the CompleteCode.zip file.

N O T E   For Macintosh users, the .zip file containing code examples can still be downloaded and decompressed on the Macintosh by using the StuffIt Expander. ▨

This file contains all the code examples used, and all the supporting graphic files. It can be downloaded and extracted onto your local hard drive to eliminate download time, and to enable you to edit and change the code.

App

E

Browser-Safe Hexadecimal Chart

Offering up a monochromatic web page can, in most cases, spell instant death for attracting lots of visitors to your site. Sensible, aesthetically appealing use of color can add depth and even aid in structuring information on a page.

With web style sheets, color becomes a bigger issue due to the interplay between text and background. To pull off a successful color scheme for your site, you need to ensure that all browsers will render your site's colors in the same fashion.

Two ways that you can specify color in the HTML code for your page are by indicating its hexadecimal RGB value or by indicating a color name. To specify, for example, that a font should appear as BlueViolet, you would use the hexa-decimal RGB value in your code as shown in the following line:

```
<font color= "#8A2BE2">
```

Likewise, you could specify the same color by using its color name as shown in the following line:

```
<font color= "BlueViolet">
```

Regardless of which manner of color specification you use in your HTML code, the following table provides a complete reference to the X11 colors that are supported by current versions of the Netscape and Microsoft web browsers and subsequently, most visitors to your site. Each color is indicated by color name, the hexadecimal RGB code, and the decimal code that you may use when rendering color in Photoshop or whatever imaging software you are using. ▦

Table F.1   Browser-Safe Hexadecimal Chart

Color Name	RGB Code	Decimal Code
AliceBlue	#F0F8FF	240,248,255
AntiqueWhite	#FAEBD7	250,235,215
Aqua	#00FFFF	0,255,255
Aquamarine	#7FFFD4	127,255,212
Azure	#F0FFFF	240,255,255
Beige	#F5F5DC	245,245,220
Bisque	#FFE4C4	255,228,196
Black	#000000	0,0,0
BlanchedAlmond	#FFEBCD	255,235,205
Blue	#0000FF	0,0,255
BlueViolet	#8A2BE2	138,43,226
Brown	#A52A2A	165,42,42
BurlyWood	#DEB887	222,184,135
CadetBlue	#5F9EA0	95,158,160
Chartreuse	#7FFF00	127,255,0
Chocolate	#D2691E	210,105,30
Coral	#FF7F50	255,127,80
CornflowerBlue	#6495ED	100,149,237
Cornsilk	#FFF8DC	255,248,220
Crimson	#DC143C	220,20,60
Cyan	#00FFFF	0,255,255
DarkBlue	#00008B	0,0,139
DarkCyan	#008B8B	0,139,139
DarkGoldenrod	#B8860B	184,134,11
DarkGray	#A9A9A9	169,169,169

Color Name	RGB Code	Decimal Code
DarkGreen	#006400	0,100,0
DarkKhaki	#BDB76B	189,183,107
DarkMagenta	#8B008B	139,0,139
DarkOliveGreen	#556B2F	85,107,47
DarkOrange	#FF8C00	255,140,0
DarkOrchid	#9932CC	153,50,204
DarkRed	#8B0000	139,0,0
DarkSalmon	#E9967A	233,150,122
DarkSeagreen	#8FBC8F	143,188,143
DarkSlateBlue	#483D8B	72,61,139
DarkSlateGray	#2F4F4F	47,79,79
DarkTurquoise	#00CED1	0,206,209
DarkViolet	#9400D3	148,0,211
DeepPink	#FF1493	255,20,147
DeepSkyBlue	#00BFFF	0,191,255
DimGray	#696969	105,105,105
DodgerBlue	#1E90FF	30,144,255
FireBrick	#B22222	178,34,34
FloralWhite	#FFFAF0	255,250,240
ForestGreen	#228B22	34,139,34
Fuchsia	#FF00FF	255,0,255
Gainsboro	#DCDCDC	220,220,220
GhostWhite	#F8F8FF	248,248,255
Gold	#FFD700	255,215,0
Goldenrod	#DAA520	218,165,32
Gray	#808080	128,128,128
Green	#008000	0,128,0
GreenYellow	#ADFF2F	173,255,47
Honeydew	#F0FFF0	240,255,240

APP

F

continues

Table F.1   Continued

Color Name	RGB Code	Decimal Code
HotPink	#FF69B4	255,105,180
IndianRed	#CD5C5C	205,92,92
Indigo	#4B0082	75,0,130
Ivory	#FFFFF0	255,255,240
Khaki	#F0E68C	240,230,140
Lavender	#E6E6FA	230,230,250
LavenderBlush	#FFF0F5	255,240,245
LawnGreen	#7CFC00	124,252,0
LemonChiffon	#FFFACD	255,250,205
LightBlue	#ADD8E6	173,216,230
LightCoral	#F08080	240,128,128
LightCyan	#E0FFFF	224,255,255
LightGoldenrodYellow	#FAFAD2	250,250,210
LightGreen	#90EE90	144,238,144
LightGrey	#D3D3D3	211,211,211
LightPink	#FFB6C1	255,182,193
LightSalmon	#FFA07A	255,160,122
LightSeaGreen	#20B2AA	32,178,170
LightSkyBlue	#87CEFA	135,206,250
LightSlateGray	#778899	119,136,153
LightSteelBlue	#B0C4DE	176,196,222
LightYellow	#FFFFE0	255,255,224
Lime	#00FF00	0,255,0
LimeGreen	#32CD32	50,205,50
Linen	#FAF0E6	250,240,230
Magenta	#FF00FF	255,0,255
Maroon	#800000	128,0,0
MediumAquamarine	#66CDAA	102,205,170

Color Name	RGB Code	Decimal Code
MediumBlue	#0000CD	0,0,205
MediumOrchid	#BA55D3	186,85,211
MediumPurple	#9370DB	147,112,219
MediumSeaGreen	#3CB371	60,179,113
MediumSlateBlue	#7B68EE	123,104,238
MediumSpringGreen	#00FA9A	0,250,154
MediumTurquoise	#48D1CC	72,209,204
MediumVioletRed	#C71585	199,21,133
MidnightBlue	#191970	25,25,112
MintCream	#F5FFFA	245,255,250
MistyRose	#FFE4E1	255,228,225
Moccasin	#FFE4B5	255,228,181
NavajoWhite	#FFDEAD	255,222,173
Navy	#000080	0,0,128
OldLace	#FDF5E6	253,245,230
Olive	#808000	128,128,0
OliveDrab	#6B8E23	107,142,35
Orange	#FFA500	255,165,0
OrangeRed	#FF4500	255,69,0
Orchid	#DA70D6	218,112,214
PaleGoldenrod	#EEE8AA	238,232,170
PaleGreen	#98FB98	152,251,152
PaleTurquoise	#AFEEEE	175,238,238
PaleVioletRed	#DB7093	219,112,147
PapayaWhip	#FFEFD5	255,239,213
PeachPuff	#FFDAB9	255,218,185
Peru	#CD853F	205,133,63
Pink	#FFC0CB	255,192,203
Plum	#DDA0DD	221,160,221

APP

F

continues

Table F.1   Continued

Color Name	RGB Code	Decimal Code
PowderBlue	#B0E0E6	176,224,230
Purple	#800080	128,0,128
Red	#FF0000	255,0,0
RosyBrown	#BC8F8F	188,143,143
RoyalBlue	#4169E1	65,105,225
SaddleBrown	#8B4513	139,69,19
Salmon	#FA8072	250,128,114
SandyBrown	#F4A460	244,164,96
SeaGreen	#2E8B57	46,139,87
Seashell	#FFF5EE	255,245,238
Sienna	#A0522D	160,82,45
Silver	#C0C0C0	192,192,192
SkyBlue	#87CEEB	135,206,235
SlateBlue	#6A5ACD	106,90,205
SlateGray	#708090	112,128,144
Snow	#FFFAFA	255,250,250
SpringGreen	#00FF7F	0,255,127
SteelBlue	#4682B4	70,130,180
Tan	#D2B48C	210,180,140
Teal	#008080	0,128,128
Thistle	#D8BFD8	216,191,216
Tomato	#FF6347	255,99,71
Turquoise	#40E0D0	64,224,208
Violet	#EE82EE	238,130,238
Wheat	#F5DEB3	245,222,179
White	#FFFFFF	255,255,255
WhiteSmoke	#F5F5F5	245,245,245
Yellow	#FFFF00	255,255,0
YellowGreen	#9ACD32	154,205,50

Dynamic HTML Tips and Utilities

The world of Dynamic HTML, although still in a state of infancy, has expanded enormously since the introduction of the first browsers capable of dynamically manipulating content in an HTML document. Now the hype is about Internet Explorer 4.0, Microsoft's new browser and operating system upgrade. If you evaluated Internet Explorer 4.0 through its platform preview releases, you understand the difficulties of getting everything to work. Also, with sparse availability of documentation at times, both the developer's and the writer's tasks were even more difficult than with Internet Explorer 3.0.

This appendix is based on the Internet Explorer 4.0 browser, Platform Preview Release 2, which reflects the vast number of features and advantages of this browser. Most of the information contained in this appendix will probably not change with subsequent releases. This appendix, although intended to be supplementary to the material in this book, is in no way a complete guide to all the wonderful things you can do with Dynamic HTML and Internet Explorer 4.0. It does, however, provide a focal point that will bring you one step closer to fully utilizing Dynamic HTML.

This appendix provides several Dynamic HTML applications, pointers, tips, and tricks. Some you can plug right into your application and others you can use with slight modifications. Other parts of this appendix feature procedures that will help you construct useful applications and other programs that will help you understand Dynamic HTML and Internet Explorer 4.0 better. This information is organized in the following way:

- **Using Scripting Languages**—Scripting languages are the lifeblood of Dynamic HTML. This section shows you how to make the best use of them and introduces some advanced programming concepts.

- **Using Visual Effects**—This section shows you some unique examples of Dynamic HTML's visual effects functionality, including a filter wizard and some interesting ways to use the DirectDraw API.

- **Obtaining Browser and Document Information**—This is always an important feature, even more so for people developing dynamic content. This section will show you how to access and manipulate browser and document information.

- **Learning More**— This section points you to additional resources, but more importantly, it shows you how to analyze examples written by other people. ■

Scripting Languages

Because scripting languages are the lifeblood of Dynamic HTML, you should have a full understanding of their uses, including when to use a specific feature or type of syntax of a scripting language, or when it's best to use a specific scripting language itself. Currently, two scripting languages are supported by Internet Explorer 4.0: VBScript and JavaScript.

Something included with an HTML page is considered *inline*, and that is also true for scripting languages. Inline scripting languages employ *sandbox architecture*, which means they are limited to how they can access and use your browser and ultimately, your computer. This security feature does not make JavaScript or VBScript very powerful compared to other languages, but it still makes them well-suited for Dynamic HTML. This security feature creates an inequality between JavaScript and VBScript, regardless of how much they otherwise seem to be alike. JavaScript, for instance, is often considered a "sandbox" scripting language like VBScript, but a few security holes have recently been exposed through JavaScript due to its C-like versatility. However, Internet Explorer prevents these security holes.

One of the purposes of this section is to acquaint you with how JavaScript and VBScript compare technically, along with the strengths and weaknesses of each language. This will be illustrated through several examples, which will help you understand Dynamic HTML better, as well. Often, how each language compares in usage seems to be more important, but a lack of understanding of the inner workings of each language can cripple a developer. This section will feature several important and often-overlooked aspects of scripting languages: how you can optimize using each scripting language; when to best use a specific language; recursion and indefinite processes; and probably most importantly, error handling and how to "gracefully degrade" a user when a possible error can occur on your page.

Selecting the Optimal Scripting Language

Determining which scripting language to use can be as simple as determining which language provides the best functionality for your intended task or application. Making this decision can also be complicated when creating an entire program specification with a project specification, requirements and definitions of first level procedures, and so forth. With such a wide range of issues regarding which language you use, how should you decide?

Consider this example: You have a form for submitting data on the page, and you want to do this manually because you want additional control over how your data is submitted. Therefore, you cannot submit the form through standard means (the Submit button). You want to use the GET method to submit your form, so how would you do this? First, you know that the GET method does not accept most non-alphanumeric characters, and it uses text-to-ASCII number conversion for these characters, translating the ASCII integer value to a hex value. So, if a user submitted data that read "John Doe," for example, you would want to use your script to submit it as: "John%20Doe" where %20 is the hex conversion for 32, which is the ASCII character for "space." Several solutions to this problem are possible. The first example examines a VBScript solution:

```
'This should be embedded inside a script block
...
sub ConvertItForSubmit(MyString)
'This Sub procedure is used to determine
'the length of a string that is passed through
'the MyString argument and use it to parse
'through the string to determine characters not
'suitable for the GET method of form submission
...
lenMyString = len(MyString)
for i = 1 to lenMyString
  MyCurrentLetter = left(MyString, i)
  ConvertLetter(MyCurrentLetter)
  strNewString = strNewString & MyCurrentLetter
loop
...
function ConvertLetter(MyLetter)
'This function takes a single character and
'determines if it is an invalid character
select case MyLetter
case "!"
     ConvertLetter = "%21"
Case chr$(32)
     ConvertLetter = "%20"
...
end select
end function
```

The program works as described in the following algorithm:

1. The Sub procedure called *ConvertItForSubmit(MyString)* is called externally from another part of the program. This Sub procedure accepts an argument in the form of a string that is to be encoded.

App
G

2. The *ConvertItForSubmit()* Sub procedure determines the length of the sting.

3. It uses this length to loop through every letter in the string.

4. In the looping process, the *ConvertLetter(MyLetter)* Sub procedure, which accepts a single character as an argument is called.

5. *ConvertLetter()* converts all invalid characters into the appropriate hexadecimal code.

6. A new string is built that is acceptable for form submission.

This task is not too difficult to program, and you could probably completely code such an application within an hour; however, the *escape()* JavaScript function does this automatically, as shown in the following example:

```
Function ConvertString(MyString)
{
//This function converts a string and parses invalid characters
return escape(MyString);
}
```

Just a couple of lines in JavaScript is all it takes to accomplish the same thing listed in the VBScript example, and if you did code such a program, you would have saved some time knowing about this function. You may not know JavaScript, so what do you do? Well, you can be resigned to just using the previous VBScript method. Note also, that you can reuse a Sub procedure to complete similar tasks.

For now, keep in mind that the need for excessive scripting you might experience in one scripting language might be significantly reduced in another. If you want to convert numbers easily between decimal, octal, or hex, for instance, you should use VBScript. For the most part, VBScript has better string manipulation. If you want control over creating your own objects, JavaScript provides the capability to create objects, but VBScript does not. On the other hand, VBScript interfaces nicely with ActiveX Controls and Java applets and also has excellent error handling. The best way to determine which scripting language is best suited for your needs might involve spending 15 or 20 minutes reading through the documentation to see exactly what each scripting language has to offer.

Recursion

Recursion is the process of repeating some process over and over again. Recursion, in programming, is a wonderful tool. By applying recursion to Dynamic HTML, you can make some pretty powerful applications. Unfortunately, when reference manuals discuss recursion, it is often limited to an application such as finding a factorial of a number. The place recursion has the greatest effect in Dynamic HTML is with animation and with changing effects of different elements on the page.

In this section, you will see some basic applications of recursion, including a "neon" sign, which you can place directly in any document. This example will be presented in both VBScript and JavaScript. In each code listing, some features specific to each language will be used to implement the neon sign, and these features will be pointed out. The implementation of these features will then be used to demonstrate the various advantages and weaknesses of each language.

Controlling Recursion in VBScript   Recursion is not hard to implement in JavaScript or VBScript. In fact, recursion can be as simple as implementing a loop as follows:

```
<SCRIPT LANGUAGE="VBSCRIPT">
'Initialize variables
dim x
x = 99
'set up do loops
do until x = -1
  alert x & " bottles of root beer on the wall"
  x = x -1
loop
</SCRIPT>
```

The *do* loop repeats the contained statements, counting down the number of root beer bottles 100 times, after which, the loop exits. Such a loop is impractical for this task because it prevents the user from doing anything else; however, the *do* loop will be useful at other times, such as in forcing input from a user.

Another form of recursion involves a Sub procedure that calls itself repeatedly until a given condition is true:

```
<SCRIPT LANGUAGE="VBSCRIPT">
'calls the recursive Sub procedure
call checkName()

sub checkName()
'This sub checks for a valid name
  InputMe = inputbox("Enter Your Name","Name:")
  if InputMe = "My Name" then
    exit sub
  else
    call checkName()
  end if
end sub
</SCRIPT>
```

In the previous listing, the VBScript calls a Sub procedure named *checkName()* that displays an input box on the screen and prompts the user for a name. If the name is invalid, then the Sub procedure *checkName()* is continuously called and the input box is continuously displayed until a valid name, in this case "My Name," is entered inside the input box. This is practical recursion in action, but how does this apply to Dynamic HTML, you may wonder. How recursion lends itself to Dynamic HTML will be shown in the following example.

The neon sign is a bunch of text that changes through a set of predefined colors, but more importantly, it accomplishes this task through recursion, style sheets, scripting, and the scripting object model. Recursion is what makes the gears turn in the following listing and causes the perpetual behavior of the color scrolling. VBScript recursion is demonstrated in listing G.1.

App

G

Listing G.1   Recursive Programming in VBScript

```
001. <HTML>
002. <HEAD>
003. <TITLE>Recursive operations in VBScript
004. </TITLE>
005. <SCRIPT LANGUAGE="VBScript">
006. 'initialize global variables
007. 'lngMyTimeOut is used to initialize the setTimeout function
008. 'strMyColorArray holds the colors
009. 'intColorCount is used to keep track of which color is selected
010. 'intWhichStyle is used to determine whether the text should
011. ' blink, or if it should change colors
012. 'bolVisVar is used to determine whether the text in CStyles()
013. ' should be visible
014. 'intSpeed is to specify the speed of span1
015.
016. dim intColorCount, lngMyTimeOut, intClrArrayLen, _
017.     intSpeed, intWhichStyle, objMySpan, bolVisVar
018. intClrArrayLen = 4
019. dim strMyColorArray(4)
020. intColorCount = 0
021. intSpeed = 1000
022. intWhichStyle = 0
023. bolVisVar = true
024. strMyColorArray(0) = "#FF89F9"
025. strMyColorArray(1) = "#8FF6FF"
026. strMyColorArray(2) = "#8E76FF"
027. strMyColorArray(3) = "#FF25B3"
028. strMyColorArray(4) = "#70FF85"
029. 'You can add as many or as few colors as you want to the strMyColorArray()
030. 'as you want by changing the array declaration, adding the additional array
041. 'variable which has the color and by changing the intClrArrayLen to
042. 'the value of the largest index array number
043. </SCRIPT>
044.
045. <BODY BGCOLOR="#FFE0E7"
046.     onload="VBScript: lngMyTimeOut = _
047.             setTimeout('call ChangeColorStyle()',1000)">
048.
049. <SPAN id="span1"
050.     STYLE="font-size: .5in;
051.             font-family:signet roundhand ATT;
052.             font-weight:bold">Enter Here
053. </SPAN>
054.
055. <SCRIPT LANGUAGE="VBSCRIPT">
056. 'This object reference is to the style object of the tag name "span1",
057. 'used to make the program more efficient and easier to write.
058. set objMySpan = document.all.span1.style
059.
060. sub ChangeColorStyle()
061. 'This is the main Sub procedure used to determine which
062. 'style to display by using intWhichStyle.
063.
```

```
064. select case intWhichStyle
065.    case 0
066.       CColors
067.    case 1
068.       CStyles
069.    end select
070. end sub
071.
072.
073. sub CColors()
074. 'CColor() is used to display a set of predefined colors
075. 'from the strMyColorAray() to the span1 tag. A simple checking
076. 'method is used to ensure that the array does not go out of bounds.
077.       objMySpan.visibility = "visible"
078.       objMySpan.color = strMyColorArray(intColorCount)
079.       if intColorCount + 1 > intClrArrayLen then
080.          intColorCount = 0
081.       else
082.          intColorCount = intColorCount + 1
083.       end if
084.       lngMyTimeOut = setTimeout("ChangeColorStyle",intSpeed)
085.
086. end sub
087.
088. sub CStyles()
089. 'CStyles() is used to rapidly switch the visibility of the span1 tag
090. 'on an off, it starts with an initial speed of 250 milsecs (fast)
091.       objMySpan.color = "red"
092.       intSpeed = 250
093.       txtSpeed.value = intSpeed
094.       if bolVisVar = true then
095.          objMySpan.visibility = "hidden"
096.          bolVisVar = false
097.       else
098.          objMySpan.visibility = "visible"
099.          bolVisVar = true
100.       end if
101.       lngMyTimeOut = setTimeout("ChangeColorStyle",intSpeed)
102. end sub
103. </SCRIPT></BODY></HTML>
```

Listing G.1 has the following parts:

- The header of the document specified by the <HEAD> tag that includes relevant information about the document (<TITLE> tag), and a scripting block specified by the <SCRIPT> tag that defines all the variables and constants that will be used in the program. These variables and constants are fully documented in the listing.

- The body of the document includes primarily the <SPAN> tag used for the neon sign and the scripting block, which holds the main program.

- The scripting block contains three Sub procedures and an object declaration. These are also documented with the code.

App

G

If you are familiar with the *document* object, *style sheet* properties, and VBScript, then you know what is being done in the code. If not, pay particular attention to lines 45–47 and line 84 of listing G.1:

```
045. <BODY BGCOLOR="#FFE0E7"
046.        onload="VBScript: lngMyTimeOut = _
047.                 setTimeout('call ChangeColorStyle()',1000)">

084. lngMyTimeOut = setTimeout("ChangeColorStyle",intSpeed)
```

You see the first line of the preceding code once in the entire document. It is bound to the *onload* event of the <BODY> tag. This means the code contained in the *onload="..."* attribute will be executed when the document loads. The code is inline to the tag, which is one of several ways you can add script to your HTML document (see Appendix C, "Using VBScript Instead of JavaScript" for more information). The scripting language that will be used is VBScript, and this is signified by the *"VBScript: ..."* statement for the *onload* event. Next, you see that the variable *lngMyTimeOut* is set to a function call, which is part of the *window* object called *setTimeout*. Basically, the *setTimeout* function waits a specified period of time (in line 47, 1000 milliseconds or 1 second) then executes the specified statement that is calling the *ChangeColorStyle()* Sub procedure.

 T I P JavaScript is the default language for Internet Explorer 4.0, which means if you create a script block with the <SCRIPT> and </SCRIPT> tags without specifying any attributes, you will use JavaScript. Similarly, when you specify inline event code for different elements, JavaScript is the default language and you must use either the someEvent="VBScript: code here..." method, where you specify the language followed by the statements in the event attribute itself, or you must add the LANGUAGE="VBScript" attribute to the tag for which you want to handle the event.

The second line of code you see twice—once in the *CColors()* Sub procedure and once in the *CStyles()* Sub procedure. It does the same thing as the previous listing of code, except the amount of time to wait is not "hard coded" into the function. Instead, it takes the form of a variable called intSpeed. Because intSpeed can change, so can the amount of time in the *setTimeout()* function.

Both instances of the *setTimeout()* (lines 84 and 101) function do the same thing; they call the *ChangeColorStyle()* Sub procedure. The *ChangeColorStyle()* (line 60) Sub procedure contains a select case structure that determines what type of effect to apply to the <SPAN> (span1) tag that was mentioned. If it is the first choice in the select case structure, then the effect applied to the span1 is that of a neon sign—a change in color. If it is the second choice, then span1 rapidly blinks.

The recursiveness of this program comes into play when calling either *CColors()* or *CStyles()*; each has a different effect on span1, and the *setTimeout()* function that is at the end of each Sub procedure again calls the *ChangeColorStyle()* Sub procedure, which then determines which style to use, and so on. The *intWhichStyle* variable determines which style to use. The style can only be changed by user intervention. So, if you have the initial value of *intWhichStyle* set to "0," then span1 will continue to behave like a neon sign. If you change the *intWhichStyle* value to "1," then span1 blinks rapidly.

You can easily play around with the speed and the display of the <SPAN> tag to create different effects by inserting the following lines right below </SPAN> in the document:

```
<HR>
<INPUT TYPE="button" NAME="btnSpeed" VALUE="Change Speed"
       onclick="VBScript: intSpeed = txtSpeed.value">
<INPUT TYPE="text" NAME="txtSpeed" VALUE="1000"
       TITLE="The higher the number, the slower the change"><BR>
<INPUT TYPE="button" NAME="btnStyle" VALUE="Change Style"
       onclick="VBScript: if intWhichStyle = 0 then _
              intWhichStyle = 1 else intWhichStyle = 0">
```

The preceding code listing is a quick user interface that was designed to investigate the different properties of the neon sign. This code's interface consists of a horizontal rule and three <INPUT> tags. <INPUT> tags specify HTML *intrinsic controls*, which are also sometimes referred to as *form controls*. The first <INPUT> tag is a button that is used in conjunction with the second <INPUT> tag, which is a text box. You enter a desired speed in the text box and click the "Change Speed" button to watch the speed of the text, "Enter Here," change. The higher the value, the slower it goes because you are specifying a larger interval. The third <INPUT> tag switches between the two styles previously mentioned. You might notice that all the code for accomplishing the aforementioned tasks is inline to each respective <INPUT> tag or control. The code entered is simple VBScript. Specifying short bits of inline code and calling external Sub procedures or functions are all that is really recommended for handling events inline.

Controlling Recursion in JavaScript   As you can see, implementing recursive tasks and adding advanced functionality in VBScript is relatively simple, as is true for JavaScript. JavaScript has a few added features that make recursion more powerful with JavaScript, as you will see in listing G.2. Figure G.1 illustrates this listing.

Listing G.2   Recursive Programming in JavaScript

```
01. <HTML>
02. <HEAD>
03. <TITLE>JavaScript example of recursive code</TITLE>
04. </HEAD>
05. <SCRIPT>
06. //declare colors array
07. var myColors = new Array()
08. myColors[0] = "lightblue"
09. myColors[1] = "blue"
10. myColors[2] = "darkblue"
11. myColors[3] = "purple"
12. </SCRIPT>
13.
14. <BODY>
15.
16. <SPAN id="span1" STYLE="color: black;font-size=.5in">Our Text</SPAN>
17. <BR><B id="test2">Hullo!</B>
18.
19. <SCRIPT>
20. //variable declarations to make code cleaner
```

App

G

continues

Listing G.2   Continued

```
21. var objSpanNeon = document.all.span1
22. var objBNeon = document.all.test2
23. function controlSpan(objMain, speed, scrlColors, whichOption, objID)
24. {
25. //Methods
26.   this.begin = begin;
27.   this.dispStyle = dispStyle;
28.   this.color = getColor;
29.   this.Timer = setTimeout;
30.
31. /* this.begin is the method that initiates the process
32.    this.dispStyle is used to switch between changing
33.                   colors and blinking
34.    this.color is a method that changes the color of an element
35.    this.Timer is a setTimeout function made part of the object */
36.
37. //Objects
38.   this.objMain = objMain;
39.   this.scrlColors = scrlColors;
40.
41. /* this.objMain is the object passed on which all the style
42.                 manipulation will occur. It is passed as an
43.                 argument to the function
44.    this.scrlColors is the array containing all the colors in
45.                 the form of "colorname" or "#RRGGBB"    */
46.
47. //Properties
48.
49.   this.bolVis = true;
50.   this.colorInd = -1;
51.   this.objID = objID + ".begin()";
52.   this.scrlLen = scrlColors.length - 1;
53.   this.speed = speed;
54.   this.TimerVar = 0;
55.   this.whichOption = whichOption;
56.   this.stopit = stopit;
57.
58. /* this.bolVis is used in the dispStyle method to determine
59.                 whether the text should be visible or invisible
60.    this.colorInd is used with the color array to scroll through
61.                 the colors
62.    this.objID is used with the Timer method to create recursiveness
63.    this.scrlLen is used to scroll through the colors and to make
64.                 sure that this.colorInd does not go over bounds
65.    this.speed sets the speed of the this.Timer method
66.    this.TimerVar sets the Timeout ID for the Timer method, in case
67.                 it has to be stopped for some reason
68.    this.whichOption is the variable used to switch between the
69.                 different styles in dispStyle. 2 exist now. */
70.
71. }
72.
73. function getColor(newColor)
```

```
74. //this method sets the color of the given object
75. {
76.   this.objMain.style.color = newColor;
77. }
78.
79. function begin()
80. //this method is what is used to start changing styles
81. //for the given object
82. {
83.   this.dispStyle();
84.   this.TimerVar = this.Timer(this.objID, this.speed);
85. }
86.
87. function dispStyle()
88. //This is the heart of our "neon sign" function
89. //it contains the conditionals used to determine
90. //which style to apply to the given object.
91. {
92.   if(this.whichOption == 0)
93.   {
94.     if(++this.colorInd > this.scrlLen)
95.       this.colorInd = 0;
96.       this.color(this.scrlColors[this.colorInd]);
97.   }
98.   if(this.whichOption == 1)
99.   {
100.     if(this.bolVis == false)
101.       this.objMain.style.visibility = "hidden";
102.     else
103.       this.objMain.style.visibility = "visible";
104.     this.bolVis = !this.bolVis;
105.   }
106. }
107.
108. function stopit()
109. {
110. clearTimeout(this.TimerVar)
111.
112. }
113. //The declaration below is used to declare a new neon sign object.
114.
115.   var spanner = new controlSpan(objSpanNeon, 1000, myColors, 0, "spanner");
116.   var bold2 = new controlSpan(objBNeon, 500, "", 1, "bold2");
117. //start the style changing for span1
118.   spanner.begin();
119.   bold2.begin();
120.
121.
122. </SCRIPT>
123. <BR><INPUT TYPE="button" onclick="spanner.stopit()" Value="Stop First
➥Label">
124.    <INPUT TYPE="button" onclick="bold2.stopit()" Value="Stop Second
➥Label">
125. </BODY>
```

FIG. G.1

You can create instances of the *controlSpan()* object any number of times with different elements on the page.

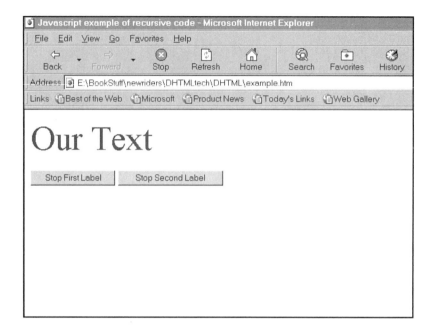

Much like the VBScript listing, listing G.2 has the following parts:

- The header portion of the document, which contains a scripting block that has general information (such as the color array definitions and so on).

- The <BODY> portion of the document, which includes a <SPAN> tag used with the first object definition, a <B> tag used with the second, and two HTML intrinsic command buttons that cancel the special effects of the first and second groups of text.

- The <SCRIPTING> portion in the <BODY> tag is the most important part of the document. With it, the object is created and two instantiations are created that correspond with the tags labeled "span1" and "test2" respectively.

Listing G.2 shows a culmination of several important parts of JavaScript other than recursion. The most important, and the one you might have noticed immediately, is that an object packages all the methods and properties of the neon sign. When everything is packaged nicely and neatly into an object, you have cleaner, more portable, and easier-to-use code, in addition to relieving some of the headaches involved with debugging the code. Furthermore, with JavaScript's instantiation capability, you can quickly create an unlimited number of neon signs on a page.

Examine what is happening in the program. First, two object references are created that reference the <SPAN> tag and the <B> tags, which are in *javaneon.htm*. An object called *controlSpan()* is created and the methods and properties are added. Then, two instantiations (spanner and bold2) of the object are created for the tags with which they are used. The *controlSpan()* object is defined on line 23:

```
function controlSpan(objMain, speed, scrlColors, whichOption, objID)
{...}
```

When you create an instantiation of *controlSpan ()*, you also create the need for arguments to initialize the contents of the object. The first argument, *objMain,* is the reference to the object that will be manipulated. In this case, the objects (or elements) called "span1" and "bold2" will be used for the *objMain* argument, as you will see in the following code listing. The *speed* argument defines the timing speed for the *setTimeout ()* function that will be used to dynamically change the styles of the two elements. The *scrlColors* argument contains the array of colors used to change a neon sign's color. The *whichOption* argument determines which style (blinking or changing colors) should be displayed for a given element. Finally, the *objID* argument sends the name of the instantiated object to itself. You will understand the full purpose of this argument later in this section.

Now that you know the purposes of the arguments this object accepts, examine the instantiations of *controlSpan* in lines 115–116:

```
var spanner = new controlSpan(objSpanNeon, 1000, myColors, 0, "spanner");
var bold2 = new controlSpan(objBNeon, 500, "", 1, "bold2");
```

The first instantiation (or creation) for the new object called "spanner" is for the <SPAN> tag. You know this because, for the *objMain* argument, the variable *objSpanNeon* is used as one of the properties for the object, which references *document.all.span1* or the SPAN element that is used in this example. Next, a speed of 1000 is given for the object, which specifies how fast objects will dynamically change styles. The higher the value, the slower the effects will occur. The *myColors[]* array contains all the colors that will be used to change colors for the neon sign. The value "0" is given for the *whichOption* argument, which specifies which dynamic style the object will use. This can be either "0," which specifies changing through colors as defined in the *scrlColors* array, or "1," which specifies an element that blinks on and off on the screen. Finally, "spanner" is given as the instantiated object name.

The second object creation is similar to the first, except during the creation of the object the array of colors is not used at an argument because there is no need for them. For this object, the only thing that is desired is the blinking effect (the effect would require the *whichOption* to be set as 1).

To start the process of dynamically manipulating the styles for each of the elements, you must invoke the *begin ()* method for each object as shown in listing G.2. Stopping each process is quite simple, and you should be able to determine how that is done by reading the script.

Now for the recursive part. As one of the methods of the *controlSpan* object, you include the *setTimeout ()* function on line 29:

```
this.Timer = setTimeout;
```

Basically, the preceding code is essential in creating the object with black-box architecture in mind, so everything is contained and the object does not have to rely on anything that is not within the function. To follow the black-box architecture, the *this* constructor is used extensively to ensure the object is not reliant on any other code except its own. A problem occurs, however, when you try to use the *setTimeout ()* function with the *this* constructor for the

App

G

controlSpan() object. Because the *setTimeout()* function is part of the *window* object, the *this* constructor points to the *window* object every time the *setTimeout()* function is called, thus eliminating the previous object reference to an instantiated *controlSpan()* object. When using the previous statement, the *setTimeout()* function is assimilated with the *controlSpan()* object, thus partly solving the problem. Finally, a string is built using the *objID* argument to tell the *setTimeout()* function which method it should call. This is done with the following property from line 51 of listing G.2:

```
this.objID = objID + ".begin()";
```

And assigned to the *setTimeout()* function on line 84 in this manner:

```
this.TimerVar = this.Timer(this.objID, this.speed);
```

The preceding statement is what causes the code to be recursive, because the *this.Timer* calls itself over and over again until it is told to stop.

You create as many instantiations of the *controlSpan()* object as you want, as long as you specify the valid arguments. If you had a <H1> tag named "header1," for instance, you would use the following syntax to make an instantiation of the object:

```
var myheader1 = new controlSpan(header1, 1000, myColorArray, 0, "myheader1")
```

In the following instantiation, you would have made an object called myheader1, given it a style changing speed of 1,000 milliseconds, and specified the array *myColorArray* as the array that will be used for displaying the different colors. You gave myheader1 a *whichOption* value of "0" (meaning you want it to display different colors) and put in the string "myheader1" for the *objID* argument, which is the name of the object.

Additionally, you can add more styles to the *dispStyle()* method, such as changing the size of text to make it appear larger or smaller, and so on. To do this, you would add another conditional statement that corresponds to a *whichOption* value for each dynamic style you want to include. You add a style, for instance, that changes the size of the font, then you add a conditional that states if whichOption = 2 then change the size of the text.

Furthermore, you can programatically control the properties of each object. If you want the object to change styles instantly, for example, you set the appropriate property of the desired object whenever a given event happens. A caution, though—if you want to switch back and forth between blinking and color changing, you must specify a color array, and you cannot leave that argument blank as was shown in the *bold2* object instantiation.

Error Handling and Error Trapping

Unfortunately, error handling is one of the most overlooked processes in programming languages. Although this concept does not relate directly to any single component of Dynamic HTML such as event bubbling, it is essential. Some browsers will support Dynamic HTML and the additional components associated with them, such as scripting, and some will not.

This can cause a potential problem to browsers viewing your Dynamic HTML site. Most browsers use truncation techniques that ignore anything the browser cannot understand. This is not true, however, for browsers that support scripting languages and *not* Dynamic HTML. For instance, how many times have you seen a web page that comes up with an "object not found" error?

Generally, errors with programming languages can be handled in two ways: by careful, "secure" programming code (error trapping), and by using built-in means to control errors. Such means are specific to each programming language. VBScript, for instance, has strong support in the language for error handling.

VBScript Error Handling   If error handling is of utmost importance in your web project, then VBScript is probably the language you should use. It provides two useful tools to accomplish error handling:

> The *on error resume next* statement
>
> The *err* object

As you know from your understanding of objects, each object can have several properties, methods, and events.

Although you can learn about the methods and properties of the *err* object and additional information about the *on error resume next* statement from VBScript documentation, this section will show a few examples of how to use these objects and statements.

The *err* object has two methods and five properties that contain information about errors that occur when your script is running (at runtime). You need to use the *on error resume next* statement to be able to ignore errors so that you can access the information they generate. The following listings are used to demonstrate error handling using VBScript components.

Consider the following code:

```
<HTML>
<HEAD>
<TITLE>This page generates a runtime error</TITLE>
</HEAD>
<BODY>
<INPUT TYPE="button" NAME="btnClickMe"
       VALUE="Click to change text box">
<INPUT TYPE="text" NAME="txtWillChng"
       VALUE="">
<SCRIPT LANGUAGE="VBScript">
sub btnClickMe_onClick()
txtWillChngg.value = "See I changed!"
end sub
</SCRIPT>
</BODY>
```

When this page is run, an error will be generated stating that an object called *txtWillChngg* is required. This means the scripting interpreter cannot find the object (that is supposed to be the text box). Now, any scripting programmer will most likely know what is going on; however, the average user probably will not. What will the user know if this error pops up and the script stops running? Now consider the following code:

App

G

```
<HTML>
<HEAD>
<TITLE>This page generates a runtime error</TITLE>
</HEAD>
<BODY>
<INPUT TYPE="button" NAME="btnClickMe"
       VALUE="Click to change text box">
<INPUT TYPE="text" NAME="txtWillChng"
       VALUE="">
<SCRIPT LANGUAGE="VBScript">

sub btnClickMe_onClick()
' the statement below causes the script interpreter to
' ignore any runtime errors on the page
on error resume next

' below is not a valid object
txtWillChngg.value = "See I changed!"

'here is our error handling conditional, checks to
'see if there is actual an error
if err then
  select case err.number
    ' the number below corresponds to the error
    ' generated when an invalid object is accessed
    case 424
     strError = "An element or object on the" & chr(13) & _
                "page could not be accessed." & chr(13) & _
                "Do you still wish to continue" & chr(13) & _
                "running scripts (Yes) or " & chr(13) & _
                "exit the part of the program" & chr(13) & _
            "that caused this error (No)?"
  end select
  ' here is a message box that informs the user an error occurs
  x = msgBox(strError,20,"One or more errors have occurred")
  ' this determines what to do based on what the user specified
  ' in the message box
  select case x
    case 6 ' when the user clicks Yes
    case 7 ' when the user clicks No
        exit sub
    case else ' to be safe
        exit sub
  end select
end if
end sub

</SCRIPT>
</BODY>
```

As you may have noticed, the error handling is robust in the preceding example. Many interesting features belong to this error handling routine. First, examine the statement that enables you to perform all the error handling:

```
on error resume next
```

This statement enables the scripting interpreter to ignore all runtime errors generated by the script. Additionally, it stores all the information about the would-be-fatal error in the *err* object. This includes a not very informative description, an error number that corresponds to the description, and other miscellaneous information.

Now, examine the conditional statement, which initiates the error handling:

```
if err then
...
end if
```

The script checks to see if an error was actually generated, then proceeds with identifying the error using the *select case* statement with *err.number* property as the test case. If the number matches a number that the routine covers, then a string will be generated and used with the message box telling the user in a more descriptive manner which error actually occurred. Then the option of what to do with the remaining script is left up to the user.

This listing shows a general use of error handling through scripting. If you want more robust error handling in your statements, you should use error handling in all your subroutines and in your main program. The primary reason for this is that all the information in the *err* object is reset every time a subroutine or function is called or when the scripting interpreter comes across another *on error resume next* statement.

For optimal efficiency, you should put most of the code in a special error-handling function, which returns the value of what the user chose for the message box. A resident *select case* statement could be in each subroutine to determine how to deal with the error, and this could allow for special cases, as well. Listing G.3 shows how to set up such a function.

Listing G.3   A Complete Error Handling Application

```
01. <HTML>
02. <HEAD>
03. <TITLE>This page generates a runtime error</TITLE>
04. </HEAD>
05. <BODY>
06. <INPUT TYPE="button" NAME="btnClickMe"
07.        VALUE="Click to change text box">
08. <INPUT TYPE="text" NAME="txtWillChng"
09.        VALUE="">
10. <SCRIPT LANGUAGE="VBScript">
11.
12. sub btnClickMe_onClick()
13. ' the statement below causes the script interpreter to
14. ' ignore any runtime errors on the page
15. on error resume next
16. ' below is not a valid object
17. txtWillChngg.value = "See I changed!"
18. 'here is our error handling conditional, checks to
19. 'see if there is actual an error then calls a function
20. if err then
21.   lngMyErr = lngProcessError(err)
```

continues

Listing G.3   Continued

```
22.   select case lngMyErr
23.     case 6 ' when the user clicks Yes
24.         ' just continue with flow
25.     case 7 ' when the user clicks No
26.         exit sub
27.     case else ' to be safe
28.         exit sub
29.   end select
30. end if
31. end sub
32.
33. function lngProcessError(objError)
34.   select case objError.number
35.     case 5   ' error handling for invalid procedure call
36.     case 11 ' error handling for divide by zero
37.     case 13 ' type mismatch
38.     case 16 ' expression too complex
39.     case 380 ' invalid property value
40.     case 424 ' error handling for object required
41.      strError = "An element or object on the" & chr(13) & _
42.                 "page could not be accessed." & chr(13) & _
43.                 "Do you still wish to continue" & chr(13) & _
44.                 "running scripts (Yes) or " & chr(13) & _
45.                 "exit the part of the program" & chr(13) & _
46.             "that caused this error (No)?"
47.   end select
48.   ' here is a message box that informs the user an error occurs
49.   lngProcessError =  msgBox(strError, 20, _
50.                     "One or more errors have occurred")
51. end function
52. </SCRIPT>
53. </BODY>
```

The *lngProcessError()* function (line 33) now contains all the code for handling the different errors that may occur. The value that *lngProcessError()* returns corresponds to which button (Yes or No) the user clicked; then this option is handled by the *select case* statement resident in the Sub procedure, which called the function. In this case, the Sub procedure is the event handler for the *btnClickMe* button.

VBScript also provides the means for *error trapping*—the process of knowing an error might occur and dealing with it before it happens. You can trap errors in a variety of ways; if you are accepting input for dividing two numbers for some purpose, for instance, and the user can possibly enter zero for the denominator, you can check to see if it is zero and inform the user, thus avoiding the "division by zero" error. You also use error trapping for validation. Suppose you require a user to enter a number in an input box, and this is the only input you want to accept; however, the user enters a letter. You can trap this by using the *IsNumeric()* function as shown in the following code.

```
Sub txtWillChng_onChange()
  if IsNumeric(txtWillChng.value) = false then
    window.status = "This is not a number"-
    txtWillChng.value = ""
  end if
end sub
```

Every time the user types in something that is not a number (a letter, for instance) and then leaves the text box, he or she will be informed that what they entered isn't valid data.

All in all, VBScript provides more versatile methods for error handling than with JavaScript. The *err* object and the *on error resume next* statement, and with the various forms of error trapping are all more versatile then JavaScript.

JavaScript Error Trapping   JavaScript has no internal support for error handling, so the only way you can deal with errors that might occur in your scripts is through error trapping. You are familiar with the process of error trapping so far. JavaScript has some internal functions and methods belonging to objects, such as the *math* object, and elsewhere that will enable you to trap for many errors. Consider the JavaScript version of the VBScript code in listing G.3:

```
<HTML>
<HEAD>
<TITLE>This page generates a runtime error</TITLE>
</HEAD>
<BODY>
<INPUT TYPE="text" NAME="txtWillChng"
       VALUE="">
<SCRIPT FOR="txtWillChng" EVENT="onchange">
//event handler for the change event of the
//txtWillChng tag
if (isNaN(txtWillChng.value))
{
  window.status = "Not a valid number";
  txtWillChng.value = "";
}
</SCRIPT>
</BODY>
```

As you can see, the JavaScript *isNaN()* function determines if the value entered for the text box is not a number, which is opposite to the VBScript *IsNumeric()* function that determines if a number was entered. Click event is fired for the text box called *txtWillChng* when the user leaves the text box. You can trap most of the errors in JavaScript much in the same way as you would VBScript.

N O T E   An event that can be handled by either JavaScript or VBScript is the *onerror()* event, which enables you to access some information an error might generate, thus providing more detailed feedback to the user if an error occurs. This event, however, provides no means to stop the error, and the standard error window will occur despite the handling of this event. ■

App
G

Optimizing Scripting Syntax

This section deals with the significance of the different ways you specify scripts on your page. This includes the specification of scripting blocks and the location of external scripts that will be used inline. This sometimes becomes handy when you are working with multipart projects or it is just too cumbersome to include all the text in the document itself. This section shows you how to call external scripting files from your HTML document.

Scripting in the Header and Body Sections   The first thing to consider is that a big difference exists between placing scripting blocks in the header section (encapsulated in the <HEAD> tag) and in the body section (encapsulated in the <BODY> tag). First, any variables, functions, objects, or Sub procedures that you want to be global to your web page—and to other pages within the same browser window—should be placed within a scripting block in the header section. Because the header section initializes before any other scripts on the page, you can declare important constants, Sub procedures, and other types of data to use on the page with your event handlers and other forms of scripting.

Second, although you can make a script global by using a scripting block inside the body, it only becomes global when the scripting interpreter reads it, which means if a script needs to access that variable before it is created, it might not be available. Functions and Sub procedures can be declared in either the head or the body and are initialized when the page is loaded because the scripting interpreter executes functions and Sub procedures when they are called upon. All event handlers and references to object properties and events should be declared in the body section, unless your page consists of a collection of frames specified by <FRAMESET>. In that case, all scripting must be done in the header section.

Specifying External Scripts   Throughout this entire book, all scripts have been included within the page. But what if the script is very large, and placing the entire script inside an HTML document becomes a daunting task? You can specify the location of external script files and use them inline through the SRC attribute with the <SCRIPT> tag, much like what is shown in the following snippet of code:

```
<SCRIPT LANGUAGE="Some_ScriptingLanguage" SRC="SomeScriptingFile"></SCRIPT>
```

The LANGUAGE attribute functions the same as always; it specifies which scripting language you will use with the scripting block. The SRC attribute, however, specifies the location of a file that contains the script that will be used within the context of this scripting block. The path to this file can be a relative or absolute URL. The convention for naming this file should be the name of the file with a .vbs extension for a VBScript file or a .js extension for a JavaScript file. If you wanted to place all the components that make up the *controlSpan()* object of listing G.2 in an external file and use inline scripting to contain your color arrays and object instances, you would take the object function and all its methods, place them in a standard text file, and call it *controlspan.js.* The code to access this file would resemble the following line of code:

```
<SCRIPT LANGUAGE="JavaScript" SRC="controlspan.js"></SCRIPT>
```

In another scripting block, you would place all your instantiations of the *controlSpan()* object. However, it is necessary that you define external scripts before you create other objects or scripts that are dependant on that external script. As a general rule, you should make your external scripts reliant upon nothing so, no matter where or how they are used, they can be used anywhere, making them more portable and easier to maintain and update.

N O T E When using an SRC attribute within a scripting block, the code contained within the block will be ignored. ■

Using Visual Effects in Dynamic HTML

If scripting is the lifeblood of Dynamic HTML, creating and deploying the numerous Dynamic HTML visual effects is the central nervous system. It is one of the most noticeable and readily available changes from previous versions of HTML. As you have seen through the many examples in this book, visual effects can be as simple as changing the color of text to creating your own transitions.

This section shows you how to accomplish many visual effects through the use of several graphics filters provided by CSS and through the DirectDraw API, which is exposed to Dynamic HTML and web pages through four ActiveX Controls (path control, sprite control, structured graphics control, and sequencer control). With these ActiveX Controls, you can create numerous visual effects ranging from simple animations and other effects on elements in an HTML document, to three-dimensional animations complete with depth, lighting, and fully controllable geometry.

The following basic example demonstrates the different components of the DirectDraw API. This example demonstrates the power behind using the DirectDraw API in conjunction with Dynamic HTML.

Using CSS

In this book, you have already witnessed that CSS provides a dramatic increase in the layout and positioning of the items on your web page, precision control over how elements are rendered, and the robust interface CSS provides to other components of Dynamic HTML, such as scripting. In addition to these features, Microsoft's additions to CSS also provide a number of filtering effects that you can apply to the elements in your page.

In general, a *filter* is some process that modifies and enhances the qualities of the elements on a web page, such as text or graphics. You have seen how these filters work on images, but they have a different effect on text. Using script-controlled processes, especially those of a recursive nature, can provide some pretty incredible effects for your web pages. You can, for example, make glowing text on the page, filter out one color, reverse text and images, and so on. The listing that is provided in this section shows you how to utilize multiple filters on any element.

Listing G.4 provides an interface that enables you to examine all the filters Dynamic HTML provides through CSS on any element, whether it is text or graphics. Figure G.2 shows this interface.

App

G

Listing G.4   The Interface and Additional Code for the Filter Generator (filwiz.htm)

```
01. <HTML>
02. <HEAD>
03. <TITLE>Testing Filters Example</TITLE>
04. <STYLE>
05. .myclassb {color: white; background-color: floralwhite;
06.        position: absolute;
07.          width: 300; height: 300; overflow: scroll}
08. .myclassx {color: #ADD8E6; background-color: lightblue;
09.        position: absolute;
10.          width: 300; height: 300;}
11. .myclassr {background-color: darkred ; color: #CD5C5C ;
12.        position: absolute; left: 320;
13.        width: 250; height: 300;}
14.
15. .myclassi {background-color: cornsilk;
16.        position: absolute; top: 320;
17.          width: 560; height: 100;}
18.
19. .myinfo   {background-color: #B22222; height: 130; width: 120;
20.           position: absolute; color: red;}
21. .labela   {font-size: 14pt}
22. .labelb   {color: blue;
23.           width:250; height: 250;
24.           font-size: 24pt; left: 10}
25.
26. </STYLE>
27. </HEAD>
28.
29. <BODY BGCOLOR="darkblue">
30. <DIV id="div1" CLASS="myclassb" >
31. <SPAN id="changetxt" CLASS="labelb">
32. The text or graphics you enter will be filtered
33. </SPAN>
34. </DIV>
35.
36. <DIV id="div2" CLASS="myclassr">
37. <H2 ALIGN="Center">Filter Generator</H2>
38. <SPAN CLASS="labela">Place text here:</SPAN><BR>
39. <INPUT TYPE="text" SIZE="30" ID="textinput">
40. <SPAN CLASS="labela">Location of graphic:</SPAN><BR>
41. <INPUT TYPE="text" SIZE="30" ID="grapinput" VALUE=" ">
42. <HR>
43. <SELECT id="selfilt" MULTIPLE>
44. <OPTION VALUE="FlipV">Flip Vertical
45. <OPTION VALUE="FlipH">Flip Horizontal
46. <OPTION VALUE="Glow(color=#FF0000,strength=5)">Glow
47. <OPTION VALUE="Shadow(color=#FFFFF, direction=225)">Shadow
48. <OPTION VALUE="Gray">Grayscale
49. <OPTION VALUE="Invert">Invert
50. <OPTION VALUE="Blur(add=0,direction = 0, strength = 3)">Blur
51. <OPTION VALUE="DropShadow(color=#0000FF,offx=4,offy=-4)">Drop Shadow
52. <OPTION VALUE="Xray">X-Ray
```

```
53. </SELECT>
54. <SPAN CLASS="myinfo" id="params"
55.  TITLE="All color values should be in the form of #RRGGBB">
56. Select A filter!
57. </SPAN>
58. <HR>
59. <INPUT TYPE="button" id="appfilt" VALUE="Apply Filter"
➥onclick="initFilter(selfilt)"><BR>
60. <INPUT TYPE="button" id="clearall" VALUE="Restore"
➥onclick="restFilter(changetxt)">
61. </DIV>
62.
63. <DIV id="div3" CLASS="myclassi"
64. TITLE="When you generate a filter for the text you specify, the CSS
65.        code corresponding to the filters is displayed here
66.        this works best with SPAN and DIV elements">
67. </DIV>
68.
69.
70.
71. <SCRIPT LANGUAGE="JavaScript" SRC="padprog.js">
72. //code generating the filter
73. </SCRIPT>
74.
75.
76. </SCRIPT>
77.
78. <SCRIPT LANGUAGE="JavaScript" FOR="selfilt" EVENT="onchange()">
79. //code for handling which option was clicked for the select box
80. myindex = selfilt.selectedIndex;
81. var gsstring = 'Color: <INPUT TYPE="text" id="gcolor" size="7"><BR>';
82. var strev = '<INPUT TYPE="button" Value="Apply"
onclick="eval(str0);udv()">';
83. var strsdir = 'Direction: <INPUT TYPE="text" id="sdir" size="3"><BR>';
84. var strgstr = 'Strength: <INPUT TYPE="text" id="gstr" size="3"><BR>';
85.
86. if(myindex == 0 || myindex == 1 ||
87.    myindex == 4 || myindex == 5 || myindex == 8)
88. {
89. //code for general filters that require no arguments
90.    params.innerText = "No Additional attributes needed";
91. }
92. if(myindex == 2)
93. {
94. //For glow filter
95.    str0 = 'selfilt.options(2).value = "Glow(color="+gcolor.value+",
➥strength="+gstr.value+")"';
96.    params.innerHTML = gsstring + strgstr + strev;
97. }
98. if(myindex == 3)
99. {
100. //For Shadow filter
101.    str0 = 'selfilt.options(3).value="Shadow(color="+gcolor.value+",
➥direction="+sdir.value+")"';
102.    params.innerHTML = gsstring + strsdir + strev;
```

App

G

continues

Listing G.4   Continued

```
103.
104. }
105. if(myindex == 6)
106. {
107. //For blur filter
108.     str0 = 'selfilt.options(6).value="Blur(add="+addn.value+",
➥direction="+sdir.value+",strength="+gstr.value+")"';
109.     str2 = 'Add: <INPUT TYPE="text" id="addn" size="2"><BR>';
110.     params.innerHTML = str2 + strsdir + strgstr + strev;
111.
112. }
113.
114. if(myindex == 7)
115. {
116. //For Drop Shadow filter
117.     str0 = 'selfilt.options(7).value="Dropshadow(color="+gcolor.value+",
➥offx="+doffx.value+",offy="+doffy.value+")"';
118.     str2 = 'X-Offset: <INPUT TYPE="text" id="doffx" size="3"><BR>';
119.     str3 = 'Y-Offset: <INPUT TYPE="text" id="doffy" size="3"><BR>';
120.     params.innerHTML = gsstring + str2 + str3 + strev;
121.
122. }
123. //places the code necessary in div3 to use in a stylesheet def
124. div3.innerText = selfilt.options(myindex).value;
125. </SCRIPT>
126. </BODY>
127. </HTML>
```

FIG. G.2

An interface to specify what filters to apply on text or graphics.

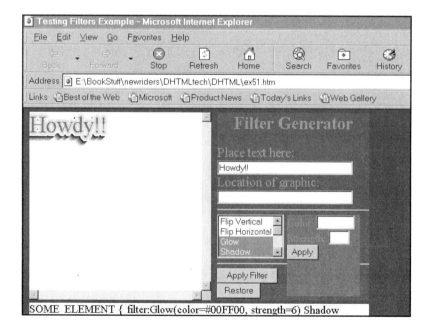

Listing G.5, *padprog.js,* is the main program used to generate the filter on the text or graphics you specify. padprog.js handles all the communication in the program, such as when you select different filters and so on, and it is responsible for creating the code you use to specify one or multiple filters.

Listing G.5   A Filter Generation Program (padprog.js)

```
01. function initFilter(objSelfilt)
02. {
03. //main procedure for handling everything involved with filtering
04. //process
05.   var imageloc = new String();
06.   var strFilter = buildFilter(objSelfilt);
07.
08.
09. //here the string that specifies filters will be created
10. imageloc = getimage(grapinput);
11.
12.
13. //here the text in changetxt changes (actually, the SPAN tag)
14.   changetxt.innerHTML = textinput.value + imageloc;
15.
16. //changetxt.innerText = textinput.value;
17. //here everything is applied
18.   changetxt.style.filter = strFilter;
19.   div3.innerText = "SOME_ELEMENT { filter:" + strFilter + ";}";
20.
21. }
22.
23. function buildFilter(objSelfilt)
24. {
25. //checks which options are selected then builds the string
26. var intSelindex = objSelfilt.length;
27. var strmystring = new String();
28. for(i=0; i<intSelindex; i++)
29. {
30.   if(objSelfilt.options(i).selected == true)
31.   {
32.     strmystring += objSelfilt.options(i).value + " ";
33.   }
34. }
35. return strmystring;
36. }
37.
38.
39. function getimage(objgrp)
40. {
41. var strmystring = objgrp.value;
42.   if(strmystring.length > 4)
43.   {
44.     return imageloc = " <IMG SRC=" + grapinput.value + ">";
45.   }
46.   else
```

App

G

continues

Listing G.5 Continued

```
47.    {return "";}
48.
49. }
50.
51. function restFilter(objfilt)
52. {
53.
54. objfilt.style.filter=" ";
55.
56.
57. }
58. function udv()
59. {
60. div3.innerText = selfilt.options(myindex).value;
61. }
```

Several important aspects of listings G.4 and G.5 should be considered, specifically:

- The primary interface constructed from several <DIV> tags that use positioning attributes, background, and foreground colors.

- The intrinsic control interface found in the second <DIV> element (named *div2*) provides an efficient way to choose which filters to apply on text or graphics. You can enter the location of the graphic file and enter your own text with HTML markup.

- The scripting involved with the page, which is found in two sections: the event handler for the element named *selfilt* and the script found in the file *padprog.js*, which applies filter settings for text or graphics you specify.

A large number of coding concepts and procedures are included in listings G.4 and G.5. The basic purpose of the program is to let the user enter some text and/or specify a graphics file, then observe the effects the different filters have on the graphics and text.

This is not all the program does, however. The program enables you to customize each filter that is supported. Figure G.3 shows you an interface for entering parameters for the glow filter. In addition, the <DIV> element named *div3* contains the default information for the filter you have selected. When you enter different settings for the filters (these settings correspond with those mentioned for each filter in Chapter 15, "Multimedia Filters and ActiveX Controls") and click the Apply button (*not* Apply Filter), the filter settings are updated in *div3*.

When you have selected which filters you want to apply (this is accomplished by selecting multiple filters), enter the text or graphics you want to filter and click the Apply Filter button; the filters are then applied to the text and graphics. After clicking the Apply Filter button, the complete code for specifying this filter as a CSS definition is displayed in the <DIV> element called *div3*. You can then cut and paste this code into your own HTML document to use with your text.

FIG. G.3

You can enter settings for the glow attribute.

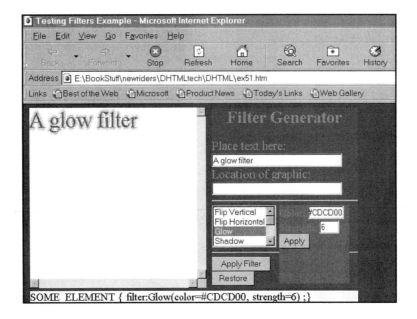

The following exercise is provided as a quick tutorial to acquaint you with the filtering program.

1. Type in both files and name them as shown in the headers.

2. Launch the file named *filwiz.htm* in Internet Explorer 4.0.

3. In the text box immediately under *Place Text Here*, type **This is a test for filters**.

4. Specify the location of a graphic if you have one available.

5. In the list box, click the Flip Vertical option. Notice how the text to the right changes.

6. Click the Glow option. Notice how the text changes again, and you see two text boxes and a button. In the Color:text box, type **#0F0A0C** and in the Strength:text box, type **6**.

7. Click the Apply button under the text boxes. Notice how the text in the lower-left corner changes to match the values you entered.

8. While pressing the Ctrl key, click the Flip Vertical option.

9. After both of these options are selected, click the Apply Filter button. Two things happen. First, the graphics (if specified) and the text are displayed to the left. Then, the code for applying this filter is displayed in the lower-left corner. You can take this code and use it with a DIV or SPAN element, and it will do the exact same thing as you displayed. Figure G.4 illustrates the results of this exercise.

App

G

FIG. G.4

Results of the preceding exercise.

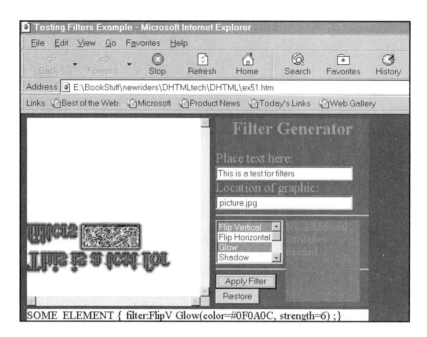

Now it is time for you to examine some aspects of the code. What you should be particularly concerned with in this example is listing G.5 (*padprog.js*). This is the program that builds the filter using a string and sets the *style.filter* property of the <SPAN> tag named *changetxt* to this string. The main function, *initFilter()* (line 1), is put into action when you click on the Apply Filter button. After the *initFilter()* function is activated, the *buildFilter()* (line 23) function is called, which determines what options in the Select box are selected. The values of these options are the filters that will be used in making your filter string. Every time *buildFilter()* finds an option that a user has selected, it concatenates the options value to the string, thus building the filter. To wrap up the code, the *changetxt.style.filter* property is set to the string created in *buildFilter()*, then the code used to define this filter or group of filters through CSS is displayed in the DIV element, *div3*.

As mentioned previously, the code that was originally part of *filwiz.htm* is used to build the interface that you use to specify the parameters of the different filters. It is a basic interface, and is nowhere near complete. Its minimal functionality, however, provides more than enough to demonstrate the versatility of filters. Some filters have been excluded, including the chroma filter, all lighting filters, and alpha transparency. You can add these, if you like, by adding an additional <OPTION> tag to the *selfilt* select box and entering a value, which is the filter code for that filter effect. Then you add the necessary code in the *onchange* event handler, which is at the bottom of *filwiz.htm*. You need to add the <OPTION> tag at the very end of the current list of option tags so you do not disturb the index order. In this way, you can easily specify additional filters with a minimal amount of coding.

The following listing is the VBScript version of *padprog.htm* for you VBScript-savvy programmers.

Listing G.6   The VBScript Version of padprog.js (padprogvb.htm)

```
01. q = chr(34)
02.
03.
04. sub initFilter(objSelFilt)
05. 'main sub routine
06.   dim strImageloc, strFilter
07.   strImageloc = " "
08.   strFilter = buildFilter(objSelFilt)
09.   strImageloc = getImage(grapinput)
10.   changetxt.innerHTML = textinput.value & "<BR>" & strImageloc
11.   changetxt.style.filter = strFilter
12. end sub
13.
14. function buildFilter(objSelFilt)
15. 'checks for filters then make them part of the string
16.   for i = 0 to (objSelFilt.length -1)
17.     if objSelFilt.options(i).selected = True then
18.       buildFilter = buildFilter & _
19.                     objSelFilt.options(i).value & " "
20.     end if
21.   next
22. end function
23.
24. function getImage(grapinput)
25. 'checks for an image, then passes the HTML back to
26. 'make an image tag
27.   if len(grapinput.value) > 4 then
28.     getImage = "<IMG SRC=" & q & grapinput.value & q & ">"
29.   else
30.     getImage = ""
31.   end if
32. end function
33.
34. function restFilter(changetxt)
35. changetxt.style.filter = " "
36.
37. end function
```

Listing G.6 is used to replace *padprog.js* in the original listing only. The interface for changing the values of the parameters of different filters will still be JavaScript because the methods you would use to accomplish the interface already established with JavaScript would be radically different. Listings G.5 and G.6 are almost identical, line by line; however, you will notice some minor differences. The most obvious difference in the VBScript version is that the + character for string concatenation is replaced by the & character. The + character still works in VBScript; however, this character exhibits strange behavior when used with numeric literal values.

The VBScript conversion is not yet complete. You must modify and replace a few lines of code in *filwiz.htm*. This includes modifying the function calls to the appropriate language and changing the scripting block to VBScript instead of JavaScript. When you come across the following lines:

App

G

```
<INPUT TYPE="button" id="appfilt" VALUE="Apply Filter"
➥onclick="initFilter(selfilt)"><BR>
<INPUT TYPE="button" id="clearall" VALUE="Restore"
➥onclick="restFilter(changetxt)">
```

Replace them with:

```
<INPUT TYPE="button" id="appfilt" VALUE="Apply Filter" onclick="VBScript:
➥initFilter(selfilt)"><BR>
<INPUT TYPE="button" id="clearall" VALUE="Restore" onclick="VBScript:
➥restFilter(changetxt)">
```

This enables you to specify that VBScript will be the language used when the *initFilter()* (line 1) and *restFilter()* (line 34) functions are called for the click event of their corresponding element. These functions are both contained, as you remember in the *padprogvb.vbs* file. One more minor thing you have to do is insert these lines of code near the end of your document in *filwizvb.htm*:

```
<SCRIPT LANGUAGE="JavaScript">
function udv()
{
div3.innerText = selfilt.options(myindex).value;
}
</SCRIPT>
```

This function is required by the filter-input interface and was included along with *padprog.js,* but because you are using a VBScript file, this function has to be specified inline.

ActiveX Controls and Dynamic HTML

A myriad of ActiveX Controls exist that enable you to fully harness the power of Dynamic HTML. Although an entire book can be written on how to use the outstanding DirectX Controls included with Internet Explorer 4.0, this chapter presents a simplistic, yet interesting, example of the DirectX functionality. Listing G.7 provides this example. A simple matrix design is created using the Structured Graphics Control. The following listing is a simple, yet attractive, demonstration of the DirectDraw collection of ActiveX Controls. Figure G.5 shows the output from this listing.

Listing G.7   A Simple Demonstration of the Structured Graphics Control

```
01. df<HTML><HEAD><TITLE>Demonstration of ArcDegrees subroutine</TITLE></HEAD>
02.
03. <BODY>
04.
05. <OBJECT id="MyPolygon"
06. CLASSID="CLSID:369303C2-D7AC-11d0-89D5-00A0C90833E6"
07. STYLE="WIDTH:450;HEIGHT:450;ZINDEX:1;">
08. <PARAM NAME="Line0001" VALUE="SetFillColor(0,255,255)">
09. <PARAM NAME="Line0002" VALUE="Polygon(4, -128,-128, 128,-128, 128,128,
➥-128,128, 0)">
10. <PARAM NAME="Line0003" VALUE="SetFillColor(0,255,240)">
```

```
11. <PARAM NAME="Line0004" VALUE="Polygon(4, 64,-128, 128,64, -64,128, -128,-64,
➥0)">
12. <PARAM NAME="Line0005" VALUE="SetFillColor(0,255,225)">
13. <PARAM NAME="Line0006" VALUE="Polygon(4, 16,-112, 112,16, -16,112, -112,-16,
➥0)">
14. <PARAM NAME="Line0007" VALUE="SetFillColor(0,255,210)">
15. <PARAM NAME="Line0008" VALUE="Polygon(4, 88,-16, 16,88, -88,16, -16,-88, 0)">
16. <PARAM NAME="Line0009" VALUE="SetFillColor(0,255,195)">
17. <PARAM NAME="Line0010" VALUE="Polygon(4, 62,-34, 34,62, -62,34, -34,-62, 0)">
18. <PARAM NAME="Line0011" VALUE="SetFillColor(0,255,180)">
19. <PARAM NAME="Line0012" VALUE="Polygon(4, 62,-34, 34,62, -62,34, -34,-62, 0)">
20. <PARAM NAME="Line0013" VALUE="SetFillColor(0,255,165)">
21. <PARAM NAME="Line0014" VALUE="Polygon(4, 38,-41, 41,38, -38,41, -41,-38, 0)">
22. <PARAM NAME="Line0015" VALUE="SetFillColor(0,255,150)">
23. <PARAM NAME="Line0016" VALUE="Polygon(4, 38,-41, 41,38, -38,41, -41,-38, 0)">
24. <PARAM NAME="Line0017" VALUE="SetFillColor(0,255,135)">
25. <PARAM NAME="Line0018" VALUE="Polygon(4, 18,-40, 40,18, -18,40, -40,-18, 0)">
26. <PARAM NAME="Line0019" VALUE="SetFillColor(0,255,120)">
27. <PARAM NAME="Line0020" VALUE="Polygon(4, 3,-34, 34,3, -3,34, -34,-3, 0)">
28. <PARAM NAME="Line0021" VALUE="SetFillColor(0,255,105)">
29. <PARAM NAME="Line0022" VALUE="Polygon(4, 26,-6, 6,26, -26,6, -6,-26, 0)">
30. <PARAM NAME="Line0023" VALUE="SetFillColor(0,255,90)">
31. <PARAM NAME="Line0024" VALUE="Polygon(4, 18,-11, 11,18, -18,11, -11,-18, 0)">
32. </OBJECT>
33. </BODY>
34. </HTML>
```

FIG. G.5

The matrix that is produced by listing G.7.

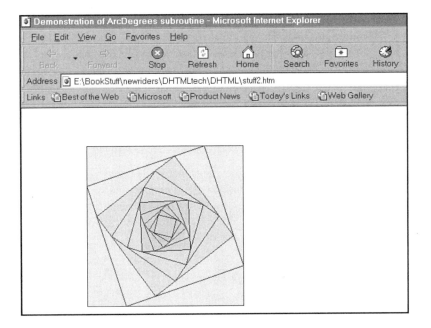

App

G

You only need to consider a few minor things in this example. First, an instance of the Structured Graphics ActiveX Control (SGC) is inserted on the page (line 5). This is identifiable by the <OBJECT> tag. The many <PARAM> tags (lines 8–31) associated with the Structured Graphics Control may seem peculiar.

<PARAM> tags, of which 24 are nested within the control definition, initialize and set values of public properties of the ActiveX Control with which they are associated. In the 24 instances of the <PARAM> tag found in listing G.7, this is a half-truth. These <PARAM> tags are specifying properties, but they are what can be considered a "virtual" property, which only exists when you need it. These properties are used for drawing various shapes, setting colors and fill patterns of these shapes, and so on.

Each one of these properties is specified by a "Line*xxxx*" value for the NAME attribute of the <PARAM> tag, starting from the value "Line0001." As you can see, all the <PARAM> tags that have odd-numbered "Line*xxxx*" values for the NAME attribute have something in common for the VALUE attribute. These specific values are used to set up the ten squares you see in figure G.5. Calling the *Polygon* method, which is part of the Structured Graphics Control, creates these squares. All the even-numbered "Line*xxxx*" values specify the colors for these boxes. Again, this listing was provided as a springboard for your future use with DirectDraw ActiveX Controls. This example shows you how to create a relatively complex example with minimal coding.

Finding Information About Your Document

Finding information about the elements contained in your document is critical for many uses in Dynamic HTML. You have seen this importance in the chapters in Part V of this book, "Multimedia and Dynamic HTML." The example in listing G.8 is a diagnostic utility that examines and categorizes the tags. The listing's main importance does not rest in the application itself, but in the methods used to extract and categorize this information. Listing G.8 takes the URL of any HTML document and analyzes which tags are on the page, then categorizes those tags. Categorizing tags enables the person using the application to know exactly how many tags are on the page, and it also makes it plain to the user if a tag was typed wrong, and so forth.

As mentioned before, there are truly incredible things you can do with the DirectDraw API. Some games, such as Microsoft's *Age of Empires* and *Monster Truck Madness 3D* are based on it. To learn more about the DirectDraw API and about DirectX, view the Internet Software Developer's Kit Internet Multimedia section at **http://www.microsoft.com/msdn/sdk/inetsdk/help/dxmedia/jaxa/default.htm**.

Listing G.8   Web Page Diagnosis

```
01. df<HTML>
02. <HEAD>
03. <TITLE>Page analyzer</TITLE>
04. <SCRIPT>
05. var EleArray = new Array();
```

```
06. var EleNum = new Array();
07. var mycounter;
08. EleArray[0] = " ";
09. EleNum[0] = 0;
10. </SCRIPT>
11. </HEAD>
12. <BODY>
13. <DIV STYLE="position:absolute;top:0;left:0">
14. <IFRAME id="placedoc" WIDTH="400" HEIGHT="400" SRC="">
15. </IFRAME>
16. </DIV>
17. <DIV STYLE="background-color: lightblue; position:absolute;top:0;
➥left:410;width:300;height:100">
18. Enter location of document: <INPUT id="myloc" TYPE="text" SIZE="40"><BR>
19. <CENTER>
20. <INPUT TYPE="button" VALUE="Analyze" id="buttonok" onclick="testfunction()">
21. </CENTER>
22.
23. </DIV>
24. <DIV STYLE="background-color: mintcream; position: absolute; top:110;
➥left:410;width: 300; height: 250; overflow: scroll" id="reporthere">
25. </DIV>
26.
27. <SCRIPT LANGUAGE="JavaScript">
28. function testfunction()
29. {
30. mylocalURL = myloc.value;
31. placedoc.location = mylocalURL;
32.
33.
34. alert(placedoc.document.all.length)
35. analyze();
36. report();
37.
38.
39.
40.
41. }
42.
43. function analyze()
44. {
45.    var objCurTagName = placedoc.document.all;
46.    for(mycounter=0; mycounter < placedoc.document.all.length; ++mycounter)
47.    {
48.      for(i=0; EleArray[i] != null; i++)
49.      {
50.        //alert(i);
51.        if(EleArray[i] == placedoc.document.all.item(mycounter).tagName)
52.        {
53.          ++EleNum[i];
54.        }
55.        else if(i == (EleArray.length - 1))
56.        {
57.          i++;
58.          //alert(i);
```

continues

Listing G.8   Continued

```
59.          EleArray[i] = placedoc.document.all.item(mycounter).tagName;
60.          //alert(EleArray[i]);
61.          EleNum[i] = 0;
62.          ++EleNum[i];
63.        }
64.      }
65. }
66.
67.
68. }
69.
70. function report()
71. {
72. reporthere.innerHTML = "<B>Reports for: " + placedoc.location + "</B><BR>";
73.
74. for(j=1; j < EleArray.length; j++)
75. {
76. reporthere.innerHTML += EleArray[j] + ":" + EleNum[j] + "<BR>";
77.
78.
79.
80. }
81. }
82. </SCRIPT>
83. </BODY>
84. </HTML>
```

The preceding example is rather straightforward. The user specifies a location of a local document; the program iterates throughout the entire document and informs the user which tags are found on the page and how many of each tag. The algorithm created to do this is a little complex and involves two loops. These loops are found in the *analyze()* function (line 43). The outer loop in line 46:

```
for(mycounter=0; mycounter < placedoc.document.all.length; ++mycounter){}
```

scrolls through all the elements in the HTML document that the user entered inside of the text box named *myloc*. These elements are accessed through the *item()* property of the *all* collection. To access each item, the *mycounter* variable references each index in the *all.item()* collection of the specified HTML document. The second loop in line 48:

```
for(i=0; EleArray[i] != null; i++)
```

accomplishes two things. First, it populates two arrays (*EleArray[x]* and *EleNum[x]*) that each contain information about the tags and how many of each tag are in the page that is currently loaded. *EleArray[0]* will usually contain the <HTML> tag, for instance, and *EleNum[0]* will contain the quantity of that tag on a page (always 1). The code nested in this *for* loop also checks to see if an element found in the specified document's *all.item()* collection exists within the array. If the element does not exist, the code allocates a new entry for that tag.

The final part of this program prints out a report for the document that you specified. In this report, the full path to the document is displayed (file://someplace-on-your-hdd) along with each tag and the number of times each tag is on the page. Although the specifics of this algorithm will not be discussed here, enough information has been given for you to dissect the code for yourself. This program not only provides you with a handy diagnostic tool, but the code used to manipulate the arrays is also useful. Sometimes using complex code that every programmer should understand is an efficient way to accomplish different tasks such as adding items to lists.

From Here...

This appendix provides a glimpse of the unique ways you can harness the powers of Dynamic HTML technology. This appendix, combined with the other premium examples in Part VI, "Real World Dynamic HTML," of the book, will give you a strong grasp of Dynamic HTML so that you can make the fullest use of this technology.

The techniques and examples shown in this appendix can be modified easily and used in many other examples. This appendix provides the final road map in this book for you to fully understand and utilize the power of Dynamic HTML.

Glossary

absolute positioning   Specifying the position of elements on an HTML page in relation to the window.

ActiveX   Microsoft's method of distributing components over the web.

Advanced Data Connector (ADC)   A Data Source Object that ships with Internet Explorer 4.0, which allows data binding to remote sources of data.

applet   A Java program that can run inside of a web page.

block   A group of JavaScript statements.

Boolean   A value that is either true or false.

Cascading Style Sheets (CSS)   A W3C specification for defining layout and style elements for HTML pages. The first official release is referred to as CSS1.

channel   A subscription-based mechanism for delivering scheduled content updates.

Channel Definition Format (CDF)   Microsoft's file format for specifying channels that can be pushed to users' desktops dynamically.

clipping   Defining a limited, viewable window for displaying elements.

collection   A wrapper that enables objects to be grouped.

COM   Microsoft's Component Object Model, the foundation upon which ActiveX Controls are built.

Common Gateway Interface (CGI)   A standard web protocol for executing a program through the web server and returning its output to the web browser.

conditional   A point in a program at which the branch of program flow is controlled by a logical expression.

container   A CSS Positioning element that can be used to relatively position child elements.

cookie   A file on the client machine used to store information about previous web page visits.

CSS attribute   Used synonymously with CSS value to specify the parameter for a CSS property.

CSS Positioning (CSSP)   Currently a W3C working draft for extensions to the CSS specification to allow tighter control over positioning HTML elements. Implemented in Internet Explorer 4.0.

CSS property   An attribute used with style sheets to configure styles for a given selector.

CSS value   The data to which CSS properties are set.

current record binding   A data binding method by which one record from a data source is retrieved at a time and bound to a series of data consumers.

data binding   The process of connecting and automatically placing data into an HTML element from a data source.

data consumer   HTML elements that are bound to data source objects and are automatically filled with data from those data sources.

Data Source Object (DSO)   A type of ActiveX Control that provides data to data consumers. Data Source Objects can retrieve data from just about any source of data, but RDBMSs and flat text files are the most common places.

database server   A storehouse of tabular data that can be accessed via a Data Source Object.

dynamic   Microsoft defines dynamic as content that is alterable at load and runtime.

dynamic content   Content in elements that is changed at runtime, such as text ranges.

Dynamic HTML (DHTML)   A collection of technologies implemented in Internet Explorer 4.0, such as dynamic styles, dynamic content, CSS Positioning, the Dynamic HTML Object Model, data binding, and Dynamic HTML multimedia—all controllable via scripting.

dynamic styles   The capability to change the style property values of an element at runtime.

element   An instance of an HTML tag in an HTML document.

event   The notification triggered when an action is done that is being monitored.

event binding   The connecting of events to event handlers.

event bubbling   The passing of events up the HTML element hierarchy.

event handler   A function that is bound to an event via event binding that responds to the event.

field delimiters   The character that separates fields in a Tabular Data Control data file.

form   HTML code that enables user interface controls, such as edit boxes or list boxes, to be placed on the HTML page.

function   A group of statements that are referenced by a name and executed when the name is called.

Hypertext Markup Language (HTML)   A generic language for defining pages for the World Wide Web.

Hypertext Transfer Protocol (HTTP)   The communications protocol used to transfer web pages from the server to the browser.

ID   A CSS property used to assign a name to an element.

InetSDK   Microsoft's Software Development Kit for Internet client development.

integer   A number that does not contain a decimal point (–3,–2,–1,0,1,2,3, and so on).

Java   A programming language and runtime environment created by Sun Microsystems to promote cross-platform compatibility and simplify application development.

JavaScript   Netscape's implementation of a scripting language that is loosely based on Java's syntax.

JScript   Microsoft's implementation of JavaScript in Internet Explorer.

layout   The precise positioning of HTML elements on a page.

letter-spacing   The amount of whitespace that appears between characters.

logical expression   An expression that evaluates to true or false.

loop   A programming construct that enables a statement or block to be repeated multiple times.

method   A function that is contained in an object.

multimedia filter   A transformation, such as a blur or a light source, which can be applied to an element.

multimedia transition   An effect, such as a dissolve or a wipe, which can be applied to the switching between two elements.

numerical expression   An expression that evaluates to a number.

object   A grouping of data and functions into one data structure.

object model   The abstracting of the functionality of a program into objects that can be accessed via a scripting language.

path   A set of geometric coordinates used to specify where an object will move.

query   A method by which data is requested from a database server.

recordset   The part of a Data Source Object that enables traversal throughout the rows of data available.

Relational Database Management System (RDBMS)   A database server that uses the Structured Query Language.

relative positioning   Positioning elements in relation to their parent objects.

repeated table binding   The capability to bind a Data Source Object to a table, causing all the rows available in that Data Source Object to automatically be placed in rows in that table.

RGB value   A color specification that utilizes the primary colors of light (Red, Green, Blue).

round trip   The process of the web browser asking for data from the web server and then receiving it.

row delimiter   The character that separates rows of data in a Tabular Data Control.

scalability   The capability of a server to handle increasing amounts of traffic.

scaling   Altering the dimensions of an image or element.

scripting language   A computer language that runs inside of a web browser, which allows the manipulation of elements on the page.

selectors   The CSS equivalent of the HTML tags to which the style being defined will be applied.

sorting   Placing things in a specified order.

statement   The smallest executable portion of code in a scripting language (usually a line).

string   A sequence of characters. This definition is a string.

Structured Query Language (SQL)   A language for performing database server queries on a Relational Database Management Server.

Tabular Data Control (TDC)   A Dynamic HTML Data Source Control that provides data specified in a static data file supplied via the web server.

text range   A selection of characters that can be addressed as an object.

Uniform Resource Locator (URL)   The WWW standard for identifying the location of desired data on the web.

variable   A named, temporary holding place for data.

Visual Basic, Scripting Edition (VBScript)   Microsoft's stripped-down version of Visual Basic designed as a competitor to JavaScript.

word-spacing   The amount of whitespace between words on a page.

World Wide Web Consortium (W3C)   A group of industry developers and institutions formed to oversee standards development for the World Wide Web.

Z-index   The order in which elements are layered on a page.

Index

A

Complete and Return this Card
for a *FREE* Computer Book Catalog

Thank you for purchasing this book! You have purchased a superior computer book written expressly for your needs. To continue to provide the kind of up-to-date, pertinent coverage you've come to expect from us, we need to hear from you. Please take a minute to complete and return this self-addressed, postage-paid form. In return, we'll send you a free catalog of all our computer books on topics ranging from word processing to programming and the internet.

☐   Mrs. ☐   Ms. ☐   Dr. ☐

me (first) ☐☐☐☐☐☐☐☐☐☐   (M.I.) ☐   (last) ☐☐☐☐☐☐☐☐☐☐☐☐☐☐

dress ☐☐☐☐☐☐☐☐☐☐☐☐☐☐☐☐☐☐☐☐☐☐☐☐☐

☐☐☐☐☐☐☐☐☐☐☐☐☐☐☐☐☐☐☐☐☐☐☐☐☐

y ☐☐☐☐☐☐☐☐☐☐☐☐   State ☐☐   Zip ☐☐☐☐☐ ☐☐☐☐

one ☐☐☐ ☐☐☐ ☐☐☐☐   Fax ☐☐☐ ☐☐☐ ☐☐☐☐

mpany Name ☐☐☐☐☐☐☐☐☐☐☐☐☐☐☐☐☐☐☐☐☐☐☐

mail address ☐☐☐☐☐☐☐☐☐☐☐☐☐☐☐☐☐☐☐☐☐☐☐

Please check at least (3) influencing factors for purchasing this book.

nt or back cover information on book .... ☐
ecial approach to the content .... ☐
mpleteness of content .... ☐
thor's reputation .... ☐
blisher's reputation .... ☐
ok cover design or layout .... ☐
dex or table of contents of book .... ☐
ce of book .... ☐
ecial effects, graphics, illustrations .... ☐
her (Please specify): _____ ☐

How did you first learn about this book?

w in Macmillan Computer Publishing catalog .... ☐
commended by store personnel .... ☐
w the book on bookshelf at store .... ☐
commended by a friend .... ☐
ceived advertisement in the mail .... ☐
w an advertisement in: _____ ☐
ad book review in: _____ ☐
her (Please specify): _____ ☐

How many computer books have you purchased in the last six months?

is book only .... ☐   3 to 5 books .... ☐
ooks .... ☐   More than 5 .... ☐

4. Where did you purchase this book?

Bookstore .... ☐
Computer Store .... ☐
Consumer Electronics Store .... ☐
Department Store .... ☐
Office Club .... ☐
Warehouse Club .... ☐
Mail Order .... ☐
Direct from Publisher .... ☐
Internet site .... ☐
Other (Please specify): _____ ☐

5. How long have you been using a computer?

☐ Less than 6 months   ☐ 6 months to a year
☐ 1 to 3 years   ☐ More than 3 years

6. What is your level of experience with personal computers and with the subject of this book?

	With PCs	With subject of book
New	☐	☐
Casual	☐	☐
Accomplished	☐	☐
Expert	☐	☐

Source Code ISBN: 0-7897-1482-5

7. Which of the following best describes your job title?

Administrative Assistant .... ☐
Coordinator .... ☐
Manager/Supervisor .... ☐
Director .... ☐
Vice President .... ☐
President/CEO/COO .... ☐
Lawyer/Doctor/Medical Professional .... ☐
Teacher/Educator/Trainer .... ☐
Engineer/Technician .... ☐
Consultant .... ☐
Not employed/Student/Retired .... ☐
Other (Please specify): _____ ☐

8. Which of the following best describes the area of the company your job title falls under?

Accounting .... ☐
Engineering .... ☐
Manufacturing .... ☐
Operations .... ☐
Marketing .... ☐
Sales .... ☐
Other (Please specify): _____ ☐

Comments: _____
_____
_____

9. What is your age?

Under 20 ....
21-29 ....
30-39 ....
40-49 ....
50-59 ....
60-over ....

10. Are you:

Male ....
Female ....

11. Which computer publications do you read regularly? (Please list)

_____
_____
_____
_____
_____
_____
_____
_____

Fold here and scotch-tape to m